Means of Transportation

←——————→ Air

·–·–·–·–·–· Road

————————— R

Gdańsk

Bialystock

Warsaw

Poznań

POLAND

Lublin

Wrocław

ue

Oświęcim Cracow

Tatras

ZECHOSLOVAKIA

Bardejov

bor Třebíč Brno Trenčín Prešov

Třeboň Liptovský-Mikuláš Levoča

mlov Košice

Little Carpathians

Bratislava Eger Miskolc

Vienna Győr Budapest Debrecen

TRIA Tihany Kecskemét

Siófok Szeged

Oradea

HUNGARY Subotica Timişoara

Voivodina

ana Zagreb

Slovenia

Croatia

YUGOSLAVIA *Serbia*

Bosnia-Hercegovina Sarajevo

Mostar Niš

Monte negro Prištinа

Titograd *Kosovo*

Dubrovnik Skopje

Bar Shkodër *Macedonia*

Tiranë

Durrës

Berat **ALBANIA**

Vlorë

Gjirokastër

Sarandë

Corfu **GREECE**

Naples

S S R

Carpathians

Suceava

Iasi

Cluj-Napoca

Sighişoara

Sibiu Braşov

ROMANIA Ploiesti

Bucharest Constanta

Craiova

Ruse

River Danube **BULGARIA** Varna

Belgrade

Tárnovo

Gabrovo

Kazaniák

Karlovo

Sofia Plovdiv

Rilski Manastir Pazardzik

Blagoevgrad

Melnik

Istanbul

Thessaloniki **TURKEY**

Athens

BERLIN TO BUCHAREST

By the same author

*The Journey Back from Hell: Conversations
with Concentration Camp Survivors*

ANTON GILL

BERLIN TO BUCHAREST

*Travels in
Eastern Europe*

GRAFTON BOOKS
A Division of the Collins Publishing Group

LONDON GLASGOW
TORONTO SYDNEY AUCKLAND

Grafton Books
A Division of the Collins Publishing Group
8 Grafton Street, London W1X 3LA

Published by Grafton Books 1990

British Library Cataloguing in Publication Data

Gill, Anton
   Berlin to Bucharest: travels in Eastern Europe.
   1. Eastern Europe. Description & travel
   I. Title
   914.7

ISBN 0-246-13485-2

Phototypeset by Computape (Pickering) Ltd,
North Yorkshire
Printed in Great Britain by
William Collins Sons & Co. Ltd, Glasgow

FOR PETER WICKHAM,
and in gratitude to Dieter, Kasia, Anna,
Iwona, Marek, Dezider, Beata, Marta, Sándor,
Ion, Oliver, Daniel, Branka and Bashkim.

CONTENTS

PART ONE

NORTH: East Germany and Poland

PART TWO

CENTRE: Czechoslovakia and Hungary

ACKNOWLEDGEMENTS

A book like this owes its existence to far more people than just its author. First of all, I thank those friends in eastern Europe who took me into their confidence and treated me with openness and generosity. In some cases I have had to disguise an individual or change the location of an event, but without ever altering what was said or what happened. Apart from also acknowledging the information and help I derived from reading articles by the eastern Europe correspondents of the west European and North American press, I should like to mention specifically the following books: *The Struggles for Poland* by Neal Ascherson; *A Guide to Central Europe* by Richard Bassett; *God's Playground* and *Heart of Europe* by Norman Davies; *A Time of Gifts* and *Between the Woods and the Water* by Patrick Leigh Fermor; Fodor's *Guides* to both eastern Europe and Yugoslavia; *Albania and the Albanians* by Ramadan Marmullaku; *Eastern Europe 1740–1785* by Robin Okey; *Poland* by Tim Sharman; and *Albania* by Philip Ward.

In western Europe, thanks must go to Archie Affleck-Graves, Neal Ascherson, E. L. Gill, Isobel Hunter, Eugen Kessler, Xavier Kreiss, Antonina Łaniewska, William Monteith, Betty Palmer, Fred Pearson, G. F. N. Reddaway, George Schöpflin, and George Stanica.

These acknowledgements would not be complete without thanking my wife, Nicola, for her constant support and forbearance, and my friends Richard Johnson of Grafton Books, and Mark Lucas of Peters, Fraser and Dunlop. Finally, I have to thank the British and Romanian authorities responsible for the retrieval and return of the notes and exposed film confiscated from me by the *Securitate* at Otopeni Airport as I was leaving Bucharest for Sofia; and members of the staff of the School of Slavonic and East European Studies at London University.

PROLOGUE

Since the end of the Second World War, eastern Europe has been the West's dark mirror. Now that mirror is shattered, and we can once more go through to the other side. Neighbours who have hitherto been strangers are no longer so. The cultural and economic richness and power of Europe could, with luck and happy cooperation, be redoubled.

Although it is still too early to know what the longterm results of the revolutions in eastern Europe will be, it is certain that 1989 will go down in history as a year to rank with, if not outstrip, 1848. Our close neighbours, for so long sequestered from us by an increasingly hollow and outmoded ideology, have finally, almost spontaneously, thrown off their shackles and set themselves on the path of freedom and self-determination.

Hungary was already on that path when I set out to make the journeys which are described in this book. As I was finishing them, Poland started to follow. Then, in an explosion which lasted from the end of October to the end of December 1989, East Germany, Bulgaria, Czechoslovakia, and finally, unexpectedly, bloodily, Romania, brought an end to a form of government which had controlled them all for forty years, and which had simply outlived its usefulness. The tragedy of the leaders, all old men, was that they did not see it coming. Their self-serving ways have been exposed to their shame; the most grotesque among them, Nicolae Ceauşescu of Romania, paid the price of his megalomania with his life on Christmas Day, 1989. Ironically, the great palace he had been building for himself at the cost of his nation's blood was just nearing completion.

The cue for these actions has been taken from the changes in the Soviet Union, and when I set out on these journeys I did so in the full knowledge that I would be recording the hopes and fears of people living in the Eastern Bloc during its last years. But nobody could have predicted that all save one of these countries would have set themselves on the road to democracy within the seven months since I completed my travels in May 1989. Even in Albania, as I write this at the beginning of January 1990, the first rumblings of dissent have been heard in Shkodër, and in the light of what has happened elsewhere it would be a brave person who would give even that isolated and entrenched regime more than half a decade with confidence.

My purpose, then, has been fulfilled in the nick of time, for I sought to introduce these relatively unknown near neighbours of ours to the West in anticipation of their frontiers' opening. In tandem with describing their countryside, history, art and architecture, I wanted additionally to record the hopes and fears of ordinary people on the brink of revolution.

This is a travel – not a political – book, and in essence its content is unaffected by the events of 1989 or by the political changes which will take place in the coming decades, as democratic electoral systems get under way in eastern Europe. However, it is fair to let the reader know that these journeys were made over the summer and autumn of 1988 and the spring of 1989. I travelled first through East Germany, then on to Czechoslovakia, Hungary, Romania, Bulgaria and Yugoslavia. I visited Poland and Albania separately in the spring of 1989. To know this will be helpful to any reader worried by apparent anomalies of the weather and the seasons described as he or she progresses through the book, for the order in which the countries appear is not that in which I visited them. The order chosen is chiefly for geographical and historical comfort and consistency.

I chose to include Albania and Yugoslavia because, although they are not members of the Warsaw Pact, their post-war politics were both born of the womb of communism, though they have turned out to be very different siblings. The obvious additional unifying factor of these countries, now an historical one, is that each had the Red Star as its national symbol. The speed with which those recently 'liberated' have reverted to their pre-communist flags and anthems is symbolic of the feebleness of the hold their former regimes had at the end. How long will it be, one wonders, before the street names are changed, the statues of Lenin go? Nevertheless, the experience of forty years of living under the old system will not be shaken off so easily. The brainwashed wretches of Ceauşescu's Securitate and the Children of the Falcon are extreme examples of dependency upon an enforced system; but even the most dedicated dissident will not have been able to escape its influence entirely.

Curiosity was my main motive for making this trip; but there was a personal reason too. At the end of 1988 I published a book called *The Journey Back from Hell*. This deals with the post-war lives of victims of the Nazi concentration camps. Many of the people I interviewed, though living now in western Europe, Israel and the USA, had been born and grew up in eastern Europe. I wanted to see where they came from, and my imagination had been fired by simply looking at the map of that unknown territory, full, as it seemed, of romantic and appealing names. I also wanted to see the camps where they had been imprisoned. Visiting Buchenwald, Theresien-stadt and Auschwitz was for me a profoundly moving experience.

Prior to these journeys, I had only been to eastern Europe briefly. In 1967 I passed through Hungary, Yugoslavia and Bulgaria on my way to India, and a couple of years earlier I had spent a long, happy summer as the schoolboy guest of a Hungarian family whose immediate forebears had become Yugoslavs as a result of the redrawing of the frontiers following the end of the First World War. With them, I learnt rudimentary Hungarian and Serbo-Croat, and made forays to Szeged. In 1985 I briefly visited East Berlin, in those days a very dingy place.

I wish I could have gone properly armed with one Slavonic language, but I found that English, French, German and Italian got me through almost everywhere, and that the one tongue the majority of east Europeans hated to speak was Russian –

until recently an obligatory second language. After leaving the linguistic ease of East Germany, I found that older people living within the compass of what had been the Habsburg Empire spoke German, and younger ones, English. The same applied in Poland, where French was also helpful, as it was, together with Italian, in Romania. In Albania the little unofficial contact we had with locals was made in English or German; as my wife Nicola was able to accompany me to Albania, my input from that country was gratifyingly doubled. Only in Bulgaria did I feel at all seriously the lack of the native language; but here also the people were most reserved. I did learn basic expressions, numerals and questions in the languages of all the countries I passed through, both to help me and as a courtesy to them.

The future of Europe has been unexpectedly galvanized. Whatever happens now, it will certainly be interesting. If this book fulfils its purpose, of reintroducing the eastern to the western half of Europe, at a time when people from either side will be bent on discovering the other, a right so long denied them, then I will be pleased. I only hope that we learn something of what is good and gentle in the east, and do not swamp it with the worst vulgarities of western materialism. There are many good ideas in communism, and they should not be thrown out with the leaders who have abused them. At the moment, however, it is perhaps enough that our friends and fellow-Europeans are able at last to make up their own minds about what they do.

Anton Gill
London
January 1990

PART ONE

NORTH:
East Germany and Poland

1

HAMBURG'S SISTER

'Ladies and gentlemen, this is your captain speaking . . . ' The regret in the voice was unmistakable and my heart sank. Delays, even on the shortest and simplest flights, are something we have grown used to, but I could have done without this particular holdup.

'We have a bag on board without an owner. As you will appreciate . . . '

If we weren't airborne within fifty minutes, I could forget about my train connection to Rostock. Looking out of the window at the rain-spattered tarmac of Heathrow, I could see a number of plump men in blue blazers and red caps lumbering about among forlorn items of luggage scattered under the belly of the plane. I tried to concentrate on my newspaper, but could not resist looking at my watch every three minutes.

'Ladies and gentlemen, we have still not been able to locate the owner of the luggage in question, and it may be necessary to ask you to disembark and identify your own luggage personally.'

Forty minutes passed. Cursing the bag's owner, I gave up on my connection.

'You'll like it in Rostock,' the lady at Berolina, the official East German travel agency in London, had told me a few days earlier, as I collected my hotel vouchers. 'It's where all the trade unionists take their summer holidays.'

I tried to imagine what a beach full of East German trade unionists would look like, spread out in their swimming costumes under a reluctant Baltic sun, but I needed all my attention for the paperwork in front of me. To get to the German Democratic Republic as an independent traveller – that is, to qualify for a visa – you are obliged to book and pay for all your hotels in advance, which means you have to know precisely when you want to be where for the duration of your stay. That was no great problem for me, and the staff at Berolina couldn't have been more helpful in suggesting how much time any East German city would warrant. My route was by train, starting at Rostock – I wanted my overall journey to link the Baltic and the Adriatic – then, using the *Deutsche Reichsbahn*, the East German equivalent of the *Bundesbahn*, I would head south to Berlin, on to Potsdam, Erfurt, Weimar, and through to Leipzig and Dresden. But timing was crucial, because the dates of arrival and departure at all these places were already fixed. I was due to arrive in Rostock on 28 July, and there was only one connecting train a day from Hamburg.

I signed my cheque and looked through the vouchers. Only two dates were wrong.

Later, when I was in eastern Europe, I would learn the wisdom of double-checking everything: the paperwork isn't just too much for the average westerner, it's clearly too much for the average easterner as well.

The hotels were all in the luxury and first-class Interhotel bracket. These are the only ones available to westerners. Cheaper places can only be used by East Germans and visitors from elsewhere in the Eastern Bloc. Selling us their biggest and best hotels ensures that we part with the maximum number of dollars – lifeblood to the East – but if prices vie with those we'd pay in the West, service is as good and often better.

'With these vouchers, they'll stamp your visa into your passport at the frontier, on the train, and there'll be no obligatory currency exchange,' said the lady at Berolina. 'Have a good trip.'

On the plane the minutes continued to tick by. I made some fretful calculations. If we left by ten past perhaps there would still be the ghost of a chance . . .

Finally the captain told us that the owner of the bag had been located on another flight and we could proceed. We took off at precisely the moment we should have landed at Hamburg. I wondered what the East German border guards would say to my arriving armed with vouchers valid from a day earlier. I knew from the odd trip to East Berlin that they didn't have a great reputation for good-humoured amenable-ness.

This wasn't the most auspicious beginning for a journey. Once we got started, British Airways and a following wind made short work of the flight, but I was still left with only half an hour to get to the station. My bag was one of the last off, but by luck there were plenty of beige Mercedes taxis on the rank outside.

'Can we get to the station in twenty minutes?' I asked.

'No. It takes at least thirty-five.'

'Can we try?' I explained why.

'What the hell are you going over there for?' The driver grinned. 'Still, if it amuses you . . .'

The taxi-driver dropped me at the station with five minutes to spare, relieved me of forty marks and wished me luck. Hamburg station is one of those palatial Victorian glass-and-cast-iron places, but there was no time to admire it. I could see the Rostock train pulling in to platform 11.

It was packed solid, mainly with East Germans returning after visits to relatives in the West. By the time I had climbed into the wrong carriage and then fought my way through the narrow corridors to the right one, I thought that I would have made more enemies than I would like to make in a lifetime. But everyone was friendly, calm and sympathetic.

My first east European companions were all women. Opposite me sat two sisters, pretty brunettes in their late twenties. Both were shy. They looked at me from the corners of their eyes, and giggled as they discussed me. Once they were tired of that, one ignored me, but the other kept stealing curious and even flirtatious glances. When I spoke to her in German she blushed, and wouldn't look me in the eye. There was also a sad-eyed academic-looking woman who turned out to be the manageress of a boutique in Bad Doberan in East Germany, and an elderly lady who surprised me by telling me that Goethe, as he had lived so long in Weimar and been a student in Leipzig, was therefore an East and not a West German. No one commented on this remark, though it stimulated eloquent looks from the silent sister and the woman with sad eyes. Looking your thoughts is an east European mannerism I became used to.

The string of dismal small factories on the outskirts of Hamburg gave way to scruffy countryside, and then to the most beautiful rolling farmland, the barley and wheat already beige-yellow against the lush green of other crops. We stopped briefly at Lübeck, and soon afterwards arrived at the frontier. First came high fences topped with barbed wire. Crossing the no-man's-land I thought of the acres of wasted farmland stretching from here south to Kassel and Hof, and remembered my first sight of this frontier years ago on a similar summer's day near Coburg, where a road leading east had simply come to a torn-up end, and where a great wooden farmhouse had been trapped between the fences, and was falling into ruin.

High concrete pylons now reared up on either side of the track, and from the top of a watchtower the bare blond heads of two young East German soldiers were visible, with bored expressions on their faces and binoculars perched on the parapet in front of them. I felt as if I were entering a prison.

The frontier guards boarded the train at Herrnburg. At least I was on schedule and would have no difficult explaining to do. The first official to arrive was dressed in a greenish khaki uniform and wore gold-rimmed sunglasses. He glanced into our compartment.

'All coming back, are you?' he asked casually, and walked on without waiting for a reply.

The women looked at me and fluttered.

'Passport control?' I asked for confirmation.

'Yes. Have you a visa?'

'No. I'd better go after him.'

Clutching my passport, I pursued the official down the corridor. When I told him who I was and what I wanted, he seemed mildly irritated, but told me that one of his colleagues would be along. I returned to the compartment and waited.

After ten or fifteen minutes another official appeared, so like the first that I wondered briefly if it was the same man, but this one was friendlier. He had a little portable desk draped round his neck. He took my passport, stuck a stamp in it, rubber-stamped the stamp, and charged me fifteen Deutschmarks. The East German mark is pegged to the Deutschmark, so that the Democratic Republic does not lose out on the exchange. Then he, too, moved on. But I still had no visa; I had simply paid for one. My original officer reappeared, and made up for his previous neglect. He took my passport and gazed from the photograph to me for a long time. Then he handed it to a young colleague, who did the same. Then they looked at each other doubtfully. They had clearly been coached by a past master of the Basilisk Stare. I took out my book of hotel vouchers, and this seemed to mollify them somewhat, but they took both vouchers and passport away and did not return for ten minutes.

'I'm sorry if I'm holding things up,' I said to my travelling companions.

'Don't worry. It's always like this.'

The older officer returned, and, opening his own portable desk, ceremoniously stamped a visa into my passport, telling me that the police in each town I stayed in would have to counterstamp it (this wearisome task, undertaken in any case by the hotels, was curtailed in Berlin, where the police put in a super-counterstamp, covering the rest of my journey). He also gave me my vouchers back. Our next visitor was a little old lady, who asked me diffidently if I had to conform with the obligatory currency exchange. I produced the vouchers again, and she disappeared apologetically. Then the younger officer returned.

'Vouchers,' he snapped.

'But he's shown them twice already,' my travelling companions piped up protectively.

'Immaterial,' said the young officer, but he was discomfited. He had poor skin and a wispy moustache. He made a great show of reading the vouchers once more, then gave them back after one more agate stare. He was soon followed by a different uniform – Customs. A fat, avuncular, bored-looking man in his fifties, with a trace of humour about his mouth.

'Anything to declare?' he asked me, glancing at my two bags. I said no but reached for the key to my main bag anyway. However, he had already turned his attention to the women.

'And what about you lot?'

Solemn shakes of the head.

'Okay,' he grinned. 'Welcome back.'

There was a longish pause after his departure, and then the woman from Bad Doberan leaned forward and said quietly, 'We are sorry about your reception. Please don't judge us by our officials.' I thought that if anyone judged any country by its officials, no one would travel anywhere, but said nothing. The elderly woman had dozed off.

Soon afterwards, the train lurched forward again. The countryside barely changed, but I had an indeterminate feeling of having travelled back in time. One of the first sights in East Germany seemed to be a good omen. Someone had built a wooden pylon near his house and set a wagon wheel on it, where a pair of storks had built their nest. They were standing on it, oblivious of man-made boundaries, flying happily to the West if need be to collect food to bring back to their home in the East. They stood so still that for a moment I wondered if they might be models of storks, so unreal did they seem. I noticed cobbled streets in the villages, where there had been tarmac in the West, and red-brick houses with high gables, where before there had been white-painted dwellings with low roofs.

The sisters got off the train at Grevesmühlen – to my regret, for the communicative one was softening by the mile. They were replaced by a large, placid schoolteacher with penetrating blue eyes. She fixed me solidly with these whenever she addressed me, and I felt trapped as in the beam of a powerful searchlight. She was reading a translation of *Kim*. Kipling is one of the few western authors whose work is easily available in East Germany, though there is no dearth of bookshops there. In eastern Europe generally people must be far more literate than they are in the West, if one is to judge by the number of bookshops; but it is more likely that with less television the book is still more important as a means of communication than it is in England.

I watched the countryside and the stations we passed through – Bobitz, Ventschow, Blankenberg. The stations hinted at a reason for the sense of having travelled back in time. When we reached Bützow I knew what it was. The name-signs were not illuminated glass, as in the West, but hand-painted on wooden boards, black lettering on a white background; and the lettering was in Gothic script. It was this above all that gave the place a pre-war air – this and the dull red-brick of the stations, which seemed for all their neatness and tidiness to have an atmosphere of depressing neglect.

'What is a "Station of Youth"?' I asked the schoolteacher, noticing that Bützow declared itself to be one.

'The Pioneers maintain it as part of their social duties. They don't run it, of course, but they are responsible for its general upkeep.'

'Sounds like a good idea,' I said politely.

'Oh, it is, and it saves wages; but of course not many of them want to do it. It takes too much of their spare time.'

'What would they rather be doing?'

'Listening to pop music, going to parties.'

She sounded sympathetic. She taught mathematics in Stralsund, and told me that most of the students who passed through her hands really had only one ambition – to leave for the West. 'And quite a few manage it. If they have official connections, and the subjects they want to read are not too controversial, they can even get permits to study abroad. One of my former pupils is doing a theology course in Chicago now. I doubt if we'll ever see him here again.'

The elderly woman continued to sleep. Glancing at her, the sad-eyed woman joined the conversation. 'Anyone who can visit relatives is lucky, but most of the time you have to travel alone, leave your family behind. That's to make sure you come back.'

'Is that what you were doing – visiting relatives? Or was it a shopping trip?'

Both women laughed. 'I wish it had been. But you can't take much western money out, and certainly not enough to match the prices in the Federal Republic. It's that as much as anything which keeps us where we are – the lack of hard currency.'

'What kind of welcome would you get in West Germany?'

'A warm one. It's written into their Constitution that any "refugee" from the DDR is *de facto* a citizen of Germany, and therefore has equal and retrospective rights of citizenship if he or she moves to the West.'

'Why doesn't everyone go?'

'It's hard to give up your home, your way of life, your friends. And of course it isn't that easy. It's unlikely that anything bad would happen to the people you left behind if you went, but there's always that doubt.'

It was late afternoon when the train pulled into Rostock, and a chill had settled on the air as we descended. On the platform, people awaiting the arrival of friends greeted them with posies. I had expected a large station, with a bank or an exchange office nearby. I found a small, battered, provincial building. I knew that Rostock, formerly a member city of the Hanseatic League, had suffered badly in the war, but guessed that as East Germany's principal port it would have been mightily rebuilt by now. I wondered whether I'd be right. The boutique manageress quickly disappeared into the crowd, but the schoolteacher, who was being met by her husband ('in our car', as she proudly told me), wouldn't leave me until she'd guided me out of the station and pointed me in the right direction.

I knew that any taxi-driver would cheerfully drive me to my destination for dollars or Deutschmarks, but I crossed the station square to the small Hotel am Bahnhof opposite and asked about trams, and whether I could change some money to buy a ticket. You cannot take East German marks into or out of the country – the same rule applies to all the lands of the Eastern Bloc, and it makes judging your budget so that you can leave the country with as little as possible left over into quite an art, since the difficulties of changing these unwanted currencies back are often insurmountable. This also explains the local hunger for negotiable, 'hard' currencies – the US dollar, the Deutschmark, and the pound sterling above all.

The receptionist gave me my first taste of the friendliness and helpfulness of the East Germans. No, she couldn't change money – that could only be done at the Interhotel where I was staying – but she could give me a ticket, and did, from her handbag, refusing any money at all. She even made sure I got on the right tram. The sun was setting, and in the golden light the number 11 took me up Rosa Luxemburg Strasse and through the Steintor, past the Town Hall with its seven spires, and the vast ship of the Marienkirche, to the hotel, across the road from the River Warnow with its ranks of derricks. I had no anxiety about finding the hotel, because without being asked, people on the tram, seeing my bags, said they would tell me where to leave it.

'Are you from the *Bundesrepublik*?'

'No, England.'

'England!' They seemed pleased. 'Nobody comes here from England.'

There are some towns, like some people, which one immediately takes to, before one knows them at all. Rostock was such a place for me. It started life as a colony of craftsmen from the west bank of the Elbe at the beginning of the thirteenth century. The fledgling town expanded onto the nearby heathland, and bought up the village of Warnemünde in 1323, becoming an important member of the Hanseatic League, and experiencing an economic boom, as a result of which one of north-eastern Europe's first universities was founded here in 1419.

Collapse came with the decay of the Hanseatic cities after the Thirty Years' War in the seventeenth century. The population declined by sixty per cent, and for centuries the town was a backwater. Its fortunes as a port recovered gradually, but this was a mixed blessing, because its importance as a naval base in the Second World War made it a principal target of the RAF, and in successive air-raids forty per cent of the town was destroyed. Since the end of the war, however, and with the division of Germany, it has risen from its ashes, and although still small – with its satellite 'new towns' its population numbers only 250,000 – it has worked its way back to something like its original status.

The university has also resumed a position of importance. It is now named after the pioneer German communist Wilhelm Pieck, who was the first president of the Democratic Republic, and whose name is given to streets and squares throughout the country. Near its neo-Renaissance building is the small garden of the Universitäts-platz, where there stands a statue of Blücher, the distinguished Prussian field marshal and ally of the Duke of Wellington, who was born here in 1742. The statue is by Johann Gottfried Schadow, a member of the family of great German sculptors of the turn of the nineteenth century. There are many seamen of the *Volksmarine* in Rostock, and on my first evening in the town I saw one of them having a quiet piss in the undergrowth by the statue; but the fact that it is there at all indicates a new readiness in East Germany to accept some of the history it shares with the Federal Republic. Elsewhere, even statues of Frederick the Great have been reinstated.

The Old Town runs along a main street, the Kröpeliner Strasse, which is now a pedestrian shopping boulevard, and which links the thirteenth-century Kröpeliner Tor in the west with Ernst-Thälmann-Platz, now a huge carpark dominated by the striking Town Hall, in the east. Beyond this axis the Old Town spreads north to the river, and south to the remains of the town walls, but little of it remains. What does has been cherished, and the churches destroyed in the bombing have been restored. The Nikolaikirche today, however, houses offices in its nave and flats in its roof. Looking up, one can see little window-boxes built into its monumental slope, each gay with geraniums in summer. By contrast, the Petrikirche, presiding over the Old Market, looks sad and neglected, and the Old Market itself is a forlorn place, turned over to use as a carpark, and flanked with small craftsmen's shops with metal name-plates which date from before the war, standing among bomb-sites still tousled with moss and fern.

There are brighter moments. Down by the Kuhtor, the third surviving medieval gate of the city, is the Kerkofhaus with its five-stepped gable, one of the best remaining sixteenth-century 'Burgher' houses. Others line the Kröpeliner Strasse, and as they have no advertising strapped to them, it is possible to enjoy them in their original beauty. The street is busy with shops and cafés, but what immediately strikes one is the quietness. It isn't silence; it is a generally muted air which is pleasant and unfamiliar.

In the shop windows there are a few familiar faces. The Smurfs and Garfield are tolerated throughout eastern Europe (but not in Albania or Romania, almost always the two exceptions). In the record stores a host of unfamiliar faces looked out at me from the sleeves. One girl, Ina Maria Federowski, seemed familiar – a home-grown Liza Minnelli.

There was no lack of electrical goods – televisions, radios and cassette players, though design and variety seem to western visitors old-fashioned and poor. People were smartly dressed, especially the young. In Rostock and Berlin, stone-washed denim was all the rage when I was there, and there was an element of positive chic in the way the girls dressed that I have not seen often in London. Paradoxically, the clothes in the shops seemed drab, and there were always clusters of people around the casual street traders who sold Adidas and Levis from park benches everywhere from the Seepromenade in Warnemünde to the Prager Strasse in Dresden.

Behind the Kröpeliner Strasse bulks the Marienkirche, a great grey brick church from the early thirteenth century. Inside it is dusty, but loved, and used. It contains two mighty artefacts: a massive organ hangs high on one side of the vast nave like some curious metallic animal clinging to the wall. It is by Paul Schmidt of Rostock, and was completed in 1770. It has 5702 pipes, four manuals, and one pedal. Although it was the first of many Baroque organs I would see, it is still the most impressive. At the other end of the church is an astronomical and astrological clock by Hans Dühringer of Nuremberg. It was built in 1472, and has only been restored twice since – in 1643 and 1974 – each time using the original parts. I asked a middle-aged woman selling Lutheran tracts from a trestle table if there was any literature about the church, but there was nothing to take away.

Returning to my hotel, I saw a large group of men and boys clustered admiringly round a big BMW which was parked outside.

'What are you looking at?' I asked one of them.

'The car, of course! You don't see many of them around here.'

'What do you drive?'

'Nothing. I'm still on the waiting list. But I'll get a Wartburg in another couple of years. One of the new ones.' Something I noticed in eastern Europe (apart from Budapest and Belgrade) is the lightness of the traffic. In East Germany, so little money is invested in the motor industry that there are only two basic types of car, the Wartburg and the Trabant, both modest models built to a very old-fashioned design, not unlike old DAFs. However, Wartburg have recently produced a new body design, with French help, which everyone is very excited about. The cars come in a very limited range of colours, but at least are no longer all black or beige, as they once were. Most of them sound like dying motor mowers, yet I rarely saw one actually broken down. The Wartburg takes its name from the castle which dominates the town of Eisenach in the south, where the car is made.

Soon after, the West German owner of the BMW arrived, and without a trace of self-consciousness got in and drove off. The group broke up, paying not the slightest attention to a girl emerging from the hotel in the tightest, briefest shorts I had ever seen.

There were some advertisements on display, and inspired by one for Bulgarian wine, which glowed from the roof of the skyscraper next door to the hotel, I decided to set off in search of some, and fish to go with it. I ended up drinking a sharp white East German wine, with roe on toast followed by turbot, in the Gastmahl des Meeres by the Museum of Navigation. This was my introduction to slow service and lukewarm food, but as there was no hint of hostility or resentment, these didn't seem to matter, and the food itself was excellent. I felt an unexpectedly warm glow steal over me which was not all to do with the wine or the sun, or even with relief at having managed to get this far. It had more to do with an unaccountable feeling of being at home – something which I would not experience again for some time.

The next day started dull, with heavy clouds that fortunately never kept their promise of rain. I decided to take the S-Bahn to Warnemünde. The half-hour trip cost one mark (transport is heavily subsidized and very cheap: my journey from Rostock to Berlin would cost less than my taxi-ride across Hamburg). We travelled in curious double-decker carriages of a type which I was to see on and off throughout my journey. They were practical. In eastern Europe, where private transport is scarce, public transport is very much used, and has to be made the most of.

The journey took us roughly north-west, with the Warnow on our right and what must have been marshland, to judge by the wildflowers growing along the railway, on the left. Large pipelines skirted the track, occasionally daubed with graffiti of the 'Hans loves Liesl' type, though here and there someone had written the names of western pop stars like Bruce Springsteen. Beyond them were the new towns, of which the local guide-books speak proudly. The need to house people as quickly and as cheaply as possible after the war was pressing, and East Germany had none of the help that the Federal Republic enjoyed.

The townships, Reutershagen, Evershagen, Lütten Klein, Lichtenhagen, Schmarl, and Gross Klein, spread themselves along the railway between Rostock and Warnemünde, separated only by the scrubland that existed before them. They are all of a piece, identical ranks of tower blocks with nothing to break them up or provide variety, not even a tree, each with a basic shopping centre, and schools.

On some of the patches of ground between them were tiny bungalows, each surrounded by a little garden in which fruit, flowers and vegetables were growing. These were the summer houses of those lucky enough to be able to own one. I could imagine less fortunate people envying the ability to grow fruit and vegetables more than the pretty flowers or the little houses themselves. Greengrocers, I had already noticed, were few and far between, and their poorly-stocked shops carried placards advertising their willingness to buy from private growers. Orange-juice at breakfast was the most expensive drink I was offered anywhere in East Germany and Czechoslovakia, and I did not see an orange or a banana between leaving London and arriving in Mostar, in Hercegovina, months later. Any other fruit was rare and poor, though I was travelling through some of the richest farmland in Europe.

Warnemünde itself is a pretty little resort town which, with its grey sky and its grey sea, reminded me of several English counterparts. A man-made inlet, the Alter Strom, shelters the trawler fleet, and along its bank is strung a series of boutiques and cafés. I tried to get a beer in one, having already introduced myself to the excellent local Radeberger (surpassed only by Wernesgrüner). The waitress looked me up and down.

'Only coffee or cocktails.'

'What sort of cocktails?'

She reeled off a list in which the name Collins appeared frequently. I opted for a gin-and-tonic, and was given a perfumed fizzy drink that tasted strongly of synthetic lemon. After that, I was ready to explore.

Warnemünde is a fishing harbour and a major freight port as well as a resort, and so it is split into three. The central part is the town itself, with the trawler moorings, a small crisscrossing of a dozen or so attractive narrow streets and a little park in which muted children rode on a carousel whose music, however soft, was a relief to my ears after so much silence. To the south is the main port, dominated when I was there by a mighty Russian ship, the *Samarkand*, almost as big as the town. To the north are the beach, the yacht harbour, the customs buildings, and a small quay whence the ferry boats leave for Denmark.

There were plenty of holidaymakers about, rather drably dressed. In the thin drizzle which had started to fall, in their tan anoraks and plastic rain hats, trying to calm squalling children enveloped in candy-floss, they didn't look unlike English families at the seaside. Despite the weather, people were sailing and even bathing. The most striking thing on the beach was a great number of enclosed double chairs, made of wood or, more attractively, wicker, and painted a variety of colours, so that from a distance they looked like a large patchwork quilt spread out on the sand. The interesting thing about these two-seaters was that they had clearly been designed for the northern climate, for they were boxed in, like porters' chairs, to protect their occupants from the wind. A few, in addition, had doors, so that you could climb in and shut yourself up completely. Not surprisingly, some of the remoter ones, thus closed, were rocking and giggling, though how anyone could get up to anything in such a confined space is beyond me.

I walked up to the Westmole, on which a small green-and-white lighthouse was perched, partly to watch the yachts racing.

'Look,' a young father was saying to his son as they watched a ferry departing for Gedser. 'That's how they used to leave for sea, for voyages of five years and more, and all the sailors' wives would stand here and wave their handkerchiefs and cry.'

'I'm glad you're not a sailor, Daddy.'

'Let's look at the yachts.'

'Can we have a yacht one day?'

The father caught my eye and smiled. 'Perhaps. If we get to be big enough fish.'

On the tram back from the station into Rostock I met Berndt. I can't remember how we got into conversation, but we were the only two people on board. He was solidly drunk, and at first inclined to be aggressive. I think I must have asked him something he'd misunderstood.

'Are you from out of town?' he said, from his expression trying to locate my accent.

'Yes.'

'From the West?'

'From London.'

His frown cleared and was replaced by a beam which sent his red moustaches shooting almost vertically up his cheeks. 'From *London!*'

He came and sat next to me, pumping my hand and giving me a bear-hug. 'Bloody hell, from London! Well, what the hell are you doing here?'

'I wanted to see eastern Europe.'

'What the hell for?'

'I think Europeans should see more of each other.'

'So do I. I wish I could return the compliment. Where're you staying? Let's go for a beer.'

He worked as a carpenter, and had been installing roof joists in a housing development nearby. He was born in Rostock in 1952, and apart from a day-trip to Prague once he had never been out of the DDR.

'It's a bugger, really, but if you don't have any clout, you don't get the *Devisen*, the exchangeable currency, to make any kind of holiday away possible. Even the packages they offer us within the Bloc cost the earth, and I don't fancy Poland or Bulgaria or any of those places. Too bloody uncivilized!' He was proud of the town, and reeled off a list of statistics relating to its growth since 1945. Then, after our third beer, his enthusiasm suddenly drained out of him. 'We're okay here, really,' he concluded. 'We've got no unemployment, and we've got no debts – not like you lot have, in hock up to your bloody armpits!' He paused and looked reflectively at his beer. 'But there's something missing. I think,' he added heavily after another pause, 'that we've lost our soul.'

'Do you think we'll ever get back together?'

'East and West? Well, most of *us* would like to, but could you afford to take us on? Would you want to? Would you trust us? And how long would it take for us to unlearn all our propaganda and learn to trust you? Christ, it's all right for you and me to sit down and have a beer, but I don't think it's in the politicians' interests on either side to give the other lot a human face. They'd lose their jobs! Anyway,' he added as an afterthought, 'it might be okay if East Germany and even Hungary came over to the West, but I don't know about the rest. Some of those poor buggers have never had any freedom, and they wouldn't know what to do with it . . .'

After we'd parted, I wandered back down Kröpeliner Strasse. The grey morning had given way to a positively balmy afternoon. It was a Friday, but the street was filled with people of all ages. One of the mysteries of eastern Europe that I never quite penetrated was that everywhere the daytime streets were always full. I remember overhearing an American tourist, buffeted by the crowd in Prague, exclaim: 'Jesus, doesn't anyone work over here?' – but my guess is that the answer lies in shift-work. Unemployment doesn't exist yet, though it is a spectre which is rising in East Germany, and has already arrived in Hungary.

The street was full of music. Across from the university, a band composed of middle-aged men were belting out German hits of the Twenties, while in unconscious competition two youths with banjos sat on a wall not far away and plucked tentative Blue Grass. The one occidental music which has taken root and thriven like a weed is Country and Western, and I have heard Dolly Parton and Crystal Gayle records playing to the twilight diners of places as remote as the Astoria Hotel in Oradea in western Romania. Along the street an appreciative crowd listened to two skinheads who were the best performers of all. They were singing medieval ballads to their guitars. One of them, which I knew, tells of a man stuck in a town and determined to break free and try his luck elsewhere. They sang it as if it had been written yesterday. The inability to travel, except in the limited zones available to them, lies very heavily on young people.

Further up the street still was a traditional German one-man band, with his battered frock coat and top hat, his drum and his accordion. Attached to his back was a little puppet-devil on a pole, which rotated and rang bells as the old man played, oblivious of the clicking Praktikas of a handful of Russian tourists.

2

'HAUPTSTADT DER DDR'

'You have the world to choose from; why on earth have you come here?'

Georg was getting on for sixty, a civil engineer from Teltow who was holidaying alone at the Interhotel – he was reticent about his family, and I never discovered whether he was married or not. He had short grey wavy hair and a serious, lined face. He lingered over his second coffee and smoked cigarette after cigarette – Kenton Blue Stripe, which he told me were the mildest available. His doctor had warned him about smoking; but he knew he couldn't give up. Blue Stripes were a compromise.

'Don't make the mistake of thinking that this is an egalitarian society. Influence and contacts are what matter here – having friends in the right places. I expect it's the same where you come from, but at least you don't try to pretend that it isn't so. The biggest problem we have here is the problem of hypocrisy.'

I asked about the private summer houses.

'Just to get one built, to get the plot of land, you need to know which strings to pull. If you know that much, then suddenly the usual problem of getting hold of building materials disappears too.'

'What about the cost?'

'That's no problem if you're a big fish, but for most of us ... Look, have you seen the travel agents' posters? They all advertise holidays here, there and everywhere in eastern Europe and Russia: "Come to sunny Romania", "Why not make it Burgas this year?" – but the costs are deceptive. A package holiday for two in Bulgaria might set you back 5000 marks, which may not sound bad until you realize that a man on 1000 marks a month is going to have to save for ages to get it, and if he's got kids, it'll take longer and cost more. With cars it's worse. Even a locally-made car costs 14,000, and you can be on a waiting list for twelve years if you want one because the factories are antiquated and can't cope with the demand. Yet the government won't invest in the motor industry. It's crazy, but we have no choice.'

'Do you think you'll ever get one?'

He looked at me shrewdly for a moment. 'What, and rejoin the West? Never. We've become a Russian province. Look at the names of our streets. Half of them are called after Russians. The great excuse is that this was the cradle of Communism – but there's a Russian soldier round every corner.'

Georg spoke with asperity, but he must have been a man of some privilege himself, or he wouldn't have been staying at an Interhotel.

***

The train journey to Berlin took three hours. I travelled opposite a young mother with her three-year-old son who was by turns excited, bored, fractious, sleepy, and then excited again as our way took us through featureless farmland planted with maize and cabbages. I once saw a roe deer by the side of the track, and there were scattered, unexceptional villages, as well as one factory which for some reason looked like a corrugated iron copy of a Transylvanian castle.

We arrived at Berlin-Lichtenberg in the middle of a blazing afternoon, and I made my way via the S-Bahn and on foot to the luxury hotel to which my western status condemned me. I'd asked directions from a flower-seller who not only told me how to reach my destination but accompanied me part of the way. He was an old man with the broad accent of a real Berliner – which is the only human thing that can ignore the Wall. He told me that he had never been out of his district in his life. 'So I never went to West Berlin, even when I could. I've never seen the Siegessäule or the Ku'damm. Daft, isn't it? But at least the Wall's made no difference to me.'

It was ironic to be enjoying such a hotel in the Eastern Bloc, but Berlin has sprouted several such, in the hope of using them to lure western currencies, for the hotels are chiefly used as business and conference centres. The Palast was the best in town until recently. It has been superseded by the newly refurbished Grand; when I passed it on one of my walks about town, it simply looked too damned Grand for me to go in.

East Berlin refers to itself rather insecurely as 'Berlin – Capital of the DDR'. This designation even appears on road-signs. I will just call it Berlin, for it seems to me that it is isolated West Berlin which requires the addition of an adjective. West Berlin is truly half a city, because, lively and vital as it may be, one is constantly aware of the lack of a centre.

This problem does not exist in Berlin, which contains the centre of the old united city, in the area surrounding the Fischerinsel. The island itself is now a desert of high-rises interspersed with a handful of crumbling Jugendstil buildings, but traditionally this is the site of the fishing village which grew to be the capital of Germany.

Berlin also has all the city's old buildings. By the hotel is the still war-blackened cathedral, and across the Marx-Engels Bridge with its lovely Regency statuary one reaches Unter den Linden. The dark red brick of the Town Hall, and of the churches of St Nicholas and St Mary, contrasts with the pale creams, apricots and dark pinks of the Baroque buildings. Most of these were destroyed by the combined Russian and Allied forces at the end of the war, and Berlin is still a city of bomb-sites and war-torn buildings, a place where the ghost of the war is still emphatically present. Although the main edifices along Unter den Linden, the Museuminsel, and beyond, have been completely restored, their modern interiors belie the promise of their exteriors, since restoration of their destroyed decor has been impossible in most cases. Nevertheless, vast sums were spent on renovation in time for the celebration of the city's 750th birthday in 1987.

Intimations of the ideology are present everywhere. Museum guides are quick to point out the vandalism perpetrated by early Christians on pagan statuary. More mischievously, the late-night film on television on my first night in Berlin was an old

American gangster movie, with Ronald Reagan, then president of the USA, as the villain. By contrast to West Berlin, incidentally, at 8 p.m. on a summer Saturday the streets were quiet and deserted.

There are eyesores. Alexanderplatz is a bleak desert of a place even in summer, when the fountains play and there are people about; and once beyond the Boden-museum, walking north-west along Oranienburger Strasse, one is back in a pre-war city, or one would be if the now-ruined and silent synagogue were open, and not a silent, fire-blackened, bullet-pocked reminder of what happened on *Kristallnacht*, the November night in 1938 when synagogues throughout Germany were smashed and burned. As everywhere in eastern Europe, there are building sites. The building site became for me the one enduring symbol of the entire area. It can take five years to complete any project, owing to irregular supplies of materials and, very often, slow labour.

Across from the hybrid cathedral, still awaiting cleaning and restoration, is the enormous and vulgar Palace of the Republic, a building of a type and under a similar name – 'of the People', 'of Unity', and so on – found in most large towns. Where possible such a building is placed in challenging juxtaposition to the old buildings which are reminders of the capitalist-imperialist past. 'We can do just as well,' the new buildings are saying. 'Look at us, celebrations of the people, built by the people for the people.'

Because their official socialist histories are short, the republics of eastern Europe are inclined to glorify the new and the recent, and to date all progress from 1945. Very often in the past the old reminders have been swept away in the belief that a country can become a modern industrial power simply by providing the trappings. Except for Romania, the countries of the Eastern Bloc have now learned that this simply doesn't happen. Nevertheless, considering that most of them have struggled back from appalling ruin at the end of the war, and have since had to cope with an enforced and exclusive trade relationship with Russia in which the USSR has always dictated the terms, the achievements of these put-upon countries are remarkable and brave.

When I was in Berlin, only the restaurants of the Palace of the Republic were open. It was still summer, and the season of concerts and plays had yet to begin. The Palace has a concert-hall, two theatres and a congress hall. On each floor, its foyers are the size of football pitches, and the walls are adorned with modern figurative paintings demonstrating the achievements of Communism, with titles like *When Communists Dream*. One is forcibly reminded here that East Germany owes its very existence to Communism.

I wandered north up the Chaussee Strasse to Brecht's house. It was closed for the summer, but I visited his and Helene Weigel's graves in the cemetery next door. The stones are irregular pyramids of rock lettered simply in gold, the plots covered with miniature begonias. The begonia and the petunia fill the flowerbeds of monuments, parks, cemeteries, and public and private gardens all over eastern Europe in summer. I thought of the sad bronze of Brecht sitting in the little square named after him outside the Berliner Ensemble, hemmed in by corrugated iron and building sites, and of the melancholy Schiffbauerdamm running down from it along the River Spree, but cut off from it by more corrugated iron.

Eventually my wanderings brought me back down to Pariser Platz and the Brandenburg Gate, built by C. G. Langhans between 1789 and 1791, across whose top rides Rudolf Schadow's mighty charioteer. Originally the group faced west, but the East Germans turned them around, as they did the statue of Frederick the Great at the other end of Unter den Linden. The Berlin Wall crosses Pariser Platz, once the hub of the city. On the eastern side you may not approach closer than fifty yards, and in contrast to the gaudy graffiti on its western side, it is painted a uniform pale beige. A low railing indicates where you must stop, and beyond it stand, rather casually, a number of the usual heavily-armed police. One, in a sentry-box, drawing heavily and furtively on a Balkan cigarette, dropped it guiltily when he saw I'd noticed.

Looking through the arch of the Brandenburg Gate I could see the Siegessäule (the Victory Column) with its golden pinnacle, far beyond along the Strasse des 17 Juni. Nearer, a flash of bright colours just on the other side of the Gate revealed where tourists in West Berlin had climbed a viewing platform on their side of Pariser Platz to look at us.

I turned away and walked back along the empty Unter den Linden, passing two youths who were breakdancing. They stopped to wave at me, and were delighted when I waved back. I looked at the bright lettering in the clothes-shop windows – a kind of advertising. We seem to need to advertise, even when all we can say is, 'Come inside and get kitted out for summer' in bright paper letters – even, indeed, when there isn't much in the shop. Is it some natural competitive urge that can't be suppressed? Turning off the main street, I headed for Checkpoint Charlie – I wanted to see that from the other side, too.

On the way I paused at Platz der Akademie to look at Karl Schinkel's early nineteenth-century Schauspielhaus, now the principal concert hall, passing on the way the modern grey box of the Comic Opera. Within, I'd been told, Semper's ornate decoration has been retained. The Schauspielhaus stands in the centre of the broad square and is guarded by a winged bronze lion and lioness. Of the twin churches to the north and south of it, the 'German' was still a ruin, but the 'French', to the north, was fully renovated, and open. There was no access to the body of the church, but one can visit the tower, whose interior is beautifully rebuilt in brick. It is a pity that the rebuilding is so unsuited to the neo-Classical exterior.

Checkpoint Charlie is called *Grenzübergang Friedrichstrasse* by the East Germans. I crossed Leipziger Strasse, uprooted by building works, and a short distance further on was brought to a halt by a railing. Several Berliners leaned on it in the late afternoon sun, idling their time away watching the frontier traffic. Cars queued, and a cyclist was let through a gate with an electric lock. In the distance, across the clutter of fencing, I could see familiar sights: the high viewing platform on the other side; the US flag over the white kiosk in the centre of the street; the Museum of Escape. It all seemed a very long way away.

It was another balmy summer evening. I walked back into town, across the

Fischerinsel and the Molken-Markt, and along Stralauer Strasse, past the large, grey, grimy government buildings, guarded by heavily-armed youths in grey uniforms. At a street corner, two *Volkspolizei* stood by their car. They wore green uniforms, with high peaked caps, jodhpurs and jackboots. Such a style of uniform has somehow survived here, together with the goose-step march. I turned into Waisenstrasse, by now the only pedestrian around, and at the end of it came to my goal. The café-bar 'Zur letzten Instanz' is Berlin's most famous. It is entirely unpretentious. Tiny, it is usually packed, but I was very early. I hadn't reserved a table, however (people seem remarkably reluctant in any case ever to take reservations for one; you just arrive, and are shunted wherever you will fit), so they sat me at the *Stammtisch* by the ornate green porcelain stove near the door – exactly where Napoleon is reputed to have sat. The place seems too modest for him. The pub (for that is what it is) is reputed to have been founded by a retired knight-errant in 1621, making it Berlin's oldest such establishment.

I ordered cold pork and beer, and wolfed it down – I'd been walking for eight hours, and all I'd had for lunch was an appalling dish at one of the museum cafés – poached eggs, raw swedes and cold rice.

In East Germany, the tendency is to fill up the tables one by one, rather than sit separate groups at separate tables, so that I rarely lacked someone to talk to at mealtimes. That evening I was joined by two young men who were hoping to go to drama school and become actors after they had done their military service. Most of what they said was familiar, describing a situation not unlike that in English theatre a few years ago. The theatre was stagnant because it was in the hands of directors who had got into niches when they were young and held on to their positions. Now they were played out of ideas, but still too young, relatively, to retire or hand over.

'It's very frustrating,' they said. 'But it's typical. It can't be like this in the West.' So often, the West represented a kind of Never Never Land where everything had to be all right simply because people were 'free'. I talked about riots, and strikes, and student unrest, and unemployment. 'Well, at least you're free to have them,' was all these two would answer.

They asked me a lot of questions about London, and they also asked, inevitably, why I had come east. 'Is there anything here that you like?'

'The streets are clean and quiet, and I've seen no drunks, no down-and-outs, no homeless people.'

'You've been to the wrong streets.'

Nevertheless, it was generally true that to walk down the streets of most east European cities at night was to be completely safe – there was no one about anyway, except for groups of aimless teenagers with nothing else to do, sitting on benches and talking, or wandering up and down, empty-eyed, dressed up to the nines.

There were two or three visits that I had promised myself. The first was to the Pergamon Museum. My first sight of the much restored and reduced-in-scale Pergamon Altar was delayed by the complication of entering the museum at all, having queued for my ticket, and again for a camera ticket, and again to hand in my shoulder bag. Once inside, I was astonished to see people, apparently members of the public, walking all over the altar steps, despite a discreetly low rope barrier at its base, but I was told that they were members of an international conference of archaeologists, who were having drinks in the upper part of the altar, where a room displays a frieze telling the story of Telephos. To reach it myself, I would have to wait until the next guided tour.

It was worth it. The guide was a raddled forty-year-old with a delightfully cynical sense of humour. 'The tour lasts three-quarters of an hour; if you don't think you can take it, drop out now.' When the time came to mount the steps, a number of opportunists latched on to our group. The guide dealt with this hitch with great aplomb. 'Only the original fifteen members of the group can come up,' she announced. 'Who they are, I leave to you to decide.'

The one thing overdone here is restoration. The altar, dating from about 180 BC and discovered during excavations of a fortified complex on the hill of Bergama in western Turkey at the turn of the century, is too much shored up with modern reconstruction to allow its antiquity to breathe. The same applies to the other great exhibit of the museum, the Babylonian Ishtar Gate of Nebuchadnezzar II. I preferred the small Roman mosaics from Ostia in one of the upper rooms – among the finest I have ever seen.

The New Museum nearby is still a ruin, in the slow process of reconstruction. The priorities of government have been to build up industry and get people housed, which is why there are still ruins over forty-five years after the end of the war. The Old Museum, a gloomy neo-Classical structure by Schinkel, adjacent to the cathedral, had a good exhibition of recent and contemporary East German painters. The subjects were, on the whole, serious and individual, not conventional paeans to Communism Triumphant. Here, painters like Otto Nagel and Bert Heller confirm that the spirit of the individual cannot be overwhelmed by a group ideology. There were also four paintings by David Hockney and Roy Lichtenstein, on loan from the Ludwig Collection in Aachen.

There was one other visit I wanted to make – to the vast war memorial to the Russian soldiers who died liberating Berlin. It is to the south of the city in Treptower Park, on the south bank of the Spree. The main part of the memorial is defined by three mighty Socialist-Realist statues – two mourning soldiers flank the entrance to the central arena, which is dominated at the far end by a gigantic soldier bearing a massive sword in one hand, while the other arm protectively clasps a little girl. The base is marked 1941–1945 (no one likes to think of the years 1939–1941, when Russia and Nazi Germany were allies).

Around the sides of the memorial are sixteen stelae containing reliefs of war scenes and quotations from Stalin. The marble for them was taken from Hitler's Chancellery. But the most moving monument of the whole complex is in stone. It is at the far end of the area, by itself in a protective semi-circle of poplars, and depicts a mother mourning her lost children.

In the grounds of the main complex a young gardener was at work, clearing away weeds. He was dressed in shorts and a T-shirt, which carried a picture of a skyline with skyscrapers and the message, *I LOVE Manhattan!*

I walked back to the quays where the White Fleet boats leave for trips down the Spree, through the sunny birch trees, almost alone in the park, passing only a woman teaching her dachshund to jump over a low fence. I realized that I was becoming used to seeing public notices in both German and Russian, but I could never quite ignore the pervasive presence of this foreign power, either in notices or monuments, or reflected in street names – particularly in East Germany, Czechoslovakia and Bulgaria.

I took the S-Bahn back to the centre. The sign by the window, NICHT HINAUSLEH-NEN – do not lean out – had been selectively scratched away to read NICHT HINSEHEN – do not look out; a sad comment. The S-Bahn, an old system of overground trains which link up with the Underground, still operates all over the divided city, though it is run by the East Germans.

That evening I had drinks with a western businessman who had spent some time in the DDR.

'One of the problems here is that Russia, which never directly experienced the Renaissance or the Reformation, has no tradition of personal freedom, or of personal intercession with God. The Orthodox Church has kept the Mystery behind the iconostasis, and the people can only approach God through the priest.'

'But that doesn't apply to East Germany or Poland, or any of the countries which used to be part of Austria-Hungary?'

'No, but all of them, except for East Germany, have been used to many centuries of autocratic rule, by foreigners, using fear and terror, informers, a secret police. Stalin continued an existing tradition, which was only interrupted between 1918 and 1938; but that was it, until today.'

'And what about Russia now?'

'We'll see. Here, everyone is waiting with bated breath. But you know, there was a joke going around Poland recently, that the only difference between Gorbachev and Dubček is that it hasn't happened to Gorbachev yet! Things seem to be moving fast – and so they should – too fast for the Old Guard to respond. But the Old Guard won't give up without a fight, and some of them sincerely believe that their way is the only way to rule these people. There's not a very strong sense of individual rights, or even individualism, and a whole adult generation has grown up here in the DDR in that way of thinking.'

When I left, I took a taxi back to the Palast Hotel. The driver was chirpy and suntanned, just back from his holidays in Hungary. 'Go there every year,' he told me. 'Even hotter than it is here and cheap as hell if you've got dollars or D-marks. Have you got any D-marks, by the way, that you want to exchange?'

I hadn't. He didn't offer me any change for my fare. 'You can afford to be generous if you're staying here,' he grinned as he drove off.

3

GOETHE'S GERMANY

When I arrived at Schönefeld to get my connection to Potsdam, I discovered that the line was closed for repair work. If the building site is the obvious symbol of eastern Europe, the world *Reparatur* in all its forms best reflects its spirit.

The train had been replaced by a bus service, cleverly scheduled not to connect with the S-Bahn, so that one either faced the prospect of a forty-five-minute wait, or took the regular bus, for which one had to pay again.

'I'll wait,' decided a fat young fellow passenger wearing a T-shirt with the message *Sport macht fit*. 'My time is paid for.'

'Good luck,' I said, cramming myself and my bags onto the already crowded regular bus. The journey took an hour and a half through dull countryside and biscuit-coloured villages whose architecture featured that uncompromising rectangularity common to all post-war German building.

Potsdam was bigger and more modern than I had imagined it, and here for the first time I was aware of a solid Russian military presence. Once checked in, I walked north to the Nauener Tor, one of the city's surviving medieval gates, which looks as if it had been deposited directly from the pages of Grimm's fairy tales, and then struck west along Hegel Strasse to Sanssouci Park. Here, one immediately crosses another kind of frontier – a frontier in time. I would become used to this phenomenon as the journey progressed. The buildings of the past are preserved and even enshrined (though in places neglect indicates that there have been other priorities), but that is all. They have no living relevance to the country they are in, and seem out of their element, like giant beached sea-creatures, or elderly relatives, tolerated, but consigned to a corner of the room.

'Don't visit the palace itself – go and see the New Chambers instead,' I had been advised by a man in the street of whom I'd asked directions. He'd also told me to look at the Friedenskirche, a neo-Romanesque church built in the middle of the nineteenth century by Persius, to the order of Friedrich-Wilhelm IV, who is buried in the crypt with his wife. It is now maintained through private contributions by a small Protestant group. It is a beautiful building, so tucked away that people miss it. If you didn't know where you were, in its grounds you would imagine yourself in Italy.

The New Chambers (*Neue Kammern*) had originally been built as an orangery, but shortly afterwards Frederick II had them converted to extra accommodation for his guests. The suite of Baroque rooms, newly renovated and decorated with illustrations from Ovid's *Metamorphoses*, seem cold today. It is hard to imagine the

vivid life which went on here when Frederick's salon was at its height, though
earnest young guide did his best to breathe life into the rooms for the dull-e
tourists, mainly Russians in flat Terylene caps, with cameras in bulky antiqu
cases dangling at paunch level. Slopping around the marble and jasper floors in out-
sized felt slippers made us all look ridiculous.

Outside, near the vine-terraces beside the steps leading up to the palace, a youth
sat on a stone bench, eyes closed, totally immersed in the music he was listening to
on his Walkman (a rare and prized status symbol everywhere but in Hungary and
Yugoslavia, where they are common, and not seen at all in Albania or Romania). A
foolish man, the father of two young children, gawped at this spectacle and tried to
distract the youth by coming close and imitating the yelping of a dog, but the young
man was oblivious. It was interesting to see the response – a childish mixture of envy
and aggression – his composure evoked.

I walked through the Rehgarten to the Neues Palais, but did not feel like visiting
another series of empty Baroque rooms. The statues outside were sad enough, still
soot-blackened by the fires of the Second World War. Some stood around the terrace
in forlorn groups, waiting to be replaced in their positions along the roofs and
balustrades. All were badly eaten by pollution.

It was getting late, and only a few small knots of people were still about. The sun
had vanished behind clouds and it was immediately much colder. City parks in the
late afternoon have a melancholy effect, and the time had come to leave. I decided not
to head north to visit the rather pompous Cäcilienhof, a mock-Tudor lodge, now a
hotel, where the Potsdam Agreement, finalizing the division of influence in Europe at
the end of the Second World War between Russia, Great Britain and the USA, was
signed. Instead I retraced my steps by way of the oddly-named Ökonomieweg, which
took me past the Chinese Teahouse, an idiosyncratic summer house in the park
guarded by life-size mandarins, and tea-girls in gold, who looked more than anything
like geishas.

To escape from the diet of pork, beer and potatoes, backed up by the occasional
canned pea, I ate in the best of my hotel's five restaurants. A single glass of Austrian
white wine at 12.65 marks rather took my breath away, but the food, a venison steak
with fresh vegetables, was excellent. Near me, a privileged young couple were
toasting each other in cocktails of a lurid colour, and a Cuban engineer toyed with
some fish. I talked with a schoolteacher who, he said, treated himself to dinner here
once a month.

'Nearly everywhere you'll find that the locals use the hotel bars and restaurants –
they're the only place to go in some towns. Here, we're much more fortunate. We
don't even suffer from pollution as much as they do further south. In Bitterfeld and
Halle, they've really got problems these days.'

'Is anything being done?'

'Our government has a very simple way of solving the pollution problem: they say
it doesn't exist. Anyway, they stick to the view that production and expansion have
to take precedence over a clean environment. They're terrified of the country going
bust.'

'But here it's better?'

'Yes, but even so ... Look, the people in West Berlin aren't allowed to eat the fish out of the Havel any more, but there's no such proscription in the DDR. And all the pine trees are dying. I even notice the effects in my own garden.'

'What do you grow?'

'A lot of fruit. The soil's sandy here, though, and it doesn't retain water. I expect you get quite a lot of success with roses – all that London clay!'

'Yes. But most of the roses in my garden are too old – finished. I must get round to replacing them.'

'There are two elderly English spinsters who live just beyond Babelsberg now that they're retired. They came here after the war to teach, and they liked it so much that they stayed. They've got a little cottage on a hill overlooking the town, and they have quite a lot of success with their roses. Must be the English green thumb!'

It was pouring when the train arrived in Magdeburg, and a wintry chill had settled on the air. I had a three-hour wait for my connection to Erfurt, but there seemed to be little point in leaving the shelter of the station. There was nothing to do except queue for a coffee from the Mitropa stand, and then settle down on a bench to read. The connection was delayed, and I asked a lady in red whether she knew anything.

'No, it's often a little late. It's a shuttle service between here and Erfurt.' She was waiting for her nephew, but she wasn't sure if he'd actually be on the train. 'Still, I've not heard anything to the contrary.'

'Well, if they didn't phone ...'

She laughed. 'You're just like my relatives in the West. If you only knew how lucky you are, to be able to take telephones for granted!'

'You don't have one?'

'No one has them except the higher-ups. Anyway, even if I was prepared to apply and wait three years to get one, still none of my friends would have one, so what would be the point?'

'What do you do if you need to get in touch with someone urgently?'

'You go to the post office and you either queue for a phone booth, or you queue to send a telegram.'

I thought about queues. In Berlin I had queued to get into a bookshop, because you couldn't enter without a little supermarket basket for your purchases, and if none was available you had to wait. Then you queued to hand your purchase to a shop assistant, who gave you a bill, which you took to the cashier's queue. Then you re-turned and queued to pick up your wrapped package. It was enough to test patience severely, but I had already noticed that the tempo of life is slower in eastern Europe. People walk more slowly in the street. A kind of lethargy is in the air. As a foreign visitor one is pampered. The hotel rooms have phones, colour television and radio, and you can buy stamps and postcards at the reception desks, for hard currency.

'I just wish my relatives in the West would reply to my letters more often,' the lady in red was saying. 'But they've forgotten how to write. They have the telephone and it slips their minds that we're twenty years behind them.' The train pulled in then and she left me to look for her nephew. I climbed aboard and found a window-seat. Not that the rain allowed me to see much. And what I could see, of course, looked much bleaker than it deserved to.

The route lay through miles of flat, featureless farmland until Güsten. South of there, hills run all the way to Erfurt, and the countryside becomes more varied. By the time we arrived, in mid-afternoon, the sun was out again, and the heat intense. It was hard to believe that an hour earlier we had been travelling through a hailstorm.

Seeing Erfurt, one thinks immediately of sister medieval towns only a short distance to the south in West Germany: Bamberg, Rothenberg, Nuremberg. Certainly these have their modern quarters, but how beautifully their old centres have been maintained. It is sad to see Erfurt as neglected as it is, for it is a lovely town. There is evidence of restoration work, though the decay of some of the medieval and German Renaissance houses is worrying, as is the state of the 600-year-old Town Bridge. Traffic pollution, the great curse of east European towns, is also taking its toll.

Erfurt is dominated by its two great churches – the Cathedral of the Virgin and the Church of St Severin, both built close together on a hill above the Domplatz, and looking like a pair of stranded galleons.

The cathedral was founded by Boniface in 742, and the church a century or so later, to house the relics of Saint Severin, though his bones, together with those of his wife (Saint Vincentia) and daughter (Saint Innocentia), have remained in the cathedral. The present buildings date from the late thirteenth to the mid-fourteenth centuries.

The cathedral is famous for its fourteenth-century oak choirstalls, which are heavily carved, the best featuring a laughing bishop and a bat-devil who could be the twin brother of the Lincoln Imp. The east window was also built in the fourteenth century, and at eighteen metres high it is the tallest in Europe; but the most striking feature for me was the Portal of the Virgins. The wise virgins on the left look suitably smug, but the foolish virgins, in an agony of self-recrimination, twist and tear their bodies away from the columnar form which hitherto in sculpture would have contained them. Their expressions are worthy of such central European geniuses as Veit Stoss, the Bamberg Master, and Paul of Levoca.

There are more astonishing treasures still. Near a mid-twelfth-century stone Madonna stands a bronze, half-life-size statue of a man, his arms held aloft to take candles. It looks so very like the 'ecclesiastical modernist' sculpture of the Fifties that I passed it by at first. Then I discovered that it was cast in 1160 by a master called Wolfram, and is the earliest such bronze in existence.

I didn't think I would get into St Severin's, as it appeared to be closed to the public in order to host a Youth Festival for Peace. Peace, throughout eastern Europe, is the great cry of the moment. Posters celebrate it everywhere, and the impression is that no one else has thought of it, or is really rooting for it. MIR – PAIX – PEACE – PAX – FRIEDEN shout the posters, over which stylized doves with olive branches fly. One wonders if this propaganda isn't some kind of distraction. In Romania, President Ceauşescu has turned himself into a prophet of peace, thereby deflecting attention from his unpleasant internal policies.

At St Severin's, no one had arrived yet. A handful of students on the temporary stage in front of the altar were testing the sound system. The church is a huge, largely bare, grey vault, and it has an airiness and lightness the cathedral lacks. I remembered the interesting phrase in the brochure describing the two churches: 'Whoever is able to respond to the stillness and the grandeur of these beautiful Gothic halls will be richly rewarded – even if he himself is unable to pray.'

In the church, selling postcards and church literature, was an attractive woman of perhaps thirty-five. 'Restoration of church buildings is a problem. There just isn't the money to get on with it fast. All the money for the cathedral has come from Roman Catholics in West Germany ... I wish we could restore some of the old houses and make them habitable rather than go on building more and more concrete blocks, but what can you do?'

She regretted not being able to travel. 'We feel so cut off here, forced to look east all the time. That is why we are so pleased to meet people from the West, from out-side. It broadens our outlook, if only by a little. I hope you won't be too disappointed by what you see here.'

'I hope you'll be able to come and see us one day.'

'I'd like to.' She looked rueful. 'But that is a long way off. Still, if you had made the same suggestion even five years ago I would have been certain that I never could; now at least I'm hopeful.'

When I left she said goodbye, shyly, in English. 'You must forgive the way I speak it. We so rarely get a chance to use it. It gets rusty.'

There was a fair set up in the Domplatz. Now, as evening approached, it was beginning to come to life. The rough, lively, gypsyish men and the bored, knowing girls who ran the stalls and the sideshows were the same as fairground people everywhere, but I noticed for the first time in the candy-floss- and ice-cream-eating crowd a few people who looked poor.

People spent their money on the dodgem cars, and on fat sausages eaten with sauerkraut and mustard with a wooden fork from little square cardboard trays. Among the entertainments was the 'Berliner Ring' – a speedway. Ancient low-powered racing cars roared around an oval wooden track. The last time I had seen such at thing at a fair was thirty years ago at Walton-on-the-Naze, when I was a little boy.

Hungry by now, I looked in vain for somewhere to eat – a problem which was to recur frequently over the next few months. I had tried one restaurant – the Hohe Lilie, where Gustavus Adolphus, the great Swedish warrior king and champion of the Protestant cause, who fell at Lützen in 1632, aged 38, had once lodged in the course of his campaigns. The woman at the door had said that indeed I could eat there, though not without an expressive look at my jeans. This was a smart place.

'Do you want me to go and change? I have a jacket and tie,' I asked her, not about to let her get away with that look.

She was embarrassed. 'No, not at all. But perhaps you should know that this restaurant is in the upper price range.'

'Can I see a menu?'

'They are upstairs.'

'Can I go upstairs and look at a menu?'

'Only if you are going to eat.'

It would not be difficult for the two Germanys to reunite. I said I would come back, and went to look for somewhere else; but failing to find anywhere that wasn't either packed or closed, and unwilling to eat in the hotel, I returned. She seemed pleased to see me.

'How much must I expect to pay? Forty to fifty?'

More embarrassment. 'Oh no – more like fourteen to twenty.'

It was a chintzy, stuffy restaurant. On the menu was more extravagantly-priced wine. I ordered beer. I had been seated with another solitary diner, but felt a little tired to talk that evening. However, after we had completed the usual furtive survey of one another we started to chat. He was a businessman from Ohrdruf. He showed little or no interest in the fact that I was from the West. He was dark, about my age, elegantly dressed. He told me he had recently moved with his wife to the Thuringian countryside from Halle. His wife was adapting worse than he was to their new environment.

'You can't compare the sticks with a big city like Halle,' he informed me.

'Does your wife work?'

'Of course! We all work.'

He'd been in Erfurt to attend a planning meeting, and would go home the next morning. I didn't ask where he was staying since I was sure it would be in the same hotel as myself and I didn't want him to feel obliged to keep me company all evening.

'Why is wine so dear?'

'They mark it up if it comes from the West. Anyway, this is the most expensive restaurant in town.'

'Are you drinking wine?'

'Lord, no. This is a dry vermouth. It's a kind of fortified wine from Italy,' he added, in sophisticated explanation. He asked me where else I was going in the Democratic Republic, and when I mentioned Dresden he became enthusiastic. 'That is a great city. And you mustn't miss the Sistine Madonna in the Zwinger, whatever you do. I've seen it five or six times, and every time it has the same effect on me – almost hypnotic – you feel that there is something else out there – some kind of world-spirit. If there weren't, Raphael wouldn't have been able to paint like that.'

He ordered another drink from the waitress. 'Tell me,' he said, 'where are the hot-spots in town?'

'What do you want to do?' she asked.

'Oh, I don't know. Have a few drinks, a dance or two.'

She named the nightclub at my hotel. 'That's where everyone goes,' she said.

Returning, I crossed the Juri-Gagarin-Ring, and briefly wondered how I'd feel if, say, Oxford Street were renamed John H. Glenn Boulevard. Gagarin, the first cosmonaut, is a Soviet hero much celebrated in street-names throughout eastern Europe. Names that also crop up frequently, along with those of other national communist heroes, are, inevitably, Marx, Engels, and, absolutely everywhere, Lenin.

The other common names stem from abstract ideals: People's Solidarity Square and Street of the Unified Workers were among the more portentous.

I looked in at the bar for a nightcap. The place was full of rich East Germans, most of whom were locals. The nightclub was still empty and silent, and there was no sign of my friend from dinner. My drink cost every bit as much as it would have done in a similar establishment in London.

I got into conversation with a man who might have been the young Brecht. Earnest, with severely cropped hair and wire-rimmed spectacles, he welcomed the chance to speak English. He was fluent.

'You can't imagine what a golden opportunity this is for me to practise it!'

Nearing the end of his military service, he was on his way to visit his wife in his home town of Suhl. Before going into the army, he had worked as a translator from Russian and English, but had given it up because all they gave him was technical tracts, and he wanted to translate literature.

'But it's meant that I've had a fairly easy time of it in the army. I teach Russian to the new recruits.' All Warsaw Pact soldiers have to have a basic 150-word Russian vocabulary at least, since it is the official language of command.

Erich seemed to be a fortunate man all round. He told me he had secured, after only nine months' wait, a flat in a privately-owned house. The old woman who owned the place would be charging him and his wife forty-five marks a month – something like £15. When he left the army, he would have a job waiting for him in the *Kulturbund* – an organization akin to the Arts Council.

'The flat's the best news, though, because we've been living with my parents in three rooms and it's been driving us all mad. And next summer I am taking Anna to Lake Baikal for our holidays. I have been there once before – I spent a year at university in Moscow – and it is very beautiful.'

It is no distance at all from Erfurt to Weimar. I sat opposite a Russian engineer with a broken nose who was disinclined to talk, but who smiled when I said goodbye to him. The only other people in the carriage were a bored woman and her mother, dressed in the black skirt, blouse and headscarf, scattered with a pattern of small white flowers, that I remembered seeing old women in West Germany wearing in the Fifties.

The mother chatted interminably in a grating whine, while eating sausage and dry grey bread from a tinfoil package. Her loose dentures made heavy weather of this task, and it was a relief to leave the train.

It was far too early to go to my hotel. In East Germany you are expected to check out by eleven and not to check in before two, so I dumped my bags in the left-luggage and caught the bus up the Ettersberg to the Buchenwald Concentration Camp memorial.

Of the camp itself, little is left; but what remains is of grim and central significance. The administration *Block* now houses a museum, where much emphasis is laid on the heroism of the communist fighters against Fascism, though the fate of the Jews is at least mentioned. The tendency to blame all the evils of the Second World

War on West Germany has been toned down, though not altogether extinguished. However, the denial of responsibility for the war by the DDR (an impossibility since the Democratic and Federal republics didn't exist at the time) has continued for so long that people have actually begun to believe that all the Nazis lived west of the Elbe, and all the socialist heroes east of it.

The gas chamber, crematorium and pathology laboratory tell their own story. In a corner of the crematorium yard there is a memorial to Ernst Thälmann, the chairman of the German Communist Party, who was shot here by the SS. The false doctors' surgery is still intact. Here, people were stood against the wall apparently to be measured, and then despatched by a shot in the neck through a slit in the wall concealed in the measuring device. The crematorium still contains original corpse-wagons, and long iron stoking-hooks. The worst buildings, however, are the gatehouse, in which the camp *Bunker*, or prison, is incorporated, where the bestial Martin Sommer held sway over its inmates with a four-edged iron truncheon, and the neighbouring house, where the commandant lived. It is hard to believe that in these orange-painted, modern, unassuming buildings such unspeakable horror occurred, and such appalling people as the notorious Ilse Koch lived, less than fifty years ago.

The *Blocks* themselves no longer stand, but the rectangle covered by each is marked by grey clinker. A small concrete post in front of each gives the number of the *Block*. In front of each, fresh flowers are always to be found. Although the day was fine, a cold wind blew across Buchenwald. Ironically, the view across the valley from the Ettersberg was superb.

I made my way back to the town and got off the tram with my luggage at Theaterplatz. The square was busy. A solitary drunk sat outside Goethe's theatre and berated the crowd indiscriminately. He was ignored even by the policeman who strolled up and down, swinging his truncheon idly to scare the pigeons. A queue was forming outside a seedy restaurant on the corner, whose window-sills were littered with dead flies.

The Hotel zum Elephant stands on the market-place, which at the time I was there was taken up by a large building site. The attractive Renaissance gables of the old Town Hall and Cranach's house looked at each other across a dug-over wasteland surrounded by corrugated iron. It had been like that for three years. The Elephant, built at the end of the seventeenth century, has been modernized, and has lost some of its character, but it is still really the place to stay. In doing so, one joins company with Goethe, Schiller, Liszt and Herder, as well as Cranach, Bach, Wagner, Tolstoy, Sholokhov, Neruda, Lilli Palmer, Helene Weigel, and Thomas Mann, who uses the place in *Lotte in Weimar*. Adolf Hitler also stayed here, though he is left off the hotel brochure's list. The old restaurant up the road next to Goethe's house, *Zum Weissen Schwan*, was closed for renovation.

Goethe arrived in Weimar aged twenty-six in the late summer of 1775, at the invitation of Grossherzog Karl August von Sachsen-Weimar-Eisenach, a few years his junior. Between them they ran the dukedom on liberal and enlightened lines, and Weimar became the literary centre of Germany. It is now a major tourist centre, not unlike Stratford-upon-Avon in atmosphere. Although Schiller's house was closed for renovation (and had been for two years and would probably remain so for at least another three), both Goethe's town house on Frauentorstrasse and his summer residence a short walk away in the Ilm Park were open, as well as the *Römisches Haus*, another gift to him from Karl August. They are austere places, though the town house is filled with his collection of majolicaware, of Graeciana, and his library of 6500 books. Filing through with me were gaggles of French and Italian tourists; a package of Swiss was being delivered to my hotel as I set out, and everywhere, travelling in modest red-and-white buses, were Russians, their faces glazed with ignorance of what they were seeing, but dutifully going through the motions. One could always tell Russian and Eastern Bloc tourists from the others by their old-fashioned cameras.

The pretty Ilm Park, through which the little river wends, contains the worst statue of Shakespeare ever perpetrated – he looks like a deranged nineteenth-century Italian actor. Groups of apprentices from Zaïre, Mozambique and Cuba danced to reggae on their ghetto-blasters, placed on the grass. Crossing the park westwards and leaving it by way of Berkaer Strasse, you come to the town cemetery, where Goethe and Schiller lie buried side by side in the vault which is now named after them. It looks like a small Russian Orthodox church, and was the last resting place of the Saxon aristocracy. Their lead coffins are still here, but all have been moved to the sides of the vault to give pride of place to the two huge and almost identical mahogany coffins of Germany's greatest writers.

Christiane Vulpius, Goethe's long-standing mistress, who eventually became his wife, is buried in the Jakobskirche, together with Weimar's other famous son, Lucas Cranach the Elder. Not only was he a highly-esteemed court painter, he was also a successful businessman and local politician. The Town Castle is now a museum holding an important collection of his work, but the building itself is interesting, since the upper floors look as if they have been untouched since the days when the *Schloss* was a private residence.

I met Heiner, Peter and Ulli that evening over dinner in the *Elephantenkeller*, where they serve, in my experience, the best food in East Germany. Ulli lived in Weimar; and the other two had come over for the day from Erfurt.

Ulli arrived first and, after we had sat in silence for a while, asked me what I was reading. I nearly always left an English book by my place as a bait to attract curiosity and draw conversation. I told him that it was a satirical novel about the British in Africa in the Sixties. He looked nonplussed.

'A political book?'

'No; but it sends up politics.'

'That's good.' He still looked doubtful. He was slightly built, in his late twenties, with a blond moustache and short thinning hair.

'I hear you have big problems with AIDS in Britain now.'

It was my turn to be nonplussed by this abrupt line of enquiry; but Ulli was interested, and was sounding me out, as he hesitantly explained, because he was gay himself.

'I have a Yugoslavian friend who is getting very worried,' he said. 'Here we have no problems yet, but they will come. These problems are worldwide. We cannot just sit around pretending they only happen in the West.' Homosexual men in Germany have not had an easy time, though in the DDR their post-war lot was better than in the Federal Republic during the time that the activity was still illegal. Hitler introduced a severe homosexuality law. After the war, it was repealed immediately by the East German government, which reverted to the pre-Nazi statute. West Germany, however, retained the Hitlerian Article 151A until homosexuality ceased to be a crime in 1969. In East Germany, all laws against homosexual activity between consenting adults in private were dropped a year earlier.

I wondered guardedly what all this information was leading up to, guessing the answer.

'Are you, by any chance ... ?' Ulli let the question hang in the air.

I shook my head. He smiled. 'Never mind. You're not offended?'

'Not at all.'

'Good. Then we'll have another beer.'

We were drinking it when Heiner and Peter joined us. As soon as he learned that I was English, Heiner launched into a discussion of English football clubs which was so informed and detailed that I was soon left far behind. The topic being fairly quickly exhausted, and as they turfed us out of the *Keller* at eight, when it closed, we went off to a bar, where the conversation turned to other things.

'The trouble with the building sites is that there's no incentive to hurry,' said Peter, a moon-faced surveyor with a walrus moustache. 'Five years is nothing. Ten isn't unusual for even a small building, from start to finish.'

I asked about rents. The figure I'd heard from Erich seemed very low indeed.

'It's possible; but he wouldn't get very much for forty-five marks,' said Heiner. 'I mean, you wouldn't get a bathroom of your own, and all you'd get for a kitchen would be a gas-ring in a corner. A modern flat like we've got, which is still small because we haven't any kids yet, is about 120 marks, though you can get them as low as sixty.'

'Where are you off to next?' Ulli asked me.

I told him.

'Quite a trip.'

All their tourism faces east, and it is relatively easy for East Germans, provided they can afford it, to visit Czechoslovakia, Bulgaria and Hungary. Apart from students, I met few people who had visited Romania, though this seemed to be due more to considerations of comfort than to any bureaucratic obstacles that might be placed in their way. Romania, however, is not the easiest country to visit for any foreigner, because Romanians are supposed to report all contacts with outsiders to the police. Not, of course, that they do.

'I've never been there, and I never want to go,' said Heiner. 'I think it's probably the one place where things aren't loosening up at last. Look, even five years ago we wouldn't have been able to talk to you like this; we'd've been looking over our shoulders to see if the people at the next table were listening to us ... ' He broke off to wave to a couple of pretty girls at a table nearby, and for a moment I wondered if he wasn't somehow obscurely demonstrating his point. The girls, who had been watching us, now turned away and became absorbed in their drinks. 'No harm in trying,' he said.

'What are the shops like in London? What is fashionable?' asked Ulli. I didn't know how to answer, since I didn't want to get into the position of making comparisons. I mumbled something about shops varying depending on where you were, and I said that as far as fashion was concerned, anything went. The Centrum Department Stores I had seen here reminded me of Woolworth's or British Home Stores of about twenty years ago; but they were better stocked than I had imagined. The dingiest shops were those selling men's clothes; but, as in Rostock and Berlin, the people on the streets, especially the girls, were more chic – in a rather glitzy, cocktail-dressy way – than in London.

'I think our girls wouldn't wear quite so much gold lamé at lunchtime,' I said.

They all laughed. 'Not all of ours do! Are you sure you haven't been chasing tarts?'

By the time Heiner and Peter left to catch their train it was late. They shook hands warmly. 'There's so much we haven't discussed, and I don't suppose we'll meet again,' said Peter. 'It's bloody; but things will have to change. Look, I'm twenty-eight, and I know things will get better before I'm much older. We can't survive economically unless we find markets in the West; and when we do, they've got to get rid of the Iron Curtain, haven't they?'

'I don't think it can last forever.'

'Of course it can't. Then I'll be able to visit you. They talk about peace, but if people can't get together, see what each other look like, what hope is there of it?'

4

GHOSTS OF EMPIRE

Trains are always packed, as they used to be in England in the Fifties. Families crowded with luggage, eating picnics out of tinfoil, drinking beer and what can only be called 'pop', soon turn a compartment into a small living room. Everyone carries a bottle opener into which a plastic stopper is incorporated.

It was impossible to reserve a seat from Weimar, and as a result I stood for the journey to Leipzig. The countryside for most of the way remained obstinately featureless, though maize, the great universal crop of eastern Europe, now began to put in its first positive appearance, as did the occasional hideous, isolated factory. Everywhere piles of lignite, the basic fuel here, were to be seen, and the factory chimneys belched smoke of a similar muddy dark brown colour to the coal.

The train started to slow for Leipzig about twenty minutes before we arrived, but as soon as they noticed the change of tempo, all the passengers who were getting out gathered their belongings and solemnly queued in the narrow corridor, blocking it completely. Leipzig's station has twenty-six platforms, and is the largest in Europe. The train appeared to be entering the maw of a gigantic cast-iron whale. A vast cathedral of a place, very dirty, with huge spans.

A voice presides over the station. It is the tired but soothing voice of a middle-aged man, making self-consciously well-enunciated announcements, the important bits of which are intoned twice: 'The train standing at Platform Seventeen will depart for Karl-Marx-Stadt in five mintues. Karl. Marx. Stadt. In. Five. Minutes.'

The hotel was modern, built with Japanese help in the early Eighties and containing the city's one Japanese restaurant. My room was on the twenty-third floor, and looking out of the window I had my first view of east European pollution. I was high enough up in the sky to be able to look down on the pale brown miasma which shrouds Leipzig.

In the streets, the central pedestrian precinct (a favourite feature of east European cities) protects you from the smell of exhaust fumes, but once you are away from it, your nostrils and the roof of your mouth turn sour and taste metallic within minutes. Leipzig was badly damaged in the war, and little of its Old Town remains – one or two churches and the attractively-named Naschmarkt in the centre. The new city is modern, grey, high-rise; by no means unpleasant, but soulless. Its business life centres around the spring and autumn trade-fairs, which are of international importance and which continue, uninterrupted by Communism, Leipzig's 800-year-old role as a commercial centre.

I went to the Thomaskirche, where Bach was organist for twenty-three years, and where he is buried in a suitably austere tomb. A rather heroic statue of him stands outside the fifteenth-century iron-grey church, a building which did not inspire me, but where, I learned with surprise, both Richard Wagner and Karl Liebknecht were baptized. Far more beautiful, and a delightful discovery, was the Nikolaikirche, surrounded as usual by builders' rubble and looking very closed, but, by a miracle, open. Its interior is flamboyant white, green and pink Baroque; the most striking feature is that the capitals of the columns supporting the nave branch out as plaster rush leaves across the ceiling, like fan-vaulting.

Since Goethe is Leipzig's other famous citizen, it was obligatory to visit Auerbach's Cellar. Although its present interior is nineteenth-century, the tavern was founded in 1530. Its owner was called Heinrich Stromer; he was known as Auerbach after his birthplace. In the seventeenth century, Auerbach's became associated with the story of Faust, and Goethe, who spent at least some of his student days drinking here, sets a scene in *Faust 1* in the Cellar. At lunchtime on a Saturday, it is a sober enough place. I had a poor chicken risotto with some very heavy and entirely unsuitable Pinot Noir (my fault), which laid me out for the afternoon.

Leipzig goes to sleep after midday on Saturdays, a habit it shares with many other east European towns. It was still too early in the summer for the Gewandhaus, the famous concert hall, to be open; I didn't feel like giving up and returning to sample one of the hotel's four or five 'gastronomic facilities', and so I walked around the emptying town, sitting for a time on a bench in the sun on Grimmaische Strasse, where a handful of other people were doing the same thing.

I'd read about the view from the tower of Karl Marx University, and so I paid my 1.50 marks for the privilege of being speeded up to the top in an express lift, whose operator, a middle-aged man with a pencil-line moustache, gave me an equally express run-down on the history and vital statistics of the tower. What he neglected to tell me was that the viewing gallery itself was closed for restoration. However, my ticket entitled me to a seat at table 15 in one of the red plush restaurants at the top, where I joined two elderly ladies, having been firmly moved by a waiter to the correct table from one of the dozen or so empty ones around it. I ordered a beer.

This was the season of weddings, and at another table along one wall a wedding lunch was coming to an end. I couldn't identify a bridegroom. The bride seemed to be sitting between two fathers. I asked my table-companions.

'We wondered that too, but the bridegroom's the one on her left,' they said. 'He's certainly old enough to be her father.'

It was far too hot and claustrophobic to stay long, any view was shrouded from us by thick, yellowing net curtains, and so shortly afterwards I left. By now even the benches on Grimmaische Strasse were devoid of life. I decided to head for the zoo.

And that was where everybody had gone – or so it seemed, and no wonder. At one mark a head to get in, Leipzig Zoo is phenomenal value. It was as full as the town was empty. It is a large, enlightened place, with a particular reputation for successful breeding programmes. Although some of the cages for the smaller cats and the larger birds of prey are still old, and too cramped, reminding me of similar cages at

London Zoo, I have rarely seen better-kept or happier-looking animals in any zoo anywhere, and I will never forget the glorious polar bears.

People I talked to in Weimar and in Leipzig told me that I'd find the Dresdeners more reserved, more conservative, and more difficult to approach.

'You won't like the accent either,' they added. 'It's very strong, very thick.'

Although the countryside on the way to Dresden became more attractive, with here and there a hill topped by what began to look like a central European castle, I began to feel that I was leaving familiar Europe behind. This was dispelled on arrival by a typically European taxi-driver who wouldn't take me anywhere as he was on his lunch-break, and by posters advertising a concert by a British group called 'The Flying Pickets'.

I don't know what I was expecting. I knew that Dresden had been a city of magical beauty, and that on the night of 13 February 1945 it had been bombed to extinction by the Allies. There seems to have been no clear military reason for the raid, which killed 35,000 people in fifty-six minutes. One argument suggests that it was necessary to strike a blow at what remained of Hitler's morale by demonstrating that the Allied air forces had the capacity and the ability to attack the remotest German city, and the jewel in the German crown; but simple revenge seems a more likely, and even, in the savagery of war, understandable explanation.

Dresden is a new town with an old core, and while the exteriors of the old buildings have been restored with painstaking care, it has not always been possible to recreate their interiors. The Church of the Holy Cross on the Altmarkt was originally built between 1206 and 1216, but in the course of its history it has been burnt down five times. When it was rebuilt and restored in 1955, the architect responsible, Stendtner, opted for a stark, Fifties-Romanesque interior in which concrete incorporates some remaining stone fragments of the original church. It is effective, but it conveys no sense of history. Not all have suffered this fate. The opera house is an architectural glory inside and out, having been completely rebuilt from Semper's original plans of the 1870s. It reopened in 1985. Across the Theaterplatz from it, Matthäus Daniel Pöppelmann's astonishing and florid Zwinger Palace is still being worked on. The buildings which comprise it, so brilliantly reconstructed, are covered with the soot of wartime fires, and the art gallery wing is closed for restoration, but evidence of continuing work is visible everywhere, in planks and scaffolding.

The Old Town, if one can call it that, centres on the Theaterplatz and covers a handful of blocks along the south bank of the River Elbe, either side of the southern end of what is now called the Georgi Dimitrov Bridge, after the first communist leader of post-war Bulgaria. Formerly it was called the Augustus Bridge, after Augustus the Strong, the Elector of Saxony, also King of Poland, who lived between 1670 and 1733. To each age its hero, though the Saxon court of Augustus' day became known as the most dissolute in Europe, and Augustus himself is reputed to have fathered 300 illegitimate children. The buildings which remain are dominated by the palace, the opera house, and the Baroque Trinity Church, which was Augustus the Strong's Court Church. The city castle and the Frauenkirche are still ruins, and seem to be in a parlous state; one can only hope that work can start on them before what remains falls down. And although one applauds the restoration, one regrets the dirty state of all these lovely buildings.

Here, as everywhere, hideous modern buildings are thrown up cheek by jowl with the old. Across the Altmarkt stands the Kulturpalast – but before condemning it out of hand as a repulsive squat greenhouse, I must remember not to judge things here by ideal standards. Remembering the lesson learned in Berlin, I also recalled that modern history, the history of the young communist countries created since the war, is as important as, and probably more important than, earlier periods. The new buildings are something to be proud of because they reflect the triumph of the working class. The old buildings, though valued as cultural relics, are officially associated with regimes of the past.

New Dresden is at its best in the two main streets, now both pedestrian thoroughfares. Prager Strasse leads north from the station to the Old Town, and contains most of the hotels, the cinema complex, and main shops. Building started here in 1965, and the uncompromising Sixties concrete-and-glass boxes would not look out of place in Birmingham. However, they are redeemed by a series of fountains in which children are allowed to paddle and play, open-air cafés and grassy areas. Winter may make it a bleaker place, though it is broad enough not to be oppressive.

The second street, Strasse der Befreiung (Liberation Street), continues north across the Elbe from the Dimitrov Bridge. It was built in 1979, and with its lower houses, incorporating some surviving old ones, and its trees and statues, it is more successful aesthetically, and more human in its proportions. Near its southern end are Dresden's best hotel, the Bellevue, and an equestrian statue of Augustus the Strong, recently given a fresh coat of gold paint.

It is much hotter here than in Leipzig, and suddenly there is the feeling of being much further south than I actually am. This is the heart of Saxony, and I find that the warnings I was given earlier were correct: the people here are more provincial, more reserved. But I am left with good feelings for Dresden: it is another phoenix risen from the ashes which were the inheritance of the war.

I had a drink in a beer garden between the river and the Theaterplatz before setting off on two walks. I must mention the beer: it was the worst I have ever tasted in either West or East Germany, and quite untypical. It was also served in a mug whose rim was so badly chipped that I was in constant danger of cutting my lips. Glasses in this condition cropped up again and again in eastern Europe, but I didn't encounter such a bad one again until (once) in Romania. Three girl punks at the next table sweated in black leather and drank local Coke.

My first walk took me along the north bank of the Elbe as far as a life-size bronze statue of an archer. My guess is that he was made around the end of the last century; but who he is and who his sculptor was I was not able to discover. The views back to the town from where he is placed are exceptional, especially late in the day.

The second walk was longer, and took me to the People's Park. This is a large area to the south-west of the city, one of whose attractions is a Pioneer railway. I'd noticed posters suggesting to young people careers working for the *Reichsbahn*, and this scaled-down network of two or three lines traversing the park is a training ground for Pioneers, for they do everything but actually drive the miniature locomotives, which are beautiful eight- or ten-foot-long models of old steam engines in gleaming blue and green liveries. Passengers are carried between five stations and, as the park is large, it is a very convenient and quick way of getting from, say, the zoo to the open-air theatre. As all parks in eastern Europe seem to be, this one is beautifully kept, with fastidious gardens – though no one can rival the public gardens of Romania.

I managed two museums in the Zwinger: the Porcelain Museum, in which the most exquisite Meissen and Dresden ware is displayed, and the Historical Museum, which is a collection of militaria. One display remains firmly in my memory, more because of a name than anything. The great armaments town of Germany is Suhl, now in the East, and the exhibit illustrates the advent and development of the sporting rifle in the eighteenth century. These guns were made then, and are still made, by a firm of gunsmiths with the superb name of Spangenberg und Weiss.

Visiting the Porcelain Museum strengthened my resolve to visit Meissen. I got up too late to catch the White Fleet boat, and so took the train – another of those double-decker carriage affairs I had encountered at Rostock. The train was cheap and quick. In the event, I was glad not to have invested time and money on a boat trip, because Meissen was a disappointment.

The town is built on an abrupt hill, crowned with a great, solid castle built for defence rather than looks, and a heavy, late Gothic cathedral, strongly reminiscent of Cologne. Both were closed and seemed to be in an advanced state of neglect, and the two restaurants on the deserted square which surrounds them were also shut. In the town, only one inn was open, and that was packed, with a long queue snaking back along the pavement from its door. No one could sell me a map, and the tourist office was closed. All this was nothing: it was the dilapidated look of the town which was depressing, the more so since it is attractive and has lost none of its medieval proportions. The Elbe snakes indifferently round the Burg, and on its other bank the porcelain factories spread themselves – piles of china clay like snowdrifts in their yards.

'I've lived here nearly all my life, and I'm not surprised to hear you say you're disappointed,' said the old lady I helped at the station. 'All the young people leave to work in Leipzig or Dresden, and there's no money to keep up the old buildings here. They spent a fortune doing up Berlin for 1987, but there wasn't a penny for Meissen...'

'Why not? It's a world-famous town.'

'... and our mayor is a philistine – a world-famous provincial! He's not interested, so things just slide downhill.' She shifted her weight on her crutches.

'Do you want to sit down?'

'No. It's just that I'm still getting used to them.' She was referring to her two porcelain false hips. She was approaching eighty, a fierce and sad intellectual whose loneliness was so strong you could almost touch it. Her son, a heart specialist, was away with his family, teaching at a West African hospital. They would not be back for another year.

'It's been very hard since my operation – I can't take my turn in the stair-cleaning rota in the flats where I live, and do you know what the neighbours say? That I should be put in a home. But I'm not going. They can't make me.'

She told me that she was grateful for a chance to talk; that often she went for days without speaking a word to anyone. She hadn't much money, either. Pensions in eastern Europe are low, and the average in the Democratic Republic is around £100 a month.

'Things would be easier if my son were a Party member; but he won't join. That's why he'll never make professor.' She says this proudly; she brought her son up alone, and they are very close. She accepts that he has to go where his work takes him; but she wishes he were there to protect her.

Most of the paintings from the Zwinger had been put on display at the nearby Albertinum while the gallery was under *Reparatur*. The Albertinum is just round the corner from one of the 'sights' of Dresden – the 'Green Vault'; but as this is principally a collection of plate and *objets de vertu* I did not respond to it. The paintings were a different matter. The recent works were spectacular enough, representing artists like Otto Dix, Karl Schmidt-Rottluff, Max Liebermann, and Max Slevogt's landscapes of North Africa and Egypt in 1914; but the Old Masters collection, one of the greatest in the world, is breathtaking.

The foundations of the collection were laid by Augustus the Strong and his son Augustus III. It was in the latter's reign that the hundred best pictures from the Duke of Modena's collection were bought in 1745, and Raphael's glorious Sistine Madonna was acquired in 1754. It is a miracle that the main collection, which had been evacuated, survived the war. Nevertheless, a catalogue published in 1963 lists 206 pictures destroyed and 507 missing from the original number. By 1979 only 27 of those missing had been recovered. In what private collection, I wonder, are the 480 which are lost?

To begin to describe the pictures that remain would fill an enthusiastic couple of books, but those that are familiar in reproductions and startlingly brilliant in the original are the Sleeping Venuses of Giorgione and Palma Vecchio. There is a rich series of works by Correggio, Veronese and Tintoretto; a Van Eyck triptych; and paintings of great power and beauty by Vermeer (*Girl Reading a Letter at an Open Window*), Rembrandt, and Poussin.

It was in Dresden that I first became aware of tourists from farther east, from countries closer than Russia, but also more remote. Dark-skinned, serious people, who might have been from Calabria or Turkey. Sturdy women with thick eyebrows and broad hips, dressed in tight cotton frocks with loud floral patterns in shades of lilac and burnt orange. In front of the Sistine Madonna I first saw the Group Photograph. This particular group was a large Bulgarian family, about ten of them, all ages and shapes and sizes, the women in brightly clashing patterns and headscarves; the men brown-suited and tieless, with heavy black moustaches. Solemnly they arranged themselves in an untidy cluster and unsmilingly faced Dad who, holding his Praktika like a casket of jewels, finally waved a warning arm, and with great ceremoney and deliberation pressed the button.

In a bar early that evening I ran into two young men who were on their way to Prague for a long weekend. One was a Dresdener; the other came from Rostock, where he worked as a merchant seaman.

'They gave me the chance of doing the Tilbury run, but I turned it down because it's just a shuttle; and that means I've been practically everywhere in the world but London.' He was on the Havana run at the moment, shipping tractors to Cuba. 'Don't dream of going there. It's a dump. Everything's going to rack and ruin, and all they want from you is dollars. The only things that are cheap and good are the women and the cigars.'

They asked me questions about how much I earned and how much I had to pay for hotels. 'Of course, we aren't allowed to stay in such hotels – some do, but they're the higher-ups, and the ones with clout. But the most we'd expect to pay for a hotel room would be around thirty marks,' said the Dresdener. This was a fraction of what I'd paid.

'One of the advantages of our beautiful DDR,' said the sailor, smiling the east European ironic smile. 'But I'm twenty-two. I'll see the end of the road.'

Later on, at dinner, found after the usual search, my companions were a middle-aged professional couple – she a teacher of mathematics, he an executive. The questions started almost immediately.

'Is it true that your economy is run down in Britain, and that you are turning into a one-party state?' Dieter wanted to know. I told him what I thought.

'You must find it very drab here after London, even so,' said his wife.

I said that was not my impression, which pleased her. After a time, during which we ordered beers and 'Tyrolean-style' steaks, I was able to start asking questions in my turn. My time in East Germany was coming to an end, and there still seemed to be an infinity of things to learn. They told me that eighty per cent of East German women work. A possibly resultant fall in the birth-rate is a problem several east European countries face. ('Why bring children into this kind of society?' one embittered Czech doctor said to me – but she had lost her right to practise after becoming a signatory of Charter 77.)

In East Germany, welfare is good. When a woman has a baby, she is allowed off work for a year, during which time she is paid eighty per cent of her salary. The child is then sent to a crèche, and subsequently to kindergarten – all this is state-subsidized, so that the parents pay minimal individual costs – before starting school.

'The problem is that from an early age our children are outside our influence for most of the time that they are awake; and even today they are taught that the Berlin Wall is there to protect us from Fascist-Imperialism, that Christianity was created to blur the workers' awareness of their fates, and crap like that. There's even a kind of fake confirmation service the Young Pioneers go through, where they swear an oath to fight Imperialism and serve the state. It can't go on like this for ever, we say to ourselves; but when we see how the children lap it up . . .'

Dieter and Ulla were also on their way to Prague, for the Čedok Open Tennis Tournament in the brand new stadium which has been built there recently. 'We say in the DDR that our shops are empty, but we have plenty of money; whereas in Czechoslovakia the shops are full – at any rate, fuller – but they have no money to buy the goods!' Dieter stressed his use of the name 'DDR' ironically. A moment earlier, we had reached a misunderstanding because I had referred to the Democratic Republic simply as 'Germany'.

'We know that you refer to the Federal Republic as West, and the Democratic Republic as East Germany,' he said, 'but when we hear the word "Germany" on its own, we think people mean West Germany – and not only when we hear it from westerners.'

There is still no unemployment in East Germany, but full employment is maintained by obliging people who have trained for a specific job to go wherever there is a vacancy.

'I was born in Leipzig and trained there,' said Ulla. 'My first posting was to Neubrandenburg. Perhaps it is better than being unemployed, but separation from your friends and family can be a bit of an upheaval. Still, we get used to it. Neubrandenburg is a hole, anyway, so perhaps I'm being unfair by being too subjective.'

No one is homeless either, but flats are allocated on a sliding scale; in general, a person living alone gets one room to live in; a couple, two; a family, three rooms and upwards depending on its size.

'If, however, you don't like this Utopia and you can get over to the *Bundesrepublik*, they'll give you full rights of citizenship,' said Dieter.

'But you'd have to give up everything,' added Ulla.

'Yes,' Dieter agreed after a pause during which the waiter delivered our food. 'But salaries here average maybe 400 English pounds a month. Rent's about a tenth of that. But pensions are small. So the tendency is for many young, and many old people to go. Our government doesn't care how many old ones go, of course – it saves them money if they do.'

'But what about leaving their families behind? And whatever property they've got?'

'Well, for some people it's worth it. And materially there's no problem. We have a friend who left, and within two years he'd made up for all he'd lost, because he got a job with a fantastic salary by our standards.'

'Have you ever considered going?'

They looked at each other. Ulla shrugged. 'Our children are still very young. And after all, this is home.'

Since I had this conversation, and since the cautious first steps towards liberalization in Hungary and Poland during 1989, East Germans, infected by the impulse to greater freedom, have been leaving their country in droves.

5

A PHOENIX ARISEN

Ewa, to whom I'd been given an introduction by a mutual friend in London, met my plane at Warsaw airport. She was a slightly worn-looking woman in her mid-thirties, whose enthusiasm only became visible when conversation turned to western Europe and her trips there, especially to Holland, where her work as a textile designer frequently took her. Her eyes shone as she described Dutch shops, making me remember a visit to Arnhem a few years ago, just before Christmas, when the goods on display easily outdid Bond Street or Fifth Avenue. From a Varsovian point of view, the streets of the Netherlands must be paved with gold.

We drove into town in her battered red Golf. Crossing the airport carpark to reach it, the very first person I saw was a Hasidic Jew. Strange, in a country which had once contained the largest Jewish community of the Diaspora, but whose Jews now numbered a bare 5000. Probably, like me, he had just got off a plane.

First impressions of Warsaw were of a city devoid of life – it was Easter Monday, and everyone was either in the town centre or at home watching *Star Wars* on television. We drove through outskirts of low buildings set in sparsely-treed scrubland, and then into suburbs which expanded on either side of main streets of a uniform grey. Buildings are mammoth rectangular blocks in whose ground floors unhappy shops occasionally crouch. In a little outpost of flats behind one of these, Ewa lived.

Just as in East Germany, it can take time to get things in Poland. Eight years for a telephone, ten for a car, and up to forty for a home. There is a joke which people tell you about a housing official who visits a family with the good news that their flat has come through. The young man who answers the door and to whom he imparts this news says, 'Sorry, it can't be for me; it must be my father you want.' The father, summoned, knows the long-awaited flat can't be for him either, so he fetches *his* father – the Mr Suchodolski the flat is actually for. All three generations share the same home, with their families. Sometimes the only way a Pole gets a place of his or her own to live is through direct inheritance.

Ewa and her husband were lucky. They lived with their two children, aged six and eight, in a flat which they had to themselves. But as I was to learn, both of them had the opportunity to travel to the West and to earn hard currency – the key which can unlock any door in Poland. 'We have two currencies, really – the złoty and the dollar, and there's no prize for guessing which one does the real work!' It was a good flat. Off a small entrance hall was a minute lavatory and a bedroom. A corridor beyond the hall led to the galley-like kitchen, a bathroom, and a small cube of a room which may have been the children's bedroom, though in the daytime it doubled as a study.

Everything was neat and tidy, as on a cabin cruiser. In this agglomeration of small rooms occupied by four people, it had to be. But it might have been much harder. It is not uncommon at all for Poles, ninety-six per cent of whom are conservative Roman Catholics, to have very large families. Until recently, Lech Wałęsa lived with his wife and eight children in a three-roomed flat. I wonder if many of those of us who are privileged in the West could stand the sort of stress this *modus vivendi* would entail.

As my length of stay in eastern Europe increased, I found the necessity of queuing for everything hard enough to take. Yet here it is a way of life: 'You just have to accept that you are going to spend about twenty hours a week standing in line – there isn't much alternative.'

The flat contained evidence of western currency earnings: ranked along the window wall of the living-cum-dining room were a Japanese midi sound system, a video, and a large, lumpy television. *Star Wars* was on for the children, who nevertheless preferred to play in the street outside in the sunshine, scampering in and out occasionally to complain of bullying by other children, or to refill the plastic lemons they were using as water-pistols – on Easter Monday it is the custom in Poland for people to squirt water at each other. In the town centre they were using buckets.

The sun filtered in through the heavy net curtains which give such a claustrophobic atmosphere to so many east European interiors, and *Star Wars* rambled on. The treatment it had been given to render it comprehensible to Poles was odd – it was neither dubbed nor subtitled, but a Polish actor did a voice-over, playing all the parts. Beneath him, the original English dialogue could still be fuzzily heard.

We sat at the other end of the room, the dining table standing between walls almost hidden by trophies carrying the horns of small deer. Above our heads, a dusty stuffed eagle spread its wings. Many Poles are still keen hunters, and Ewa's deceased father had been no exception. On the walls beyond hung two enormous abstract tapestries done in wool – a craft at which Poles excel. 'My mother did one, and the other is my college apprentice-piece.'

There were few other decorations, and a noticeable absence of books, which are one of the few things which are cheap here. However, the large-format art books in colour which Ewa needs for her work are not. 'They cost about 18,000 złotys apiece, and I earn 25,000 a month.' 25,000 złotys, roughly translated at the official rate of exchange, then amounted to about £25, and the average monthly salary hovered around the 75,000 mark. Academics and teachers are paid least well, manual workers and miners best. Ewa only worked part-time at her official job. To make ends meet, though, most Poles must take at least two jobs. Ironically, there are several hundred Polish free enterprise millionaires, and if a Pole is fortunate enough to get a job in the West, a year's work there can set him up for life at home. His savings, invested in a hard currency bank account in Poland, will yield him enough interest to live on in comfort. However, since the period of martial law at the beginning of the Eighties, most Poles have not trusted the banks, fearing that in a similar state of emergency (or rather, state of war, since the Polish Constitution makes no distinction), bank accounts will be frozen. Up and down the country, dollars and Deutschmarks can be found in mattresses, or hidden in socks stuffed up chimneys.

The problem with accepting hospitality in Poland is that you don't know what sacrifices have been made to provide you with it, and yet you can hardly refuse, for to do so would offend, and the Poles, because they have been oppressed for generations, are a proud people. We lunched on bread not unlike German *Bauernbrot* but lighter, good butter, *myśliwska* sausage, and smoked pork, which was followed by *śledź* (herring) with onions and pickle. Beetroot forms the basis of many Polish dishes, and the salad was beetroot and horseradish – a superb combination, though eye-watering. With the meal we drank black Indian tea, and afterwards a bottle of sweet Russian wine, which reminded me of British sherry. Almost all wine is imported, as the Poles grow hardly any vines. What wine Poland produces herself is raw stuff. 'The only people who drink it are the alcoholics – and then only when they can't get vodka!'

There was an Easter cake, made of chocolate (a rarity), with coconut, cream and poppy-seeds. The poppy-seeds gave rise to speculation on the part of Ewa and her husband about the drug problem of the West. They were both fascinated by our social problems and seemed disappointed to hear that unemployment and racial tension in particular were not as bad as they evidently assumed them to be. 'We do have our own drug problem,' they told me when I asked. 'Some of the young take the stalk of a certain poppy and boil it up in water – that produces a kind of drug-drink. But it's a cultivated poppy, not a wild one, and farmers have been forbidden to grow it any more.' I saw only one small group of young men in my entire time in Poland who were high on something. They were in the plac Zamkowy in Warsaw, and whatever it was they'd taken, it was certainly stronger than poppy-stalk tea.

The question of racial tension interested them more, and in talking to them I was struck by a certain racism behind their comments. These, however, may have stemmed more from naïveté than dislike. Travelling around Poland, I saw only five black people altogether. The only one I met was in Poznań. He was a traveller like myself, an American, who had had the misfortune to have all his luggage stolen.

Once a richly heterogeneous nation, with a Jewish minority alone accounting for ten per cent of the population, Poland was radically changed by the Second World War. Only a tenth of the Polish Jews survived, and the majority of them emigrated in the years following 1945. With her newly-defined frontiers causing the entire country to be shifted about 200 miles westwards, Poland also lost her German and Ukrainian populations. Today, she is populated almost entirely by ethnic Poles, and Poles of the Catholic faith at that. There is no more homogeneous state in Europe, and with a population whose average age is twenty-eight, Poland is, after Albania, the youngest nation of the Continent.

Students come here from Iran, Iraq, Vietnam and Central America to read engineering. Their success at learning Polish easily enough to speak it adequately within a year was held out to me as proof that the language was not as impenetrable as it appears, and indeed once you have sorted out the difficult consonant-clusters that typify it, you will find that pronunciation is almost entirely consistent. To look at, though, it is daunting. I discovered one town called Szczyrzyce, and there is a famous tongue-twister about a singing beetle which even Poles (they tell me) find difficult: '*w Szczebrzeszynie chrzaszcz brzmi w trzcinie i Szczebrzeszyn ztego słynie . . .*'

It is an inflected language, but it behaves regularly, which probably makes it easier to learn in the long run than English, though I found it unassailable. I was fortunate that English is quite widely and enthusiastically spoken, together with French, and German among older people. Russian, which the Poles are obliged to learn, is used with reluctance and is – like everything connected with the USSR – cordially loathed.

Poland looks west. It is from western Europe that her influences and traditional cultural associations have always come. Her affinities are with England, France and Italy, not with her close neighbours. Although she has always been firmly rooted in the East geographically, her strongest links in every other sense have been with the West, where her leaders received their education, and whence several of her kings and queens came. The attachment remains fierce, despite the disappointing support and broken promises of recent history. Always trapped between two traditional enemies, Germany and Russia, Poland today is further separated from where her heart lies by the encirclement of the Eastern Bloc – she shares no common frontier with a western country – and her immediate neighbours are not well-disposed towards her. Though she spoke with enthusiasm of Holland, Great Britain, and even West Germany, Ewa had travelled little in eastern Europe, and had never been to Russia. 'Why go east for more of the same? In fact, it's even worse there than it is here. Warsaw is clapped out, there's nothing in the shops – and yet Russian tourists who come here think they've hit Eldorado!'

As my journey progressed, I became aware of the lack of curiosity one east European country has for another. If there was travel, it was to tourist resorts in the mountains or by the sea; and though there are business connections, little cultural interchange goes on, or is desired. Relationships are sought with the West rather than with each other. The great fear is of being left out, even forgotten. Many people were worried by the impression they had that when we in the West talk of Europe, we only mean the lands between the Atlantic and Austria, and that beyond our easternmost frontiers we believe a nebulous collection of Russian provinces begins.

One of the saddest things I had to accept as a result of travelling here was that, although Poles may be as different from Romanians as the English are from the Italians, and although relations between one country and another may be coloured by events which occurred before the communist era, and by the successful Stalinist 'divide and rule' policy which has kept these nations under Russia's thumb, the similarities are more striking than the differences. Subjected to the same kind of administration, economic mismanagement and deprivation, the reactions of the various peoples have been the same, breeding a similarity in their personalities. Czechs and Poles may mistrust and even despise one another for various historical reasons, but the face they present to the outsider is the same. And despite the strong national pride which exists in every one of the countries of the Eastern Bloc, itself a result of severe curtailment of self-determination, all too often national differences appear to have been leached away by the shared method of rule. Only in Albania, undeveloped enough for that method of rule still to be of benefit, and supported by her own fierce independence, was optimism still discernible.

The other factor here is the suppression of the expression of individuality. This may form the crux of the matter; but I never had the sense that suppression would lead to extinction. One Polish underground artist said: 'The strongest plants grow in the roughest soil. We are the weeds in the concrete of totalitarianism. They can't get rid of us, and once we are free again the road back to a real sense of individuality, though it may be a long one, will be covered quickly. What I miss is unrestricted access to western trends, to the art and music of Africa, South America, Alaska – you name it. Here, I feel that my influences are filtered, out-of-date. But I've got to stay here. This is home. If I were an exile, I couldn't work at all, because my work has to be directly linked to what I know.'

Life is hard in Poland, and frustrating. In a country with 50,000 square miles of forest, there is a shortage of paper and matches. The trees are also under attack from industrial pollution, which poses a great threat to the country. Control remains a low priority, despite the fact that Poles have been aware of the evils of pollution for a long time. Supplement 29 to Point 16 of the Gdańsk Protocol, concluded on 31 August 1980 between the government and the Interfactory Strike Committee, requests an undertaking 'to ensure the cleanliness of air, soil and water, especially of coastal waters'. Yet for some, life is remarkably sweet. These people hold the reins of power, enjoy the privileges of special shops, avoid queues for anything from food to housing, get preferential medical care, and have access to western travel and the hard currency that makes it possible.

The so-called *nomenklatura* of Poland is actually illegal in terms of the Constitution, which guarantees the equality of all citizens, though it is run by the cadres department of the central Party Secretariat. It is composed of two separate lists, one of reserved posts in State and Party bureaucracies, the other of people entitled to fill them. The second list is secret, though the names on it are those of people from every conceivable walk of life. They have one thing in common: they form the ruling core of Poland, and they control every aspect of the country. 'We're run by a Mafia,' one journalist told me. 'That is the simple truth. All that is being altered today are the appearances. Beneath the token reforms, things go on as before.' His scepticism did not prevent him from having strong faith at least in the possibility of Solidarity – which was reinstated as a legal organization while I was in Poland – being able to press for real and fundamental changes for the better.

Meanwhile, incomes are low, and it is the dollar which makes all possible. 'The problem that may arise from this situation is that we Poles will become the next generation of guest-workers in the West, after the Turks and the others have gone home. Or that we will be exploited for cheap labour at home. Already there is a furniture factory in Elbląg which is wholly owned by an Englishman. He has absolutely no trouble with his workers because he pays them $80 a month – $30 more than they'd get elsewhere. Being paid in hard currency makes all the difference in any case. You cannot overestimate the power of the dollar in this country.' At the same time, Lech Wałęsa has wrily described himself as the only Nobel Peace Prize winner in the world who has to get up at 5 a.m. every morning to go to work – though with the revival of Solidarity his days as a working electrician are over.

Ewa had dropped me at my hotel, and on the way down to dinner I passed a group of young Israelis – the first of many such groups I encountered travelling around Poland, visiting the towns their parents and grandparents came from. Dressed in bright T-shirts and tracksuits, with tanned, confident, arrogant faces, they were a world away from the gaunt, apologetic figures in the photographs which are virtually all that remain as a record of life in the *shtetls* of Poland. They were sitting on the floor of the television lobby on the sixth storey while an elderly Jew gave them a lecture in English: ' . . . Poland was the worst hit country of all in the war, and got the least out of it. She lost forty per cent of her wealth, sixty per cent of her schools, fifty per cent of her public transport. And twenty per cent of her population. That compares with 11.2 per cent in Russia, and 2.5 per cent in the United Kingdom. Twenty per cent. Nearly six million people. But never forget that half of them were Jews.'

I dined with a Norwegian journalist – an eastern Europe correspondent who had just been allowed back into the country for the first time since 1981. We drank imported beer in cans; Polish beer is cheaper, but hotels don't offer it eagerly as they can make a bigger profit on western brews – you pay for the can as well as the snob value, and your beer costs as much as your main course. Stein had had an adventure coming from the airport which was typical of what one comes to expect here. There had been a long queue for taxis, so Stein returned to the airport building in search of an alternative means of transport into town. It wasn't long before a man offered him a lift in exchange for dollars. The man turned out to be an off-duty bus-driver who had simply taken a bus from his depot and driven it up to the airport to tout for custom and earn a few bucks. He ended up by agreeing to transport the entire taxi queue to their various hotels in Warsaw for a flat fee of $5.

There are, of course, more conventional and less surprising ways of earning dollars. At 1 a.m. on my second night there was a knock at my door. I opened it to a rather matronly blonde in far too short a skirt who smiled winningly and said, 'Are you waiting for my friend?'

'No.'

'So you are alone?'

'Yes.'

'May we come to you?'

This was the only direct approach I had. Stein was phoned up in his room by girls twice in the course of that night, and I had variations on the experience elsewhere in Poland. Taxi-drivers had their own approach, and everywhere little difficulties were invented or presented which vanished at the sight of a dollar. My friend Maciek in Wrocław said: 'In the past 200 years, what it boils down to for us is twenty years of freedom, between 1918 and 1939. And even then we only got six years of real democracy. So it's hardly surprising that we've developed into a nation of wheeler-dealers. The more you get kicked around, the lighter on your feet you become. In that way, the Poles and the Jews have a lot in common – in fact, if you took a "stage" Pole and a "stage" Jew, they'd be virtually indistinguishable; at best, noble and brave; at worst, whining and grasping.'

There is a much-quoted joke in Warsaw, that the best place to see the town is from the top of the Palace of Culture. 'Why?' you ask. 'Because that is the only place in Warsaw from which you *can't* see the Palace of Culture!' The building was an unsolicited gift from Russia in the mid-Fifties, and from one point of view could be seen as a symbol of Big Brother's unwelcome presence and power. It is grey in colour, and looks like a cross between the Empire State Building and the University Library in Cambridge. It is even uglier than either, and if the outside is hideous, the inside has to be seen to be believed, with its grey marble, dreary Socialist-Realist statues, and sub-Art Deco light fittings. Unable to find any access to its summit, I escaped with relief into the fresh air. Lying at the centre of the vast central European plain, which covers all of Poland but its mountainous southern frontier, the city is subject to extremes of temperature. Now, although it was only early spring, the weather was hotter and more humid than London ever gets.

I took a taxi to Łazienkowski Park. I was lucky; this taxi-driver was one of the few who charged what was on the meter and didn't engage me in a long discussion involving dollars. He even offered me change at the end of the ride, and seemed pleased to get a tip. Taxi-drivers, I later learned, are freelancers, and among the best-paid workers in Poland. Dodging the scruffy little boys who haunt tourist areas and the entrances of hotels, holding out packets of poor quality postcards and crying, 'Dollar, dollar,' I entered the park.

The park is known to everyone locally as 'Łazienki', which means 'baths', for the palace the park contains was built on the site of a former royal bath-house. The place was laid out by King Stanisław-August Poniatowski, who reigned from 1764 to 1795. He was the last of a long line of Elected Kings of Poland, a sensitive and cultured man who had the misfortune to preside over the erosion and final partition of his country, when Poland ceased to exist. Both he, and the system of elected kings, deserve explanation.

There were two great dynasties in Poland. The Piast line, founded by Prince Mieszko I in the tenth century, was terminated by the death *sans issu* of Poland's greatest king, Kazimierz III, who died in 1370. The succeeding dynasty was that of the Jagiełłonians, founded by the marriage of Queen Jadwiga to Jagiełło, Grand Duke of Lithuania, in 1386. It lasted until the death without issue of Zygmunt August in 1572.

The Jagiellonians were followed by the Elected Kings – a system set up in a spirit of democratic post-Renaissance enlightenment by the great Polish statesman Jan Zamoyski. There were eleven elected kings over the next 223 years, of whom seven were foreigners. They were elected by the nobility, and performed the function of a managing director under contract. The first was Stefan Batory, Prince of Transylvania, who is still a national hero; he was followed by a Swede, Zygmunt III Wasa, who transferred the capital from Cracow to Warsaw to be nearer his northern domains. Later Polish kings of significance were Jan III Sobieski, the saviour of Vienna from the Turks in 1683, and Stanisław-August.

Stanisław, a former lover of Catherine the Great, had been put on the Polish throne a Russian puppet – by the eighteenth century the democratic system of election had become wide open to corruption, and was further hampered by the misuse and abuse in parliament of the ultra-democratic *liberum veto*, by which no law could be passed if even one delegate disagreed with it. During the time of August III, Stanisław's predecessor and a singularly useless king, who reigned for thirty years, only one session of the Diet succeeded in passing any laws at all. But Stanisław would not simply do Russia's bidding, and despite his relatively powerless position he did much to consolidate Poland's sense of nationhood, and to establish a cultural identity which would stand his country in good stead in the years to follow, when her name was blotted off the map, and even her language forbidden. He was not, however, strong enough to withstand the inexorable encroachment of Russia, Prussia and Austria. In 1772 and again in 1793, whole tracts of Poland were annexed by these powers, and finally, in 1795, the country was swallowed up completely. It would not re-emerge for 123 years.

Walking in Łazienki I was able to shake off some of the mournfulness which hangs over Warsaw. I am not sure how to define it, but I am not the only one to have felt it. It isn't just that few people smile, and it isn't just that Warsaw is a recreated city, one which, despite brilliant rebuilding after German destruction in 1944, has lost its true age, its patina of history. Perhaps it is born out of the frustration of a people who have not forgotten their eight centuries of democratic tradition, and who even now are sceptical about the light which may at last be at the end of the tunnel they entered in 1795. The twenty years of freedom between the two world wars are cherished like a jewel, and though there are no streets named after Piłsudski, or public monuments, his portrait and his statue are to be found in art galleries everywhere, and his tomb in the crypt of Cracow Cathedral is all but buried under fresh flowers. Józef Piłsudski, born in 1867, was a patriot and freedom-fighter who was also a distinguished soldier and politician, though the high reputation he has always enjoyed is now coming in for reassessment in some quarters. With one interruption, he was effective ruler of Poland between the wars, and ushered in a new age of independence. He died in 1935.

It wasn't very long before I came upon the Chopin memorial statue, a sentimental, sugary piece of work which has nothing to do with the composer or the strong delicacy of his music. Passing it quickly by, I made my way through the sullen afternoon to Łazienkowski Palace, built as a retreat by Stanisław. He must have found the role forced on him by history difficult and distasteful.

The restored palace is built across a long sliver of lake. It is all of white stone, and in the fading light looks like what it is – the ghost of a vanished age. By a miracle the Germans had no time to raze it during their two-month orgy of destruction, though they did burn out the interior in preparation for blowing it up – the fate which befell seventy per cent of Warsaw.

South from it on the lake shore is an oddity: a reproduction ruined Roman theatre, where performances are given in summer.

I wandered on through the park under dark trees, noticing the hooded crows which seem to come this far west from Asia, but no further, and passing loving couples, and beautiful girls in hilarious and impenetrable little groups. I made my way around the side of the Belvedere Palace, a sprawling wedding-cake now occupied by the president, past the ubiquitous soldiers, and on to the Parisian Aleja Ujazdowskie, which is wide and green, and full of embassies. It is amusing to see unlikely countries juxtaposed and in buildings of such different styles: the crumbling country-house of the Swiss next door to the modern concrete-and-marble pile of the USA; and along from them the mediocre neo-Classicism of the Bulgarian Embassy. Large photographs in glass cases outside some of them display the ruling elite of that particular country quaffing and shoulder-slapping – obedient to the rules of the awful hypocritical bonhomie common to leaders.

I had been warned about the vast queues that I would have to expect when visiting any building or monument which was a particular reflection of national glory. One of these, perhaps the most obvious, is the Royal Castle, whose rose-pink walls dominate one side of plac Zamkowy. Arriving there only a few days after Easter, I found no queue, and even the group which I was obliged to join was a manageable size. We donned our felt slippers (to protect the floors) and set off at breakneck speed with a diminutive elderly lady whose voice was so light that even had she been speaking English I would not have caught one word.

The castle, resurrected by the Poles from the rubble left behind by the Germans, is only one example of the heroic reconstruction of their capital. Its symbolic import- ance is clear, but how easily the decision might have been made to rebuild Warsaw as a functional communist new town, in the Fifties. The castle was rebuilt over three years in the early Seventies. It is a very odd experience to visit a Renaissance palace which is effectively brand new. What is missing here, as so often, is a sense of history which only time can bestow on the fabric of a place; though perhaps its absence is balanced by the astonishing craftsmanship employed to reproduce it. The stucco work and the incredibly fine parquetry floors are beyond comparison.

Although much furniture has been donated by patriotic Poles abroad, and some of the original fixtures and fittings were saved in the nick of time in 1939, what was destroyed and lost forever is conspicuous by its absence, for what has survived cannot fill the rich succession of rooms. To counter this, the castle also contains many paintings, notably by the great nineteenth-century painter of Polish patriotic and historical subjects, Jan Matejko, but also by Bernardo Bellotto. This Venetian, confusingly called Canaletto (to whom he was related) in Poland, was employed by

Stanisław-August in 1767. He executed a large number of canvases of contemporary Warsaw, recorded with photographic attention to detail. These documentary paintings were of cardinal assistance in the reconstruction of Warsaw after the war. Indeed, the new city was an ideal version of the old, since Bellotto had recorded unrealized architectural projects. At the same time several ugly nineteenth-century buildings which had also been destroyed were not resurrected.

Beyond the castle immediately to the north lies the Old Town – a small area perched on a hill above the Vistula, comprising a grid of narrow side-streets centred on a fine market square. What is impressive is that it is all new, all recreated. In 1945, this was a pile of grey rubble. Ironically, its juxtaposed medieval and Renaissance buildings, with their jaunty gables, are reminiscent of a German town of the same period. Along one side of the square, a group of houses contains the National History Museum. Though marvellously displayed, the paucity of the exhibits is one more indication of how much in Poland has been pillaged or destroyed.

I met Dorota for lunch at the well-known Bazyliszek Restaurant. She is a shy, serious girl who has her share of problems. She lives in a small flat in the centre of town with her husband, her seven-year-old daughter, and her mother-in-law. But she is in the process of getting a divorce. While this is proceeding as amicably as possible, it is hard to have to continue to live with someone from whom you wish to separate, and the effect of the tension on the little girl is grim, for she doesn't understand what is going on, but senses that it is bad. But there is nowhere else for Dorota to go. For two summers she has 'moonlighted' in London, working in hotels to earn the foreign exchange she needs to extricate herself from the situation. This year she hopes to do so again, but the problem, as always, is, will the British grant her a visa? The perspective has changed subtly. Since the beginning of 1989, Poles have been allowed to have their own passports, which they may keep (not hand back at the end of a trip abroad), and which are valid for five years. 'Our government doesn't care where we go, and if we stay away permanently they're pleased – one less person to have to worry about. But of course you lot in the West, confronted with the possibility of an invasion of hungry Poles – well, naturally the barriers go up!'

Behind her conversation – as was the case with several in Poland – was the hope that I would be able to help her in some way, or that she could use me as a link with the West, even as a source of dollars. Close to desperation, she made little attempt to disguise this. As we settled down to eat, her opening remarks were disquieting:

'Have you noticed how down in the mouth everyone is?' She lit a cigarette, an Opal, and inhaled deeply. 'It's not just the drab imitations of western clothes that make us look shabby, you know. It's the sense behind our eyes that we've been lied to once too often. You don't know how lucky you are to have been born in the West. I feel like a prisoner in my own land.'

The need to talk, to get things off her chest, hurried her words. Successive governments have let the Polish people down again and again since the war, each promising an economic regeneration which they have been unable to achieve, bogged down by corruption, the difficult balancing act of keeping just enough to the Party line to prevent direct intervention by Russia while preserving at least the semblance of Polish autonomy, and shortsighted policies which have, for example, been responsible for the inefficiency of Polish agriculture. But above all, people are dominated by the feeling that currents for change are more illusory than real, and it will take a long time for Poles to shed their scepticism. 'But hope is a disease we are prone to,' Dorota added, and perhaps the dramatic shift towards western democracy which occurred within six weeks of my being in the country will have lightened the burden on Polish hearts.

'I don't trust Gorbachev at all,' said Dorota in answer to a question, and reflecting the cynicism and suspicion displayed by almost every Pole I met towards *perestroika*. 'But some good may come out of having even just a handful of genuine liberals in the government. Even if they are guaranteed never to be in a majority, some of their opinions might rub off. That is, if the powers that be haven't just got them in to propitiate the people, or to batten on some new ideas. That's the trouble with our government. It is intellectually bankrupt.'

Already a spirit of economic reform has indicated that the only way out of the mire of debt in which Poland has been plunged since the Seventies is through free enterprise. But the communist government wanted that to come about as far as possible without relinquishing its own power and privileges – and those of its supporters. Thus until the summer of 1989 the one-party state remained. 'Which made rather a nonsense of the old official concept of democracy that we have here. For you, democracy is represented by freedom of choice of government – free elections are enough to keep the kind of power blocs that jeopardize equality in check. For us Marxist-Leninists,' Dorota smiled drily, 'only the abolition of capitalism achieves that. And it follows that once you've got rid of capitalism, elections involving different parties will be unnecessary too, since the different class interests the parties represent will have disappeared!' She laughed. 'Poor old Karl. Poor old Lenin! I bet they never expected it would work out like this. They must be spinning in their graves. But what do you expect when you try to keep a set of hundred-year-old theories dreamed up in Victorian England strapped onto a group of European states today? And whatever else old Karl learned in the British Library, he sure as hell didn't learn anything about people.'

The Polish free enterprise millionaires deal in products not subject to government control – anything from mayonnaise to cut flowers. But these new rich have nowhere to invest their money, so they buy things like expensive cars and hi-fi systems, and build palatial homes. Warsaw was peppered with new BMWs and Mercedes, and in Poznań I saw my first Polish Porsche – a 928S, at that. By contrast Dorota, working as an English teacher, earns a low salary, and because she doesn't have the right contacts, cannot break into the field of translation, where her ambitions lie. She would not believe the suggestion that a similar set of circumstances might thwart her ambitions in the West. Nothing must besmirch the image of the West. 'Not that I would want to live away from Poland; but I want Poland to become like your country.

'And in the meantime, I make my life bearable by retreating from reality, inside myself. I read a lot, too much, to get away from the here and now. It's a kind of drug, but it'll keep me going until things get better. Don't imagine for a moment that I am the only person who does this.'

She took me to the National Museum, and guided me through its treasures, her eyes shining with pride, pleasure and knowledge. The most obviously beautiful galleries display the severe and remote eighth-to-twelfth-century frescoes of saints and archangels from the cathedral at Faras in the Sudan, which were discovered and excavated by the great Polish archaeologist Michałowskiego earlier this century. Their solemn faces stare down at you with a Byzantine vitality undiluted by time.

But it was the Polish painters I had come to see. The best known of these is Jan Matejko. In the second half of the nineteenth century, at a time when the Polish language was forbidden, his massive canvases depicting decisive moments of Polish history served as a source of inspiration to his countrymen – and still do. The most magnificent here is the impossibly crowded and active *Battle of Grunwald*. At this battle, fought in July 1410, the Polish king Władisław Jagiełło won a decisive victory over the Teutonic Knights, who had been a thorn in the Polish side ever since they had been shortsightedly invited to Poland in 1226 by Conrad of Mazovia to help him subjugate the pagan Prussians. The Knights – a group of unemployed ex-crusaders – got rid of the Prussians, but proceeded to occupy the Baltic coast on their own account, and took Gdańsk in 1308, establishing a base for themselves at the vast castle of Malbork. The Order of Teutonic Knights was not finally dispersed until 1525, when the last Grand Master, Albrecht von Hohenzollern, swore an oath of allegiance to Zygmunt the Old in Cracow – which, inevitably, is the subject of another Matejko painting.

A more intimate painter of historical subjects is Józef Simmler. Among his best is *The Death of Barbara Radziwiłł*. She was the second wife of Zygmunt August, son of Zygmunt the Old and the last of the Jagiełłonians. Although of high birth, she was not noble, and so the marriage – which was a love match – was opposed by his parents. She died only a year later, and though he subsequently married again, Zygmunt August was inconsolable and died childless. Simmler treats the subject with considerably more muscle than a contemporary English artist would have done. Nineteenth-century Polish painting is infused with a strong nationalistic pride which seems to have gone unnoticed by the German and Russian censors. 'The Radziwiłłs are still with us,' Dorota told me. 'I have a Radziwiłł girl in my class at school. Although of course we are all equal now.' Again the ironic smile.

The polymath Wyspiański comes next. He was a poet and dramatist as well as a painter; here he is represented by the design for Caritas in the stained glass of St Francis' Church in Cracow, and by several of his delicate pastels and watercolours, especially of children. Later painters, of the first half of this century, tend to drift into derivative and unfocused modern styles, though Leon Chwistek stands out, as do the paintings of another polymath, Stanisław Ignacy Witkiewicz. He died in Russia in 1939, and his paintings, many of which are still in private collections in Poland, are worth a fortune today. 'The Russians didn't return his body to us until 1988, and even then it was discovered that there had been a mixup, and the wrong body had been delivered. But nothing was done about it, so all poor old Ignacy has here is a symbolic grave. Still, the situation might have appealed to him. He was a famous eccentric,' said Dorota.

The greatest Polish painter is Jacek Malczewski. He lived from 1854 to 1929, and his disturbing paintings, where they are open to direct interpretation, concern themselves with the long period of darkness Poland endured in the nineteenth century. Here in particular his *Sunday in a Mine* stands out. It shows a group of Polish dissidents who have been sent to Siberia. The lassitude, boredom and desperation of the prisoners in their brown greatcoats is palpable to a frightening degree. Even their guard, almost hidden in shadow on the left of the picture, is hunched in a misery of ennui. All are trapped. I was not surprised on my journey to discover people for whom again and again Malczewski is *the* painter, and my own enthusiasm for him was to help cement several friendships. He should be better known outside Poland. He speaks to us all.

Like most teachers, Dorota supplements her income by giving private lessons to the children of those who can afford it or who are prepared to make the sacrifice, and as a teacher of English she is in great demand. 'But therein lies another of the ironies of our system,' she said. 'Teaching is a poorly paid profession. Therefore in general it is not attractive. Therefore very often inadequate teachers are employed. And therefore people seek private tuition for their children – from teachers, who give of their best at private tuition because it augments their salaries. We live inside a vortex of vicious circles.' We parted company soon after leaving the museum and I watched her small, deliberate figure cross Aleja Jerozolimskie and vanish into the crowds on Nowy Świat. How soon the new democratic government will be able to implement much-needed reforms is an open question, but most Poles I have talked to since Solidarity effectively took over the reins of power feel that Wałęsa showed a proper degree of sceptical caution in declining to become Prime Minister.

My own route lay north-west, across the pleasant Saski Gardens, and past the lovely neo-Classical Skarbowe Palace, to Muranów, the suburb which was the site of the Warsaw Ghetto. The monument to its victims stands in a wide grassy square which must once have been a busy labyrinth of streets. Today, broad empty avenues divide featureless, interminable blocks of flats. The sunny day, the cheerful old men basking on park benches by the monument, even the large bunches of fresh flowers at its foot, could not dispel the presence of the dead of this place. At its centre lies another monument, on the site of the infamous Pawiak prison, at its worst during the German occupation, whose basement cells remain – sweltering in summer, frozen in winter – reminding one of all those who suffered here.

My spirits did not lift until the following day when I met Tadeusz. News had just come through that Solidarity had been reinstated and would have the right to be represented in government. Despite his elation, Tadeusz, a sports journalist who had strong links with the militants in the trade union, was still cautious, though his conversation bounced and reverberated as he discussed figures with me, arguing the pros and cons of any representation at all, and doubting if the move would ever lead to the Party letting go of the overall majority it had guaranteed for itself in the event of elections.

We celebrated in a café with ice-cream and glasses of tea. 'Who knows,' said

Tadeusz. 'Perhaps the ship isn't sinking after all! In any case now that we've got the "Mafia" on the run, we won't let up.'

He also looked forward to the day when he'd be able to cover sports events abroad without the restrictions he now has to put up with. 'When I last went to the West, to cover an athletics event in Madrid, I travelled with our team unofficially and shared a hotel room with the coach to save money.' He laughs at the idea of expenses. 'What happens is that I pack a bag with all the food I'll need while I'm away, and live on that in my hotel room. It saves foreign exchange. My paper knows where I'm staying, and they phone me up at a prearranged time for me to file my story – that saves hard currency too. I look at my western colleagues with their access to fax machines and expense accounts, and I just have to smile. Do you know what my paper gave me as expenses for a six-day trip to Birmingham a few months ago? £11. Of course the worst thing is that it stops me getting to know the country I'm visiting.'

We ordered some more ice-cream, delicious in Poland, and Tadeusz went on to tell me about his younger brother, who is an economist with practical experience in Paris and New York, and now specializes in international finance at Gdańsk University. 'I think he's mad to stay here, myself. He's paid peanuts and he and his wife have to live in a one-room flat. They have two kids, so God knows how he gets any work done.'

'How would he go about getting a better flat?'

'With dollars. He'd have to go abroad and earn enough to jump the housing queues, then buy himself one. They're there for the asking if you've got the dough. Even luxury places. But it's easier said than done, and there's no such thing as a mortgage here, yet. I'm not married, but I really wouldn't mind a modest flat of my own, rather than having to share as I do. It'd cost me about $15,000 to buy – but of course I don't have such a sum, and I'll never earn the złoty equivalent in a lifetime. If I had a relative living in the West who could send me money, or help organize work for me, I'd be considerably better off, but I don't, so all I can do is wait for better times. But my brother – he speaks fluent English and French ... Well, as I've said, I think he's mad.'

'Doesn't the government value his services?'

Tadeusz grinned. 'Listen, the worst paid are the skilled professions. We've got a real crisis in medical services here now, because the doctors are leaving in droves. Three thousand last year alone – far more than graduated. My one consolation is that at this rate the system really can't last much longer!'

But there are other sides to the question of changing horses. 'Most Poles would love to be capitalists and have a free economy – we all adore Mrs Thatcher, and most of us think she's the best thing since Joan of Arc or Elizabeth I; but there's a problem. We don't know what living in a sink-or-swim society like yours would be like. We haven't any experience of it. The idea sounds fine, but take us to the edge of the deep end and say to us, "Off you go", and would we? I think many Poles would draw back when it came to the crunch. They'd feel insecure. So that's something else we have to deal with.'

6

CRADLE OF SOLIDARITY

On the train I shared my compartment with two elderly couples. One of the wives had been a textile worker before retiring, and told me in German that as far as she was concerned, her career had been a complete waste of time. 'If I'd been working for a capitalist, even a real so-and-so, at least I'd have known that someone was making a profit!' Their husbands wore the brown double-breasted suits favoured by the majority of men over fifty throughout the country, and both had their combat medals in miniature pinned to their lapels. The four of them soon settled down to sleep as the endless green plain swept past, wakening now and then to plunder a seemingly endless supply of grey bread sandwiches neatly wrapped in white paper, and consume them with bottles of very pungent beer.

The farmland we passed was divided into strips – a result of the complicated system of private ownership in Poland, where through inheritance and purchase a farmer may find himself in possession of several little plots separated from each other by a dozen kilometres. Apart from the occasional half-hearted undulation, the terrain remained resolutely flat, unrelieved even by villages. I was struck now, and in subsequent rail journeys, that apart from plough-horses I never saw any livestock of any kind from the train – not even a cow, although the fields were always busy, and sprinkled with small farms.

The massive fortress of Malbork finally loomed up on the left, glowing like a giant ember in the late afternoon sunlight. Gdańsk would not be much further. The fortress, as big as a small town, rambles along the bank of the River Nogat, and comprises a labyrinth of red-brick corridors, gloomy rooms, and sightless walls. The great fortifications withstood the power of Poland for fifty-five years after the Battle of Grunwald. Needless to say, it later became a focus for German fantasies of empire. At the turn of this century when Henryk Sienkiewicz was writing *The Teutonic Knights*, Kaiser Wilhelm II was holding fancy-dress parties at Malbork (then still called Marienburg), with himself as the Grand Master. Perhaps this was a prelude to Heinrich Himmler's far more sinister version of resurrecting with costume and ritual the medieval days of German supremacy in north-eastern Europe.

As in East Germany, the presence of the Second World War is never very far away. Gdańsk, then the German-controlled town of Danzig, suffered more than any other city of modern Poland. When they liberated it, in a spirit of revenge on a par with the bombing of Dresden or the razing of Warsaw, the Russians destroyed ninety per cent of it. The renovation of the Renaissance Main Town, which is chiefly made up of one long impressive street, the Długa, and the Długi Targ, or market, is almost uncanny, though the soot which clings thickly to every surface makes one wonder about the degree of atmospheric pollution here – something which I would soon know more about.

The Długa is dominated by the Town Hall, whose pencil-like spire points confidently heavenwards, though it seems almost too slim to be safe. The building is now a museum, and although modern decoration and a dearth of contemporary furniture indicate what was lost in the destruction of the war, the wonderful Red Room, which I guess was the main council chamber, has been restored to its original glory, as its impossibly ornate ceiling was sensibly removed and stored at the beginning of the war. The centrepiece is a delightful, pompous painting celebrating trade and the union of Gdańsk with Poland, by Isaac van den Blocke.

In the terrace next door to the Town Hall are two of Gdańsk's most prosperous houses: the Dwór Artus, the extravagant windows and clean lines of its façade making it look perhaps 250 years younger than it is – it was built on to a medieval structure in the early seventeenth century; and the richly decorated Golden House, with statues waving from its parapet. Everywhere, in the meanest street, one discovers ornate doorways, heavily carved window-cases – marks of what was once one of the wealthiest cities in the world.

With its bright colours, Dutch gables, and towering terraced houses, Gdańsk reminded me vividly of Rostock, her sister Hanseatic city. The atmosphere and architecture of Gdańsk owe far more to Holland and Germany than to Poland, which is not surprising, considering the town's history. However, since 1945, the influence of foreign powers in Polish history has been played down, to the extent that modern Polish maps may not show the old German names of cities. A television producer who resigned during the period of martial law in the early Eighties told me that she did so because the censor required that a documentary she had made on Gdańsk in the seventeenth century should have excised from it all references to Holland and Germany. 'That was really the last straw. Working under those conditions wasn't working at all.' Sadly she reflected that now she would be happy to work in television again, but in her late thirties was too old to stand a chance of getting a job. Kasia's story has a happy end. In August 1989 she told me that she had got back into television, as a presenter for Solidarity. I can only keep my fingers crossed for her.

Like Rostock, Gdańsk is dominated by a great barn of a Gothic church, also called St Mary's. Its interior, plain white, is dull, but its size is impressive – though I couldn't believe that even its bulk could accommodate the 25,000 it is said to be able to hold. The chief treasure is the magnificent altarpiece, done in 1517 by the Augsburg master, Michael Schwarz. It is sad that it is set against an unsympathetic modern stained-glass window. The other great treasure of the church, Hans Memling's *Last Judgement*, has been removed to the National Museum – and even that action is interpreted by some people as a slight to the Church by the state. There is, however, another masterpiece, of woodcarving, in the form of *The Beautiful Madonna of Gdańsk* – though I found her less than appealing, with her soapy smile and hydrocephalic head. For me the chief glory of all the Gdańsk churches was their delicate brick tracery.

The sun, which had kept me almost unwelcome company since my arrival, so hot had it been, was now beginning to hesitate, and there was a suspicion of rain in the air as the wind ushered clouds into the sky above the red-brick church towers of the city. I made my way north towards St Bridget's, Solidarity's church. Like all the churches here except the Russian Orthodox, which was spared, St Bridget's has been restored. The interior is light and spare, uncluttered by ornament and dominated by a striking modern altarpiece in bronze. Inside, by the door in the south wall, an elderly lady and a tough, cheerful young man were selling Solidarity badges and photographs of Wałęsa – on his own, with his family, with the Pope, with Mrs Thatcher, with Father Popiełusko, who was killed by the security police – along with devotional cards, and pictures of Jesus and the saints.

In the north aisle there is a monument to the murdered priest, his figure realistically sprawled across it in death – a life-size bronze. Near him, a cluster of large white crosses commemorate other Polish martyrs. Prominent among them is the cross for Katyn – where several thousand Polish officers were massacred by the Russians during the war: their offence, simply that their existence as an elite presented a potential future threat to Stalin. It had been a taboo subject. Only recently had Russia publicly accepted responsibility for Katyn, and the effect was electric – it was as if the killings had just happened, though there was a grudging admiration for Russia and the Polish establishment for 'coming clean'. Zbigniew, whom I met in a bar later in the day, told me: 'The people have been at war with the government in this country since 1980, and they are getting tired. Just coping from day to day, with the queues, the delays, the bureaucracy, the lack of the simplest goods – it wears you out, takes all your energy. And I have no doubt that that is precisely the government's objective. But with God's help we will not be completely ground down. Katyn is a concession. It is like food to us.'

I walked back along the quay, quiet at this time of day but for three or four dilapidated ferry boats, and a sprucer white one with KØBENHAVN painted on it in red letters. Nothing moved except an elderly grey naval patrol boat, crewed by two self-important young sailors. Green wooden signs on churches and buildings of historical interest give their names in English – a mark of retained cosmopolitanism which goes well with the old tombstones in German let into church floors. Here, too, there is a smattering of French and West German tourists.

The quay is dominated by a fifteenth-century crane, now housing a maritime museum, its wooden superstructure and roof making the whole building look like a house improbably stretched upwards. Close by is Mariacka, a little street whose houses are encumbered with heavy stonework open terraces and wrought iron. In days predating egalitarianism, the well-off could afford houses three windows wide, the moderately rich, two, and I suppose the failures, just one. Nowadays, one finds expensive jewellers in the basements, specializing in amber.

Reaching the end of the quay I turned into town again and found myself passing buildings so shabby, sooty and forlorn that I wondered how anyone doomed to live in them could ever feel hopeful or happy. But immediately, as if someone had sensed that thought, out of a window came the sound of a saxophone playing jazz sublimely well. I couldn't stop to listen long, for the wind was whipping up rain.

In the foyer of the hotel I was, inevitably, asked if I wanted to change money. The black market is so open in Poland that I fatally lowered my guard, and entered into a transaction whereby I was royally cheated. Never do deals with touts in hotel foyers – or indeed, anywhere, except with people you already know. I later discovered that the Polish nickname for such operators is 'newspapermen', because the bundle of proffered złotys is often hidden under or in a newspaper, thus facilitating the scam. I dined gloomily, reflecting on the fruits of my own greed.

The next morning I visited the Pewex hard currency shop in the Great Mill – a solid brick building which is nearly all gable – to see what you could get for your dollars. The shop, spartan and functional, was crowded, as all such places are throughout eastern Europe. Here you could buy a bottle of vodka for a dollar, but a bottle of Heinz tomato ketchup would set you back double that. Vodka, incidentally, has had its price astronomically increased recently, in a vain attempt to check alcoholism.

I noticed a solitary refrigerator on offer at $250; but a washing machine at $900 would have been out of reach for most people. The eagerness of the shoppers reminded me of something I'd been told in Warsaw: 'We Poles always carry our cash about with us; supplies of anything are so unpredictable that our motto has to be: "If you see it, buy it!"'

A short walk north-east brought me to the gates of the Lenin Shipyard, familiar from television news. Near it is the monument to the workers who died here when the strike of 1970 was so harshly quashed. Created by shipbuilders, three tall, slender steel crosses rise in a tight group. Near their bases, bronze plaques depict scenes from the yards – they are reminiscent of medieval art. In place of the figure of Christ on the crosses, bizarrely, there are anchors – but in Poland the anchor symbolizes redemption and struggle, as well as the sea. Behind the crosses there is a low concrete wall. At its centre there is another cross, made up of white plaques bearing the names of those who died. In front of it, a rectangular tin box bearing Solidarity's name carries an eternal flame. It is flanked by a green plastic bucket and a green paint tin, both full of fresh flowers. On the wall itself, there is a quotation from the Psalms, in a translation by the writer Czesław Miłosz, who delighted his country by winning the Nobel Prize in 1980, and subsequently returned home after thirty years in exile. It reads: '*The Lord giveth His people strength; the Lord giveth His people the blessing of his peace.*'

Tadeusz had given me Halina's telephone number. They'd been at Gdańsk University together in the Seventies. Now she worked as a graphic artist.

'The name of the game,' she was now telling me over lunch, 'is selling in the West. That way, you can jump the queues and get what you want today, not when you retire.' She poured herself another glass of Bulgarian white, and spooned up the remainder of her *barszcz* before polishing off the small meat pasty that is always served with beetroot soup. 'This sure as hell beats eating at home,' she added, smiling. 'Did I tell you that there's a medium here who has been in touch with Marx? She says the man never stops apologizing – says he had no idea what it would all lead to!'

'How do you go about selling in the West?'

Halina shook out her red hair and lit a cigarette as the waiter cleared the first course. 'A friend of mine is a painter who sells a lot of his work in West Germany. He teaches in an art school in Poznań, his work's approved of, he's an asset to the country – a "privileged artist". They aren't that thick on the ground, but it's not impossible to become one.' She paused. 'Academics needn't do so badly either, if they can get work in the West. There's a guy here who taught in Montana for a whole year. He could have stayed. They wanted him to. But he preferred to come home, because with twelve months' worth of saved dollars he's become a Paul Getty in Polish terms. Mind you, he still moans.'

'What about?'

'The pyramid system. The bane of our lives. You know how it works: power percolates down from the top and gets dissipated through the chain of command. No one will take responsibility for anything, and most of the people locked in the pyramid spend their time engrossed in office politics. It's one of the reasons nothing ever gets done, which is unfortunate for those who think the machinery of the state is there to help them. But since everybody owns everything, no one's responsible for anything, and so: poor transport, poor telecommunications, poor supply. Except, of course, for the private sector. How often did you have to dial to get me on the phone?'

'Five times.'

'That's good. It can take twenty. But things are improving. We've just got International Direct Dialling. It doesn't work very often, yet, but at least we know it's there, and the few times I've used it, it's been far better than, say, booking a call to Amsterdam and then having to wait two days for it to come through – because that can be galling if you happen to be out or on the loo when it does.' She put out her cigarette and immediately lit another. 'Beating the system is almost a full-time occupation. Have you noticed the people in the queues?'

'I thought everybody queued.'

'The people who queue are the people with no clout, or the old – the retired. They've got the time to queue, so they pick up the ration tickets and shop for the family, liberating son and/or daughter to look after the children or put in a little extra work. If you're single of course it tends to be more difficult. If you've got a large number of children and the grandparents have already popped off, or live elsewhere, it's worse.'

What Halina told me would be repeated often. A kind of secondary society has developed to make life easier, but it carries its own restrictions; and while jobs are secure, mobility within a career can be very difficult. The reasons converge. They point to the existence of yet more vicious circles.

'Let me tell you one little story,' said Halina, who had already told me several, as we waited for coffee and – as a special treat for which she insisted on paying – more wine. 'The artistic director of the theatre near here has had it – he's completely out of ideas, he's bored, and he should probably retire. But no one can force him to leave his job, and he doesn't dare to for reasons which I'll come to. Now, recently he directed a production of *A Chaste Maid in Cheapside*, in which he played The Goldsmith – that way, he could carry a ledger around as a prop, which was useful, because he'd written out his part in it, thus avoiding the necessity of learning it. In any case, he was drunk at every performance. Of course, everybody was pissed off; but as I said, he can't be dislodged. And if he wanted to leave he probably wouldn't, because that would mean moving to a new town. And that would mean starting again, getting back into line for a flat, building up a new network of contacts.'

'Theatre contacts?'

'No. Life contacts. A doctor, a decorator, a butcher, you name it. People who help you sidestep the system, who make life easier, make life possible. That's why people with doctorates at university *A* rarely accept professorships at university *B*. They prefer to stay where they know and are known. And so it is that we all get locked into little prisons, where we stagnate. And in the meantime the only thing for the younger professionals to grow into is dead men's shoes. So anyone with any mind left either escapes into dreams, or gets out to the West. I am ashamed that I can't afford to buy you lunch. I am ashamed that my country is not, in truth, a developing one. It is an *un*developing one. We are slipping back into the Third World, and unless something happens soon we will slip back even further – into the Fifth World, maybe.' She stopped, and lit another cigarette. 'I think the two wickedest systems of government ever invented are Communism and Fascism.'

The coffee came. 'By the way,' she said. 'I hope you don't use milk. None of it's pasteurized.'

One problem which is becoming increasingly difficult to ignore is pollution. In eastern Europe chemical waste and air-polluting by-products in factory smoke are not filtered out or treated before being released into the rivers or the atmosphere. Throughout Poland, eighty-seven per cent of tap water is unfit to drink. Eleven per cent of the water supply is thought to be sufficiently clean for human consumption, but most of that is reserved for industrial purposes – it is the only water pure enough for the machines to use. Drinking water is available, but the people of Gdańsk, at least, have to get it from twenty miles away. Poland has the same amount of drinking water per capita as Egypt; but she is not alone in her water crisis. Bulgaria, having overspent on nuclear reactors, now cannot afford to maintain her reservoirs, with the result that several hundred towns and villages run dry every year.

I took a large packet of coffee out of my case and went downstairs to find a taxi. It had turned very cold and after the mildest winter in living memory there was a hint of snow in the air. There was a queue at the taxi rank and so I walked the short distance to the station, where there were plenty of free cabs. Why had no one else in the queue done as I had?

The taxi-driver couldn't locate Filip's house exactly, so I paid him off and with the help of my map walked the short distance that remained. The suburb was new, an odd mixture of rough park, building site, smart streets of detached timber-faced houses in their own gardens, and teetering blocks, clearly run up at speed. I noticed that some of these were clad with unprotected asbestos sheeting, although the practice is now illegal. Some kids were kicking a ball against one wall, sending up dust.

Filip and his wife welcomed me, thanked me for the coffee (and the chocolate for the children and the lipsticks for Anna which I'd also brought from England), and took me through to their living room. It was large and simply decorated – white walls and a pine floor, upon which Turkish rugs were strewn. A split upper level contained an upright piano and a dining table, and along one wall the television, hi-fi and video equipment were ranged. We drank tea and ate Anna's delicious cheesecake. We were new acquaintances. All Filip knew about me was that I was interested in discussing ecology with him. We were to talk about many other things, and I finally came away deluged in statistics passionately communicated. Filip is one of Poland's few dedicated crusaders for the environment. His voice is lonely and his battle hard.

For the moment, we talked of this and that. I told him who I was and what I did, and we waited for Maria to arrive. Maria, Filip explained to me, spoke fluent English and would translate for him when things got too complicated. She was married to an architect and lived only a short distance away. As he spoke there was a ring at the door – I never met a Pole who wasn't punctual to a fault. Maria was in her mid-thirties, ash-blonde, and wore large silver-framed glasses. She was very beautiful, and had the alabaster skin and china-blue, unnaturally clear eyes, like a doll's, which one often sees in Poland.

Filip seemed braced for an interview rather than a conversation, so I stumbled through the handful of questions which had sprung to mind since my arrival. They were enough. We sat in enormous, sagging armchairs, drank cup after cup of tea, and Maria effortlessly kept up a translation as information poured out and I tried to absorb it. Filip and Anna's small children – three of them – meanwhile scaled the balustrade separating the room's levels, played peek-a-boo behind the armchairs, and consumed Cadbury's Fruit-and-Nut with concentrated delight.

The subject which occupied him most was the building of two water-cooled reactors – one some way to the south, and the other only thirty miles from Gdańsk. For a country so crippled by its debt to the West that it is unable even to pay back the annual interest, merely to undertake such an exorbitant project seemed curious, but when one learned that the Gdańsk power station would only contribute three per cent to Poland's overall electricity supply, and would not even replace existing plants, one wondered about the sanity of the scheme. But such things are not peculiar to eastern Europe. What was more disturbing was the additional strain the existence of the power stations would put on the Polish environment. Already the statistics are chilling. In central Silesia, the industrial heart of the country, heavy metal pollution in air and water is so great that one child in every five is born mentally or physically disabled, and this is a percentage which has doubled in the past ten years. The effect on adults is no less alarming, since the incidence of pollution-induced brain damage is also doubling every decade.

Cracow, the ancient capital, jewel of Poland's architectural heritage and one of the few towns not destroyed in the war, is fast becoming a victim of the huge industrial complex of Nowa Huta only three miles away. The medieval and Renaissance buildings are mainly built of sandstone and limestone, which are especially susceptible to damage. At the moment, surfaces of such materials are being eaten away at the rate of half a centimetre a year, with the result that many of the medieval statues still exposed to the air have the look of lepers, and soon will have no features left at all. Cracow, one of the country's greatest tourist attractions, is also one of the most heavily air-polluted towns in the country, but across the whole of Poland sulphur levels in the air are 250 per cent above Polish safety limits – themselves four times higher than those set by the USA.

It goes without saying, therefore, that the forests, Poland's great natural asset next to coal, are steadily dying. In any case they are being cut down remorselessly and sold to Sweden, which buys the timber cheaply with hard currency. There is no plant for processing timber in Poland, so Sweden is able to make a handsome profit and conserve her own forests at the same time. 'The purpose of our economy is to shore itself up all the time – but it's so rickety that it's a full-time job to stop it from collapsing completely. Obviously, there isn't the time, the energy, or the money to spend on the areas which we could develop sensibly, and thus have a chance to enter the world markets.' Filip spoke with bitterness. If the West would – or could afford to – let Poland off the hook of her debt, she might be able to begin to help herself. As it is, the polarization of East and West only gets worse.

That question led us back to the one which often dominates Polish conversations – the difficulty of getting things. Supply is so erratic that one week there might be, say, a glut of soap in the shops in one town, but no matches. 'If you want matches, you have to go to another town, which probably has a glut of them, but no soap!'

Anna and Maria, both hating to queue all the time, had developed another system. 'If we see a queue, let's say at the baker's, because that's the one most frequently faced, then we'll hunt round for another baker's where there's a smaller queue. Sometimes it works, though often you can bet that where there's no queue, either the shop has run out or it's closed; and you can spend as much time hunting round as you would have standing in the original queue anyway. But at least walking you feel you're doing something, even if it's only getting some exercise!'

Queuing can take more abrading forms. Passports may now be freely available, but Maria's queue number to get one is 4050. This number – according to a system used in a variety of long-term queues – is entered against one's name in a book. Every two days she has to go along and reconfirm her position. 'It will take me eight weeks to get the application form, and then there will be another queue for the passport itself, for which I'll have to go to Warsaw. Then at least I'll have the thing for five years, after which it lapses and the whole business starts again.'

Anna had to wait a year to acquire a television set. She was allocated a queue number at the outset, and had to pay a form of retainer to keep it. This money is paid by the government to support the producer. When the set was finally ready for collection, it had to be paid for at the price it cost then, not the cost when it was ordered. 'And that is a consideration – inflation's been running at eighty per cent; salary increases average forty per cent, of which twenty-six per cent is subject to tax.' Of a person's total income, some thirty per cent is deducted 'for the Health Service – but of course what the government actually does with it is their little secret.' The grim humour with which this information is imparted is explained by the fact that state-run hospitals are so poorly equipped that people fortunate enough to get treatment at all have to supply their own medicine – to the extent of getting it from the West for which, naturally, they have to part with hard currency. 'The bosses of course have private clinics, and there are special military hospitals.'

At the other end of the scale, for those unable to work, and those on pensions, income is very low – just over 20,000 złotys when I was there. 'They live on cabbage, potato, and dog meat. That's all you can afford at that level. And God help you if you're ill. 20,000 złotys would buy you a month's supply of cotton wool,' said Anna. Filip told me that in one generation, life expectancy has decreased by ten years.

Interspersed with these topics a theme emerged whose burden was to lay the blame for all woes at Russia's door. The Russian leader Gorbachev's new and apparently liberal policies were greeted with bitter cynicism, and it was clear that my hosts were horrified that the West had been so completely taken in by him. Filip went so far as to comment that Orwell's *1984* was still the most accurate depiction of what life in contemporary Russia was like and he didn't hesitate to describe Gorbachev as no different from Stalin. 'Of course, circumstances have changed. They've finally realized that their economic system is rubbish, and now he wants to regroup without losing power. But the first thing they need to do is get their farming organized, or they really will have a counter-revolution on their hands. In any case the economy won't stand the grain imports they're obliged to make, and which are increasing. So he's wooing the West to get its technology. But you'll notice that no economies are made where the army is concerned.'

The bitterness is understandable. Russia controls Poland's oil supply and exploits her industry. When a Russian ship is built at Gdańsk, the Poles have to buy the parts needed from the West in dollars; but the Russians pay for the finished vessel in roubles. 'We are caught in a poverty trap which is not wholly of our own making, and between the debt owed to the West and the state of dependence we are kept in by Russia, there is no chance for us to get up off our knees.' By now he was more sad than bitter.

In the face of all this I was reluctant to impose myself for dinner, but my hosts insisted that I stay, laughing with slight embarrassment at my deference. 'Perhaps we've made things sound worse than they are ... ' My own feeling was that my friends suffered more from intellectual than material frustration; but the stress caused by the fact that every simple act of acquisition was a struggle couldn't be denied.

We dined on cold meats, cooked and smoked, sausage, a variety of salads based on beetroot and green peppers, and cheese, accompanied by yet more cups of black tea.

After dinner, the four of us sat down to a bottle of Cinzano rosé in honour of Anna's birthday, which Filip had, apparently genuinely, totally forgotten.

'I think what really hit us below the belt was martial law,' said Maria. 'Although after all the other times since the war, you'd think we'd've got used to it. But all our attempts at getting things changed have come to nothing so far.' Martial law was especially bad. Not only was it brutally applied, with random searches both in the street and of people's homes, but it had a crippling effect on industry and trade, added to which basic goods suddenly became completely unavailable. 'Mind you, nothing's changed in that department. But it was quite something not to be able to get any ink.'

Martial law ended in 1983. Six years later, and a matter of weeks after I had been in Poland, Solidarity convincingly won all the seats available to them in the first elections held in the country for forty years. There is now a Solidarity-backed democratic government – the first in eastern Europe; all this within three months of my visit to Poland.

I mentioned the reserve I'd sensed, and been told about. 'It's true,' Anna told me. 'During martial law, people just went into their shells, and they haven't come out again yet. They have to do with their immediate circle, family and friends, and that's it. You help your own, and you turn your back on the rest.'

'But there's also the sheer grind, which I know we've gone on and on about,' said Filip. 'I'm sorry about that, but just imagine how it would be for you if you had to make a trip to buy shoes for your kids to a town a hundred miles away, simply because none were available anywhere else. It's the time everything takes, and the effort. Most of us have to take two jobs to make ends meet, and the net effect is that you end up with no energy to think clearly or develop any clear line of action for your life.'

I thought that his own example gave the lie to that, but he was exceptional. When I told him, he smiled and said that I was paying him a great compliment. 'We live in a country which is essentially ruled by mediocrity, for only the mediocre are trusted not to make waves. The interesting, the original people either get out, or go under.'

'I think you are exaggerating.'

'A little, but only to make my point. What is true is that many good people – most – who do make a career in the establishment end up with their sensibilities numbed. Otherwise how could they stand it?'

Poland, I thought, was not the only country of which that could be said.

The Długa was for some reason full of soldiers the next morning – national servicemen being shown the sights. National service is long – two years – and comes immediately after school or university. Maria had been quick to point out that it was designed to knock any non-conformist ideas acquired during education out of people's heads as quickly as possible; but even she admitted that if that were the case, then the system wasn't often successful. The army and the police offer several advantages to those willing to make a career in them, notably no waiting lists for flats, and prompt and efficient medical care; nevertheless recruitment is always difficult. The call of freedom must be greater. I remembered that in its heyday Solidarity had claimed ten million members – an astonishing number for there to have been no revolution, one might have thought. But the union remained disciplined, and determined to win its aims by legal means.

The sun had returned, but there was no warmth because of a freezing wind from the sea. I hurried through the Golden Gate, a sooty white Renaissance wedding cake designed by Abraham van den Blocke in 1612, and turned south towards the National Museum.

The collection here has treasures to match Warsaw's. There are two very fine Malczewskis – possibly the best anywhere. A weird scene portrays the painter in the countryside, holding an ear of green wheat upon which a grasshopper perches. On either side of him a little boy has a songbird on his finger. The picture is called *The Sounds of the Meadows*, and would be less exceptional if it weren't for the fact that in the background a half-glimpsed group contains a nude with enormous wings, and the little boys are staring at the birds in their charge with expressions of consummate evil.

In a corner of the same room in the museum, a frightening dwarf by Malczewski stares out at you from amidst a swirl of colour. His eyes dance with malevolent life. Beguilingly, he is simply called *The Country Boy*. Matejko is here, and Wyspiański, who Maria thinks is Poland's best poet after Mickiewicz. Mickiewicz, a close contemporary of Byron, has the status of a national hero. His statue is everywhere, unavoidable, for at the time he wrote Poland was in the deepest darkness, and he both represented the flame of her spirit and kept it alive. Many streets and squares are named after him, and after the great military hero of the period, Tadeusz Kościuszko. No streets or squares here are named after Soviet heroes or socialist ideals.

The other nineteenth-century painter, whom I had only encountered briefly before, was Piotr Michałowski, a proto-impressionist whose horses were much admired by Picasso; but the centrepiece of the collection is Hans Memling's *Last Judgement*. I am glad that it is no longer in St Mary's, for here you can approach close enough to appreciate its detail. It is extraordinarily fine, and the facial expressions, especially of the damned, have a psychological realism which is vividly precise. Among the judged souls is a black man, drawn with great accuracy. His face in the crowd reminded me of something I had heard a couple of days earlier. Someone returning from several months' work in Zaïre had had his portrait painted – for a joke – as a negro. The joke had been a great success, I was told; I doubt if that would have been so in a more heterogeneous society. Poland misses something by having so very few representatives of other races, and I frequently wondered about the unmistakable strand of racism which ran through so many conversations – could it merely be laid at the door of parochialism?

We stood surveying the little carpark just beyond the Main Town wall. The area was a scruffy no-man's-land wedged in between the medieval wall and the Victorian red-brick police headquarters. Behind us, just visible, was the grim, dominating bulk of the Prison Gate, the medieval prison and torture chamber which now houses the university's Department of Criminology.

'The theatre was here,' Janek told me, sweeping an arm over the roofs of the assorted Fiat Polskis, Polonezes, Ladas and Skodas in the carpark. We had come here as the result of a conversation about Elizabethan and Jacobean drama in general, about which Janek knew considerably more than I did, having translated several of Shakespeare's contemporaries into Polish, and written a book on something I knew nothing about at all: English travelling players of the period working in central and eastern Europe. It transpired that they didn't travel so much as take contracts to work for this or that prince or grand duke for a season – or longer. German translations of Shakespeare's plays were already being performed in Gdańsk during his lifetime. 'But in those days the town was a great cosmopolitan city, of course.' The English Comedians, as they were called, are generally thought to have used pirated Shakespeare scripts translated into German.

Janek had discovered the theatre by chance, noticing it in an old print of the city he'd discovered while researching his book. It was a three-thousand seater, and based squarely on the design of the Fortune Theatre in London. 'It was built here in the early seventeenth century, and I am sure the design was roughed out by an English actor from his memory of the Fortune. The Fortune wasn't a complicated structure like the Globe or the Rose – it was just a box, after all – something which the local builders and carpenters could knock up without too much specialized knowledge.'

I asked whether there might be any chance of getting the carpark dug up so that he could excavate the site, but he looked gloomy and replied that it all depended.

'On money?'

'No. On outside interest. Do you think the BBC might want to do a programme? Is there anyone there you could ask?'

He asked after Halina as we walked back to his car. 'Did she tell you about my *Chaste Maid in Cheapside*? It wasn't as bad as all that, you know.' He went on to say that he was considering translating a selection of Ben Jonson's comedies, and which did I think would be best to do?

We drove out to Sopot for lunch – 'It's where I was born, and you can't leave Gdańsk without seeing it!' – but not before Janek had given me a whistle-stop tour of the northern part of the town, casting all thoughts of petrol rationing from his mind. The giant sword which is the monument to those who fell defending the promontory of the Westerplatte – the first victims of the Second World War – is massive socialist art at its rare best. Across the town from it, on the western side, is the beautiful red-brick Gothic cathedral of Oliwa, which must have one of the longest naves in the world. With its narrow façade and high curved roof, the cathedral looks like a liner. Its elegant wooden Baroque western doors lead to an interior which is a glorious if surprising mixture of Romanesque and Baroque, with an altar floating on plaster clouds, and at the west end a massive eighteenth-century organ in dark wood, decorated with angels carrying gilded trumpets, and a golden sun, stars and moon – all of which 'perform' when the organ is played, the angels blowing their trumpets and the spheres moving across a wooden sky.

On the way to Sopot, Janek switched on the car radio, but hearing a news programme he switched it off again. 'Have you heard the joke about our news broadcasts? The power stations register a drop in consumption when they are transmitted, as everyone turns off their radios and television sets!' Much later, back in England, I heard from friends in Poland that Solidarity, which by then had its own radio and TV broadcasts, was having great difficulty in overcoming traditional and ingrained mistrust of everything said through the media.

Sopot looks like most similar opulent and suburban seaside towns. Fittingly, we lunched at the Grand Hotel, built in the Twenties to accommodate the people who came here to patronize the casino (long since defunct). A handful of early holi-daymakers were here, but most of the other diners were locals. The hotel is built right on the beach, and the Baltic looked crisp and inviting across fifty yards of clean, pale beige sand, the brisk wind whipping the dark water into fresh white breakers. Bathing, however, is forbidden. The Vistula, stiff with chemical waste, debouches into the sea here. The waters of the Polish coast are dead to a depth of fifty metres. Despite the pollution and the warnings, people do bathe. 'They like to get their money's worth out of their holiday,' Janek explained simply, though not, of course, without irony. This was the northernmost point in my entire journey, however, and whenever I encounter the sea I have to wet my hand in it, and so I did here.

'Actually it's worse up the coast at Kaliningrad,' Janek said, though he called it 'Königsberg'. 'The Russians are even worse dumpers than we are. Königsberg's a closed town these days, it's a naval base; but a friend of mine was invited there to design a set for their theatre, and when he came back he said he'd never seen such poverty. Here,' he indicated the impeccably maintained opulence of the hotel, 'we still manage to keep up a certain style, though I have to say that the longer we stay in the Eastern Bloc, the more Balkan our standards of service become.'

He apologized for abandoning me soon after lunch, but he was about to move with his second wife into a new flat which he'd been lucky enough to acquire after only a seven-year wait. I was quite pleased to walk off the heavy lunch of *bigos* – a Polish staple made of cabbage, sauerkraut, onions and a variety of meats, predominantly pork and sausage – and *zrazy zawijane*, which is minced steak wrapped around mushrooms and then covered with sour cream and served with *kasza*, buckwheat groats. The weather remained sharp and sunny, and I had no fear of rain today, for Maria had told me that it never rained on Saturdays. 'It is a very Polish belief, though – Saturday is the day the Blessed Virgin does the celestial washing. Therefore it cannot rain.'

7

GOATS IN THE CLOCK TOWER

A last conversation in Gdańsk is worth recording. Recently, the authorities discovered that one country house and its estate had escaped confiscation and was subsequently forgotten in the plethora of bureaucracy in the years following 1945. An investigation was set in motion and the house was found still to be run by a member of a family of the *szlachta* – the nobility – which had always owned it. What is more, his workers had remained loyal to him. No one had invited the state's intervention, nor was it welcomed when it came.

With some embarrassment, the authorities pointed out to the owner that the property should have been forfeit to the state over forty years ago, and could still be, though of course, they hastened to add, in these post-Stalinist days it would be a question of purchase rather than compulsory takeover. He replied regally that as they were discussing the family home he would have to refer the matter to his relatives – now all living in Paris. Those in authority acquiesced.

'They did so,' my informant told me, 'because even after this long they slipped back into a peasant-master relationship with the aristocrat, though he had no power at all. It is an oddity of our culture today, and another of the paradoxes that make up society here. You see, those who took over in the late Forties – the Russian appointees – and all those who followed them are precisely the people with no breeding or background. All the key positions were filled from the rank and file, regardless of aptitude or experience – people's poets, people's professors, people's factory managers. Originality and integrity spelt individualism, and that was bad. We took all the goodness out of the soil, and now we wonder why nothing will grow.'

I pondered this as I gazed out of my window at the ferocious snowstorm which had blown up in the night and covered everything in a grey pall. The best answer I could come up with was from the same source as the story. My informant, seeing doubt creep into my face, had laughed and slapped me on the back. 'I can see what you are thinking, that we are a nation of right-wingers, who cannot bear to see any good in this system at all. And you meet me, and see my house, and you think, well, he at least doesn't exactly seem to be suffering. But the real point is that we are fed up – fed up – with having a government imposed on us, fed up with having no say in how we are run, in having no choice, in not being able to speak and do for ourselves. Of course it is true that in the years of Partition most of the administration in the Prussian, Russian and Austrian zones was carried out by Poles. My view is that nothing has changed: Poles are still running Poles on behalf of others. That is what frustrates us, and it would even if our government was one hundred per cent efficient. I think that is the hardest thing for you to understand, coming from a country which has had almost uninterrupted democratic development, and which hasn't even been occupied by a foreign power for a thousand years. I'd like to give some of your armchair communists a taste of living here for a few months and see how they'd like it! Not, of course, that this has anything to do with real Communism any more.'

He lived with his wife and two children in a large, modern detached house, filled with English books. He frequently worked abroad, and was himself descended from a *szlachta* family. His Anglophilia extended to his dog, a golden labrador puppy called 'Tamisa' (Thames) – 'Because there is always an unexpected risk of flood with her!' Something else he'd said lodged in my mind: 'No Eastern Bloc nation is temperamentally suited to this form of government, but my guess is that the Poles are the least suited of all!'

By the time I was due to shoulder my pack and walk to the station, it was as if the snow had never been. The sun had already melted most of what had settled, and when the train pulled out there was no hint of it in the countryside south of the town, though in the course of the four-hour journey to Poznań we rode in and out of storms, lending at least a variety of climate to an unchanging landscape. My travelling companions, dressed in the predominant browns and beiges, were uncommunicative, and as I did not feel like reading I dozed to the rhythm of the train. Only occasionally was the view from the window gloriously enlivened by the sight of a giant hare, disturbed by the noise, bounding across a field away from us; and south of Bydgoszcz a field full of fighter planes added variety to the interminable flat farmland, dotted with nondescript villages.

What town in the world presents a good first impression to anyone entering it by train? Poznań is heralded by a string of hideous factories. It is a sprawling place, and the little Old Town at its centre, once again heavily but impressively restored after war damage, is like a museum quarter. Over half of it was destroyed by the Germans, but now it is impossible to see what is original and what reproduced. Traffic is banished from its centre, as in Warsaw and Gdańsk, but here it is so much quieter that it is easy to allow the past to enter your imagination. The elegant little houses painted in a variety of bright pastel colours cluster tightly round the Town Hall, a piece of Renaissance ebullience bordering on the vulgar. The original building was brought up to this level by Giovanni Battista Quadro in 1550, two years after the death of Zygmunt the Old, whose wife, Bona Sforza, had brought considerable Italian influence in her wake when she married him – and was also instrumental in getting the Poles to eat vegetables. She later went on to have several of her political opponents poisoned, though not necessarily, one assumes, with minestrone.

'Have you seen the picture of her in Matejko's *Raising of the Zygmunt Bell*?' asked my friend Ignacy, as we wandered round the old Market Square. 'Poor Zygmunt. She certainly wore the trousers in that relationship.' But all the credit for the influence of the Renaissance cannot be placed to Bona Sforza's account: the Poles embraced Italian architecture and ideas with enthusiasm.

During Zygmunt's reign, the astronomer Mikołaj Kopernik (Copernicus) developed his idea that the sun was the centre of the solar system. Having a healthy respect for the Church, which didn't share his view, he told only a handful of close friends of his discovery, and withheld his full findings from publication, though there is a legend that the first copy of his book *De revolutionibus orbium coelestium*, which appeared in 1543, was presented to him on his deathbed – an example of perfect timing, if true. In the following reign, the poet Jan Kochanowski and the statesman Jan Zamoyski rose to prominence. All three men were educated at either Bologna or Padua and at Cracow, one of the oldest European universities. Poles wryly point out that their cultivated king, Zygmunt August, was at war then with the Russian tsar Ivan the Terrible, a man whose name is associated with near-criminal barbarity. I heard it said that Russians could not properly be considered European, and the opinion implied that in this context 'European' was synonymous with 'human'. Poles told me that in the past they had always been happy when Russia had had problems on her Eastern frontiers, as it kept the Russians off their backs.

The clock tower of the Town Hall is distinguished by two metal goats which emerge at midday and butt heads – commemorating two real goats whose battle once roused the burghers of Poznań to awareness of a fire. I didn't see them. 'You have missed nothing,' Ignacy consoled me later, adding, in his lugubrious way, 'There are only three things to see in Poznań: the Old Square, the parish church, and the cathedral.'

The parish church, with its ornate, dim interior and its towering pink Baroque façade, cramped into tiny Swietosław Street which leads up to it, is like a ponderous Spanish church which has been transplanted, although in fact it is the work of Italian architects. The first side chapel to the left is dedicated to Maksymilian Kolbe, the Polish Catholic priest who laid down his life in Auschwitz so that another man might live. Father Kolbe has been recently beatified, and chapels to him, and votive paintings, are everywhere to be found. Hanging in the nave of this church too were red-and-white national flags bearing the emblem of the Second World War Polish Resistance.

The cathedral lies some way away, on the island which was the site of the original settlement of Poznań, though now it is chiefly occupied by Church administrative buildings. The Reformation never took firm hold in Poland, only influencing the German northern coastline, and the Counter-Reformation when it came was swift and severe. Roman Catholicism is entrenched and conservative, commanding a powerful and populous priesthood and a devoted following. Abortion, AIDS, and homosexuality are all regarded with almost superstitious horror.

The tall red-brick towers of the great church are visible as soon as you leave the Old Town, and it is quickly reached by crossing the River Wárta, which here is the colour and consistency of Brown Windsor soup, and slicked with oil. Dodging several cheerful drunks ('It's the beginning of the month, so they've got money to spend,' Ignacy explained apologetically), we made our way there.

The interior is odd. The brickwork is all new, since although this building dates from 1347 it was used as an ammunition dump by the Germans, and blew up in 1945.

After the war, it was restored to its pure Gothic form, apart from the Baroque spires and one or two other features. The austere and vast empty space thus achieved is therefore at variance with the Baroque furniture, such as the pulpit with its extravagant baldacchino. Behind the fifteenth-century carved altarpiece, which is too far away and too dimly lit to see properly, there is a chapel which marks the site of the tombs of the first rulers of Poland, Mieszko I and his son Bolesław the Brave. The chapel itself is Victorian-Byzantine and an oddity. If you are lucky enough to have a five-złoty coin on you, you can put it into the slot of a machine at the gate and get the place illuminated.

Opposite the chapel a corpulent marble bishop reclines on his tomb, sleeping his last sleep. Though his posture looks uncomfortable, his expression is serenely satisfied. Working back along the north aisle, I discovered a sixteenth-century stone bishop designed to lie flat but now giddily set into the wall. At the west end of the aisle is a superb twelfth- or thirteenth-century brass. Again, it is a full-length portrait of a bishop.

The acoustics here are eerily good; the slightest rustle is amplified all over the church. And here, as in every church I entered, there were at least a dozen people at prayer. Services were always packed.

Leaving the cathedral, we walked north up Gabary to the park which covers the land once occupied by the citadel. On its south side lies the Poznań Old Garrison Cemetery, divided into sections – Russian, Polish and Commonwealth – of graves of the fallen of the Second World War. Each section has its own style – the Russians have terraces of grey granite stones bearing red stars, the Polish headstones are individually designed and are laid out less formally, as in a country churchyard. The Commonwealth section, maintained by the War Graves Commission through the Polish Government, is composed of neat rows of white tablets beneath a towering cross, though not all those buried here are Christian. One pilot who lies especially far from home is Flight-Lieutenant A. G. Henriquez, a Jamaican Jew who died aged 28 on 17 August 1944. In one corner a group of graves marks the resting places of the men who were captured and shot by the Gestapo after the POW breakout from Stalag Luft III featured in the book (and film) *The Great Escape*.

Heading back through the north-western corner of the town centre, we passed through pleasant suburbs largely composed of nineteenth-century villas and ornate imperial buildings. There is an unexceptional neo-Classical opera house, and close by an ugly grey rectangular castle, built as a residence for Kaiser Wilhelm II. In the square which separates it from the university stands a statue of Adam Mickiewicz, and the monument to the workers killed here by the police in 1956. The other dates marking similar events in Poland's recent history are also recorded: 1968, 1970, 1976 and 1980. A popular cartoon shows Poland as a nervous slalom skier, still upright – just – after having negotiated a series of gates marked with all these dates.

Ignacy's flat in a quiet side-street beyond the zoo was airy and comfortable in an untidy, bookish way. He teaches linguistics at the university, and his wife has made a good living out of a private School of English – her problems now being to recruit enough teachers and rent enough extra space to meet the demand. Both were born in

Poznań, and had lived here all their lives.

Ignacy was bullish about his country's future. 'I think we are on the right track at last. They're even making it more attractive to own złotys, and at last they're doing something to counter the black market.' He was referring to a recent move whereby the PKO (National Savings Bank) could now offer close to 3000 złotys to the dollar – on a par with the black market rate. 'And we can buy dollars now too, at a slightly higher rate. Added to which, there's talk of private currency exchange businesses being given the green light.'

'So you'll all become capitalists?'

'Some of us already are.'

He and his wife were so loud in their praises of the capitalist system that I felt bound to mention some of its disadvantages. 'Are you a communist, then?' asked Helena, only half joking.

She was dark, volatile, humorous; and oddly proud of the fact that her brown eyes and black hair meant that she was frequently taken by her fellow Poles for a foreigner. 'One or two of my students are convinced that I am Jewish, and they are quite suspicious of me,' she laughed.

By contrast, Ignacy was bear-like; tweedy, bearded and bookish. After tea, he drove me back into town in his ramshackle beige Lada, narrowly missing dusty green trams which rang angry bells at us as he cut across their tracks. He told me more about why he felt optimistic. 'I think our new Prime Minister has pulled together a really progressive cabinet. We've got a Minister of Labour who, admittedly, is a Party member and a big wheel in state finance, but he also spent a long time in the private sector and he's a millionaire.' He caught my expression. 'I can see what you're thinking, but believe me, a communist-capitalist is just what this country needs.' His own boss, the Vice-Chancellor of Mickiewicz University, has been appointed Minister of Education.

'We've developed into a nation of opportunists anyway, because supplies are so erratic. And whatever you do, don't get ill or have an accident here – we're a good two decades behind you and some of the drugs we still use would probably see you off!'

'I remember that in our first flat, which was a tiny place provided by the university, we only had a put-you-up to sleep on. It was very uncomfortable, so we decided to buy a mattress. It took a year to find one! And later, when we found another, we bought that too, although we didn't need it, simply because it was there.

'The other thing that is always impossible is shoes. There are shoe-shops, sure, but are there ever any shoes in them? All of us get used to "organizing" on every level, and we build up a network of contacts to help us. As for free enterprise,' he laughed, and swerved to avoid another tram, 'since it's been possible to get to West Berlin without a visa, people have been getting up at the crack of dawn, boarding the first train, and whisking across there loaded with butter and vegetables which they've bought here at subsidized prices. They set up unofficial markets there and sell 'em – even undercutting local prices by fifty per cent and they still make a handsome profit. The West Germans have put a stop to that now, but our own customs authorities simply wink at our nationals bringing in anything they've bought in the West with their own hard currency – from colour TVs to personal computers. There's rather a nice story about a bunch of Poles who are travelling back from Istanbul, loaded with goodies, via Sofia. They book a Balkanair flight to Warsaw, pay the phenomenal excess baggage charge, load up their stuff and get aboard. The Tupolev starts up, taxis down the runway – puts on power – but it can't take off! It's too heavy! So the Poles have to get off with their stuff, and Polish Airlines have to send down a special plane to collect them!'

To the south-west of Poznań, beyond the station, there is a thieves' market, where clothing smuggled in from Turkey is sold – at inflated prices, but there are always buyers, because the stuff is at least there. It's at Rynek Łazarski, but look out for pickpockets if you go.

The following day was Monday, when most museums are closed. Nevertheless I walked up the plac Woloności to the National Museum in the faint hope that I might be lucky. The door was open – an unexpected bonus – so I went in, but only to be told by the motherly group of ladies at the kiosk that the museum was indeed shut. I smiled and appeared not to understand. This would be my only chance to see the place, and as I had got this far I hoped that someone might take pity on me. After a few minutes a small bald man of about thirty-five with bright eyes and appalling teeth appeared. We discovered that we had French in common. I told him my plight, and said that if it were possible I should like to see Malczewski's *Melancholy*, probably his greatest painting.

As soon as I mentioned the picture, any remaining reserve was put aside. Wacław (as he introduced himself) told me to sit on a bench and wait while he fetched keys. When he returned he gave me a two-hour personal tour of the museum, which by luck was mounting an exhibition of Polish history through its painting and had thus amassed a number of works from other collections.

Painting is the most poignant and immediate means of expression of the period of Partition. The curious view Poland has of herself as 'the Christ of nations' – so-called for her suffering, and because, Wacław suggested, she was between two thieves: Russia and Germany – was represented in a number of popular lithographs, where, for example, fighters in the two major uprisings, of 1830 and 1863–4, are shown in defeat, hanging their swords on a life-size crucifix. Poland was also represented as a woman shut out of her own home; and a glass case displayed the black mourning jewellery worn by Polish women after the failure of the 1864 ('January') Uprising.

Battle scenes from the Napoleonic Wars to Piłsudski's campaigns against the Bolsheviks and on to the Second World War were plentiful, for the history of Poland is a history of battle, occupation and resistance. The most striking exponents of these were the father and son, Juliusz and Wojciech Kossak. Wojciech was one of the two painters responsible for the astonishing *Panorama Racławicka* which I was soon to see in Wrocław. A small study for it was displayed here. Of the few Socialist-Realist paintings depicting post-war prosperity, Aleksander Kobzdej's *Pass me a Brick* was the most ponderous example.

The painting which sums it all up, and upon which not only the exhibition but also nineteenth-century Polish history seem to pivot, is *Melancholy*. Painted in 1894, when Malczewski was forty, it is a representation of the whole period of Partition. We are in a vast room, part studio, part cell. At the extreme left, his back to us, bent in an attitude of despair, the painter sits in front of a canvas which he has barely touched, but from it, floating and swarming across the room towards us, comes a horde of people – young, old, artists, prisoners, madmen. Their goal is the broad window which flanks the right-hand side of the picture. Beyond it, friendly normality – a pleasant building in a spring garden. The window is half-open, but just outside it, guarding the opening, stands a figure in black, who may be Melancholy, or Death; but who prevents the onward movement of the crowd. Siberian prisoners lean, broken-spirited, on the window-sill; others are thrown back into the room, swirling towards the black-and-white banner at its centre.

The painting was done on the centenary of the uprising against the Russians led by the Polish hero Tadeusz Kościuszko, the failure of which induced the final collapse of Poland in 1795. On the back of the canvas, Malczewski wrote: 'Prologue of a vision/the last century in Poland – Tout un siècle.'

8

RENAISSANCE AND INDUSTRY

Tired horses ploughed shallow furrows in small fields, encouraged by elderly couples dressed in black. The farmland remained as green and flat as ever, although for a time halfway between Poznań and Wrocław it conceded a handful of gentle undulations. The weather had changed its mind again, and turned bitterly cold. In our compartment the heating didn't work. '*Alle pölnische Bahne kaputt,*' the well-kempt businessman sitting opposite me confided before folding his arms and settling into a frowning sleep. I was too uncomfortable to follow suit. I curled my toes up in my shoes to try to get them warm, and beat my fingers against my thighs to encourage some circulation.

About an hour before Wrocław, we moved into a snowstorm, though by the time we reached the outskirts of town it had changed to freezing drizzle. Luckily taxis are in greater supply in Poland than elsewhere in eastern Europe. I plunged through the large, crowded station and found one without difficulty.

I had managed to avoid too many new hotels and the one here was a comfortable turn-of-the-century building, furnished in Edwardian mahogany. I took myself to the restaurant to have lunch and wait for the rain to stop. At last I was beginning to get Polish beer, which is heavy and rather malty. Lunch was served by the most imperious waiter I have ever encountered.

Feeling warmer, I set off into the town. Wrocław has only been Polish since 1945 – before the war it was the German town of Breslau, and despite the fact that many Poles from eastern towns like Lwów, absorbed into Russia in 1945, have been resettled in Silesia, the area's capital is still distinctly German in its atmosphere, though this may be due to the German domestic architecture – even the cobblestones are laid in the German way. The continuing interest the Germans have in this part of the world is a source of irritation to the Poles. One, who has a smallholding on the outskirts of town, told me that every year the children of its former owners come over from Munich 'and make sure that I'm keeping the place up all right. Don't worry, they seem to be saying, this is really ours, and we'll be back.' There is no love lost between the Poles and the Germans. In the hinterland of Wrocław, the countryside is dotted with closed, degenerating German cemeteries, in some of which the graves have collapsed. Together with the rotting, neglected cemeteries of the Jews, these present a woeful picture.

But Wrocław is undeniably a German town, and if people speak a second language here, it is German rather than English or French. The Market Square is of the same pattern as at Poznań – restored medieval and Renaissance houses surrounding an imposing Town Hall – but here traffic is still allowed right into the centre, and the effect of the dirt it creates on the buildings is all too obvious.

I crossed the square and headed north up Kuźnicza to the university, a huge grey Baroque pile whose façade is weighed down with crumbling stucco. It is cramped in a narrow square where its whale-like proportions cannot be appreciated, though it is a fine building, the work of another Italian architect, Domenico Martinelli. Beyond it lies the cluster of small islands which formed the original settlement. The cathedral, on the north bank of the Odra, is, as in Poznań, at the centre of a number of buildings devoted to Church administration.

You reach it by making your way past the grim red-brick pile of Our Lady of the Sand, and on over an iron bridge painted blue, past the Church of the Holy Cross. Both these churches are Gothic, but they look like the sooty Victorian piles you might find in some grimy northern English industrial town. The Church of the Holy Cross is particularly sad, dirty and crumbling without, broken windows looming behind gates secured with rusty chains. The cathedral lies just beyond. It is also of sooty red brick. Its stumpy twin towers look as if they had been robbed of their spires.

The interior is crepuscular. There is a carved altarpiece which may be from the studio of the late medieval woodcarver and sculptor Veit Stoss, but it is far too dark to see it in any detail at all, even when the sparse illumination is switched on. At first sight, the cathedral appears to have little more to offer, but I was lucky enough to be able to tag on to a Polish tourist group, whose leader pressed an electric bell set into the wall by a wrought-iron gateway halfway down the nave. It summoned a nun, who opened the gate and ushered us through, past the high altar, to visit the three chapels which lie behind it. The central one is dedicated to the Virgin. It is severely Gothic, and contains what looks like a crusader's sarcophagus, the stone polished as smooth as marble with age. On either side (barred and unlit unless a group descends) are two unexpectedly luxurious Baroque chapels.

To the south is St Elizabeth's, built for the Cardinal Duke Frederick by Giacomo Scianzi. Frederick was Elector of Hesse, a convert to Catholicism shown in an extravagant attitude of prayer opposite an austere Virgin, who rides on a collection of awful overgrown putti. The sculptors were pupils of Bernini, and though they do not seem to have learned much about lightness of touch, the master's influence can be seen in the figure of the duke, and in the drapery which flows around his supporters. To the north, the Corpus Christi Chapel is a far more sophisticated affair, which is not surprising, as it was designed by no less an architect than Fischer von Erlach. It has an airy lightness which is surprising in this gloomy Gothic barn, and it is dedicated to Franz Ludwig Neuberg, Archbishop of Breslau and Elector of Trier. I was not able to find out how he conducted his affairs in two such widely separated places.

Nuns flitted like bats through the nave as I made my way out, crossing the plac Katedralny and returning to the town over Pokoj Bridge. Doubling back across a small park, I reached a building like a concrete crown of lamb. This houses the *Panorama Racławicka*.

It is an enormous circular painting completed by Jan Styka and Wojciech Kossak in nine months in 1894, the centenary of the battle which gives its name to the panorama. It was the most famous victory the Poles scored over the Russians in the course of the insurrection inspired and led by Tadeusz Kościuszko in 1794. Recently, the village of Racławicka was visited by Lech Wałęsa, dressed in the white peasant's costume of the period – an act (in spring 1989) of great contemporary significance.

The panorama form predates the epic film by about twenty years, and naturally was superseded by it; but this kind of 'living history' exhibit used to be very popular. The *Racławicka* is one of the few surviving examples, and among the best. It is also profoundly important to the Poles because of its subject-matter, even though the insurrection was ultimately a failure. Kościuszko was a professional soldier who had already distinguished himself in the American War of Independence. He had made his way clandestinely from exile in France to Cracow, and drummed up an army composed largely of the peasantry, who armed themselves with scythes, turning them into formidable weapons by the simple expedient of fixing the blade in line with the haft, instead of at right angles to it.

The picture, which shows various stages of the battle in quasi-strip cartoon manner, is full of energy and incident, and its history is as interesting as its subject. At the start, the two painters had to travel illegally to the site of the battle for their research, as it was then in the Russian zone. The panorama was originally set up in Lwów. Damaged at the beginning of the Second World War, its mighty canvas was then taken down and rolled up – a job which took two months in itself – and stored in a specially constructed box. The Russians let the Poles have it back as early as 1946, but refused permission for it to be exhibited until 1985, when it was finally resurrected, restored, and put on display in Wrocław. Tours of the painting run every twenty minutes each day (almost) from 8 a.m. to 9 p.m., but demand to see it is so great that tickets are booked weeks in advance, and I was very fortunate indeed that one of the staff took pity on me and 'organized' one for me.

The picture is 15 metres high, and 114 long. Very brightly lit, the extraordinarily convincing three-dimensional effect is achieved in two ways. High skies and distant hills, with tall birch trees in the foreground, give an illusion of great depth, and as you walk round and look back, your eye deludes you into seeing a change of perspective. This deceit is compounded by a 'real' constructed foreground of muddy field and wrecked pieces of cavalry equipment. The 'real' elements, be they a fallen tree-trunk, a broken harrow, or a cannon trolley, are continuations of ones in the painting. Thus it is very difficult to see where two dimensions end and three take over.

The water in Wrocław, I notice from brushing my teeth, tastes of metal and chlorine, and I understand why attached to my room key ring there is a bottle opener. It is for the mineral water I should have purchased in the restaurant.

***

The rain did not go away and, though the weather became warmer, the battered streets and crumbling houses looked more forlorn than ever. The rain turned the surface of the streets to black glass, and muddy pools appeared where the paving stones had broken. Huge red-brick churches with enormously steep gables tower everywhere, some covered with wooden scaffolding. In an underpass, people sell sheepskin slippers and chunky woollen sweaters from huge bags.

The Polish section of the National Museum was closed for renovation, and so was the floor of contemporary art, but here the fact was not disclosed by a notice, nor was the area roped off, so I innocently wandered its rooms, switching lights on and off as I passed through them and wondering vaguely at the lack of supervision, until a wardress noticed me and saw me off. The modern art I had seen, most of which was done in the Seventies and Eighties, was very strong, especially over the last ten years, but cruel and brutal. Mockery of Christian imagery is evident in a lot of work, but most reflects frustration. Browns and greys predominate, and one major piece was made up of thousands of concentration camp identity photographs. Many of the sculptures were of fractured bodies, and one was of a black, sloth-like creature emerging from a ruined pram, of which it was also part. Another, easy to interpret, showed a group of grey life-size figures in a queue; as the queue progressed, the figures sank into the floor.

There was a good collection of foreign paintings, among which the best was an *Eve* by Lucas Cranach the Elder, but two other collections drew me – one for its content, the other for the people looking at it. The first was Polish medieval church art. There is a particularly attractive local *Madonna Enthroned on Lions* – a wooden group in which a plump, cheerful peasant Mary, supported by angels, carries a rather pompous Christ-child standing on her knee. Beneath the folds of her dress two lions peer out. They seem to be carrying everybody and they look fed up about it. By contrast, the Pietàs and Depositions here, as elsewhere in Poland, are the cruellest, and the most bloodily realistic, that I have ever seen.

The other collection was an exhibition of a long series of photographs of the USA taken for *National Geographic Magazine* by the Warsaw photographer Tomasz Tomaszewski. Apart from the few landscapes, they are all critical and negative – but, perhaps you could argue, how could they be otherwise? What has attracted Tomaszewski are the eccentric extremes of American society. The reactions of those looking at his photographs were interesting: horror and wonder. What can that mad country really be like? Schoolchildren confronted with a photograph of guests at a New Orleans drag ball gazed with serious and completely bewildered eyes. And yet, in dog-eared advertisements culled from heaven knows where, all over Poland, in shops, travel agents and hotels, the American Dream is held out for inspection, and as a temptation. Kodak girls, their colours long faded to a uniform pale blue, grin chirpily in dusty corners and continue valiantly to show off their legs and pert bottoms; on a glass case full of tired cakes in a baker's, a flyblown picture draws your attention to a competition run by Hershey's in which the first prize is a Toyota Celica. But travel to pretty well anywhere is available from here to those with the necessary hard currency – the national tourist agency shops, nearly always crowded, offer package tours to places as diverse as China and the Costa del Sol.

There is another exhibition of photographs in the Architectural Museum, telling the sadly familiar story of the destruction of the town. How must it feel to live in a country where most of your heritage was destroyed during enemy occupation, and which was then taken over? Looking at old photographs, I thought of the other culture which has all but vanished from Poland – that of the Jews. In Wrocław there had been a massive synagogue, of which no trace remains. Among the scientists, artists and historians of Breslau was the writer Emil Ludwig, whose family name was Cohn. There is a photograph of plac Solny, formerly Blücherplatz, showing a whole terrace of shops with Jewish name-plates. Near my hotel was the Jewish-owned luxury department store Wertheim's, on Schweidnitzer Strasse (now Świdnicka), a splendid Art Deco structure. The building still stands, and it is still a department store, though it is a DT Centrum now. Inside, you can buy a 'Laura' model bicycle for 100,000 złotys, or a fridge for about 65,000. It is crowded with people, milling about with an air of expectancy, though there are very few goods on display. The wood-effect lino on the stairs must be original, and what hasn't been worn away is chipped and cracking. The tiled floors are broken, and the concrete underneath lies exposed.

Back in the Market Square, the bareness of the interior of the Town Hall, now a museum, once more testifies to what was lost in the war, as the guide-book sadly confesses. But astounding restoration is an act of heroism and a statement of national faith which is not expressed in this way for the first time. Wrocław was destroyed by the Tartars in 1241; thirty years later, the Town Hall was completely rebuilt.

In the hotel I dined alone – to my relief the regal waiter was off duty, replaced by one who actually smiled. I had not arrived early enough to avoid the group – rhythm and bass guitars, alto sax, drums and vocalist. The purple and red lamps were switched on, and the mirror-balls scattered their dull light over the lumpy parquet of the dance-floor. Two or three broad-hipped couples – the women in lilac, the men in beige – gyrated slowly or jived to a succession of standards in which 'My Way' and 'Yesterday' predominated. I had to make a very early start, and hadn't packed. I went to my room to take care of it.

While I did so, I listened to the radio. A long programme exhaustively discussed the musical career of Leonard Cohen.

9

A JEWEL IN THE DUST

The British Council runs something called 'Studium'. It has centres in all major Polish cities, and its purpose is to teach English to university academic staff, other than those in English departments. 'Actually, its effect is very simple,' one of its teachers told me. 'We teach 'em English, and as soon as they're halfway proficient at it, they emigrate to the United States. I actually had a man accuse me of breaking up his marriage, because as soon as she had completed her Studium course, his wife did just that.'

At the time we were sitting over beers in a brass-and-glass hotel half a mile or so to the south-west of the Old Town of Cracow. Outside, a thunderstorm was looming. I had arrived in the late afternoon, after a long journey south-east from Wrocław enlivened by the sight of a stork picking its solemn way across a freshly ploughed field and looking, as storks do, more like a clockwork model than the real thing. At Cracow station I had joined a long queue for taxis (unusually, there wasn't one in sight), only to be plucked out of it after a few minutes by a cabbie who cheerfully pointed out that there was no need to wait if I was prepared to part with a couple of dollars. I was tired, and so I undemocratically succumbed. As we drove across town, he said: 'I bet you want to visit Auschwitz while you're here. Everyone does. I can offer you a package: trip there, a couple of hours to do the Main Camp and Birkenau, and the trip back. Say six hours in all. Twenty dollars. You want to do it today? There's still time.'

It was true that I wanted to visit Auschwitz, or Oświęcim, to give the town its Polish name. The most notorious German concentration camp is now a museum, about forty miles from Cracow. I hesitated, knowing that Oświęcim wasn't the easiest place to reach by public transport.

'Okay, fifteen dollars,' said the cabbie, drawing the figure on his dashboard with a stubby finger and turning to grin at me. I told him I'd think about it. I was still wondering how he'd identified me as a foreigner as I stood in the taxi queue. I was dusty from travelling, and wouldn't have thought I looked any different from the assortment of Poles who'd formed the rest of the line.

The thunderstorm never happened, and later I ventured out. Cracow is a university city and a seat of ecclesiastical power. Pope John Paul II was archbishop here. It was also the capital of Poland, and although that was nearly 400 years ago it has not been forgotten. The atmosphere is busy, bright and cosmopolitan. Its spirit is independent, and since the war it has been a centre for intellectual opposition to the government.

The Old Town is small, surrounded and defined by a two-kilometre-long strip of park, called the Planty, which marks where the city walls stood. These were only dismantled at the beginning of this century, in one of those fits of civic vandalism so deeply regretted today. The pattern of the town is typical – a cluster of narrow streets surrounding a main square. The Main Square here is of vast size, and only kept under control by the huge Cloth Hall, the Sukiennice, which occupies its centre, next to the tower which is all that remains of the Town Hall. The Sukiennice was for many centuries a covered market, and its arcaded ground floor is still filled with small shops selling, on the whole, tourist souvenirs.

Upstairs, where former storage attics were later converted into state rooms, there is now an art gallery. At first it doesn't look promising, as the walls of the first rooms are hung with poor eighteenth- and nineteenth-century portraits, and some sketchy pieces by Michałowski which do not seem to be worthy of him. The only other room, however, is a delight. It is enormous, and its main exhibits are five or six massive canvases. There are two major works by Matejko: *Kościuszko at Racławicka* and his own version of *The Prussian Homage*. The spot where Albrecht von Hohenzollern formally submitted to King Zygmunt the Old is nearby – it is marked by a plaque in the Main Square near St Adalbert's Church, a few yards to the south-east of the Sukiennice. Once again, I was impressed by the extraordinary detail in these paintings. Where had the man done his research? I thought that one Teutonic Knight had an unlikely decoration in his helmet, which was feathered like the head-dress of a Red Indian chief. But I was wrong, for the following day I saw armour both in Wawel Castle and in the Czartoryski Museum adorned in a very similar way.

There is a touching small Malczewski here, *Christmas in Siberia*; but the most striking painting of all is by Henryk Siemiradzki. Siemiradzki lived from 1843 to 1902, and although both the paintings I saw by him were on the theme of Christian martyrdom under Nero, I wondered if the intended symbolism was that the martyrs should be read as Poles, the Romans as the Partition Powers. Whatever the case, this enormous canvas, done in 1876, is very powerful indeed. In it Nero, a tiger on a golden chain near him, lolls on a raised dais below which various courtiers and concubines sprawl. In front of them a large number of Christians tied to garlanded stakes are about to be put to the torch. At the centre of the painting, drawing the eye, is a lovely, erotic, half-clad girl dancer, holding a large tambourine and looking unintelligently doubtful about what is going on. She does nothing to defuse the savagery of the subject, and Siemiradzki, a kind of Alma-Tadema with balls, reinforced my feeling that Polish nineteenth-century painters had considerably more edge than our own.

The National Museum was closed for renovation, and looked set to be so for some time to come. That I couldn't visit the Collegium Maius was a greater disappointment, for it contains the museum of the Jagiellonian University, founded in 1364 and one of the oldest in Europe. An apologetic porter told me that the burglar alarm system had to be overhauled, and gave me a booklet outlining the theories of Copernicus as a consolation present.

I was almost unlucky in my visit to Wawel, too. Wawel is a small, abrupt hill on the Vistula at the southern end of the Old Town, and the site of the earliest settlements here. Today, it is crowned by the castle and the cathedral. But I was not in a group, and when I finally located a ticket office I was told that no further tickets for that day would be issued until 5.40 in the afternoon. As it was only about eleven in the morning, this seemed extreme; but the clerk relented and suddenly issued me with a ticket anyway – and not only that. She wouldn't charge me for it, presumably because it was supernumerary to the quota. Of course you don't just get one ticket for all the castle – you have to have a separate one for each section of it, and then another for the especially interesting bits of the cathedral – but the clerk remained on my side and obliged me with a fresh bit of paper every time I went back to her until she shut up shop at lunchtime, so that I managed to see most of the place.

The castle has been subject to so many battles, fires and changes of ownership that its last rebuilding after the Second World War was its twenty-first. Its dominant style is Renaissance. Cracow fell into the Austrian domain during the period of Partition, but the Poles were able to take back control of it in 1880, and apart from the interruption in the Forties, when it was occupied by the Nazi governor, Hans Frank, it has remained in Polish hands ever since.

The legend of the foundation of the castle and the town concerns a dragon which lived in a cave under Wawel Hill. It made a nuisance of itself by devouring anything it could get hold of, and laying waste the countryside; it successfully killed all the knights who came against it with shield and lance, and caused great distress, until one day along came a man called Krak, who decided that the only way to destroy the monster was by stealth. He killed a sheep, stuffed its body with sulphur, and left it where the dragon would find it. The dragon greedily and recklessly gobbled up the spiked carcass, and then, driven into a frenzy of thirst by the sulphur, rushed into the Vistula and drank and drank until it exploded. Krak was duly elected chieftain by the grateful locals and gave his name to the community he founded. An ugly bronze statue of the dragon stands near the site of the cave. Children clamber about on it, which seems dangerous, as every few minutes real flames shoot from its mouth.

The restored state rooms are prosaic. They are gloomy and sparsely furnished, but you can borrow a mimeographed guide-book and shuffle through on your own in your felt slippers, which beats being dragooned past everything in a group. The great glory of these rooms is a number of sixteenth-century Brussels tapestries, the chief of which depict the stories of the Tower of Babel, the Flood, and the Creation and Fall. In the Flood sequence, which is magnificent, there is one detail which I found mysterious. As well as the animals, several curious mythological beasts – all of evil aspect – are admitted to the Ark. In the Disembarkation scene, they are shown again. One of them has immediately set about attacking a lion, itself on the point of eating one of the corpses of the drowned, who are graphically displayed. All the faces, human and animal, are vividly expressive, the best belonging to two worried lions, reluctantly boarding the Ark. Although African and Asian animals suffer slightly from being unfamiliar, the artists handle European species with accuracy and delicacy.

One room is notable for its coffered ceiling. Each of the coffers was once filled with a carved and painted life-size human head, and two dozen or so remain, gazing giddily down. They seem to be portrait heads, representing people from every level of society, and were conceivably put there to remind the king of the population he served – an interestingly liberal concept, but not an impossible one for the end of the Jagiełłonian dynasty. They seemed uncomfortable and unpleasant; but they are a staple of the tourist industry, and reproductions of them can be bought everywhere. The frieze in this room, and one or two others, was painted by Albrecht Dürer's brother, Heinrich – a man who, to judge by these efforts, had absolutely none of Albrecht's talent. I was pleased to see a small painting in another chamber which was of the wife of a Russian tsar by the name of Demetrius the Spurious. There were three 'False Dimitris' during the Time of Troubles which followed the death of Boris Godunov. Which one this lady was the wife of, I have been unable to discover.

In the Armoury is *Szczerbiec*. Although the name means 'jagged sword', this Sword of State, used in the coronation ceremonies of the kings of Poland, is not jagged at all. It is a businesslike straight-bladed affair with a mildly decorated black-and-gold hilt. The sword has a room virtually to itself and is displayed in a spot-lit glass case. This revered relic is all that remains of Poland's crown jewels.

But the cathedral is crammed. Only four of Poland's kings are buried elsewhere, and the dark interior is a clutter of dusty tombs and ornate side-chapels, hidden behind heavy, decorated iron gates and barely glimpsed in the gloom. The whole of Wawel, even this early in the year, was dense with tourists, and the atmosphere of the cathedral was about as churchlike as that of Westminster Abbey; but there were compensations.

Dominating all, in the centre of the nave, is the ponderously sculpted seventeenth-century tomb of Stanisław Szczepanowski. He was bishop of Cracow in the eleventh century, at a time when Church and State were on nearly equal terms in the struggle for power. Stanisław must have overstepped the mark, for King Bolesław the Bold had him murdered in 1079. This was not a good move, for subsequently Bolesław was forced into exile to do penance, and Stanisław was canonized. The blackened silver coffin is too ornate to be beautiful, but it is a mark of the profound respect in which powerful church leaders have always been held here. A simpler and more dignified tomb in red Hungarian marble marks the resting place of the splendid Kazimierz the Great. During conservation work in 1869, the tomb was disturbed and fell open, revealing the king's remains, together with his crown, sceptre, orb and spurs. Jan Matejko, who lived in Cracow all his life, was summoned to make drawings of the find, and then the tomb was resealed, to be followed by a second funeral service for Kazimierz. It would be very cynical indeed to regard the decision to hold such a ceremony as merely politically motivated; but the effect on national feeling at such a time, when Poland had not existed on any map for seventy-five years, need not be described.

In the north aisle, across the nave from Kazimierz, is an unmarked, plain vault just wide enough to contain the massive stone coffins of the two great Romantic poets, Adam Mickiewicz and Juliusz Słowacki. In a country far more aware of its cultural and literary heritage than Britain is, these two men commanded a wide reverence for being champions of Polish nationalism, and for holding up a mirror to the Polish psyche. One wishes, for the sake of greater understanding, that their works were more easily available in translation, for from conversations I had it was clear that Mickiewicz's *Dziady (Forefathers' Eve)* is of deep significance to the Polish consciousness.

Two entrances off the north aisle lead to the Zygmunt Tower and St Leonard's Crypt. The tower contains the cathedral belfry, and here, reached by narrow, dusty wooden stairways which rise between the bells like a set from *The Hunchback of Notre Dame*, hangs the greatest bell of them all. The Zygmunt Bell, raised 400 years ago, is now only rung on Easter Sundays, and on days of national triumph and disaster. These, I suspect, must be carefully gauged. Was it rung, for example, on the day Solidarity was reinstated?

St Leonard's Crypt is a labyrinthine necropolis of the great. Here, often crowded together and in surprisingly modest tombs, lie Józef Piłsudski and Tadeusz Kościuszko (who, when he died in 1817, left all his money to the cause of emancipation of the slaves in North America; a plaque from a grateful USA commemorates this, and the service he gave that nation in its War of Independence), King Stefan Batory, and (rather neglected) King Zygmunt the Old.

Rain had cleared the streets and polished the cobblestones by the time I emerged. I hurried into town in search of a restaurant, but was sidetracked, stumbling accidentally on the Czartoryski Palace. It was open, and following the rule that if something is open, see it at once for you never know when you'll catch it open again, I went in. Immediately an official confronted me and jerked his thumb in the direction of the usual hamper of felt slippers.

The Czartoryskis were one of the great noble families of Poland; at the turn of the nineteenth century, Prince Adam was a Polish minister of state and a confidant of Tsar Alexander I, though later in life he was to become a leader of the nationalist movement and an émigré leader at its headquarters in the Hotel Lambert in Paris. The risks taken by those who opposed Russia were high, as was the price paid for failure. Political prisoners sentenced to exile in Siberia were often also condemned to walk there in chains, as was the case with Prince Roman Sanguszko (1800–1881).

The art collection housed at the palace was started at the beginning of the nineteenth century by Izabela Czartoryska at the family seat in Puławy, but was moved to Cracow when the family had to leave the Russian zone after the failure of the 'November' Uprising in 1830. It is a lovely, intimate museum, and it seems as if little has changed since it was first laid out. Silver and glass artefacts are crowded in elderly glass-fronted wooden cabinets, bearing labels handpainted in gold, in Polish and French. There is some splendid sixteenth-century majolicaware, a musty bearskin, a small, unlabelled nineteenth-century sleigh decorated at the front by a wooden 'figurehead' of a busty girl bursting erotically out of her blouse as she twists round to look adoringly in the direction of the sleigh's single seat.

Various bits of armour follow, and a richly decorated Turkish tent, together with two suits of oriental chain-mail, captured during Jan Sobieski's Austrian campaigns. The succeeding rooms contain a series of extremely fine medieval church paintings on wood, which in turn give way to a catholic selection of oils, in which the Dutch seventeenth-century landscape predominates – the best represented by Cuyp, Teniers, Wouwerman and Ruysdael. There are also some quaint engravings by one Jeremiasz Falck – particularly two stilted ladies representing Earth and Air, each with a short verse giving their attributes in French, with a Francophone translation into English, where 'sell' is spelt 'sil', and 'birds', 'bourdes'. There is also a collection of miniatures of famous Poles and Englishmen and women. Among the English are a boyish Henry VIII, Anne Boleyn, Captain Cook, Newton, Francis Bacon, and Shakespeare, who is depicted with a bushy beard and a full head of curly ginger hair.

The collection contains two famous pictures. Rembrandt's *Landscape with the Good Samaritan*, set proudly apart on an easel, glows from its plain dark wooden frame; in the room next door is Leonardo's *Lady With an Ermine*. The ermine is not well observed, and the hand of the lady which clasps it is enormous, but her face has the same liveliness and luminous tranquillity as the *Mona Lisa*, or *John the Baptist*. The gilded frame, with its tracery of trailing flowers, looks early enough to be the original.

The rain had stopped when I left, but I could find nowhere other than a hotel to eat. Restaurants below the top level are at the mercy of the unpredictable supply, though one can normally count on pork and cabbage. On this occasion, I was prepared to forego both.

One of Kazimierz the Great's achievements was to open his country to the Jews, on the correct assumption that their presence would give a boost to Poland's economy. The suburb which is named after him was not originally designated as a Jewish settlement; it was a new town to take the overspill population of Cracow. Founded in 1335, it had its own market square, of a size to rival Cracow's, its own walls, and its own charter. However, just over 150 years later, King Jan Olbracht, as a result of a dispute between Jews who were turning to the crafts as a means of making a living and the established guilds, decreed that Jews could only live in Kazimierz. The town, soon to be absorbed into Cracow, became a Jewish quarter, and has remained so; though the population was all but destroyed by the Germans during the Second World War, the few survivors still remain here. They are nearly all old; only two bar-mitzvahs have been celebrated in Poland since 1945. In the fullness of time the older Jews will die, and the few younger ones who choose to remain will perforce marry Gentiles. Thus within a generation the Jews of Poland will have disappeared.

Kazimierz today is a Dickensian place; a poor quarter where dirty urchins run beside you in the street and bony adults in tattered clothes eye you from doorways. Unexpectedly, many synagogues still stand, though few function. The Reform synagogue is only open for High Holy Day services; another has become a museum of Jewish culture. On a wall here, a plan rather sadly explains the former significance of different areas and rooms, and one Jew I spoke to told me that the presence of the museum gave him the distinct impression of being buried alive. But in the same square a small synagogue was open, and as it was Sabbath a service was in progress. Next door lay a well-tended graveyard, and surprisingly, laid into the wall were two commemorative plaques in English. The congregation was large, and although the people were cautious they were not unfriendly.

Poland had for many centuries been host to the largest population of Jews in the Diaspora – a situation which accounts for the vein of anti-Semitism which existed here, and still does to an extent, though the likelihood of many Poles under fifty having ever met a Jew is small. There are two puns in Hebrew on the name Poland – *poh-lin* ('here one rests'), and *poh-lan-yah* ('here God rests') – dating from the time of their welcome by Kazimierz. The Jews were later tolerated, although the tendency was for them to lead separate lives, remaining faithful to their own culture and traditions within their adopted country.

It was not until the time of Partition that they were even required to register as Polish citizens officially – which meant that they had to acquire family surnames, contrary to Jewish custom but necessary for administrative purposes. Thus it is that many Polish-Jewish surnames derive from towns (Pinsker, Warschauer), or are of German origin. A story is told of the German writer, E.T.A. Hoffmann, who was a registrar of new names in Warsaw, then the capital of 'South Prussia', and where, incidentally, he wrote his *Tales*. He would whimsically issue names according to his mood, or deriving from any striking impression of his day or immediate experience. Many modern Rosenblums, Rosenthals, Rosenzweigs, Rosensafts, Rosenstocks, and so on, will owe their names to the inventiveness (or lack of it) of German officials two hundred years ago, as will the Helfgotts, Gottliebs, Weinstocks, Goldfarbs, Silbersteins . . . The list goes on.

Today the strongest traces of a vanished way of life can be found in the graveyards. Many are neglected, locked up and overgrown; but those in Kazimierz are still tended. The Old Cemetery, destroyed by the Germans, has been restored. The New Cemetery, whose graves go back about 400 years, was also vandalized, and a Wailing Wall has been constructed here from fragments of the broken monuments. It is a large place, whose newest graves are only two or three years old. The worst enemy today, eating into the sandstone, causing it to flake away, eroding names and dates, is air pollution, which sets its dead hand on Jewish and Gentile monument alike.

The street names of Kazimierz give the district's origins away: Meiselsa, Estery, Izaaka, Jakuba, Józefa . . . But it is hard to imagine them teeming with Jewish life as they once were. An American-funded move is afoot to restore Kazimierz; but however much you restore the buildings, you cannot bring back the life. Perhaps it would be better to give in to history.

My friend Maria in Gdańsk had given me the address of her old university friend, Jurek. He lived with his wife, three children, mother-in-law and scruffy dog in a small house surrounded by fruit trees in a suburb to the south of the Vistula. The next day there was brilliant sunshine, accompanied by hot summer weather, and Jurek suggested a drive in the country. Taking a short cut from his house, we bounced over a dirt road which might have daunted a Land-Rover, let alone a Fiat Polski, and made our way through little villages with houses painted bright blue in the local style, to the Benedictine monastery of SS Peter and Paul at Tyniec, on the banks of the Vistula to the west of Cracow.

The monastery church is a plain and dignified Baroque pile which serves a community of fifty black-clad monks. The place is set on a hill overlooking the Vistula, and the original fortifications, built to withstand the Tartars, are still evident. Cracow is a thriving religious centre, and the local telephone directory has four pages of religious houses. Below the hill, pleasant grassy banks line the Vistula, but even as far upstream as this the river is already polluted by the effluent from the chemical works at Oświęcim – the town is now a centre for the plastics industry. The water is warmed by the pollutants, and nowadays never freezes in winter. It therefore attracts flocks of thousands of swans to the Cracow area at that season. They are known locally as 'chemical swans'.

Across the broad, shallow valley defined by the river lies the home of a far more severe Order. There are seventeen Cameduli monks here now, all old. They are curious men: small, shrivelled, dwarfish, in white habits stained by age and use, their cropped pates covered by white woollen skullcaps, and their cheeks shaved, but wearing long white beards. There are younger monks too, but these have been sent here from their own Orders for a few months' corrective training, having become too lax in the observance of their vows.

The setting is idyllic. The monks live behind a high cream wall in beautiful grounds. Each has his own tiny cottage, surrounded by a vegetable garden which he must tend and which provides his only source of food. In summer, these little gardens are a riot of colour, though no visitor will ever see them. I only know about them because a Jesuit friend was for a time their confessor. The casual visitor will be lucky if he even sees the monks, for only the vast, chilly Baroque church is open to outsiders. Except for when they are at prayer, the brothers maintain a vow of silence.

The Order was founded by St Romuald in 961 at Campo di Madoli in Italy, whence the Order's name. Women may not even visit the church, except on twelve days of the year, including Christmas and Easter and St Romuald's feast days. Young men, visitors like us, knelt in prayer on the bare stone floor. Jurek crossed himself devoutly. I wondered what it must be like to come here to pray in winter; but there is a chapel under the east end of the nave which the monks use then because it is easier to heat. The interior of the main church must be many degrees below freezing at that time.

To the side of this chapel is another, a narrow undercroft where the monks are buried in oven-like openings in the wall. The oldest occupant had died in 1788, the latest two years ago. It seems that, subject to space, the length of tenure must be about two centuries before the remains are removed elsewhere to make room for later generations. Most of the monks had joined the Order young, in their late teens, and lived within it to very great ages. Few were under eighty when they died, many over ninety. One wonders how many novices join the Order now. The Church in Poland, however, is never short of recruits, and in no other country had I seen so many monks, priests and nuns – most of whom were under forty.

The monastery is built on the so-called Silver Mountain, and is set in woodland, chiefly of birch trees. The church is a popular place of worship on the great feast-days. I met very few Poles who weren't regular and ardent church-goers. Jurek, who as a Cracovian has several hundred churches to choose from, doesn't always go to the same one. In the back of his diary he has a list of his favourites, with their Mass times.

Jurek had spent many years in university administration earning very little indeed; but this year he had just managed to save enough capital to start his own business as a picture framer and supplier of 'instant' frames. He was having to work long hours, but that in itself was a hopeful sign, since he'd clearly identified a market for which there was a demand. The small factory/workshop was on the outskirts of town, where the rent was low. His wife, Urszula, who'd studied Fine Art at the Jagiełłonian University but who, in a society not yet fully geared to careers for women, had never used her training, was now hoping to do so. The youngest of her three children would soon be going to school. Then, maybe . . .

All this I heard over a late lunch. Urszula had pushed the boat out. There was a gigantic dish of braised veal in cream sauce, potatoes, sweet beetroot, beetroot with horseradish, sauerkraut, and cucumber salad, followed by the same sort of delicious cheesecake I had had in Gdańsk, this time with the added distinction of a chocolate topping, which I knew was an unheard-of luxury. We drank *kompott* – pear and plum juice made from the fruits of the trees in her garden.

They were teaching their children English, and looked forward to the day 'when we will no longer be obliged to learn Russian'. Urszula's mother told me, with the strength of commitment of one who is eager to convince herself, that the best news coming at the end of the twentieth century was that Communism was on its last legs. Jurek and Urszula are sceptical of this, but she wouldn't listen to them.

Her late husband had been a doctor, and during the war ran a small hospital in Radom, where he sheltered both partisans and Jews. This he did at great personal risk, since billeted on him were a *Wehrmacht* colonel and a female officer of the Gestapo. It was, however, this woman who saved him by warning him when his name appeared on an interrogation list at Radom Gestapo HQ. He was able to go into hiding until the German managed to bury his file. After the war, and seven years after his death, a tree was planted in his name on the Avenue of the Righteous at Yad Vashem in Jerusalem.

After lunch, Jurek and I drove into town. I wanted to leave the brass-and-glass monstrosity of a hotel I was staying in and move to a small, old-fashioned Polish place I'd discovered a dozen yards from the Main Square, and we had to collect Jurek's twelve-year-old son Ryszard, who was returning from a skiing test in the mountains above Zakopane, a hundred kilometres to the south on the Czech border. He had passed the test, which would admit him to a ski training club. I checked into my new hotel, and Jurek suggested a walk.

As we recrossed the Market Square to descend Grodska Street, the hour sounded from one of the lopsided spires of the Mariacki – St Mary's Church. Every hour a trumpeter (drafted from the Fire Brigade, to whom this honour now belongs) blows a call. It is known as the *hejnal*. The melancholy fanfare breaks off abruptly before it is finished – a tradition based on a fourteenth-century legend. During that time of Tartar raids, a watchman in the church tower once sounded the alarm at the barbarians' approach, but his call was cut short when an arrow caught him in the throat. If it's true, it seems unlikely that the present call is based on the one played then, since it has no urgency whatever, and is sonorous and sad. But it is a moving thing to hear, especially late at night across the lonely square. The trumpeters work by twos in twenty-four-hour shifts, and I can imagine the time passing slowly for them, so perhaps it is selfish of me to pray that they are never replaced by a tape-recording.

We walked down to the Church of SS Peter and Paul. This is a large Baroque temple, bare and dignified within, but having (as is often the case) highly ornate side chapels and lovely funerary monuments – in particular one of an eighteenth-century cavalry officer and his wife. Their miniatures show them in the prime of life, smiling cheerfully out of pale gold backgrounds. In front of the high altar a small crypt contains a tiny metal coffin with the remains of Piotr Skarga (1536–1612), an influential Jesuit who was the first confessor to Zygmunt III Wasa. Skarga was a champion of the Counter-Reformation and an enemy of religious tolerance. His last resting-place is lonely and bleak, lost in this great pillared void, but the coffin is surrounded with flowers, and prayers scribbled on bits of paper.

Outside the church, its west front is defended by a row of life-size statues of the Apostles, surprisingly uncorroded. (The statues on Wawel Cathedral and on the Sukiennice were in a much more serious state.) All becomes clear, however, when you learn that these are reproductions. The earliest of them, Saint Peter, was blessed by the Pope in 1980, as a small brass plaque testifies. In the yard of the church stood three plaster-casts of the originals (themselves now in a museum), which show the leprous state they had reached.

Just south of the church is a convent of Poor Clares, and next to it is their Church of St Andrew, for me the most attractive in Cracow. It is Romanesque, though its twin towers are capped with Baroque spires. But it is the interior which is wonderful. The church is unexpectedly small inside, and it is crowded with pure, soaring Baroque decoration. The stucco work is brilliant and the silver pulpit a masterpiece. It is in the shape of a ship, as is frequently the case in Polish churches, but this ship floats on foaming, fish-filled waves, has a mast, sail and rigging, and is manned by angelic mariners. Crowded behind it is the lovely little bow-fronted organ. At the west end there is a gallery behind a grille above the main congregation, where the nuns attend services – for the Order is strict and closed. From a hidden side chapel we heard them at prayer as we stood in the nave. I had at first mistaken their voices for children's.

Not surprisingly, Ryszard was beginning to flag. A cake shop known to Jurek since boyhood ('and unchanged in thirty-five years,' he told me happily; 'only the *patronne* has grown older') was just closing, but we found a *kawiarna* able to provide coffee, orange squash, and ice-cream. These cafés are old-fashioned, almost Viennese establishments. All that is lacking are the smell of cigars, and *Sachertorte*, and newspapers in wooden clips.

Afterwards, we walked down Dominikańska to the Dominican Monastery and Church of the Holy Trinity. Within, there was a buzz of activity. In one chapel off the cloisters a packed meeting was being held about raising pensions. Outside again, I noticed a young Dominican showing a group of children around the cloisters. He looked exactly like a British subaltern, with his round, fresh face and curly blond hair. But the monks here are in a tough tradition. During the period of martial law, the monastery provided sanctuary for those suffering political persecution.

The basilica itself is High Gothic. It was destroyed together with all its original wooden furniture in the great fire of Cracow in the mid-1850s, but everything has been fully restored. There is an unnatural sense of newness about the place, although the high-spired oak confessionals, intricately carved, must be as ebullient as their originals. We stayed for Latin Sung Mass, celebrated by two hundred white-clad monks, none of whom was over thirty. Hearing their unaccompanied voices soaring confidently up to God was a moving experience, which opened up a brief view of the Middle Ages.

The Church has inspired all kinds of artistic tribute, and in Cracow there are two precise high points. The first is the stained glass of St Francis, designed by Wyspiański. The colours of the windows, burned into life by sunlight, are staggering enough for their depth and tone, but the representations – especially the figure of God in the West Window – contain an energy and movement which are frightening. The second is equally alive, though executed almost five centuries earlier by the master carver Veit Stoss. This is the giant triptych behind the altar in the Mariacki. Open, it shows six scenes from the New Testament. The principal subject, dominating the central panel, is the Annunciation, which shows a group of Apostles supporting Mary, who is fainting, framed by an arch in which tiny figures are perched. They are drawn by Stoss from contemporary Cracovian society, which he had twelve years to observe in the course of this job. It is sad that this great work is underlit, and that one cannot get closer in order to really appreciate it. What is inescapable, however, is the astounding realism of expression and arrested movement. The painted wood seems as soft as flesh; it would seem quite natural if this frozen moment of theatre thawed and the action continued.

After such rich food, it was good to taste something lighter and drier; and so it was appropriate to end at the university church of St Anne, by the Dutch architect Tylman of Gameren, whose work is also everywhere in Warsaw. The interior contains lovely stucco by Fontana, and the side chapels are glories of delicate Baroque. The tomb of the university's patron saint, a former professor called Jan Kęt, is a masterpiece, even if the spirals of the rear right of its four columns twist the wrong way.

Poor Ryszard was by this time frankly tired, and I said goodnight to him and Jurek, taking a walk north through the Planty to bring myself back down to earth, and turning back into town to look at the Stary Teatr, where the film and theatre director Andrzej Wajda cut his teeth. It was the weekend, and amiable drunks were already tottering here and there, faces flushed with vodka. I had planned to eat at Wierzynek's – Cracow's best restaurant, on the corner of the Main Square; but I suddenly didn't feel like it any more. A sense of foreboding, which the events of the day had kept in abeyance, now crept up on me. I knew why. In the morning I had to make a pilgrimage to Auschwitz. I was fortunate that Jurek had offered to take me. It is not a place to go alone.

The route from Cracow was a pretty one, through countryside which was almost hilly and little villages still containing a number of traditional blue houses, though many of these have now been replaced by angular modern villas. The crops were potatoes, corn, wheat and beetroot, and the farmland was interspersed with little woods – no more than clumps – of birch and silver birch.

Oświęcim itself is an unexceptional small industrial town of mainly modern buildings which straggles along the banks of the Vistula and the Sola, the two rivers joining a few kilometres to the east. It comes as a shock to find that the original camp, known as Auschwitz-Central, or Auschwitz-I, is right in the town. The car-park was by no means full – a dozen coaches and perhaps thirty cars. There is a cinema which shows a film edited from footage shot at the time of the liberation of the camp by the Red Army in January 1945. The images are familiar, but never lose their effect. The flickering ghost of a half-demented old man, wrapped in a black blanket, appeared on the screen. A survivor. The narrator of the film informed us that the man was forty-two. In the course of the film the Jews are mentioned precisely once, as part of a list of the 'nationalities' incarcerated here.

You leave the cinema and walk out into the forecourt of the camp. Fifty metres away are the gates, so familiar from photographs, topped by the grotesque motto, *Arbeit Macht Frei*. Details not perceived before become apparent. The metalwork of the motto, for example, is attached only to the right gate – it does not split in two when the gates are opened. The gates themselves are far smaller and less imposing than I had imagined.

Beyond them, the red-brick *Blocks* are laid out in orderly rows. Their gables are dropped at the peak in a style typical of the region. They are very ordinary brick military barracks. Trees line the 'streets' between them, which today are neatly gravelled and bordered with grass. It was a bright day, and the air was loud with birdsong. There was a terrible ordinariness about the place.

How modern it all looks! The most horrifying thought is that this place was ful-filling its foul purpose well within living memory. But one can hardly believe it, walking between the *Blocks* – each with its original blue-and-white number on a plaque. One of them is given over to a large new museum specifically chronicling the persecution of the Jews here. Not far away lies one of the former hospital *Blocks* – if such places can be dignified by the word 'hospital' – and opposite it, the two *Blocks* with the grimmest reputation of all – numbers 10 and 11.

In *Block* 10 were housed the women upon whom the Germans performed medical experiments connected with mass-sterilization. Few escaped with their lives, and still fewer were left wholly unmutilated. The SS gynaecologist Carl Clauberg burned their genitals with X-rays in pursuit of an effective method.

Block 11 was the *Bunker* – the prison within a prison. The ground floor rooms are spartan offices, except for a bedroom and a dormitory opposite for guards, both of which retain their original wallpaper. At the end of the corridor stands the gallows used in the execution yard which separates the two *Blocks* – a small, black, evil thing of ghastly simplicity. Next to it is a *Bock* – or whipping horse. The cells are in the basement, half buried underground, and are reached by a concrete stairway whose walls are also wallpapered, in a red-and-grey zigzag pattern halfway up their height, in the fashion of the period.

The cells are terrible – minute, damp rooms, seemingly identical, but having subtle, crucial differences. The priest Maksymilian Kolbe spent his last days in Number 18, where today a bright splash of fresh flowers relieves the iron grey. The window of this cell is at least of human proportions. Next door, cell number 19 has only a tiny aperture, not quite six inches by four, to let air in through the thick walls. There would have been no light. People committed to these rooms were often starved to death as a deliberate means of execution, and death by suffocation was not unknown. Worst of all are the *Stehbunker*. These are four narrow cells, perhaps three feet by three, each with a tiny air hole in the wall. Access to them is by an opening eighteen inches square at ground level, which could be barred and then sealed with a wooden door. Into each of these standing pens four people singled out for special punishment were crammed. After their day's work in the camp, they would have to spend the night here, unable to sit or even squat, without food or any provision to relieve themselves. According to the severity of their sentence, they might spend eleven nights in these cells. None survived more.

Between the two *Blocks* stands the execution yard with its 'black wall'. This wall, where prisoners were despatched with a *Genickschuss* – a bullet in the neck – is now strewn with flowers. Above it, the blue-and-white concentration camp survivors' flag ripples in the wind.

At the other end of the camp, near the modern exit, stands the simple gallows where the commander of this hell-on-earth, Rudolf Höss, was hanged on 16 April 1947. Next to it are the gas chamber (disguised as a shower room) and crematorium, small by the standards of the nearby sister-camp of Birkenau – where over three thousand people at a time could be 'processed'. Here, standing in the half-darkness where so many died, one looks instinctively at the false shower heads. Little was done to disguise them. The pipes to which they are attached are simply strung by wire from the ceiling – they end in mid-air. But in the darkness and confusion, who would have noticed, and if anyone had, what could they have done? In the crematorium next door, the four ovens stand, still with the metal trolleys on which the bodies were run into the furnaces. Beyond them stand the long-handled hooks and pokers used by the prisoners of the *Sonderkommando* – those delegated to do the burning.

The other *Blocks* are uniform in design. A series of large cold rooms open on each floor off a central corridor. The walls are painted grey halfway up, then cream. Exhibits are in old wooden cabinets, and the atmosphere is not unlike that of a dilapidated school building. The corridors are lined with innumerable photographs of prisoners who died here, nearly all within three months of arrival – testimony to the accuracy of the words addressed to new arrivals by one of the camp commanders, SS-*Hauptsturmführer* Fritzsch: 'If you are a Jew, you will be dead in a month; if you are a priest, in two. The rest of you will be dead within three months. There is only one way out of here, and that is through the chimney.'

On the second floor of *Block* 4 a mountain of human hair is displayed – now all turned by time to a nebulous grey-blond colour. One cannot accept it for what it is, nor the material in bolts in another glass case in the same room, rather like fine hessian, which was woven from women's hair. In room 4 of this *Block* there is a large plaster model showing precisely how the major gas-and-crematorium complexes of Birkenau were managed: the people herded down the sloping path to the under-ground disrobing room, then into the 'showers', then hooked out as corpses into the crematoria. In the same room, there are grey-blue tins of Zyklon-B, the size of two-litre paint cans. The poison was provided in the form of pellets, which turned to gas when exposed to the air.

In room 1 of *Block* 5 a glass case set into the wall contains nothing but brushes: shaving brushes, hairbrushes, toothbrushes. There are so many that they cease to be personal: you must look at single ones and try to imagine the vanished individuals who used them. In room 2 are the shoes – muddied and turned by the years to a uniform grey, though among them is a pair of yellow basketweave sandals, and a pair of high-heeled red leather slingbacks, lodged in the centre of the heap. The shoes are piled up anyhow, not sorted. That they are just dumped makes them all the more poignant – the tiniest fraction of what the Germans looted from those they murdered. But some sorting has gone on – for in a room nearby there are only children's shoes, another monstrous pile. Near them are tiny dresses, trousers and shirts in a glass case covered with flowers. There is a child's letter from Auschwitz – '*Liebe Mutter! Ich bin gesund und fühle mich gut ...* ' – 'Dear Mother, I am fine and in good health ...' The letter is rubber-stamped '*Inspected*' by the SS.

Then there are the piles of suitcases, their owners' names and addresses painted on them with pathetic care (no doubt in response to some directive), together with an identifying number. With the suitcases lie straw shopping baskets. In this *Block* too, there is a pile of enamel pots and pans, red, white, blue, black – bowls, coffee-pots, steamers, frying pans. Then there are the ranks of corsets and artificial limbs, spastics' leg-braces, a broken wooden hand clawing the air. And the spectacles: a jumble of wire-framed glasses making a wild anarchic sculpture, or perhaps they look like a legion of delicate, silvery crabs clambering over each other in confusion.

A couple of kilometres away is Birkenau, the massive camp which at its peak held 250,000 prisoners and the one which is associated in most people's minds with the name 'Auschwitz'. You come upon it so suddenly that it is anti-climactic. You had expected something more. The squat tower of the Gateway of Death, the building through whose central arch the railway-line ran into the camp, is neither as high nor as big as I had imagined. So terrible a building should be more imposing. From the tower over the arch one can look across the camp, which spreads as far as one can see. Much remains, though most of the wooden *Blocks* have gone, survived only by a skeletal forest of brick chimneys which belonged to their primitive heating system. To the right, one long row of wooden *Blocks* remains. They were originally designed as stables – each one for forty-eight horses. In Birkenau, over 2000 people were crammed into most *Blocks*.

To the left are the brick *Blocks* of the oldest part of the camp. The size of the place is astonishing – one vast flat field edged with the pretty silver birch woods that gave the place its name. The trees are lovely in the sunlight. There is grass where there was mud; wildflowers grow by the railway line, and birds sing again.

Among the brick *Blocks* lies a handful of wooden ones. Approaching them, we passed a line of reconditioned Second World War German army trucks. They had SS number plates, and as they were open children were climbing in and out of them. I visited the camp on a Sunday, and there were many families there with their children, despite a notice discouraging anyone under thirteen. There were women with babies in prams walking the paths which trace the outskirts of the camp, and the occasional cyclist. Beyond the trucks was a collection of small caravans, each with an actor's name stuck to it on a card. The names were of unidentifiable nationality – Barbara Gazelle, Carlos Weider, Leon Roman. After the caravans, an elderly coach marked 'Make-Up' was parked near the padlocked entrance to a *Block*. On the door another notice was posted, in English and Polish. It read: 'Actors Only'. Below it, in explanation of what both Jurek and I couldn't help regarding as a black joke, another sign: 'Wardrobe'. The area was deserted, and we never found out what film they were making, or who was making it.

A little further on are the ruins of Crematorium 2, a shattered wreck of brick and massive concrete pylons. Beyond it, where the railway track ends, is the memorial to those who died here. Of the twelve million who met death in the camps, four million perished in the Auschwitz complex, most of them in Birkenau. The memorial is a large, paved open space along one end of which is a row of abstract sculptures in granite. In front of them, plaques in every European language, and in Hebrew, commemorate the fallen. Fresh flowers show that they are not forgotten. Immediately next to the monument is the broken back of Crematorium 3, its entrance still clearly discernible, though cluttered with thistles and wildflowers.

A path leads away under trees, past the odd, circular brick buildings where the Germans experimented in making methane from human excrement, to the Disinfection and Disinfestation Centre, and the almost obliterated Crematoria 4 and 5. Near them, the pits used for burning bodies when the crematoria were overburdened are still there. Little children were thrown into them alive.

The return of birdsong to this place seems appropriate and good, and is a better memorial than silence. There is an atmosphere here which it is beyond me to describe, and which in any case everyone would experience in his or her own way. For me, there is something in it that is not entirely evil, negative or bad – that part which is contributed by those who died, and those who survived, without ever sacrificing the dignity which is the rare ennobling quality of human beings.

As we drove back to Cracow, the sun disappeared behind clouds, and by the time we reached the city limits, a thunderstorm had broken again.

PART TWO

CENTRE:
Czechoslovakia and Hungary

10

THE GOLDEN CITY

At the frontier the passport control officer actually smiled, especially when I spoke my stumbling handful of Czech words. My next visitors were the currency-exchange officials, a gentle, bald man of about forty and a motherly woman who carried and counted out the cash. The daily rate when I was in Czechoslovakia was a stiff $16.20 – but of course there is also a thriving black market because everyone wants currency (*Valuta*) that's got real purchasing power. Here, even vouchers for the Tuzex hard currency shops have a fat street value. I was to stay for some time, and so had to exchange a pile of traveller's cheques for a very thick wad of korunas. My 'statistics' paper, on which all currency exchanges and all hotel stays would be recorded by an eventual mosaic of rubber stamps and cramped signatures, received its first scribbles, and I stuffed the money into my wallet, which bulged as never before (or since). Formalities over, the train trundled into the Czechoslovakian Socialist Republic.

Arriving at the main station of Prague can be a problem if you aren't aware that the exit is on the lower of the two modern levels. Above them, the old Art Nouveau ticket hall still exists, though deserted, the interior of its domed roof bearing the coats of arms of the vanished kingdoms the station used to serve. Around its base stand proud, stark white, and very grimy statues of austere-looking Victorian ladies who, I think, represent those kingdoms. Below them still are two much heavier-duty ladies, draped either side of a large lozenge bearing the message, '*Prag, mater urbinum*'. Trying to leave the station is virtually impossible because the building is now an island surrounded by a very fast motorway, and the pedestrian who fails to go down the two floors and out through a little park has to pick his way along narrow kerbs by crash-barriers and finally get onto a pavement which passes a forlorn little early nineteenth-century theatre by the architectural team of Helmer and Fellner, equally beleaguered by traffic. Then comes the pompous bulk of the National Museum, and you have arrived at the southern end of Wenceslas Square. As the famous statue of Saint Wenceslas appeared I felt great elation. Prague is another of those cities one takes to at first sight.

The square is not as we would think of one, but a long enclosed boulevard. Standing at the foot of the Wenceslas statue (he's a brawny young man, with Czech features, on a rather ponderous horse, surrounded by four pious saints), one can look down the gentle hill the length of the place. It is a tremendous view, but there crept into my mind the thought that this was the last sight to meet the eyes of Jan Palać, the student who immolated himself in protest at the Russian invasion, in January 1969, aged 21.

The square is cobbled, with islands down its centre and an avenue of trees. It is packed with pedestrians – large, stout women tottering along arm in arm and svelte girls in shorts, with lanky boyfriends. In the middle of the east side is the Hotel Evropa, where I was hoping against hope for a room. The hotel was built in 1905, and has retained every last detail of its Art Nouveau design. Recently renovated, it is one of the most attractive buildings in town, and indeed in all Europe. Because it isn't expensive, its drawback is that it is often used by package tours. I was lucky. The elderly, donnish porter spoke to me in the courtliest German I have heard in a long time, and, giving me a key, pointed my way through the mob of stone-washed denims in the foyer towards the most delightful room, complete with gilded cherubs, of my entire journey.

Prague is not a large city, and its population of just over a million has now been pegged by the government, so that no one can move into it without first having a job and official approval. Its outskirts are full of hideous blocks of flats, but its core, spared bombing during the war, has kept all its considerable beauty, in layers of Gothic and Baroque. Its atmosphere is more provincial than cosmopolitan, which adds to its attractiveness. Some tastes may find it a little sugary.

The city owes most of its plan to Charles IV, Holy Roman Emperor from 1355 to 1378, and King of Bohemia and Moravia, who made Prague his capital. Its international importance, however, was inhibited by the strife following the martyrdom of the Protestant leader Jan Hus in 1415, and subsequently by the dynastic and religious conflicts within central Europe which led to the Thirty Years' War. It wasn't until the rebellious Protestant Bohemians had been crushed that Prague, firmly back under Habsburg control, but now only a provincial city of the Empire, began to re-establish herself. The architecture was now Baroque, the style in which the ecclesiastical buildings of the Counter-Reformation were expressed.

The juxtaposition of Gothic and Baroque styles results in a town that sometimes reminds one of Italy, sometimes of Germany, but positively belongs to neither. Slow and careful restoration was nearing completion in the areas of the castle (Hradčany) and the Malá Strana, and work was in progress in the Old Town. The Teyn Church, closed for some time, was open again. Inside, there was a dusty, mainly Baroque clutter, though the church is Gothic. Best of all is the red marble tombstone of the Danish astronomer Tycho Brahe, who died near Prague in 1601. Brahe spent much of his career trying to disprove Copernicus' heliocentric theory, but ended up by providing his own pupil, Johannes Kepler, with enough material to vindicate it conclusively. He lost his nose in a duel in Denmark before coming to Prague, but it is restored for the full figure relief which adorns his stone.

With the medieval Town Hall and its complex astronomical clock opposite, the church dominates Prague's central square, the Staromětské Náměste, now given over entirely to pedestrians and one of the loveliest squares in the world, despite a rather nasty large early twentieth-century bronze group in one corner, commemorating Jan Hus. Diagonally across from the Teyn is the Baroque church of St Nicholas, by Kilian Dietzenhofer. I found this church more beautiful than the other, more famous one of the same name by Kilian's father, Christoph. The interior of the former is restrained, and the spaces relatively uncluttered by statuary. It has a melancholy atmosphere, since it is now owned by the State and no longer functions as a place of worship. A side chapel near the door has been converted into a repository for the ashes of the cremated. The urns stand in cabinets formed by hundreds of little glass-fronted receptacles. In front of each urn is a photograph of the deceased, and a little posy of plastic flowers. The most recent arrivals here date from the mid-Seventies. I find Christoph's church, just west of the Malostránke Námeste in the Malá Strana, a heavy and pompous affair, in which larger-than-life statues of pot-bellied, bored bishops spear or trample on a selection of overmuscled, craven demons.

North up the Pařižká from the square, one arrives at what was the medieval Jewish ghetto, and the perfectly preserved Gothic Altneu Synagogue, where Rabbi Löw's chair can still be seen. The creator of the Golem, he died in 1609; his pink tomb is near the walls of the Old Jewish Cemetery just along the road. It is adorned with a lozenge in which the relief of a lion, emblematic of his name, appears. Tiny stones and pebbles have been placed on every ledge provided by the design of the tomb, not the only one to be so adorned.

Because it was in a ghetto, the cemetery's bounds were strictly constrained, and thus burials had to be stacked one on top of another. The long-term result is that now, surrounded by its high walls and dark under heavy trees, the terrain of the cemetery is hilly and uneven, and the tombstones tumble and twist like broken teeth or the plates on the back of a stegosaurus.

It was easy to use the Underground. There are three lines which effectively cover the city; and the flat fare was cheap at one koruna a trip. The Russian-built trains (identical with those in Budapest) were clean, fast and comfortable. They saved time and shoe-leather, and took me south as far as Gottwaldova Station, where the modern Forum Hotel rises like a silver obelisk and where the view over the town from the Palác kultury is magnificent. Not far away is Vyšehrad, the citadel which was one of the first buildings of Prague. All but totally destroyed in the Hussite wars, its walls now surround a park and a small residential area. Walking north-east from here through quiet streets, I came to the U Kalicha in Na Bojište – a restaurant dedicated to the Good Soldier Svejk. It was full of German tourists being treated to a dish which I found practically inescapable in Czechoslovakia in one form or another – pork and potatoes – and the Svejk references were limited to large colour reproductions of the book's illustrations. Not much is made by the present regime of Czechoslovakia's subversive unofficial national hero.

I turned the corner into Ke Karlovu, to find the Dvořak Museum. This is in a house built as a summer residence by Kilian Dietzenhofer, called the Villa Amerika. The composer's music plays as you wander round, looking at manuscript scores, Dvořak's doctoral robes, his spectacles, his walking stick, and his piano.

Despite the attractiveness of the Old Town, with its labyrinth of little streets between the main square and the river, the part of Prague that appeals most is on the west bank. The River Vltava itself, with its flocks of swans, Corot fishermen in little boats, and lazy brown water, sweeps under the Charles Bridge, originally commissioned by Charles IV in 1357, which is busy with people and small-time traders and street artists. It is heavy with statuary, and as a piece of architecture is the greatest achievement of Peter Parler, who designed it when he was twenty-seven. Under Saint John Nepomuk in the middle of the bridge, three young guitarists were singing 'All My Loving' in English to a small, pleased crowd. On the scaffolding surrounding another saint, people sunbathed.

Behind the Mostecká, which leads up the hill on the west bank from the bridge, is the Malá Strana. This district is a network of backstreets which seem entirely Italian. It is a world away from the tower blocks and wastegrounds of the suburbs.

'It's deceptive, living here,' one of the residents of the Malá Strana said to me. 'Sometimes you forget about the battle with bureaucracy that you have to fight every day if you want to get anything done, and the queues for everything. But I will say that it makes life more pleasant.'

From the Charles Bridge the bulk of the castle can be seen straddling the hill above the town, and as I made my way uphill through narrowing and twisting cobbled streets, I wondered whether this was the original of Kafka's castle. Outside the Matthias Gate, the main entrance to Hradčany, two soldiers stood rigidly to attention, holding outmoded ceremonial rifles made of pale wood, with silver fittings. A small boy wearing a Rambo T-shirt admired them as they sweated in the sun in their heavy khaki uniforms and white nylon gloves.

On either side of the Matthias Gate, beyond the soldiers, are beautiful slender flagpoles in wood, designed by the great modern architect Josef Plečnik, whose work on modernizing the castle in the Twenties has given rise to some lovely details within courtyards. The castle has always been, and still is, the seat of Czech administration, and the Baroque buildings which comprise most of it are dull to look at. But in the centre is the Cathedral of St Veit. This had also recently reopened following restoration. The interior is dauntingly vast, and sometimes confusing, since the church was started in the mid-fourteenth century but not completed until 1929, owing to the interruptions of wars. The Wenceslas Chapel, with its red walls set with semi-precious stones, contains the tomb and relics of the saint, who died aged about twenty-two at the hand of his brother in 929 (the exact date is disputed) as a result of his unpopular alliance with the German king, Henry the Fowler. The frescoes in the chapel are of the ancient Prague school, and the chapel itself was executed in the mid-fourteenth century; but a casual glance might mistake it for a piece of nine-teenth-century neo-medievalism. Beyond it, in the depths of the church, is the gaudy silver tomb of Saint John Nepomuk, by Fischer von Erlach. In the centre of the nave is the sixteenth-century Monument of the Kings, beneath which (their modern coffins are to be seen in the crypt) lie the monarchs of Bohemia.

In a corner of the courtyard to the south of the cathedral is the Gothic Vladislav Hall, a great bare space once used for assemblies and tournaments. From one of its balconies there is a magnificent view across the valley in which Prague lies, and from a window of the adjoining Judiciary two Roman Catholic councillors were thrown in 1618 by Protestant Bohemian nobles made impatient by Catholic interference. This action, though not fatal to the councillors, who landed on a dung-heap, was still sufficient to spark off the Thirty Years' War.

Walking to the east end of the precincts to look at Golden Lane, a street which once housed the royal goldsmiths but whose pretty little terraced houses now provide accommodation for a number of souvenir shops and small cafés, I passed the second church, St George's. The oldest parts of this plain Romanesque basilica date from the tenth century. Before leaving the castle I could not resist a glance at the picture gallery. The collection once belonged to Charles I of England, but after his death it was sold, and then lost, not to be rediscovered until the early Sixties. There are some good paintings by Rubens and Tintoretto, and one famous portrait of a woman by Titian, but they have all been so enthusiastically restored that they look like reproductions. A patina of age should be left on old paintings: our eyes are so used to seeing them in muted colours that something in our aesthetic sense is surprised at seeing the brightness in which they may have appeared originally. They look almost garish.

As I left I passed the immobile sentries again. They had been drenched by a brief, violent thunderstorm.

From the castle I walked west to the Loretto Church, built by the Dietzenhofers at the beginning of the eighteenth century. It was closed, as churches in Czechoslovakia so often are, but its delicate façade provided a welcome contrast to the ugly bulk of the Černin Palace opposite. I sat on the terrace of the café next door and drank tea served by a grumpy waitress, until another thunderstorm drove everyone inside. There was nowhere to sit for the fugitives from the storm but the restaurant, which was, a spindly waiter informed us, closed. To prove his point he drew a curtain across it; but Czechs are able to allow reason to prevail over rules, and seeing that he could hardly have twenty damp people clutching drinks standing crammed together in his entrance hall he drew the curtain back with a sheepish grin.

On the long walk back into town another burst of rain allowed me to dash into the Cavarna Malostránske on the square of the same name. They gave me a glass of dry Moravian white wine. Also on the menu were various alcoholic coffees – Gaelic, Irish and so on, but also *English* – which turned out to be coffee with gin. I sat and chatted with a young Czech who had been travelling in Hungary and East Germany during the gap between school and university. 'At least, I'm hoping it's going to be university. Anything to put off military service!' He'd also done some travelling by train in Russia, which he told me was very difficult. 'The Russians don't like us. We're second-class citizens. They save their real welcome for westerners, because westerners spend dollars.' He said that this was his favourite café in all Prague, and that he liked to imagine Kafka sitting here after work, writing at one of the terrace tables. His own travels in eastern Europe had made him very discontented with the state of political play at home. 'Everywhere in Hungary people are looking hopeful, happy, as if a burden had been lifted from their shoulders. If only 1968 could have happened here now; but perhaps our turn will come. Do you realize that we have one of the three old-guard regimes? The old men put in to keep the people toeing the Party line. Hušak here, Honecker in the DDR, Zhivkov in Bulgaria.'

'But they are old men.'

'Yes. We'll ride it out. And change is coming. Even Ceauşescu's an old man.'

I asked him what his ambitions were.

'To go to America and make films,' he answered, promptly and confidently.

Back at my hotel the professorial porter whom I'd first met was off duty. He'd been replaced by two others I knew – a man who looked uncannily like Svejk, and a plump younger porter with long brown hair who had questioned me closely about Wimbledon's chances of defending its position at the top of the football league. He favoured Liverpool himself. I had to book a room in Karlovy Vary, and together they battled with the telephone for twenty minutes to get the number I wanted. Instead, they got hairdressers' salons, a greengrocer and even the local museum.

'Is it the right number?' I asked.

'Oh yes, but there's something wrong with this phone. It won't connect numbers properly,' they grinned. 'Look, just go to the hotel you want, and if the porter says it's full, slip him a 100 note and see what happens.'

'I'll remember that. How much do I owe you for the calls?'

'Nothing. You're a good sort.'

What I'd done to deserve the compliment I will never know. Perhaps I was just polite. I remembered a conversation I'd had with the donnish porter, in the course of which I had asked him if this had always been his job.

'Well no, not really.'

'What did you do before?'

He smiled sadly. 'Something a little more interesting, but that was twenty years ago. One learns nothing here if not how to be adaptable.'

11

TAKING THE WATERS

Zdenek arrived promptly at eleven. He hadn't brought his car because there is nowhere to park in the centre of Prague, a capital more busy with traffic than Berlin, and so we travelled to his flat by tube and tram. It was right out to the north-east of the city, in one of the grey blocks built soon after the end of the war.

'You could have stayed here, there's plenty of room,' he said expansively, his smile revealing a set of teeth so yellow and snaggled that they reminded me of the tombstones in the Jewish Cemetery. He must have been about sixty, a bulky man with thin yellowish-white hair, and the kindest of natures. The flat was certainly large, each of the three main rooms appearing to double as sitting room and bedroom. Heavy modern furniture managed to clutter the rooms, big as they were, and the hall, which seemed to serve both as dining room and meeting point, was dominated by a gigantic television set. Rents are heavily subsidized, and Zdenek paid about the same per month for his flat, including all services, as I did for two nights in my modest hotel.

'I also have a summer *dacha* about a hundred kilometres into the country.' This, it appeared, had five bedrooms.

He knocked loudly on the one closed door of the flat, from behind which I had already heard muted signs of life, and from what turned out to be the master bedroom his youngest daughter appeared, tousled with sleep. She was a nurse, at present on night-shift. 'She's the only one left at home now; both the others have left the nest.' He told me that his middle daughter, now a schoolteacher in her late thirties, had gone to England to study. 'She was there in 1968 – she could have stayed away, but she was too homesick, so she came back. To this day I don't know whether she regrets that decision.'

He had driven back from his *dacha* the night before, and was clearly still tired from the journey, but he insisted on taking me out for the entire day. Since I had already quite happily travelled around Prague by myself, we decided to go and look at two monuments of the Nazi occupation, both of which lie near the capital – the site of the village of Lidice, and the town of Terezín. Zdenek had been a political prisoner of the Germans and done time at Dachau, so he was an ideal guide.

Terezín, formerly called Theresienstadt after the Empress Maria Theresa, was built in the eighteenth century as a garrison town, which it is again today. But during the Second World War the Germans converted it into a large Jewish ghetto. It was intended to be a show-camp; if the Red Cross wished to see for themselves how the Germans were treating the Jews, they would be invited to visit Theresienstadt, which on the occasion of these visits was deliberately cleaned up and sanitized – even to the extent of having false school and bank signs erected, for no such facilities existed officially. In its daily routines and conditions, Theresienstadt was barely better than any other concentration camp, and from here many thousands of victims were deported to Auschwitz. Within the camp was the Malá Pevsnost – the Little Fortress. This was an eighteenth-century fort whose impregnable construction made it ideal for the SS to convert into a prison for those inmates of Theresienstadt who were, in their eyes, over-troublesome. It is now a museum and monument. The red-brick courtyards each have large cells leading off them which were filled far beyond their capacity. But the Second World War was not the first time the Malá Pevsnost was used as a prison: one of the single cells once housed Gavrilo Princip, the assassin of Franz Ferdinand at Sarajevo, and a revered hero in eastern Europe. His cell is now a shrine.

The Nazis, however, added refinements of their own to the fort. They built a wing of concrete cells with glass roofs. The effect of these special punishment *Blocks* was to increase the heat in summer and the cold in winter, and in this part of Europe both are extreme. The *Blocks* now house exhibitions of children's art on the theme of peace, and satirical and political cartoons of the Thirties and Forties. We were there on a hot day, and even though the rooms were empty and the doors and windows open it was still uncomfortable.

'A chap was in here the other day with his wife, in this very *Block*,' said Zdenek. 'And he was pointing out to her where his bunk used to be, and she was clinging to his arm and crying.'

We lunched on hot sausage and black bread in the former SS canteen, which has been converted into a snack bar. It is a modest place, but it has all the trappings and some of the atmosphere of a genuine *Bierstube*. All it lacked was stags' heads mounted on the walls.

Zdenek had been a Party worker all his life, and so I approached the subject of Dubček and the Prague Spring with caution, but as we were within a week of the twentieth anniversary of Russia's invasion, I couldn't let it go untouched.

'Yes, I remember very well,' said Zdenek, carving a large slice of sausage. 'It was a shambles. You see, Dubček wasn't a great man – he was an opportunist. I think everything happened too fast for him. Things were pushed through very quickly, but the infrastructure wasn't affected. I remember that we got no orders in our department about what we had to do. We just sat around. I was a statistician, and I think we could have done some useful work for the new leadership. He wasn't ruthless enough. There were plenty of people left free who were only too glad to step into the shoes the Russians provided for them after Dubček and the rest had been removed.'

He wouldn't discuss the question further, and whatever he may have been in the past he was now a supporter of Hušak. 'Don't forget that I have been in the worst kind of prisons for my communist beliefs, and I hold to them. I believe firmly that only through Communism can a human being realize his place and his potential in society – as fairly as it is possible for him to do so in any kind of society that man creates, at least. Sure, we have problems, but we have no debts, and we stand on our own feet.'

As we walked back to his new but badly dented white Skoda 120 the clouds gathered with their customary speed. It was a long drive back towards Prague and Lidice; by the time we arrived in the city it had grown dark, and the rain was sheeting down. Zdenek was the worst driver I have ever met, and as we lumbered from lane to lane looking for road signs I decided that whoever had dented him was probably not to blame. Few people hooted us. Aggression didn't ever appear to me to be a Czech quality.

At Lidice, the monument and museum by the road above the site of the actual memorial were closed for restoration, but it is possible to drive past them through the little village of New Lidice, where those of the survivors of the massacre who wished to remain were rehoused after the war, in a place overlooking the green valley, at the bottom of which a tall crucifix marks the former centre of the village. There is nothing else, but the emptiness is eloquent.

Following the assassination in 1942 of the SS governor of occupied Bohemia and Moravia, Reinhard Heydrich, by Czech agents parachuted in from England, Hitler ordered the complete destruction of this little village; all the men were executed, and every building was razed and ploughed under.

'They chose Lidice because it was sufficiently near Kladno. They knew Kladno was an important resistance centre, but they couldn't do anything about such a big place. So, like the bullies they were, they took it out on somewhere small enough to succumb to their strength.' Zdenek's voice was flat, but his eyes shone with tears.

To get everywhere I wanted to in Czechoslovakia, a car would be essential. Hiring one took a little time. I'd been told when I first asked that there was nothing and that there were in any case people on a waiting list already, but then I had the luck to meet Zina, an attractive brunette who spoke fluent and accentless English. How she had achieved this, since she told me she had never been out of Czechoslovakia, I was never able to discover, as both flattery and questions were greeted with friendly coyness. She confirmed that there were no cars according to the books, but added that she had only just come back from her summer holidays and would see what she could sort out. Could I ring her the following morning?

It didn't look as if she were holding out much hope, and so I decided that I would stoop to bribery. I had brought a copy of the current *Vogue* and a bottle of scent from England. The *Vogue* I had given to one of the hotel girls in Dresden, but the perfume was destined for the wife of a friend of mine in Prague, whom I had not been able to contact as he was at his *dacha*. I fetched it from my bag and before the car rental office closed that evening took it to Zina, telling her it was a thank-you present in advance for her help, which had already been considerable as she had given me a straight answer and avoided vagueness as far as it seemed possible for anyone in a remotely official position to do. She was pleased by the bribe, but a little on her guard, and she may have thought that I was trying to pick her up – a not inaccurate guess, though I had noticed the large and obvious wedding ring she wore. We said goodbye in mutual embarrassment and I wondered if I hadn't been stupid. But I didn't regret giving her the scent.

The next day was Saturday 13 August. 'I never do anything on the 13th of any month,' cautioned Zina cheerfully as she handed me the keys to ADA 1980 outside her office at the Forum Hotel. She showed me where the ignition was and how to open the boot, and then, looking cool and beautiful, was gone. I tried to open the boot again and failed, but was taken care of by a young hotel doorman in a grey frock coat and top hat, who showed me how everything worked, including the catch to open the engine, which was concealed behind one of the back doors. ADA 1980 was a beige Skoda 130, my trusty friend for the next few weeks and 2500 kilometres.

I set off for the spa towns, once Karlsbad, Marienbad and Franzensbad, but now Karlovy Vary, Marianské Lázně, and Františkovy Lázně. Although they have long since ceased to be sophisticated international centres, they are still full of people taking the waters – usually factory workers and trade union members on their annual holidays, staying at what were once hotels and pensions but which are now official holiday homes for the various cadres of working people. I'd decided to go to Karlovy first, taking the E48 west through sunny, rolling farmland, and wondering again why countries so agriculturally rich seem incapable of producing one vegetable or fruit worth mentioning. Because they don't figure in the traditional diet? Because they export it all for hard currency?

I had no map of Karlovy because it is nearly always impossible to get a map of one town in another. This meant that I would frequently arrive 'flying blind'. In this case I was fortunate because the route into Karlovy brought me straight along the Koněvova, which runs beside the River Ohře and past the Hotel Adria. Here I parked and booked a room before setting off for Lenin Square, armed with a map I had bought at the hotel. I ought to have been armed with a thorough knowledge of Czech road-signs as well, for I was suddenly horribly aware that mine was the only car on a narrow promenade by the little River Tepla. All around me were pedestrians. I asked one of them and had my fears confirmed. I had driven into a pedestrian precinct.

The Adria turned out to be one of the friendliest places I stayed in, and although the food was along the pork/potatoes/dumplings lines that I was already familiar with, it was good and generously supplied; and the beer was not the sticky Pilsner Urquell from which it is often impossible to escape in western Czechoslovakia.

Karlovy has the usual modern developments of grey high-rises, which spread north of the Ohře and spill over the south bank, but the streets behind the Koněvova are pleasant nineteenth-century blocks with mature gardens and plenty of trees. The core of the spa town lies in a steep, narrow valley covered with dark pine trees, which give the place a claustrophobic air. Along the floor of the valley runs the little tributary River Tepla, and on either side of it are the pedestrian streets where those taking the waters stroll, carrying odd little oval mugs with a spout built into the handle, through which the water is sucked. The large nineteenth-century hotels are here too, and there are moments when one could imagine oneself in a sequestered east European Bournemouth. As one walks towards this enclave, however, the first building one sees is the giant modern block of the Thermal, a black monstrosity concrete white rotundas at either end. It lives very unhappily with the terra houses on the river bank, which might have been imported from Bath.

The colonnades which run along the river are filled with people. The only visito. from outside seemed to be from both Germanys, though there were some Italians and a handful of English. Nearly everyone was over forty, though there was one young man in a multicoloured, wispy straw hat who was sipping from a jug. He had pale, blank eyes; his figure was too thin, and bent. Anywhere else I would have taken him for someone coming off drugs.

The shops and cafés have a Parisian elegance. Small bands play popular tunes of the Twenties in the arcades, and walkers stoop to replenish their mugs from small fountains with brightly polished, gushing brass pipes. There is an ornate theatre by Helmer and Fellner – who seem to have monopolized theatre building in eastern Europe in the nineteenth century – and a beautiful Kilian Dietzenhofer church. On the Sunday that I was in Karlovy, I tried to attend Mass but couldn't get in. Watching the service from the door, I saw one youth kneeling unselfconsciously on the marble of the aisle, there being no room in the pews.

The slopes of the valley on either side are criss-crossed with pathways. Formerly, visitors would take their constitutionals here, and I followed suit, past the red-brick Gothic Victorian English church, actually barely more than a chapel but still in use, and as uncannily and uncompromisingly English as those in Simla and Bombay. Here, the feeling of being on the other side of a divide simply doesn't exist, because the divide itself is artificial and the sense of the past is strong enough to extinguish it in one's mind.

I will call Marianské Lázně Marienbad, though there is little now to suggest more than the palest ghost of Edward VII and his circle, who patronized it in its heyday. The Hotel Weimar, where Edward used to stay, is renamed the Hotel Kafka, and the monarch's portrait has recently vanished from it. But the imperial yellow of the buildings remains.

The valley here is broader than at Karlovy, surrounding the town on three sides, but the hills are equally densely clad with pines. From the north, the road follows the Tepla down through prosperous and lush farmland, but the usual vista of high-rises greets one's eyes when one arrives at the rim of the valley.

Jaroslav came to meet me at the station, where I had ended up lost as usual, and whisked me off to his flat nearby. We had made contact through a mutual friend in Munich, and he had invited me to drop in, apologizing for the fact that as two nieces were spending the summer with him he couldn't put me up. His flat was opulent, and he explained that his family moved into the small block when it was first built in 1949; now they had bought up all four flats in it, and a branch lived in each one. Born into the Czech community in Vienna, as a teenager Jaroslav had been arrested by the Nazis for belonging to a workers' youth group and been sent to the concentration camp of Mauthausen, where he met and befriended his future brother-in-law. They elected to go to Czechoslovakia after liberation, for the community they had known in Vienna was destroyed. Greeted in Czechoslovakia as heroes, they had no difficulty in settling down. Jaroslav became a master metalworker and in that capacity worked for the Marienbad council all his life. He spent four years restoring the cast-ironwork decoration on the town colonnades.

While both he and his brother-in-law were happy to talk about the war and their subsequent careers, they shied off as soon as the conversation veered even slightly towards politics. Neither, however, seemed discontented with the regime. They told me firmly that in 1948 the people had democratically voted the communists in, that President Beneš had abandoned the country, and that there was no question that Jan Masaryk's fall from a window was anything but suicide. Their reaction to my mention of the events of 1968 was simply a shrug and a regretful look.

Jaroslav was eager that I should not miss the music that was played regularly each evening at seven o'clock by the ornamental fountain at one end of the colonnade. This was preceded by a tour of the town, which began with a visit to a new workers' holiday home, about the only piece of mock-Tudor architecture I have ever seen which actually works. Not far from it is Marienbad's English church, a desolate, abandoned little brick chapel, totally bare inside, with all its windows broken.

'There are plans to restore it,' explained Jaroslav. 'It's just a question of time.'

We drove down to the main square, where a large empty space is bordered on three sides by Victorian wedding-cake hotels and houses, dating from the time when Marienbad burst into prominence as a resort. Hot summers and long, hard winters play havoc with the stucco and the ironwork, but the battle to maintain the buildings is sustained. The fourth side is taken up by the main colonnade, whose enclosed arcade has been restored, lino-floored, and renamed after Gorky. At either end stand the small cupola'd buildings housing the springs. One has been completely restored; the other, which was falling down owing to vibrations from lorries passing nearby, is being moved further away from the road, and reinforced.

We were just in time for the music, which to Jaroslav's disappointment was piped. 'You should hear it when it is live,' he lamented. What I lamented was that I had no camera with me to record the over-ornate but irresistibly lavish façades of the buildings surrounding us, their pale yellow stone darkening as the sun set over them. The music was modern-light-classical, and Jaroslav told me that the young man who had written it had spent a week here, wandering around to soak up the spirit of the place. 'But to listen to it, I think he must have been unhappily in love as well.' The fountain played for ten minutes, sending a variety of jets high into the air, and then it was all over. The small crowd dispersed silently.

'What is going to happen in the middle of the square?' I asked, indicating the open space, clearly a building site turning into wasteground, surrounded by a corrugated iron fence.

He gazed at it gloomily. 'They say they're going to build a splendid new clinic, but most of us who live here think the designs are appalling – we'd rather see it converted into a small park.'

'I agree,' I said, thinking of the Thermal building in Karlovy.

'We live in hope. It's been like this for at least two years and nothing's happened. Perhaps nothing will.'

Accompanying us were Jaroslav's wife Yelena and one of the young nieces, a pretty, dark girl with beautiful legs. She knew this, and showed them off well, but such is the effect on one's senses of what is familiar that I wished she would shave them, for they were covered with thick, curly black hair, like a man's. As we made our way to the car, an elderly couple hailed us. Jaroslav introduced me and they said to me in English, 'We hope you enjoy your stay here, and please give our regards to London.' They were Jews who had spent the war in exile there.

Jaroslav guided us back to the car. 'Being English, you will want to see the links,' he said. We drove up one of the hills behind the town and along a tree-lined road until we emerged at a luxurious golf-course, opposite which stood a hotel.

'This is the Hotel Golf, our answer to your Savoy,' said Jaroslav. 'We will have a drink.'

The carpark was full of Mercedes and BMWs, mainly with West German plates. 'We will cut a dash here with our Skoda,' said Jaroslav; but there was a hint of annoyance in his voice. Two elegant girls stood a short distance away by a long, burgundy limousine. As we got out, they were joined at the trot by two stoutish balding men in suits, and amid much tinselly laughter drove off.

Jaroslav drew me aside slightly as we walked towards the entrance. 'Those are Czech girls,' he said, 'and the men are West Germans. It works like this. The Germans come over here and change what they have to for their visas legally; the rest they do on the black market. Even a poor West German can live like a king here, because most Czechs are desperate for foreign exchange – we're allowed so little officially. In any case the average worker's wage works out at about 3000 korunas [£200] a month. And so these girls come to batten on the fat cats,' he continued. 'There's not much to choose between the East and West Germans, they all lord it over us; but the West Germans are worse.'

The last of the spa towns was the smallest and the least affected by modern times. It lies on the road towards the frontier, just beyond Cheb. Driving along, I saw signs to Nuremberg, so near and yet so far. I skirted Cheb, and drove on to Františkovy Lázně.

Sunday afternoon – a hot, lazy Sunday, and early afternoon, and not a soul, not a sound as I switched off the engine in the muddy little carpark. After cutting through the scruffy garden courtyard of two small concrete blocks of flats, I emerged in a broad avenue, a park on one side and a stately row of nineteenth-century buildings on the other, all painted *Kaisergelb* (imperial yellow), glowing in the sunlight, and relieved only by the green of doors and shutters. My tempo slowed instantly, and I found myself strolling into town. As I approached the centre, I began to notice that what had clearly been hotels and pensions were now *dûms* – workers' holiday homes. People ought to have been dressed in long skirts, white suits, Panamas. Instead them majority were wearing modest, casual clothes.

There were far fewer people here than in the other towns, and we seemed remote from the present. A crossroads led to the right through a small park, past a bandstand and a beer-garden, to the station; in the other direction the town's main street led down to the principal source, housed in a little Greek rotunda, named after the Emperor Franz-Josef, and superintended by a plump blonde in a white coat who never ceased to polish the brass pipes which conduct the water from the spring. I tried the water here. It was beautifully cold, looked like pink gin, and tasted like weak ginger ale. The street contains the sleepy Hotel Slovan, which is the kind of place a Victorian writer might have retired to for the whole summer in order to write The Novel, and a house whose entrance arch contains a plaque to Beethoven, who stayed here in 1812. The picture of the composer shows a younger and less severe man than we normally see.

Beyond the source runs the small and pretty colonnade, in front of which is a flowerbed. In the middle of this there is a bust of Lenin in red granite. I wish I had counted the number of busts and statues of Lenin I saw on these travels. They all have one of two basic expressions: the Heroic and the Defiant. Lenin's shrewd, modern face does not lend itself to heroification, and the official sculptors are prisoners of too rigid a tradition, so the great man ends up looking either smug or cunning. Here, of all places, his presence is unsuitable, a gross imposition, a Tartar invader. Devoid of any artistic merit, these reminders of Big Brother would disappear overnight in a changed political climate.

But Franzensbad, as one must truly call it, is a place out of its time as much as Lenin's bust is out of place. The people that made these towns and the Europe which they inhabited are long gone. The buildings continue to exist in a world that has moved on. I looked at the people here now. Most were old, and as the afternoon wore on, fewer and fewer were to be seen. I walked in the park, discovering another large pump-room – an all-but deserted hall. The town was a place where one might easily feel buried alive. The heat of the sun grows more intense as the afternoon progresses, and has a quality here, so far from the sea, that we rarely experience in Britain. At its worst it is oppressive and debilitating. I glanced through the open doors of the deserted casino, its overblown decor running to seed, and turned away, sensing death in the air. I wondered how it would be never to be able to leave this sleepy, warm, yellow mausoleum.

I made my way to the beer garden. An orchestra was playing Viennese waltzes from the peeling white bandstand. The waiter told me he'd visited England with the junior national football team fifteen years earlier. Normally he worked in Prague, but had come away to escape the tourists. 'Most of them come from the two Germanys and Austria, but we get plenty from Italy, a few from France, and thousands from South America – the Venezuelans are the best tippers.'

From the spa towns my route lay back to Prague and then due south past the ancient town of Tábor. The road passed through increasingly lovely farmland, dotted with villages which were reminiscent of their counterparts in Austria, and also punctuated with such aristocratic eccentricities as Hluboká – a scaled-down, snow-white copy of Windsor Castle. The road itself is good, but quite often road works are not identified, and so I quickly learned not to spend too much time admiring the scenery – dips, bumps, and sudden unmade sections loomed up without warning, and when they did I thanked God that the Skoda, for all its ugliness, was built to cope with them. Dead animals – dogs, cats, and once a wolf – were also frequent obstacles on Czech roads.

My destination was the Českys – České Budějovice and Česky Krumlov, Budweis and Krummau in German. The first is a large town, the capital of South Bohemia. It presents the usual daunting, soulless modern architecture as you arrive, but the day was warm and kind and dispelled some of the gloom this inspired. Penetrating what is a fairly thin shell of this unpleasantness, and armed, for once, with a map of the town, I nosed my way in through the nineteenth-century layer and arrived at the old core – Žižka Square. There are many Žižka Squares in this part of the country, named after the local leader of the Hussite movement, who might also claim to be the inventor of the tank – one of the armoured wagons he introduced into warfare can be seen in the Hussite Museum in Tábor Town Hall.

The square in České Budějovice is unique. It is one of the largest in Europe, and is surrounded by a collection of some of the most perfectly preserved Renaissance domestic buildings in existence. Basking in the sun, and mercifully free of cars, you would imagine that the colonnades surrounding it might harbour any number of small cafés and restaurants, but apart from that of the seedy hotel there was only one, in a back-street and packed, where poor food was doled out by tired waitresses.

The streets leading off the square contain medieval and Renaissance buildings of great quality and beauty, and restoration everywhere is thorough and sensitive. But I was not sorry that I was pressing on to spend the night at Krumlov, a smaller town a short distance to the south-west. Krumlov lies on a road lined with somnolent, pine-clad hills, set in countryside which is the model for fairy-tale illustrations. Along it is one of the two fortified monasteries of the region, founded in the Middle Ages but refurbished and redesigned in the Baroque era. Zlatá Koruna lies on the Vltava halfway between Budějovice and Krumlov, a short distance off the main road. The lane leading to it carried patrols of profoundly healthy and tanned rucksack-bearing holiday hikers, but the village itself and the monastery were deserted. Only down by the river were there signs of activity in the campsite, where more people in enviably good physical condition were busy getting in and out of kayaks.

Mercifully the modern development at Krumlov is not only better designed than elsewhere, it is set some way from the Old Town, and partially hidden by trees. The Old Town is a miniature medieval city, with high terraces along cobbled streets clambering up from the riverside to a modest square. It was founded about 1250 by the Vitkovci clan, who also built the castle which dominates it – the largest in Czechoslovakia after Hradčany. Taken over by the Rožmberks (Rosenbergs) at the beginning of the fourteenth century, Krumlov remained in their hands for the next three hundred years as the seat of their power. The castle, despite the attractive graffito decoration on the outer walls of the main courtyard, is a rather desolate and sober place, though the tour through it ends in the 'cartoon hall' – the great hall of the castle which was decorated in 1748 by a local artist called Lederer with a series of dreadful caricatures of people in Venetian carnival dress. Their effect on me was oppressive, and I was glad to escape into the gardens.

I managed to find the 'new' theatre. It is actually thirty years old, built to a special design of which only one other example exists, in Scandinavia. The 800-seat auditorium revolves, so that when a scene changes, the audience is spun to face the next aspect. This was explained to me by a couple of the stagehands, who were getting things ready for that evening's performance. I asked them about the castle's original eighteenth-century theatre, but they told me it had been closed for restoration for the past eighteen years – which cannot be right, since it is mentioned with enthusiasm by more than one recent guide-book. Nevertheless, when I found it, it was very closed and had a dusty, neglected look about it. A pity, because it has its original stage machinery, dating from 1766, and ten original sets – probably the oldest surviving in Europe.

I ended up at a small beer-and-sausage stand with a few tables under trees on the edge of the castle grounds overlooking the red roofs of the town. There was no queue, so I dived in and refreshed myself. The local beer, Krummau, is excellent, and I said as much. The proprietor, a bearded, bellied giant, started an earnest discussion with me on the relative merits of Bohemian beers. I had been sorry not to have an opportunity to drink Budweiser in Budweis, but Krummau more than made up for it.

Sitting opposite me at the table under the trees was an old man who was spending his summer evenings as an usher for the open-air theatre. He was balding, with white hair, but still fit and wiry, dressed in grey slacks and a tan check shirt. He was seventy-eight years old.

'It's a great pleasure to talk German again,' he told me. 'Nowadays fewer and fewer people can speak it here, and I miss the sound of it.' He had spent the early years of his career working as an accountant for the Schwarzenbergs, the dynastic ruling family which had succeeded the Rosenbergs. 'Days I miss now,' he said. 'They looked after you well, and when I think of the pension I would have got if my career hadn't been interrupted by events ... The Schwarzenbergs would never have treated me like this. Oh well, I am an old man now, and I don't care what I say.' He broke off, and asked me abruptly if I spoke French.

> '"Que peu de temps suffit pour changer toutes choses!
> Nature au front serein, comme vous oubliez!"*

– do you remember that? It's from Hugo, the *Tristesse d'Olympio.*' The old man's voice caressed the words. 'It is a beautiful language, but no one can speak it here. No one has been learning western languages for two generations now, and the Slav tongue could never get round French.'

He seemed lonely, somehow isolated, but he told me that he was married and that his wife was still alive. They had lived all their lives in the town, and not left Czechoslovakia since 1948. 'No doubt you have noticed all the posters reminding us that this year we celebrate forty years of Czech–Soviet friendship,' he said. 'They are there, of course, to deflect our thoughts from what the friendly Russians did in 1968.'

---

* *How little time is needed for all to change!*
Nature, serene of brow, how you forget!

His daughter, he told me, had married a West German and now lived in Cham. His son was an engineer in Ostrava. 'We rarely see my son; my daughter, never – although geographically she lives less than half the distance away in West Germany.' He asked me where I was going after Czechoslovakia, and cheered up when I told him. 'You'll like it in Hungary,' he said, adding judiciously: 'The girls are prettier, but alas, much flatter-chested.'

He would not allow me to buy him another drink. A small knot of people had gathered, waiting for the theatre to open. The sun was setting behind the hill which shelters the town, and the shadows of the trees were long on the grass.

'I cannot say *auf wiedersehen*, because we will not meet again; and I do not wish to say *adieu* because it is too sad; so I will just wish you a good journey, here and later.' He shook my hand briefly and left.

It was chilly after the sun had gone down, and I walked slowly through the gardens and the deserted courtyards of the castle back into the town. The shops were closed and no longer slung their din of loud pop music into the streets. I walked for some distance and met only one other person, though from some hidden bar came the sound of a small brass band playing Bavarian music. I walked up the hill to the square, crossing the bridge over the Vltava with its solid town gate, and looking up at the black slab of the castle above me. Another ghost.

Much later, back at home, I looked up the poem which the old man had quoted to find out how the stanza ended:

> *Et comme vous brisez dans vos métamorphoses*
> *Les fils mystérieux où nos coeurs sont liés!**

---

* *And how, metamorphosing, you break*
The mysterious cords which bind our hearts!

12

TOWARDS BRATISLAVA

I followed the Vltava south along its thickly wooded gorge, almost to the Austrian border, to the castle of Rožmberk, an ugly chunk of a place built for defence not beauty, and then on west to Vyšši Brod, the second great fortified monastery of the region. The town here is a tourist centre now, and packed with suntanned canoeists, though for the more academically minded the monastery houses an important library. I did not stay, for this was a detour into country less and less distinguishable both in scenery and architecture (and indeed tradition) from Austria, but turned east again and headed back to České Budějovice via Dolní Dvořište. Dolní is right on the frontier, and as you turn left back into Czechoslovakia up the E55 you see the red and white pole-gates of the Czech passport and customs control.

I had got up early, but I'd dawdled over my usual breakfast of rolls and strawberry jam – apparently the only flavour available to Czech hotels – because my coffee was hot and good and there was a lot of it. Even so, I was making good time, and as it was a lovely day I decided to drive further than I had originally intended. My route took me through Třeboň, its castle rising above the modern outskirts, and then onto the D23, which leads more or less due east towards Brno. This road must be among the most beautiful in Europe, certainly in August, when the early wheat has been harvested, leaving a glorious golden ruin of fields which glide in great swathes between the dark green woods running down from the hills.

By-passing Jindřichův Hradec I made my first stop in Telč. I had heard that the hotel on the main square had an excellent restaurant, and as I was now in the heart of fish-farming country I thought I might get some carp, or at least trout, for lunch.

My mind was on this more than on any aesthetic treat as I made my way from the carpark to the centre of the Old Town – almost everywhere the Czechs have sensibly banned traffic from the centres of their cities. Nothing had prepared me for Telč. I crossed the little bridge over a river that was more of a brook, went through the gate in the town walls and walked along a broad cobbled street which sloped gently upwards. It emerged in a corner of the square.

The square *is* the Old Town. It is a long rectangle; quieter and more dignified than Žižka Square in České Budějovice, with a well-carved plague-column towards one end, it lay open like a sunbather to the midday heat. All around it, without a break, were the gently curved gables of Renaissance houses, consistent in height and varying subtly in design. They were painted in pastel colours – blue, peach, and yellow, and the grander of them were decorated with rich stucco designs. This is the most beautiful town square I have ever seen. I wandered around the perimeter, unable to break away, and unable to believe that something as perfect as this could still exist. Some way along, a middle-aged man was playing jazz on a trumpet. He was a good player, and the music did not sound inappropriate as it echoed gently round the lovely houses. I walked over to him. He wasn't playing for money; he was just playing. He probably had to do with the jazz festival I'd seen advertised on a couple of hoardings. A small crowd had already collected round him as I left.

Driving eastwards, I passed through Třebič. From the road, it is an uncompromisingly modern town, though it contains the ruin of a once great Benedictine abbey. It is famous today for the manufacture of Christmas cribs. Then on, through the villages of long, low, whitewashed houses with deep-set windows, strung out along the road. Roadside crucifixes had by now replaced the modern concrete or metal monuments to Russo–Czech amity, but in each village loudspeakers were either slung on wires along the road or attached to lamp-posts. I never heard them utter, but suppose they are still used to dish out homilies on the noble purposes of their leaders to the people. All the villages had noticeably well-kept graveyards, each gaudy with fresh flowers.

This is deep country, and in it one senses great spaces stretching out far beyond the range of one's vision, the vastness of the central European hinterland; but after Třebič one begins to anticipate the end of this rural belt. Sure enough, the wayside shrines give way to concrete monuments again, and before long the little D23 arrives at the motorway which links Prague, Brno and Bratislava, and will eventually join them with Budapest. Brno itself is a huge, modern, sprawling city built over several low hills, and interrupted by tracts of green land. Despite the serried ranks of high-rises, the town is still dominated by two gaunt giants: the Renaissance castle on the Špilberk, and the equally brooding hulk of the Gothic cathedral of SS Peter and Paul. The impression of this vast town, appearing abruptly from countryside and just as quickly disappearing into it again as one heads south, is eerie.

Away from Brno, vineyards begin to appear by the side of the motorway, and in the distance long low ranges of hills rise. It was late on a Friday afternoon, and the sun slashed the dusk with fire as I joined the thundering Czech and Hungarian lorries, and the cars full of tourists from Poland, Russia, Hungary and East Germany on the road to Bratislava.

I arrived at six, just in time for the rush-hour. Once again I was armed with a map, but to my dismay the street-name plates in the capital of Slovakia were not the large, clear, red-and-white ones of Prague, but small, indistinct, and black-and-white. My map can't have been too clear either, for although I was on the right road into town to begin with I soon ended up on something which didn't seem to be in Bratislava at all, and I couldn't find the Danube either to help orient myself. After nearly getting killed by a bus on a busy crossroads I found myself following a dust-cart and ended up at the town dump. Extricating myself, by luck I passed the bus station and asked a taxi-driver if he would lead me to the hotel I was seeking. He told me that wouldn't be necessary, asked me where I got such an antique map (answer: the Czech National Tourist Office in London) and put me on the right road. This involved the same crossroads, and this time, turning left, I was almost ploughed under by three oncoming Ladas in line abreast. Later I walked back to find out why this particular intersection seemed to spur me on to such suicidal attempts, and discovered simply that the traffic lights were out. I hadn't noticed this, and so must have been queue-jumping, but the Slovaks are as polite as the Czechs. I hadn't got the barrage of abuse I probably deserved; just a mild hoot or two.

After that, it was a relief to climb into a bath. I was rewarded for my labours by a room which overlooked the Danube, and the new Slovak National Uprising Bridge which spans it. It was good to see the river. I would come across it again now and then for the rest of my journey. As I gazed at it idly, the first of many great barges made its way by with infinite slowness, the lorries which were its cargo looking like Dinky toys. Unwisely, I opened the window to my balcony and let in a cloud of bloodthirsty mosquitoes, which I had to wage war on for the next fifteen minutes.

The following day I wandered down to the tourist office to see about buying a train ticket in advance from Košice to Debrecen. It wasn't possible, as the ticket office section was closed, but I got into conversation with a man who suggested that I take a guided tour of the town. It started at two, he said, and included dinner that evening. He himself was the guide.

The group was small for the large bus that was laid on. Everyone else was from East Germany. There were a mother and father of about the same age as me, with their two young sons; an older woman with badly crippled feet, but able to walk unassisted, and her twenty-year-old daughter, who was a nurse. The only other person was a man of perhaps thirty who was a traffic circulation consultant.

Karel was in his early sixties, a retired engineer who started by telling me that he did guiding as a hobby but later admitted that it was also to supplement his pension. Men retire here at sixty and women at fifty-seven, though they may retire one year earlier for every child they have borne. Karel had lived in Bratislava since coming here as a student. His work had taken him abroad a good deal in the early years, and he had been to Paris, Rome and London; but he had not risen high on the ladder of advancement, he told me, because he had never joined the Party. His career took a dive after 1968. He spoke good English, French and German: 'I was educated before 1948, you see!'

He was a good and conscientious guide, though given to lists of statistics. By the end of the tour, which lasted four-and-a-half hours, we had covered every major aspect of the town except for museum interiors. There weren't many people on the streets apart from us, for not only does Bratislava follow the example of most east European towns and close down with the shops after noon on Saturdays, but this particular Saturday was the twentieth anniversary of the Russian invasion of Prague.

Police were everywhere, most of them too young to have been born much before 1968, and many looked embarrassed; there was no need for such a display of force, and ordinary people were clearly showing their disapproval by their absence. But the police duly did spot-checks on cars, especially if the drivers were pretty girls, and asked to see the papers of passers-by when senior officers were near. Otherwise they leaned on street-corners, smoked furtively, and chatted to one another. My group was unanimous in its condemnation.

'Though of course it's not really them, but the guys who give them their orders,' said the traffic consultant.

'If they didn't obey the orders, where would the bosses be?' asked the nurse.

'Well, we all obey orders, more or less.'

'Then we should stop.'

Our first halt was Gottwald Square, named after the first post-war communist leader of Czechoslovakia, and the site of the modern faculty buildings of Bratislava University. Its large open space is dominated in the centre by a large fountain symbolizing a cluster of lime leaves. The lime is Czechoslovakia's national tree, though I think it should be the rowan, for there was hardly a country roadside that wasn't lined with them. At the far end of the square is a large, uncompromising stone monument to Gottwald, who ran the country as a dictator in all but name from 1946 until his death in 1953.

Not far from here is the Baroque Grasaković Palace, named after the banker to Maria Theresa who built it, and occupied during the war by the infamous Monsignor Josef Tiso, who ruled Slovakia as a German puppet state. Passing it, we climbed to the Slavin Memorial to the Russian troops who died in the liberation of Slovakia. The fighting around and for Bratislava was bitter and desperate; Hitler had declared it *Festung Pressburg* – Fortress Bratislava, and stated that on no account was it to be surrendered. However, Russian troops were supported by naval vessels which sailed up the Danube through Romania from the Black Sea. The memorial is in the form of a spire, and the statues at its base are strewn with fresh red gladioli and tulips. Karel pointed northwards from the hill on which the monument stands to a nearby church. 'When this monument was erected, the Russians had the spire of that church taken down. They couldn't brook the competition.'

We walked past a row of red-and-white Russian tour buses. Below us, the new piles of the Youth Bridge were visible. The bridge is designed to complete the motorway link between here and Budapest, but it will take five years to build. 'On average, everything takes five years; for one thing, we prefer having a drink or a nap to working; for another, supplies of materials can dry up for months for no apparent reason. And yet the French are building a Forum hotel in town which is scheduled to open in September – eighteen months to the day from the moment they cleared the site. How? By working ten hours a day, seven days a week.'

Bratislava has suffered from over-enthusiastic replacing of the old with the new. The motorway which feeds the Slovak National Uprising Bridge on the north bank of the Danube gashes the old city, passing within a couple of metres of St Martin's and slapping the church in the face. Built in 1975, this road had serious sacrifices made to it: the synagogue and a section of the Old Town surrounding it were pulled down to make room. 'If it had been sited only a few metres upstream, that would not have been necessary,' said Karel. 'But there were not enough Jews left to protest, and in any case the psychology here is not based on respect and love for the old, but for the thrusting, progressive new. We are attempting to synthesize a post-1948 culture.'

That is only partly true. Destroyed by a fire early in the nineteenth century, the castle lay in ruins for 150 years until it was restored shortly after the war in the Baroque style it assumed under Maria Theresa. I visited the interior on another day, and among the austere but perfectly recreated interiors discovered a large museum dedicated to Moravian and Slovakian history. Bratislava is a sister city to Vienna, only a few miles to the west and visible from the towers of the castle on a clear day.

Although Bratislava's former cosmopolitan atmosphere – Hungarian, German and Slovak – has gone since Czechoslovakia joined the Eastern Bloc, it was here that the Hungarian crown jewels were once kept, and it was in St Martin's Cathedral that the Habsburgs were crowned until the middle of the last century. Since the town is situated on the frontier – only a couple of miles upstream, the Danube *is* the frontier – the Czechoslovak authorities no doubt wish to emphasize its continuing import-ance under their rule – Bratislava is every bit as good as 'Pressburg' was – and to play down the Austro-Hungarian element in its history.

The frontier here is the most strictly guarded in the country; but just as in East Berlin it is impossible to prevent people from watching West German television, so here people switch to Austrian Broadcasting. 'They try to counteract any evil influence western television may have on us by propaganda programmes,' one Berliner had told me; 'but above all you see the adverts, and you can't help dreaming about the availability of such things, from language courses to holidays in Thailand. I think the worst thing for me is having to watch the commercials for foreign travel.'

The views across the Danube from the castle walls are impressive, but the dominant sight is a new town. It was built over the last ten years but until recently has had no facilities whatsoever, not even a shop – residents had to come across to Bratislava for everything. Bratislava has trebled its population since the war, and the new town houses 150,000 people. It is an Orwellian place. There are only seven variations in the tower blocks' design, and the impression is of complete uniformity. And yet all is clean and orderly, and there are no graffiti.

'They were built to house people coming in from the country. As agriculture gets more mechanized, there's no need for so many workers. So they come to the towns for work. Thus we have too few people living in the country, and too many in the towns. Soon it will be hard to guarantee employment for everyone.'

I said that in districts at home like the one we were looking at, the streets and open ground would be neglected, there would be vandalism, the people would be frus-trated and take it out on their environment. Didn't that happen here?

'Most of the people living there are middle-aged or old. That's one thing. And as yet we have no unemployment, so that is one frustration we are spared. As for vandalism, well, that's a kind of self-expression; it could be interpreted as an act of political sabotage. No one would dare to be a vandal over here – punishment would be swift and severe.'

There is still an elite. They live in big villas on the hill below the Slavin Memorial, and near it is the discreet white hotel for visiting dignitaries only. Karel pointed it out to us as we drove back down to the Old Town. 'For the big fish,' he said. The East Germans laughed knowingly.

During the long walk through the town that followed I became quite worried for Michaela, the elderly crippled woman; but she wouldn't give up.

'Do your feet hurt?' Karel asked.

'Always; but as it makes no difference whether I walk or sit, I'll walk.'

I kept with her most of the time, but the only thing she complained of, as we all did, to each other, was thirst. Karel, however, was relentless. He had a schedule to get through and no break was allowed. The tour was detailed and more informative than anything comparable in the West. It must have taken it out of Karel, too.

At the foot of the castle hill we passed a little apricot-coloured Baroque house, 'At the Sign of the Good Shepherd', which houses the city's clock museum. The motorway shoulders its path between it and St Martin's, and thus the care with which the house had been preserved seems almost a mockery.

Beethoven's *Missa Solemnis* had its premiere in St Martin's, and the city has many other associations with great composers. In houses not far from one another on opposite sides of Jiráskova, the main street of the Old Town which leads north up to Michalská and Michael's Gate, Liszt and Mozart gave their debut concerts, aged nine and six respectively. Bartók studied here, and the tiny house which was the birthplace of the city's native composer, Johann Nepomuk Hummel, is preserved as a museum within the courtyard of a more recent building.

In the shadow of Michael's Gate, one of the surviving entrances to the medieval walled city, is the Red Crayfish pharmaceutical museum, with its large model crayfish signs – the first of many medical museums I found throughout eastern Europe. By now we were on the northern edge of the Old Town, and to the south of us was the principal square which, like the bridge, was named after the Slovak Uprising of 1944. Slovakia, always regarded as the country cousin of Moravia and Bohemia, first found an identity through the work of Lodovit Štur, whose struggle for his country's identity and language – there are slight but precise differences between Czech and Slovak – during the first half of the nineteenth century is celebrated everywhere.

Turning back into the Old Town, there is a concentration of churches and palaces around Radnicá and 4 April Square. Behind the Town Hall, a Gothic building overlarded with Renaissance additions and topped with a Baroque tower, is the eighteenth-century Archbishop's Palace, closed for renovation when I was there, in whose Hall of Mirrors Napoleon signed the Peace of Pressburg with Francis I in 1805. The Franciscan Church – which is really three churches in one, since it has Gothic, Renaissance and Rococo parts – was packed for Mass in Hungarian. Despite the years that have passed, there are still German and Hungarian communities in Bratislava. In the Gothic chapel of St John reposes the body of St Reparatus in a glass coffin. Dressed in the red robes of a seventeenth-century bishop, the venerable relic looks like a prop from a Hammer film.

Across from the church is the Mirbach Palace, among whose art collection is a complete set of six tapestries depicting the story of Hero and Leander. They were woven at Mortlake in Surrey in the early seventeenth century, and how they got here is a mystery – though it seems that they were bought privately by a local collector in the nineteenth century. The palace contains other treasures, including two rooms completely panelled with coloured eighteenth-century graphics – copies of works by Rubens and Boucher; and a collection of contemporary cartoons and visual jokes (though none of them contentious or political), the best of which was a witch's broom suspended from the ceiling, equipped with a bicycle saddle, handlebars and a rear-view mirror.

The best art collection in town, however, is that in the Palffy Palace in Nálepkova ulice. The great painters Martin Banka (1888–1971) and Gejza Bošaćky, who was working at the end of the nineteenth century, are represented here; and the top floors are dedicated to modern art. None of the paintings and sculptures in the modern exhibition I saw was earlier than 1985; it was clear that there is a vigorous contemporary art movement, though there is also a directionlessness which stems from the artists' lack of exposure to outside influence and the absence of social comment or criticism. In the Slovak National Gallery, a piece of daring architecture in which a modern building has been tacked to the front of a Baroque barracks, there is a superb collection of heads by the mad eighteenth-century sculptor Franz Xaver Messerschmidt – part of a series in which he explored the extremities of facial expression. The busts have a frightening modernity.

All this, however, I saw later, on the rainy days that followed. Our tour now took the bus again for the fortress ruins of Devín.

Devín (the name means Maiden Castle) has always been a fortified spot, commanding a broad curve in the Danube from a wild, surging rock. The earliest remains are Roman, but the most substantial date from the time of the shadowy Moravian Empire, which lasted between 400 and 900. It is also the site of the 'Slav Days' – celebrations of nationalism inaugurated by Lodovit Štur as part of his campaign to establish an independent identity for Slovakia. Devín is still a sensitive site. Where it overlooks the river, the river is the frontier. The hills on the other side are Austrian. Though there is nothing at all to see, photography in that direction is forbidden, and Czech frontier guards prowl their side of the river in patrol boats.

The road linking Devín with Bratislava where it follows the frontier is flanked by a high barbed-wire fence. Another image of prison. 'We feel like convicts sometimes,' Karel told me. 'But the division can't be all our fault, can it? Isn't the West to blame as well for this separation? What seems so tragic is that none of the people on either side wants it, and yet it continues to exist. Is this the final polarization, after so many combinations of divisions throughout history – into just two, East and West? Or will they melt and redivide again, like their predecessors?'

We drove out to the Little Carpathians for dinner. The outskirts of Bratislava are full of chemical plants, for which the city is famous, and Karel launched into another round of statistics; but soon we were in green countryside, and he fell silent.

13

SLOVAKIA

The day I left Bratislava the weather broke. The rain was sheeting, driving stuff, the kind one gets in hot countries after a long drought. I hadn't intended to start so early, but I could see the first accident from my hotel window. A bus and a car had collided with a tram, blocking the lines. As a result the following trams were piling up in a queue and soon they would block any left turn.

My goal was Liptovský-Mikuláš in the Low Tatras, and the route I was to follow should have been scenic. At the moment the cloud squatted so low on the land that it blotted out the slightest hint of any view, and reduced everything to a brownish-grey monochrome. I avoided the fast road out of town and took a smaller one to Trnava, one of the most venerable towns in the country and a major religious centre until it was eclipsed by Esztergom, now in Hungary. Much of the old part of the town has been swamped by new development, and the rain did not encourage me to stay long. I wanted to reach Topol'čany from here by way of Nitra, but halfway there, at Sered', signs abruptly indicated that the road was closed. There was nothing for it but to turn back, although I cut across country for a while and drove through a pale green mist, totally lost but for the reassuring presence of the River Váh on my left, still just visible. If I kept it there, I knew I would end up at Piešt'any, and so I did, turning right there for Topol'čany, where despite the rain I hoped to catch a glimpse of the famous castle and the Lippizaner stables. The weather mocked me as I drove through Radošina and Bojná and oncoming cars flashed me. This, I had learned by now, is usually meant as a warning of something unpleasant ahead – a police speed trap or an accident. In this case it was an accident: an articulated lorry, rare in this land of ultra-slow exhaust-belching four-tonners, had crushed a car as effectively as a man might squash a beetle.

There was no reward awaiting me in Topol'čany. The weather was so vile that it was as much as I could do to find my way through the grey modern part of town, and even then I did not escape being yelled at by a policeman for omitting to drive with my headlights dipped. Morosely, I made my way back to the main road by way of Bánovce.

Once back with the Váh, however, the clouds relented a little, and I was able to get a good view of the magnificent castle of Trenčin, which still dominates the town. The road shone slickly, and was treacherous where huge ponds had formed in the many depressions in the tarmac. Approaching bleak Zilina one was aware of tree-covered hills laced with cloud on either side of the road, but shortly afterwards the weather closed in again, and the rain hurled itself down as spitefully as ever.

One of the reasons I had chosen this route was that it took in the ruined castle of Strečno – all these fortifications were built as defences against the Poles – but shortly before arriving at it, we were diverted from the main road, which had been closed by another grim accident involving a large lorry and two cars. All traffic had to pass through the narrow muddy streets of the little village below the castle, which may have been charming on a sunny day but which now looked like the set for a film of *Mother Courage*. At least I saw the castle; but through a curtain of rain it fell far short of the photographs which had built up my expectations in England.

Beyond Ružomberok the road drops right down by the river, which in turn soon opens up into a lake, at the eastern end of which Liptovský-Mikulás lies. This is an attractive little town surrounded by mountains. I trekked through the streets in the rain and checked into the third hotel I tried. My room overlooked the Váh, and as I changed I watched a shepherd driving his small flock home along the track by its bank. The journey of some 180 kilometres had taken well over six hours, and I was in need of *slivovice*.

Drinking here can be quite an uninhibited matter. In the restaurant, where I had been lucky enough to get chicken (though admittedly wrapped in ham and cheese, so the escape from pork wasn't total), I watched a middle-aged woman in a 'Roller Disco' T-shirt dining with her husband on kebabs and dumplings as she drank beers washed down with peach brandy chasers. I stayed with beer and enjoyed dinner, despite being joined by a miserable man in a brown suit with a faded apricot shirt done up to the neck but with no tie. (Incidentally, this mode of dress, often associated with east Europeans, seems to be on the wane: these days men wear ties, or open-necked shirts.) My dining companion took a cool hour to demolish one tiny braised steak, which he paid for in crumpled vouchers. My attempts at conversation in fractured Czech drew nothing but a quarter-smile and an averted look. The waitresses, in their universal uniform of black dress, ankle-socks and white heel-less boots, have especially good deportment here. When I complimented mine on hers, she gave me a grin and said, 'It's because of all these bloody hills.'

The next day ushered in more unremitting rain, but as I drove past Poprad, and Kežmarok, with its eighteenth-century wooden church, and up into the High Tatras, I was impressed and gladdened above all by the emptiness of the hills. I began to climb out of the rain, and after driving through several villages battened down against the weather I arrived at Stará Lubovnă, a larger village now overtaken by industrial environs but having above it a massive and practical castle. Nearby is an open-air museum of village architecture, featuring the various styles of wooden house, with blue caulking between the planks, which can be seen in the villages around but not as easily visited, and a wooden church of the kind you can also find in the tiny hamlets of this region. This particular church is nineteenth-century, though you would think it much older. Here for the first and only time I met a package group of fellow Englishmen. They were wrapped in a variety of pacamacs and we had a brief and comfortable commiseration about the weather.

I kept on the lonely little road east, passing the ruined castle of Plaveč, of which only one wall remains, all but straddling the road on its isolated rock, and headed for Bardejov, where I hoped to spend the night. On the map, the road looks remote but in fact it is dotted with huge factories and hydro-electric power stations which rise out of nowhere. It is criss-crossed by a dense forest of pylons.

Bardejov is another town with a pretty centre surrounded by a modern ring, and in this case also by an outer ring of the most dismal and forlorn building sites. As it has a one-way system which seems to have been devised as a Mensa test, and as by now it was once more raining with a vengeance, I did not get the impression the town deserves, for its square is dominated by a beautiful medieval church and Town Hall. It was all I could do to find a place to park legally; several people whom I asked for the town centre had simply smiled and said, 'You can't get there from here.'

The only hotel in town was full, and the posh one just outside charged dotty prices. Deciding that Bardejov would have to wait for a return visit, but not sorry to say goodbye to its outskirts, I headed south towards Prešov, in the Šariš region of the Tatras, and a centre of Czechoslovakia's Ukrainian population.

Prešov is the kind of town one might normally drive past. I had the usual difficulty in finding the centre and ended up in a remote suburb before I could find anyone to ask for directions. One of the two men I met took pity on me, got into the car, and conducted me to one of the two hotels, designed for itinerant businessmen rather than tourists, for Prešov is a working city. As we drove he told me that he had once taken driving lessons but never bothered to pass his test because the waiting list for a car was so long. When his turn came he was caught on the hop, and had to surrender his place. I wanted to thank him and buy him a drink when we arrived, but he smiled, shook my hand briefly, and vanished into the rain.

A short walk from the broad, Stalinist piazza on which the hotel stood took me to the elliptical Old Town square, lined with Renaissance and Baroque merchants' houses, now mainly shops and flats, and having at its centre the large cream late Gothic cathedral of St Nicholas, the Renaissance Evangelical church, and the Baroque Uniat (Greek Catholic) church. Inside the Uniat church, which was packed to the doors although this was an early-evening service on a weekday, I noticed queues for the confessionals. The church's interior contains an iconostasis, and in plan is barely distinguishable from an Orthodox church, nor does the service differ greatly, for although the Uniat Church acknowledges the Pope it retains its own structure and liturgy, and its priests are allowed to marry.

People in East Germany and Czechoslovakia stare. It isn't a rude stare; it's unselfconscious and frankly curious, but I couldn't ever fathom the reason why I attracted it. It was far less apparent in the other countries I visited, except Albania where circumstances were rather different. It couldn't have been my beard, for beards weren't unusual, nor, I am sure, could it have been my clothes. Apart from an expensive anorak, I was dressed in the jeans, pullover and shirt outfit worn by nearly every man who wasn't in a suit. The stares were the more disconcerting as they were never a prelude to conversation.

One of the hardest things about travelling so close to home is that one *doesn't* look too obviously different from the local people, and thus in general one has to send out some other signal if one wants to stimulate talk. I used to put a guide-book or an English novel by my place at table, and that usually had the desired effect. Nowhere did I ever find the slightest trace of resentment at my being a westerner, and curiosity focused on my material status, never on life in general in what to them is a more foreign half of Europe than theirs is to us.

The plumbing in my room spent the night doing impressions of the last moments of the *Titanic*. In the morning I unglued my eyes and set off to find a bookshop, which actually produced a map of Košice, my next stop, and the last town in Czechoslovakia in which I would be staying. Every town abounds in bookshops, though stocks are limited in variety, the bulk of the books being technical works. Foreign-language editions are predominantly in Russian, and there is always a great number of Russian children's books.

I'd awoken to feel sunshine on my face, and although it was still early I saw that the streets were virtually dry already. The road to Košice lay due south, but I was making a detour west to Levoča, once a rich city on the Baltic to Black Sea trade route. The road runs through a fertile plain which lies between two mountain ranges, and in the middle of it, halfway between Prešov and Levoča, on the only hill that rears above the plain, is Spišský Castle. Originally built in 1209, and a ruin between the time of its destruction by fire in 1780 and recent reconstruction, the castle is the most imposing in Slovakia. Visible for miles, it is as positive a symbol of dominance as any Egyptian monument, rising from the calcite rock on which it stands (in August ablaze with cornflowers) as if the rock had given it birth. Painstaking work has restored its former glory without depriving it of its atmosphere. There is a superb museum.

Levoča lies in gentle countryside just to the east of Poprad. Once, as Leutschau, it was a German settlement, but the war changed that and now the only evidence of German influence is in the architecture and layout of the town, though its long rectangular main square, with Renaissance houses covered in graffito decoration, is purely Slovak. The town is dominated by the spire of the fourteenth-century St James's Church, and although the official brochures and maps, here as elsewhere, doggedly refuse to mention places of worship, this was recently the site of a pilgrimage of more than 100,000 Czech Catholics. Such demonstrations have alarmed the authorities, since pressure to worship freely may be construed as the forerunner of pressure for greater freedoms still. Nevertheless, the churches are open, and always full. Levoča is also the scene of much building activity, but this is mainly concerned with restoration, for the town is almost unique in having no grey, modern second city. It is still bounded by its extensive medieval (and very Germanic) town walls.

Sharing the centre of the square with St James's is a Renaissance Town Hall, the first floor of which is a provincial museum, while at one end of it stands a domed 'cage of shame' – a large birdcage which served the purpose of a pillory for minor malefactors in the seventeenth century. But it is the church one remembers, and that not so much for its architecture as its furniture, for it contains a fine collection of carved wooden Gothic altars. Five of them are by the late medieval Slovak master, Paul (Pavel) of Levoča, and the main altar is his masterpiece. It is the largest wooden

altar in the world, at over eighteen metres by six, and features three larger-than-life
figures, St James the Greater and St John flanking the Virgin. Beneath them, on a far
smaller scale, the Last Supper is depicted in the predella. The disciples (presumably
apart from Judas) are portrait figures of local merchants who were Paul's contemporaries. Paul is a master to stand with Adam Kraft and Veit Stoss, and his approach to
physiognomy is as individual and instantly recognizable as Tiepolo's – in his case
the hallmarks are narrow eyes set wide apart in broad faces; and his command of
facial expression is daunting in its immediacy: it is quite a shock to see such realism
in a Gothic artist. That his work has survived so many centuries is a miracle, but the
altarpiece could not withstand the ravages of woodworm, and its restoration by the
brothers Kotrba in the early Fifties is also miraculous, not least because it was
undertaken at the height of the Cold War and Russian dominance; but Czechoslovakia has never been a country to neglect its national heritage.

I didn't want to take main roads to Košice, so I set off south-east from Levoča,
aiming for Krompachy in the centre of the Slovakian Erzgebirg. I'd seen plenty of
brown-and-white cows in the fields, and occasionally whole armies of geese, but few
people. This beautiful area seems devoid of tourists, and its isolation appealed to me.
But I thought I knew better than my map, and set off on an even smaller road than
the one I'd intended to take. It climbed further and further into hills which were
lower than the Tatras, but darker, denser, and more wild. For a time the road
followed a valley carved by a little river, along whose banks the occasional vast,
rusting metal hulk of a factory would appear.

The villages that straggled along the road were sharply divided in their populations. There were the Slovaks, and alongside them a smaller, darker race, wholly
eastern, often Indian or North African in appearance, with gold rings and gay
clothes. These were Gypsies, who live in this area in great numbers. Although it
wasn't evident in the villages, in Košice I learned of considerable and growing racial
tension between the groups.

The road was getting narrower and even emptier. But I passed wagons drawn by
horses like Suffolk Punches, the occasional truck and even a bus, so I assumed that I
must be going somewhere. I wasn't. I ended up in a tiny mountain village, where the
road gave up all pretence and became a rutted track, which debouched at a
rubbish-littered clearing near yet another of those mysterious, gargantuan factories.

There was nothing for it but to backtrack. I had noticed the curious and not
entirely friendly stares levelled at me by pedestrians as I drove through the village,
and now saw that clusters of them were gathering in the fading light at the corners of
the clearing. They all looked alike; stony expressions and silence greeted my smile
and stumbled explanation that I'd got lost. I turned the car round, eager to be off, and
the engine shuddered and died.

I turned the key, but there was nothing. This was a bad moment. I had erred by
fifty kilometres and would not, unless I got my skates on, arrive in Košice before
dark, with the risk of losing my room reservation. I sat in the car and smiled at the
villagers, who did not smile back but moved closer. I forced myself to consider what
might be wrong with ADA. Too hot? Flooded? I checked that all the doors were
locked and the windows wound up. I kept mine open a little.

Something distracted the villagers from me for a moment. It was the arrival of a large, elderly woman, leaning heavily on a stick and flanked by two other women who may have been daughters but who had the bearing of acolytes. Their clothes were gaudy with clashing patterns, and their headscarves were weighted with coins. The woman approached the car directly. She looked stern. She tapped the car with her stick. I had no idea what this was a prelude to, nor in what language we might communicate – if we communicated at all.

'No function?' she said in German, her expression unchanging.

'No,' I replied.

'Who are you? What are you doing here?'

'I'm an English tourist, and I'm lost.' I tried a grin again, but it must have looked sickly.

Her expression cleared like the sun rising behind mountains. The first to notice were the two girls, who immediately sent me timid smiles. Then the old woman threw back her head and laughed, showing me a solid gold mouth. The villagers reacted to this indecisively for a moment, and then, the change hitting me like a breeze, they relaxed. Smiles appeared, they came forward.

'Where are you going?'

'Košice.'

'Will you eat first?'

'I must be there by nightfall.'

'Then we will get you on your way.' She signalled to a couple of men, and five came forward. But the road lay uphill out of the village and it was pitted and uneven. Any kind of bump-start would be difficult. I said I would try the motor once more. It started first go.

They cheered me on my way. I reached the real road to Krompachy soon after, and then drove directly through forests up and over the dark mountains, and down the other side to my destination.

Košice is the second principal town of Slovakia, and rank upon rank of high-rise suburbs surround its centre, not far from the little River Hornád. In plan it has the usual elongated main square (here called Leninova), with, at its centre, the black Gothic cathedral church of St Elizabeth. Its high altar rivals that of Levoča, though little of it was visible as it was under restoration. Delicate wooden statues of saints preside over the church just inside its doors, and in the gloom the vaulting loses itself in darkness. Just beyond St Elizabeth's, the neo-Baroque theatre (it could perhaps be yet another by Helmer and Fellner) was in a sorry state, surrounded by corrugated iron fencing; but energetic restoration seemed to be going on. Beyond it was an ominously cleared building site. I doubt if it will become an extension of the delightful little park which separates the theatre from the cathedral.

Mastering the one-way system with the aid of my map, I parked in Osloboditel'ov Square, a large open space given over to cars, on whose fringes Gypsies gathered in the dusk, and walked over to the soaring slab of concrete which is the Hotel Slovan, terminating Leninova. The hotel, which more than lives up to its reputation for poor food (except for superb chocolate pancakes – and one tended to draw the line at *rosbif anglicky*), was offering a twenty per cent discount because the hot water had been cut off for a few days.

My first job was to visit Čedok, the national tourist office next door. I queued here for only forty-five minutes for my train ticket across the frontier to Debrecen in Hungary; since I was a westerner I was obliged to pay in hard currency. This enabled me, through the kindness of the booking clerk, to skip the cashier's queue and the queue to collect the ticket, but the special treatment caused many heads to turn enviously and a little critically in my direction. I could feel waves of disapproval from a large Russian redhead next in line behind me. I left and performed my second task, which was to deliver ADA to the Pragocar office, and bid her a fond farewell. She had been a true friend.

Off Leninova, the streets of Košice are quiet and sleepy, where there are no building sites and roadworks. Turning right past the Tuzex hard currency shop and up along back-streets beyond it, I came across the synagogue, closed, crumbling, and long abandoned. This was one more sad reminder of the culture-within-a-culture which has vanished in central Europe.

At the other end of Leninova, Maratónu-mieru Square is flanked by imposing twin Victorian buildings, recalling the powerful imperial administration that stretched this far within living memory. One of them is now the town museum, which I entered without much conviction. Donning the outsize felt slippers, I paid and made my way round, followed by an attendant who switched lights on in the rooms in front of me and off behind me. The building was more interesting than the exhibits, which were eclectic and featured everything from a stuffed boar to the usual bits and pieces of Beaker and Roman pottery, and a splendid Gatling gun; but the displays were new, well designed and excellently laid out. I teamed up with a pair of Hungarian girls who were waiting for a sufficiently large 'group' to form to enable them to visit the museum's treasury in the basement. My presence created the necessary quorum, and off we went, to the delight of an elderly attendant who had been pressing me to 'see the gold'.

We went in through a massive safe door, and were confronted with a huge exhibition of gold coins, mainly sixteenth-century, which had been discovered recently – part of a forgotten hoard. Rooms opened out endlessly, and the coins gave way to jewel-encrusted crucifixes, altar candlesticks and chalices, and then to jewellery – emerald hat-pins, platinum cigarette cases inlaid with diamonds, as well as brooches and earrings, some late enough to be Art Deco, which had clearly belonged to the deposed and dispossessed aristocracy.

The girls were both science students – one of maths and the other of physics – and lived in Győr and Mosonmagyaróvar respectively. Sára, the mathematician, spoke fluent English and Russian. They were here with friends on a camping trip, and had been washed out completely by the recent storms.

'We're down to our last pair of jeans; but we're going home this afternoon. The coach is picking us up at four.'

It isn't too difficult for Hungarians to travel, even to the West if they have the means, and after I had crossed the border I was struck immediately by the signs in travel agents' windows advertising holidays in Spain, Italy, and even India and Thailand. 'The Czechs think we're rather frivolous, but it's less easy for them – even to come to visit us,' said Sára.

These two were fashionably dressed, less self-consciously than the Czechs, and in a more western style. They were more relaxed, too.

'What will you do after university?'

'Teach, if we get good enough grades. It'll mean one more year's study, but there are still plenty of openings for teachers.'

We left the museum and wandered back down Leninova. When we parted they recommended another museum set in the town walls. 'It's really creepy though – they have torture chambers in the cellars. There was no one around, so we put on manacles and climbed onto the stocks and took photos of each other – it was a gas!'

The museum is innocent enough in its upper chambers – the rooms, which appear to belong to an ordinary fifteenth- or sixteenth-century house, exhibit pikes and swords of the period, as well as contemporary maps and prints of the town, together with an assortment of legal documents. Outside, there is a minute walled garden tangled with ceanothus. But once you descend an unspectacular staircase which might lead to a coal cellar, you are in a different world. The dungeons run out in all directions, dark and dank as they must always have been. Along the corridors lie tin lids containing rat poison, which oddly intensifies the atmosphere, despite the sparing but reassuring electric lights. Two central chambers contain strappado pulleys, benches with leather thongs to which victims were attached before being beaten, manacles, thumbscrews, and racks. Large reproductions of medieval prints graphically show the use to which these instruments were put. Tongs seem to have had particularly revolting applications.

To rid myself of the taste of this place, I went to the museum of cannon- and bell-founding, a craft for which the region is famous. The museum is in the tower which is all that remains of a former church near St Elizabeth's. I was hoping for a view over the town, but the windows were tightly closed and too dirty to see through. Only the polychrome tiled roof of the cathedral next door was clearly visible.

As I left, the girl who'd sold me my ticket asked me where I was from. When I told her, she switched to good English, which I complimented her on, regretting my basic, stumbling Czech.

'But why would you speak Czech? What use would it be to you?'

'I could talk to you properly in your own language.'

'But I want to speak to you in English. How often do you think I get an opportunity to practise? Some of my friends speak it, and we talk together, but then we don't know if we're going wrong, or how to correct it.'

She was just coming off duty and we sat and talked in the little park outside for half an hour. It was a good way to say goodbye to Czechoslovakia, but as I saw another potential friendship forming, I was sorry that I had to move on.

'It's not even very easy to get English books to read. I'm really scared that without practice I'll never improve.' She looked at me hopefully. A dark girl with long legs and large eyes. Brown hair which was almost black framed her face, the ends almost meeting under her small, firm chin.

I wished that there was a way in which I could respond as she wanted me to; but she was asking for more than a few hours' conversation. She was asking for me, or rather, what she thought I represented, and it would have been wrong to fob her off with a ghost when I could not give substance, or to start something which even had I been free could have gone nowhere.

'I have to leave tomorrow,' I said.

Her eyes widened as the words caught on her heart, and then she lowered them.

I was waiting for a train again. It was early in the morning, too early, and the only other people in the great grey box of the station concourse were a group of gangly Russian soldiers in their early twenties, who looked far too young for their jackboots and the peaked caps with enormous crowns. I was tired, and I was sad to be leaving; the combined effect was to make me irritable.

The train was about fifty minutes late. I sat in a compartment with a man and his son. The man told me he'd been down to the frontier the previous day to buy Hungarian currency, only to be told after an hour's wait that he had to purchase them in Košice after all. The bureaucracy is not selective, not designed merely to ensnare and bewilder westerners. In this case it was working for me, since I was under no obligation to change money into forints before crossing the border; Hungary imposes no such condition on visiting westerners.

At Čana, the Czech passport officials were polite, but it was 7 a.m. and the storm which had been brewing again since six had broken. The men smelt of coffee and damp, and the first cigarette of the day. They had been preceded by Customs, in the shape of a pallid man who clearly wished he was in bed and a vigorous blonde of about forty-five, who decided to give me the treatment. She had all the contents of both my bags out and scattered around the compartment, looking through every notebook and even opening the packets of aspirin in my sponge-bag. Finally she seized on my £16 Sony radio and shouted that it wasn't listed on my 'statistics' form, which she had perused with the thoroughness of a German tax inspector. I explained that no one had asked me to declare it, but as Customs officials all seem to be (perhaps intentionally) monoglot, I could not reach her. She continued to shout until I produced the receipt from the shop where I'd bought it in London. I don't know what it meant to her, as she couldn't read English, but she calmed down, and even let me keep everything.

While all this was going on, two troop-trains full of soldiers passed us, headed north. Once Customs had finished with me, I asked my neighbour if they were Russians.

'Yes, alas,' he said. 'They've been with us in strength since 1968, and by the look of things we're saddled with them for a good time to come. Sorry about that cow, by the way. They like to throw their weight around sometimes.'

His son was about twelve, and we managed a few shy words; but he enjoyed looking at the collection of visas in my passport and my handful of western currency notes. By the time we'd discussed them, two men in green uniforms had arrived.

'Got a camera?' one of them asked me in English, once he'd established my nationality. I showed him my battered Yashica, its case held together with tape. He waved at the window. Beyond it the rain lashed down on grey anonymity. 'No photos here,' he said. Seeing my expression he added: 'Of the frontier,' and, acknowledging the ludicrousness of the order, given the conditions, he grinned.

I was in Hungary.

14

A TOWN ON THE PLAIN

The train continued more or less due south through unabated rain to Miskolc, an industrial town which is Hungary's second city. Here it stopped to let the majority of its passengers off before turning east. We then travelled across a dull plain covered with fields of sunflowers which hung their sodden heads; but soon after Taktaharkány small hills began to rise on either side of the track, and despite the continuous downpour the countryside held a promise of beauty as we approached Tokaj, on the River Tisza. This small, unpretentious town, hardly more than a village, lies at the centre of one of the most famous wine-producing regions in the world. No one has ever been able to reproduce Tokay, the rich, heavy wine best known to us in its sweet form, Aszubor, but also available as the dry Szamorodni, which is drunk as an aperitif and is not unlike sherry.

Trains become slower the further south-east you progress. We finally arrived in Debrecen about midday. Walking north from the station across Petőfi Square, along Hunyadi útja and thence up the main street, Vörös Hadsereg útja (Red Army Road), one notices immediately the depredations concrete- and glass-boxes erected in the mid-Sixties and Seventies have made on the original architecture – refined Baroque, and austere, solid nineteenth-century buildings. Some attempt has been made to redress the balance near the Great Church by building a new complex just to the south-east of it in a style far more sympathetic to the town's original plan, but as the architect has now given up his profession to become a radio journalist one can only hope that others will follow the example of his design.

What other first impressions? That there are more shops than in Czechoslovakia; that there are more smaller shops, too, and more variety and greater quantity in them. There are no queues. Private enterprise manifests itself even more obviously in the melon sellers, whose huge piles of green globes invade the pavement every twenty or thirty metres. In the newsagents' kiosks there are girlie magazines and pictures of Garfield, the Smurfs, Samantha Fox, Michael Jackson and Bruce Springsteen. For a country which has produced some of the world's greatest post-war film directors, the cinemas were incongruously showing *Where Eagles Dare* and *The Bridge on the River Kwai*. The cigarette everyone smokes is Marlboro, made here under licence. On television, there are advertisements; and the Hungarians produce their own pop videos. Though these still have some way to go before they achieve the polish of, say, *Thriller*, they have much more innocence and charm; singers still smile, and flirt with the camera.

On the roads, there are Shell petrol stations – a brand-name coming as a shock. You could almost be in the West, and the strongest impression of all is that Hungary would dearly love to rejoin it. The then Prime Minister, Karoly Grosz, faced with making something of a near-ruined economy (Hungary has a greater foreign debt than any other east European power), had already said that it would be impossible for him ever to be remembered as a popular leader, but he seemed bullish. He was an admirer of British economic policies in the late Eighties, before they faltered. Faced with high inflation and unemployment, he had to take unpopular measures, such as cutting back subsidy to such areas as the steel industry, Russian-inspired years ago and never suitable for Hungary with its lack of raw material resources.

Hungary is the first Eastern Bloc country to have to deal with unemployment, and has introduced limited unemployment benefit, as well as income tax and VAT. Unemployment, especially in the industrial north-east, is expected to rise drastically.

'Everyone knew the steel industry here was a non-starter from the beginning; but we did as we were told, we had no choice. Let's hope it's not too late to salvage something from the wreck,' a dentist I met in Budapest told me later. 'But at least Russia won't squash us again – things have moved a long way since 1956, and even since 1968 – the USSR has so many troubles of its own, it'd be only too glad to get rid of us, except as a defence buffer.'

I stayed at the Aranybika – the Golden Bull – an Art Nouveau building of enormous charm, despite ruthless renovation in the Seventies whose legacy is a lot of unpleasant stained glass. But the central hall is magnificent, with high Moorish arches and sensual statuary, marred only by a horrid modern bar in one corner. However, this serves excellent *barack palinta*, which is the delicious apricot schnapps of Hungary, and by its entrance stands a glass case with photographs commemorating the man who founded the hotel, Bojás Alfred (Hungarians put their surname first), who also won enough medals for swimming at the 1896 Montreal Olympics to cover his chest. His serious, thin, moustachioed face stares out at you full of nineteenth-century confidence and pride.

I met two Finnish tourists in the bar, who told me they'd come here in search of cultural connections between their country and Hungary. Finns and Hungarians may share the same forefathers from the time of the great westward migrations of the Dark Ages; their otherwise isolated languages and mythologies have many elements in common.

There are two restaurants in the hotel. The large one used to have a Gypsy orchestra, and may still have, for it is mentioned in the brochure; but while I was there all that occupied the central podium were the instruments that go with a four-man band, and they were never used. Instead, there was piped muzak, and for this reason I used the corner restaurant, which is much smaller, has no music, and serves excellent food. At one end there is a counter from which cakes are sold – Hungarians are positively Austrian in their affection for extravagant gâteaux – and at lunchtimes a constant stream of people, already bursting out of skirts or trousers, would come in and buy a chocolate cake or a *dobostorta* and eat it hastily from a little cardboard tray with a wooden fork, drinking nothing, before continuing on their way.

I was joined at my table by two men, the older earnest, the younger drunk (but never losing the friendliness and courtesy that Hungarians are born with). They deferred slightly to my silent company and when the drinks arrived we toasted each other. The old man switched to German and explained to me that he collected antique postcards (which have to be at least eighty years old to qualify). The young man was a dealer, and had a rare 1902 card to sell, which was postmarked Klausenburg 18 August despatched, and Paris 21 August received; but the price was far too high. The old man further explained that he lived in Vienna, where he'd been born in 1908, but as he was now retired he came here for three months or so every year – it was cheap, he liked the country, and as a born Austro-Hungarian he had grown up speaking both languages. He told me how, as a young man, he had driven with a friend from Budapest across the Great Plain, the *puszta*, in an Adler to visit a cousin. 'We were royally entertained then – we thought the first course was the main dish, but then came the paprika chicken. I remember my friend telling me on the way back to Budapest, "It's good to see that they still know how to entertain properly in the country."'

They resumed their conversation, which I realized by now was restricted to hard bargaining. The old man had even stopped eating his *székelgulyás*, so I knew things were getting serious.

The rain continued to fall as I went for a walk. I found a memorial to the fallen of the First World War, a pillar surrounded by Austro-Hungarian soldiers in *Stahlhelm* and *Stachelhelm* and surmounted by an imperial eagle. It was curiously moving.

My room was equipped with a sofa-bed which was about as comfortable as a park bench, but I was compensated for this by a view across Kossuth tér to the Great Church. Debrecen is a Calvinist town, and this mighty, uncompromising building was erected in the nineteenth century. Its interior is more like a parliament than a church, with three broad white aisles leading off at right angles to each other from the central pulpit. In fact it was used as a political meeting-place, and it was from here that the nineteenth-century revolutionary nationalist, Lajos Kossuth, declared Hungarian independence from the Habsburgs. The plain wooden chair he used on that occasion is preserved *in situ*, commemorated in the Hungarian style with a small wreath.

The building is in some contrast to the delicate Baroque St Anna's, the Roman Catholic church. Roman Catholicism was forbidden here for two centuries, and the church was built after its reinstitution. It is as gentle as the Great Church is severe, and it is high and quiet. Near the church, the theatre has a fine façade topped by statues of what, I swear, are hermaphrodites with beards.

Breakfast came as a shock. The hotel had been invaded by a small army of elderly West German package tourists. Because of a reasonable rate of exchange and the (to us) low cost of living in Hungary, the country is popular with westerners, and Austrians, who no longer require a visa, flood over the frontier to shop cheaply. I waited for the mob to subside and then went to the buffet to help myself to delicious, fatty *Debreziner* sausages. I still hadn't escaped pork in one form or another, but it occurred to me that I had not seen any pigs anywhere. However, in Hungary I was occasionally to pass lorryloads of the anxious-looking creatures. From the road I also saw battalions of geese frequently ranging across the fields, though never once was goose available in a restaurant.

To the north of the town lies the Nagyerdő. The word means 'great forest' (Hungarian shares with German the tendency to create compound words), which is something of an exaggeration; but this pleasant park contains a modest zoo, one of the almost-silent fairgrounds eastern Europe seems to specialize in, various sports facilities and stadia, and the university, where I had a date.

Apart from the fact that he wore a white cotton coat rather than a black gown, my friend the professor was every inch an academic. This was the university he had attended as a student, and he was proud of it, especially as the Humanities were housed in the best building – a neo-Classical block constructed in the Thirties. In its high, galleried main hall a competition was in progress involving ultra-light model aeroplanes made only of cellophane and slivers of balsa-wood, more delicate than butterflies. The little machines drifted aimlessly around the atrium in an atmosphere of profound seriousness.

'From my office there used to be a splendid view over an old quarter of town, but they pulled it down in the Sixties to build apartment blocks. A great shame. I think everyone regrets it now, but then the thinking was that everything old was automatically bad, and everything new, good.'

The science block is a modern cube, mitigated by tall trees nearby and marble facing. Across from it are student hostels – 'They sleep in dormitories. It's cheap, but of course most of them prefer privacy, and those who can afford it rent rooms for themselves in the town.' Nearby, the university church has been converted into a computer studies centre. That is something else one sees again in Hungary – the computer. When I add up the amount of time in queues which computers in booking offices might have saved me, and consider the poor clerks ploughing through piles of paperwork, equipped with pencils and ancient typewriters, I realize that I will never take those machines for granted again.

We returned to the professor's office after my conducted tour, and drank brandy and smoked cigarettes. Like many Hungarians, he is not convinced that his country will emerge from its economic difficulties for a very long time, but he is sure that the battle will be won. A large photograph of Karoly Grosz hangs on his wall; I was struck by it because it was the only one I saw. I realized that in none of the countries I had visited so far were there many portrait photographs of the head of state. I had seen none in East Germany or Poland. The same would be true of Bulgaria. Only in Romania is the case different, and in Albania and Yugoslavia the recently-deceased hero-leaders Hoxha and Tito maintain a high popular profile.

At parting, the professor invited me to look him up at his holiday bungalow by Lake Balaton, where he would be by the time I reached the area. My own route lay first towards Hortobágy, because I felt that I really ought to look at the *puszta*. I already knew from previous journeys in southern Hungary, and Voivodina across the border in northern Yugoslavia, what these vast, flat expanses were like; but since the *puszta* is a principal feature of Hungary, covering most of its south-eastern half, it would have been difficult to ignore.

The train journey was short and dull. The plain begins soon after Debrecen is left behind, and the line passes through a series of minute stations, at each of which a brief stop is made. Much of this part of the plain has been developed as farmland, and it is not until you get to the village of Hortobágy and beyond that you see something of it as it was, though the village itself is an uninspiring place, whose main square is given over to catering for the busloads of tourists who are deposited for an afternoon's 'experience' of the *puszta*.

I was staying not at the *csárda* in the village, but at an inn two kilometres up the road out of town. This was a simple place, but it had two essentials: effective mosquito netting and bicycles for hire. I was given a heavy red monster with an immovable saddle far too high for me, and set off shakily back to the village. Then I wobbled off along the road that led into the greyish flat expanse of grassland.

People use the word 'flat' loosely of countryside to denote 'not hilly', but the *puszta* is really flat. No croquet player could ever ask for more perfect ground to play on, and I wonder if the Hungarians will not one day think of turning parts of it over to football pitches and tennis courts. Nothing interrupts the plain, except for the occasional cattle shed or shepherd's hut, eaves reaching the ground and roof turfed in the same way as Icelandic nineteenth-century buildings – another place where native architecture reflects the need for protection against the elements where none is provided by nature. At intervals, lever-wells stand stark as gibbets.

The traditional occupations of the *puszta* have been horse- and cattle-breeding, along with the keeping of spiral-horned *racka* sheep, solid animals with cream or black shaggy fleece which are well adapted to survive on the meagre grass. The grey long-horned cattle are still bred, too, but they are no longer as important as they were for the quality of their meat and their usefulness as draught-animals. In this area the traditional *puszta* occupation which is still seriously pursued is horse-breeding. The Nonius, originally a workhorse, is now bred for show-jumping and has international status. The Duke of Edinburgh recently came to the village of Máta to buy stock.

There is almost no rainfall here, but the recent storms had turned some of the unmade roads into morasses. I decided to ride as far as I could. The bike promptly sank a good six inches into greenish, pungent mud, tilted, and deposited me in it.

Once I'd cleaned up as best I could with clumps of grass, I retreated to tarmac and reconsidered. I was not a good enough rider to be allowed out onto the plain on a hired horse, even with a guide. The only other possibility was to join a group in a covered wagon. We ended up a caravan of five wagons, three of which were loaded with unremittingly jolly, singing Germans from a coach. We were trotted out a few kilometres to see a flock of *racka*, and then a little further to a large herd of cattle.

Here I managed to get away from my own herd for a while. The cows look larger than they are because of their stone grey colour and their enormous horns. They are the gentlest creatures; even those with calves were unperturbed if you walked right up to them. Their principal interest in life appears to be sleep, and this gives them an enormous dignity. Two cowherds were standing by a hut not far off, surrounded by half-a-dozen villainous-looking *pumi* dogs, like shaggy black four-legged devils. These were well used to strangers, however, for they came over to be patted. The cowherds were dressed in the traditional high-necked long black waistcoat with silver buttons. With their black hats which are not unlike tricorns, they looked like a pair of down-at-heel eighteenth-century gentlemen-adventurers, but this is not a costume they put on for the tourists. They succumbed to the snapping cameras with the weary aplomb of guardsmen outside Windsor Castle.

The stars of the *puszta* are the *csikós*, the horseherds. *Csikós* do not wear the Balkan handlebar moustache, which in this area begins to adorn most male faces. As skilful horsemen as the Mongols, they use a conventional bridle and bit, but the red leather saddle is minute and has no girth: it just sits on the horse's back. The *csikós'* costume is also striking. There are no trees on the *puszta*, and consequently no shade. The clothing takes this into account, and also the extremes of temperature. It is made of a thick blue cotton cloth like denim, and consists of a shirt and trousers. What distinguishes it is that shirtsleeves and trouserlegs are enormously wide, giving maximum ventilation. They also wear a tight black waistcoat and a tricorn hat with a high raised brim, and carry slung over one shoulder a long whip with a decorated handle. The cracking of this whip enables them to herd their horses. *Csikós* still do a serious job, and are not just a handful of men in fancy dress putting on a show for the tourists (though they do that too). Most of those I came into contact with were middle-aged, though there were two or three in their early twenties, already acquiring the walnut skin that life in this open, wind-scoured place gives you.

'I do this because I was born to it, and because I love the *puszta*,' István, one of the young ones, said to me. 'You find that with most people, the plain gets on their nerves after a short while – they can't stand the monotony of it. But they are never here long enough to see what lies behind. In reality, it isn't monotonous at all. Many of the people I grew up with have gone to work in Miskolc and Debrecen. One has just lost his job, and he says he might come back here. But this isn't an expanding business.'

What István had said made me open my eyes. The plain is a great nature reserve, attracting and maintaining life which elsewhere is rare or non-existent. Scudding barely above the ground, little birds fly – you can see ringed plovers and stone curlews by the cart-tracks, and in the taller grass godwit and redshank nest. Storks and tern are common, and one early morning I saw a spoonbill emerging from the reeds by a tractor-track near my lodging. To my regret I saw no eagles, only buzzards, and once, I think, an osprey. I also saw an otter flash wet in the sun for a moment before splashing back into the marsh, but the fox and the wolf remain far deeper in the *puszta* than I was able to penetrate. If I were ever to return, it would be in the spring, for the plants suggest a display of wildflowers then which must be unrivalled in Europe. Despite the pollution generated by industry and towns, and a tendency to prairie farming, one still sees more wild flora along the roads and in the hedges of eastern Europe than we have experienced in the West for twenty years.

After a breakfast of buttery omelette washed down with (of all things in this country of good coffee) Gold Blend, I loaded my bag on my back and set off early for the station. The sun beat down hard from 9 a.m. and I did not care for the thought of the two-kilometre walk. Trains here run on time, and after my hour of happily empty-headed waiting in the sun, chatting as best I could to a wizened old man half-hidden behind his moustache and pipe and dressed in a Norfolk jacket and plus-fours, I boarded the 11.01 for Füzesabony, en route for Eger.

Lajos was on his way to Eger too, to complete his military service. He had been able to break the eighteen months into two parts on account of a business studies course and now, employed by a soap company to explore western market possibilities, he was returning to the army for six months. He wasn't looking forward to it, and he hadn't liked saying goodbye to his wife, to whom he'd only just been married. 'But it's not too bad. I'll get some sort of job instructing the rookies, and I can go home every other weekend.'

He was born in Debrecen, which he referred to deprecatingly in perfect English as 'rather a cow town'. 'But I've got my eye on Budapest.' He was sanguine about his chances of getting a flat without too long a wait, since flats can be awarded according to educational status. Lajos had been to university and passed with honours in business studies. He was not boastful, just matter-of-fact and practical. 'Normally, there's a four- to five-year wait for a flat; of course it's also possible to buy, but they are prohibitively expensive, although you can apply for a mortgage to the state bank.'

I asked him where he had learned his English. 'At school.'

'What about Russian?'

'I speak a little, but there's no point in learning it for me, and it's no longer an obligatory second language. We're learning English, French and German these days, and some Japanese. Far more useful for the future,' he smiled.

He told me that commercial administration was divided into a department for internal and eastern trade, and another for western trade, and explained why this was cumbersome and mistaken. For him the greatest worry in Hungary at the moment was that people would lose faith in Karoly Grosz because of his unpopular but necessary economic measures. It would be a disaster for the country if those in the parliament who saw the present crisis as a direct result of flirting with the West, and the only cure for it a return to fundamental, hard-line Communism ('By which they mean going back to Brezhnev rather than Marx'), were to gain the upper hand. 'Our problems now are the problems of the West – inflation and unemployment; and the answers must be found in the West, too.' Events in the months that have passed between our conversation and my writing this have gone some way to allay his anxiety. In June 1989, the Hungarians were already considering replacing the red star with the crown of Saint Stephen as the national emblem.

At the time of our conversation, basic aid was being given to the unemployed to tide them over for six months, but since then Hungary has become the first country in the Eastern Bloc to introduce full unemployment benefit. 'To rescue the economy, support in the form of subsidy to non-paying industries is reduced or withdrawn, and more unemployment will be the result before we can right the ship,' Lajos said. 'It is unfortunate, but inevitable.'

As in Poland, all those who can supplement their incomes by taking on one or even two 'extra' jobs, usually extensions of what they do anyway. I met a university lecturer in English who taught Hungarian as a foreign language in a summer school and to private students in the evenings, an airline pilot who drove a taxi in his spare time, and a doctor who was both a senior consultant and an assessor for a life insurance company. Lajos had no second job. He was learning German. 'The tuition is costing me money,' he said. 'But I regard it as an investment for the future.'

We had to change trains at Füzesabony, and as we did so Lajos, who had never been to Eger either, pointed out a nervous-looking gaggle of youths with freshly-cropped heads.

'New recruits,' he said. 'Poor buggers.' But there was a tremor in his voice and I knew he wasn't looking forward to being back in uniform. 'It's so boring, you see. For the first three months or so you learn things, how to drill, how to strip a gun and clean it, and then maybe more useful things, like engine maintenance; but after that you repeat everything again, and so it goes on. It seems such a waste of time when one could be getting on with one's career.'

It was only a short distance up a branch line to Eger, and we parted with mutual regret. I wondered if Lajos would join the others as they marched off to a waiting bus, but he said he preferred to travel independently. We shook hands and parted. The station square didn't look very prepossessing, and my map was rudimentary, giving only the faintest clue to where I was, so I climbed on a bus which seemed to be heading for the centre. After fifteen minutes it still showed no sign of moving, and as a rare taxi hove in sight I jumped off and hailed it before anyone else could.

There were two hotels. One was a horrible concrete egg-box run by supercilious porters in headache-orange blazers. The other, round the corner but connected to the egg-box by an umbilical corridor, is old and quiet. After I'd established myself there, I set off into town. Eger is one of the prettiest places in Hungary, and since it isn't on a main railway line it has been spared much unwelcome modern development. In common with other Hungarian towns, it has few streets named after Soviet heroes and politicians, though there is a Lenin Street here which debouches into a Lenin Square, complete with another unfortunate statue of the great man. Happily one barely notices it as the eye is attracted by the yellow mountain of the basilica above and beyond it. The cathedral dates from the early nineteenth century, though there has been a church on the site since Saint Stephen founded a bishopric at Eger a thousand years ago. Inside, the church is ponderously impressive, with lots of red Hungarian marble. My visit coincided with an organ recital. Music which I did not recognize but which must have been by some strong-minded and God-fearing nineteenth-century composer thundered confidently out, loudly enough to shake the solid building and wholly in keeping with it.

Eger is formed by two squares linked by a street. The first square is dominated by the cathedral and the stately Lyceum, built a short time before the basilica and now a teacher training college. The second, Dobo tér, is dominated by the Church of St

Anthony of Padua, probably by Kilian Dietzenhofer and built around 1730. It is one of Europe's great Baroque churches. Inside, there are signs of the ravages of damp in corners, but the frescoes, depicting scenes from the life of the saint, are intact and very lovely. The exterior is impressive. On the façade, two towers rise from a bow-fronted porch supported by two massive columns. Above the door a decorated plaque gives the name of the church. I spent an hour sitting in the square below as the sun set, watching as the fading light changed the colour of the stucco.

Two uninspired statues celebrate the victory of István Dobo, the city's garrison commander who held out against a Turkish siege in 1551. The city finally fell in 1596 and remained in Turkish hands for almost a century, though here, as elsewhere in eastern Europe, few traces of the Turks' occupation remain. A solitary minaret at the intersection of some side-streets north of this square is all that remains in Eger. One of these streets leads attractively up to the castle, which nestles close to the town. Guarding it are elegant narrow-bore cannon, designed to shoot through the equally narrow gun-slits in the walls. The castle itself is fun, and gives good views of the town, but its ruins have been over-enthusiastically restored, with too liberal a use of concrete. I didn't have to pay for a ticket as the booking clerk couldn't tear himself away from a phone call for long enough to sell me one.

The Kossuth Lajos útja links the two squares. It is lined with elegant Baroque houses, especially two near the bridge over the River Eger which intersects the town, though the most outstanding is the dark-pink-fronted palace at number 4, closed for extensive renovation at the time I was there. If you don't use this route to get from square to square, the back-streets are a good alternative as they contain a number of elegant shops and restaurants. Eger seemed a kind of Hungarian Bath – more sophisticated and better-dressed than Debrecen, and within easy stabbing-distance of Budapest, while lying at the foot of the lovely deep-green Bükk Hills. One of Hungary's other great horse-breeding centres, this time for Lippizaners, is not far away, at Szilvásvárad.

But I knew none of this before I arrived. I only knew Eger as the home of 'Bull's Blood' – Egri Bikavér – the heavy dry red wine easily available in any off-licence or supermarket in Britain. Both hotels had restaurants full of packaged Germans and Austrians, but nearby I had discovered and booked a table at a cellar-restaurant called Fehérszarvas Vadásztanya. Its speciality was game.

I had been in Hungary long enough by now to have noticed that the Hungarians tip generously, and that although service will always be good it will be impeccable if you tip a little in advance. This practice not only got me a table, but to my surprise it got me a table to myself – not that I would have objected to company, but at least one couple turning up without a reservation was firmly turned away while I sat in solitary state at a table which would easily have seated four. I decided to allow myself a celebration, since earlier in the afternoon I had managed not only to hire another car but also to take delivery of it. 'Are you *sure* you want a Lada?' the hotel receptionist, who'd arranged it and acted as my interpreter, had asked with great misgiving. 'It's a *Russian* car, you know. And they could easily bring you up an Opel from Budapest.'

I started with fish soup, *halászlé*, with some cold, dry Tokay, and followed it with venison, whose obvious accompaniment was Bull's Blood. This is served here in a way I had not seen before, and which at first I wrongly assumed was a tourist gimmick. The wine is drawn from a barrel into a jug. Then the waiter takes a pot-bellied glass bottle with a mouthpiece at its base, and a narrow, two-foot-long spout. Using the mouthpiece he sucks wine from the jug into the bottle, and then spurts it through the long spout into your glass from a great height, so that it froths and foams. If this seems an odd way to treat wine, the result was delicious, served slightly warmer than room temperature, and drier and lighter than I remembered it. I rounded off this self-indulgent session with *palatsinta*, the superb Hungarian pancake adopted by the Czechs and the Austrians as well. In this case the filling was of chocolate sauce, cognac and cream, topped with chopped nuts and icing sugar. The only thing to drink with this was a 5-butt Aszú.

A bizarre scene was developing at the table to my left as a Dane from a group of compatriot bathroom equipment salesmen attempted to chat up two Swiss girls in English ('Ve leaf tomorrow,' they told him firmly), so I concentrated on the band, a clarinettist/saxophonist and a pianist, who were knocking out everything from 'Moon River' to 'The Lady is a Tramp'. Since my experience of Gypsy orchestras so far had consisted of remorselessly loud and jaunty renderings of 'Solvejg's Song' and 'The Merry Widow Waltz', my evening was made. Feeling round-bellied and self-satisfied, I went for a final walk in the warm moonlight, giving my white Lada a proprietorial pat before retiring.

15

CORVINUS' COUNTRY

It was the perfect travelling day – clear and sunny, but not too hot. I had a leisurely breakfast because I was reluctant to leave Eger, and I even toyed with the idea of staying another day, but there was a lot of ground to cover and so I packed, paid, and walked across the street to the Lada.

It wouldn't start. The engine turned merrily enough, but simply wouldn't catch. I went back to the hotel and got them to ring the hire people. But the husband was in Budapest for the day, and the wife didn't know where to reach him and couldn't help. There followed an hour's worth of phone calls. The Hungarian automobile club said there was nothing they could do. A local garage promised to chase up a roving mechanic and send him along within fifteen minutes, but he never materialized. One of the hotel staff looked at the engine and said he thought it was an electrical fault. By half-past eleven I told the receptionist that I would wait until the car hire representative got back that evening, and would stay the night.

Then one of the hotel's managers, who had just arrived for his shift, asked me what the matter was. I started to tell him, but at that moment there was an explosion in the small bar off the foyer. It was the espresso machine. Blackened and steaming, exhaling the smell of burnt coffee, at least it didn't seem to have done any damage to the bar. The barmaid slowly emerged from below the counter where she had cowered, spattered with flecks of coffee but otherwise unhurt. We mopped her up and she accepted a brandy; 'I think we all need one,' said the manager. After that, he took me out to the car, got in, and started it after two attempts.

'How did you do it?'

He grinned. 'Pure genius,' he replied. 'But I have the advantage of having driven one of these before. They are temperamental. This one is basically okay. What you have to do . . . ' He went on to explain that all I had done was flood the engine, since Ladas need virtually no choke. 'You could have had a western car, you know.'

Relieved that the day was not so far advanced that I couldn't set off, and with his assurance that the drive to Kecskemét, which looked longish on the map, wouldn't take more than two hours, I took myself to the restaurant for a brief lunch. The manager asked me where I was travelling after Hungary. When I told him, he looked grave. 'Romania is a very beautiful country, but make sure you eat plenty here before you set off; and watch who you talk to. I've heard that half the people are part-time secret policemen.'

'What about the other half?'

'They're full-time,' he grinned, completing a joke I was to hear again. He'd never been to Romania himself, though he'd travelled in most of the east European countries, and in France and Spain. There is little love lost between Hungary and Romania, not least because of President Ceauşescu's notorious 'Romanization' programme, which involves suppressing or getting rid of Romania's ethnic minorities, of which the principal groups are Hungarians and Germans, established there for several hundred years. But there is more to it than that. Hungary's nascent liberalism runs counter to Romania's conservative policies; and Transylvania has been a bone of contention between the two countries since well before it changed hands in 1920.

I drove up into the Bükk to look at some hills and trees before setting off across the plain south. Most of the land between Eger and Kecskemét is former *puszta*, now largely farmland occupied by maize. Here the horse and cart are still the main means of transport, even more noticeably so than in rural Czechoslovakia, and as the road is narrow progress can be slow. The route passes through a number of towns whose names begin with the prefix 'Jasz-', grouped on or near the rivers Tama, Agói-patak and Zagyva, which flow together at Jaszberény. Patrick Leigh Fermor's route of fifty years ago and mine coincided at certain points, and it was in his book *Between the Woods and the Water* that I finally discovered the origin of the prefix. It recalls the Jazyges, Iranian-speaking Sarmatians, a branch of whom found their way this far west. But of them and their culture only this clutch of place names remains.

The police stopped me at Jaszberény. It was either a routine check or I had forgotten to slow down to the correct speed for passing through a town. Pleasingly, the police are called *rendörség* in Hungarian, and wear pale blue uniforms. '*Dokument,*' they said tersely when they discovered that I was an *angol*. For once I was lucky that my basic Hungarian didn't permit conversation with a monoglot native. They looked through my papers with the intimidating slowness all policemen affect, occasionally darting me steely looks; then they let me go.

I drove on through the unvarying countryside. Now and then poplar-lined stretches of road gave it the appearance of northern France. The two hours had extended to well over three, and shadows were beginning to lengthen, but there was less traffic on the road now, and I soon reached Cegléd, the last considerable town to be negotiated before my destination.

Kecskemét is at the centre of a rich, fruit-growing area. The apricots which form the basis of *barack* are grown here. The city sprawls over the plain (just to the south of it is the sandy Bugac *puszta*, which explained why the hotel, about as far from the sea as you can get, is called the Golden Sands), but its centre is compact. Two large squares edged by the town's principal buildings lie cheek by jowl, and although modern architecture is not far away, most of it is low-rise and bearable. The hotel itself and a nearby block of flats on Kossuth tér are the only ugly buildings, and they were both mitigated by hundreds of window-boxes, copious with geraniums and dangling petunias. Several churches, medieval and Baroque, jockey for position, but they are easily outclassed by the Town Hall, a perfect piece of rose-red Art Nouveau by Ödön Lechner, hunched in the centre of the south-west side of the square like some decorative brick tank. The interior has leafy ceilings which might have been put there by William Morris.

The squares are open and airy, but for Hungary there was a surprising dearth of cafés. In vague search of one I walked north-east past the severe Calvinist church to Szabadsag tér. Here the synagogue is large and imposing, but I discovered that it is now a workers' club and cultural centre. Along from it is another piece of Art Nouveau wedding-cakery, even more flamboyant than the Town Hall, and picked out in pink and pale blue, with curls and portholes. It is called the Cifra Palace, and nowadays also houses a workers' social centre.

The composer Zoltan Kodály was born in Kecskemét in 1882 and a third imposing building on the south side of the square houses the internationally famous school which disseminates his teaching technique. There is an artists' colony a little way south-east, but it was devoid of life when I walked through it; and although lights were on in the theatre I found I was two days too early for the opening night of the season.

From Kecskemét the road leads more or less due east to the Danube, here called the Duna, which it crosses over an iron bridge between Solt on the east bank and the pretty little town of Dunaföldvár on the west. This was my first encounter with my occasional companion since Bratislava. There, I had been impressed by the speed of its stream; here, it was its sheer size. I would see it again before long, but further upstream, where it changes its mind about flowing due east and makes a right-angled turn south before heading east again at Belgrade. The river shoulders aside time and frontiers alike, confident in its geographical certainty, in its great age, and in its ancient and indispensable usefulness to man. It has an allure as undeniable as the desert's, and only a half-promised appointment near Siófok, on the southern shore of Lake Balaton, kept me on my way.

Balaton is the largest lake in central Europe. It is about eighty kilometres long and has 170 kilometres of shoreline. The southern shore is flat, and has sandy beaches; the northern climbs into gentle hills whose vineyards produce the Badacsony white wines of which the dry kéknyelü is one of the best anywhere. At eleven o'clock I reached the south-eastern corner of the lake from countryside which had, since the Danube, become increasingly varied, broken up by trees and undulations. Turning left after Enying, and driving along the southern shore, I was abruptly transported into another world. If it hadn't been for the pine trees and the language, and perhaps the blazingly hot weather, I could easily have been in a crowded British seaside resort. Amiable and mildly overweight people ambled about in shorts and sports shirts; shops sold shrimping nets and buckets and spades in bright plastic. Every second house offered rooms to rent, and fine sand inched its way into every crevice. Siófok, late in the season as it was, was packed, and I joined the hot queue of cars running the gauntlet of traffic lights through town, the road now parallel with the little railway which travels all the way round the shore, punctuated with stations like scaled-up models from a Hornby-00 set.

I found the professor after much driving around in dusty side-streets containing neat holiday homes behind well-trimmed hedges. His wife was out boating on the lake. No one, he told me as we walked to the local supermarket to buy vodka and beer, is allowed out further than three kilometres on account of fierce currents which can be lethal. Apart from pleasure-boats and yachts, Balaton provides mooring at Siófok for the half-dozen little gunboats which make up the Hungarian navy.

'I'm glad you've come, but I'm sorry you're driving,' said the professor. 'No vodka for you.' He poured himself a huge one and lit a fresh cigarette from the stub of the last. It was peaceful, sitting on the veranda of the little bungalow he occupied in a small compound of similar houses, filled with the keen scent of pine. We talked of the impossible tasks set by the Hungarian language for those who attempt to learn it, and of a mutual friend in England who had done just that under the professor's teaching twenty years earlier. When I told him about Hortobágy, he smiled.

'I have lived in Debrecen all my life, but I have never been there, though every year the students on my summer course go down to look at the *puszta*. We have a saying in Debrecen: if you are mad enough to want to visit the *puszta* once, you deserve fifty whacks on the bum; if you go twice, you deserve a hundred!' Most Hungarians, he added, headed for Balaton if they could for their holidays. I mentioned that it seemed pretty crowded, and he laughed. 'You should have been here at the weekend. The season's over now, and most of the people went home on Monday. Before that, you *really* couldn't move!'

When the conversation turned to Hungary's present difficulties, he skirted the issue; but I had the impression that this was less from caution than from the feeling that he could safely leave it to the politicians to sort them out. 'But we must deal with the ailing industries which have been bleeding us dry for too long, and we must, I think, encourage individual entrepreneurialism. It's something we are good at, like you. But like you, we are not always very good at selling ourselves, and we should work at it. Even so, things are changing. Do you know there is even a family here where the parents have given up their jobs to manage their daughters' careers – they've brought up three chess internationals!'

Leaving the professor, I made my way round the shore, since there was a daunting queue for the ferry across the lake to Balatonfüred. If Siófok reminds one of Southend, Balatonfüred is Brighton. The town is a spa, the oldest on this side of the lake, dating from Roman times, though it reached the peak of its popularity in the early years of the nineteenth century. It is still a small place, although there is plenty of modern development strung out along the shore on either side of it, engulfing some of the *csárdas* which once provided *buts de voyage* for excursions into the country.

The centre of the town is Gyogy-tér, flanked by clinics and convalescent homes specializing in heart conditions, for the water here (earthy and metallic to taste) is good for cardiac diseases. The Indian poet Tagore, who has a street named after him, convalesced here in the Twenties, as did another poet, Salvatore Quasimodo, forty years later. The streets in the immediate vicinity of the square are in keeping with its sleepy, nineteenth-century atmosphere, but a little further on the incursions of modern architecture are evident, principally in the large and unsympathetic Hotel Annabella, while older buildings crumble in evident neglect. Along the shore there is a concrete-and-candy-floss 'seafront', where people drink beer and eat sausage and chips from cardboard plates. The posher people stay at large modern hotels a little way out of town, where German and Austrian holidaymakers lie on the lawns by the lake like dugongs, or waddle lethargically about on the water in pedalos. The atmosphere poignantly preserved in the vicinity of Gyogy-tér does not carry, but it's a pleasant place, and after the plain the vicinity of hills, trees and water comes as a strong relief.

The September sun slanted over the vineyards as I made my way west to Tihany, a village on a hilly peninsula which has also been developed as a tourist resort. The village itself is rather self-consciously pretty, but my view of it may have been jaundiced by the fact that I wasn't able to shake off the coachloads of trippers who are dropped here to admire it and the views of the lake it commands. I was unhealthily pleased that workmen restoring the roof of the abbey church hurled debris down regardless of the tourists beneath, who scattered like geese, uttering German imprecations in outraged tones. Away from the church, villagers sat on a wall selling green grapes and apricots as hard as nuts for forty-five forints a kilo. The gardens behind their dry-stone walls were loud with geraniums, petunias and begonias, tumbling over the walls and into the narrow roads. The embarrassment of riches reminded me of a box overflowing with gaudy Christmas decorations.

Beyond the church and the steep street that leads up to it, which is lined with bijou restaurants and antique and souvenir shops, Tihany slept in the sun. A few people pottered in their gardens; a dog barked drowsily behind a fence; from a window came the clatter of crockery and attendant smells as a family sat down to an early lunch.

I turned north through the Bakony Hills to Veszprém, an artistic centre within an uninspiring modern shell. From a distance it still has the form of a medieval town as it rises on its five hills, abruptly surrounded by countryside. Villages sprawled along the road in much the same manner as in Moravia, but free of loudspeakers, and the road itself was free of concrete monuments to Soviet friendship. I passed occasional lorries and, more frequently, horse-carts piled high with green fodder, like mobile haystacks. After Zirc, with its noble yellow twin-towered church, I reached a curve in the road which revealed, on a rock in the middle of the valley beyond, another castle – as yellow as Cotswold stone and ruined, but as proudly romantic as Spišský Hrad. It rose like a flame on the top of a green candle. This was Csesznek. It is in the heart of the Bakony Hills, and as I drew closer I could see that it was not entirely neglected. A large carpark was set off the road opposite it, served by a small café and souvenir shop.

It was from the owner of the café that I learned the name of the castle. It had shared a similar fate to that of its cousin in Slovakia, having been built in the twelfth century and destroyed by fire in the nineteenth. 'It is being restored now,' he told me. 'In two years' time people will be able to visit it again.' He added that he was building a hotel in the woods behind the road which he was planning to open at the same time as work on the castle was completed – 'building materials permitting'. The site, he explained, was already perfect for walking holidays, and the castle's proximity would clinch things. 'And Pannonhalma's not far up the road.' He was already canvassing western holiday companies. 'It's business suicide to attract customers from the Eastern Bloc,' he said. 'No hard currency.'

Distances are short in Hungary, and in next to no time I saw the tower of Pannonhalma rising out of the enormous bulk of the monastery to the right of the road. Despite its size, the building seems to soar into the air, and the impression is not lost as you get closer. It is a Benedictine foundation, dating from 996, though the first building you see after a steep climb from the village is a pleasant grey modern block which houses the school. The school, which is privately run (one of the paradoxes of this communist-state-despite-itself), has 320 boarding pupils. They are, says the guide-book, 'taught by priests following the state programme of courses'; but it adds: 'Religion is certainly taught at this Catholic grammar school,' and concludes smugly: 'The students having their final examinations here don't have any disadvantages when continuing their studies at a university or college.'

There are sixty working monks, supporting a community which also includes eighty 'retired' members and eighteen novices, a respectable size for a monastery in even the most Catholic of states today. Unfortunately you have to visit the abbey in a group, but I was able to join one conducted in German and Russian by an urbane man in sunglasses and a brown suit, who was serious without being grim and humorous without being flip. A gaggle of us, including a quartet of attractive Russian blondes, walked through sombre courtyards relieved by flowerbeds packed with refreshingly vulgar summer bedding and open to the view down from the hill across the broad valley on the western side. The bulk of the building here is nineteenth-century in restrained Baroque style. The entrance to the massive tower is decorated by a 1930s 'Byzantine' mosaic commemorating the abbey's foundation.

The church is Romanesque-Gothic, dark and claustrophobic, and surprisingly small. It is built on three levels, one for the monks, one for the clergy, and one for the laity, and is crowded with decorative detail, its heavy carved columns very like Durham's. Outside, in a more modern corridor – the church gives the impression of being buried in a later building – a small oil painting of the Virgin and Child is proudly pointed out, because it isn't an oil at all but a mosaic composed in the last century of 'more than three thousand minute stones' by Venetian craftsmen working in Rome. It is a copy of a painting by Sasso Ferrato, and technically it is very impressive; though as a work of art it is *kitsch*. Another door from the church leads more promisingly to the ambulatory and a sundial high on a wall. The time it reads is an hour behind. A Latin inscription explains that this allows for the Last Hour that comes to us all: *una vestrum, ultima mea!*

It doesn't seem possible that the rather Regency library can hold 300,000 books, until one realizes that the area is larger than it looks, having several deep bays. Two statues depict a self-consciously dignified Saint Stephen and, by contrast, a definitely rakish Francis I. A large globe dominates the centre of the room, and on the curved ceiling a fresco unsurprisingly shows Pallas Athene. What is impressive is the freshness of the decor, given that nothing has been touched since the library was built in 1836. I was reluctant to leave this academic haven, but the tour was over, and as the smells and sounds of a meal in preparation wafted out of the lower windows of a courtyard everything indicated that the monastery was preparing to turn its back on the world outside for another day. I set off for Győr, where I would turn right and follow the Danube east again to Esztergom.

I got lost in Győr. Hungary is not always generous with her road-signs, especially in towns. Here, I toured up and down wide boulevards flanked with pleasant but overpowering blocks of flats painted pastel shades until, finally defeated by a diversion caused by road works, I threw myself on the mercy of a small, tough-looking policeman, who was extremely helpful, with the result that I was out of town in minutes. I am not sure what I missed in Győr, but I know from friends who have penetrated it that it still has a pleasant Baroque centre.

It was good to pick up the Danube again, but though the countryside between river and road was flat, and only occasionally planted with trees and bushes, the river was in too deep a cleft to be visible for much of the time. I had ended up not very far downstream from Bratislava, and the river when I saw it was familiar. It is the frontier here, and the other side is so close that it is hard to believe what an ocean of bureaucracy and suspicion actually separates one from Czechoslovakia. Further on, I drove through Komárom, a ribbon-development town stiff with barracks and Hungarian soldiers in their soft kepis. There is a frontier-post, for Komárom is a town split in two. On the opposite bank it is Komárno. Beyond it, at Almástuzito and Almásneszmély, lay the only ugly factories I saw in Hungary.

Esztergom made up for all this. It is a place which a tourist could cover in a morning, for it isn't large, and the main buildings are obvious, but I wouldn't be surprised if the story that Marcus Aurelius wrote the *Meditations* here were true: Esztergom rewards time spent on it. It is the Hungarian seat of the Roman Catholic Church; the Primate of Hungary is Archbishop of Esztergom and the cathedral church, a vast nineteenth-century basilica occupying an abrupt hill to the east of the town centre, dominates the city. It is simply too big to be dismissed as pompous, and alone in it as daylight faded, my footsteps echoing as I walked around with increasing timidity, I felt almost drummed into belief.

A red marble chapel to the left of the entrance on the south side stands apart. The Backócz Chapel, named after a primate who only narrowly missed election to the papacy, is a rare example of early sixteenth-century architecture, all that remains of the church of that period. The foundation is very early indeed, for it was in a church on this site that Saint Stephen, the first king of Hungary, was crowned in 1000.

A plain side door diagonally opposite the chapel leads up a spiral staircase to the treasury. Nothing prepares you for the opulent array that greets you. The first room displays racks of medieval jewel-encrusted copes, mitres and shoes, looking as if they had just been made. Beyond them, guarded by elderly women who sit knitting but are as watchful as Madame Defarge, glass cases are packed with gold and silver chalices, crucifixes and reliquaries, candlesticks and patens, so encrusted with rubies, emeralds and raw grey pearls that the precious metal is scarcely visible. The quality and delicacy of the work of these distant jewellers and enamellers not only astonishes by its technical skill but by what it has survived, in a part of Europe riven by war and factional fighting throughout its history.

This is one of the great treasuries of Europe, able to stand with the collections of Topkapi and the Tower of London, even with the late Shah's treasure in Iran. There is an easily recognizable centrepiece, the later fifteenth-century *Mátyás Kálvária*. On a sapphire, pearl and ruby base, enamelled gold sphinxes crouch, supporting a central stand decorated with dolphins. Above this, Christ tortured is bound to a grey column, surrounded by saints. The eye is carried upwards to the crucifixion itself, a tiny, enamelled skull no larger than a pearl indicating Golgotha, while the Virgin and Saint John stand half-mourning, half-guarding the tiny, shining figure on the cross. The piece was made for Matthias I Corvinus, the great unifying king of Hungary who reigned from 1458 (he ascended the throne at about fifteen) until his death in 1490. He brought Bosnia, Moravia and Silesia under his sway, and in 1485 occupied Vienna. The son of another Hungarian hero, János Hunyadi, Matthias is revered throughout the country, though he is also claimed by Romania, and there is a large nineteenth-century statue to him guarding the cathedral church of St Michael in Cluj-Napoca (Kolozsvár in Hungarian), for it was there that he was born.

Descending from the basilica past the ruins of the medieval royal palace which flanks it, and past an incomprehensible, massive piece of modern martial sculpture, I passed through a small park, where lovers walked in the fading day. It was pleasant to see them, though it made me feel lonely – Hungarians are affectionate and demonstrative, and this does not cease with the passing of youth. Later, I was to find Budapest more ardent than Paris.

I left the park, turned down the hill, and came to Viziváros, the Water-Town, where elegant Baroque buildings line the streets. At the corner of Liszt Férenc útja, there is a fine modern life-size bronze of the composer. I dropped into the Balassi Bálint Museum, attracted by its buildings and its jumbled courtyard untidy with ivy and pleasantly scattered pieces of statuary; neglected in a corner was a woman's head in terracotta as beautiful as anything Clodion ever did. Inside, however, there was nothing but an exhibition of crude and dreadful modern mosaics which would have been in place along the Bayswater Road or in some Greek souvenir shop.

Not far away, on the corner of Bérenyi Zsigmond útja and 19-es Hősök tér, is the Keresztény Museum in a large building that both inside and out looks and feels like a deserted public school for boys. As its name indicates, it houses a collection of Christian art. All of it is medieval, and it incorporates statuary as well as paintings. Although a handful of masters are represented, none of the work is of the first rank, though the place itself has a certain atmosphere, with its high dark rooms and polished parquet floors.

I walked across the Kossuth Bridge over the Little Danube which loops away from its master for a moment to create Esztergom Island, and down to where the ferry docks. The ferry has replaced the bridge which once spanned the river here, and only locals may use it. Of the bridge, only the first pier projecting from each side remains. I crossed back into town over the Bottyán Bridge, passing what looked like a good fish restaurant and on to the main square, Rakócki tér, where the cinema advertised its offering, *The Bridge on the River Kwai*, with a huge poster done either by a child or by a master of naïve art. Modern buildings jostle uneasily with old, so I turned round and walked down to the lovely Baroque Széchenyi Square. The day was coming to a close and few people were about. As always the setting sun deepened fantastically the colour of the stone buildings.

After dinner, I took another walk through the town. Although it was barely ten, the cinema was closed and deserted, and apart from a few small clusters of teenagers chatting on street corners despite the cool air, and a handful of customers in restaurants, the town was empty. The silence was broken only once, by three boys roaring expertly through the back-streets on diminutive motorbikes. Once that sound had faded, the quiet was absolute, and as I turned onto Lenin Quay to walk along the Little Danube, lit by clusters of white globes mounted on Edwardian cast-iron stands along the river-wall, the melancholy descended on me of the traveller who does not want to leave, but must, for his condition is to keep going. Two lovers sat on a bench under one of the lamps, foreheads touching, the light casting hard black shadows behind them. I walked far enough past not to embarrass them, though I don't think they were aware of me at all, and leaned on the parapet listening to the water gently slap the sides of the moored boats. A large dark cat ambled along the wall and butted my arm with its head.

16

TASTING THE WEST

Visegrád lies on a small loop, almost a curvet, which the Danube makes before plunging southwards. The steep hill above the town has been fortified since Roman times, though the much-restored castle ruins which are to be seen today date from the thirteenth century. Hungarian and foreign tourists flock here for the views over the Danube and the surrounding countryside, and as it is so close to Budapest it is always crowded. The hill on which it stands has been landscaped into park; there is a golf-course and a smart hotel.

Below, the dull little town gives almost no hint that it was once the seat of the Hungarian kings. Matthias Corvinus built a palace here, and his court was seen as the centre of the civilized world; but within a generation the invading Turks had razed it and now only the ruins remain, among which some hints of former splendour survive, such as a red marble fountain bearing the royal coat of arms.

Until recently, the area was under threat from a massive joint venture between the Hungarians and the Czechs to build a hydro-electric plant here. The chief customer would have been Austria, which would have received all the electricity generated for several decades in return for a loan of $600 million. But latterly Austria took the line that she would not object if the project were abandoned altogether. It was deeply unpopular with the Hungarian people, and Austria was uncomfortably aware of a similar project of her own at Hainburg having been vociferously shouted down. The problem was that the Czechs had completed three-quarters of their share of the work. Hungary had only done one-fifth of hers, and the Czechs were furious when in 1989 the Hungarian administration, bowing to popular pressure, called a halt. By doing so they have redeemed an area of great natural beauty at the heart of the Danube Bend from oblivion; they have recognized the importance of conservation, and they have saved a tourist attraction which will be more profitable to them in the long run.

East from Visegrád lies Szentendre. Originally a settlement of Serbian and Greek refugees from the Turks, this small Baroque town on the northern edge of Budapest is too pretty for its own good. The centre is Marx tér, an attractive little cobbled place surrounded by jostling gables in pinks, creams and yellows. Little shops sell traditional handicrafts to streams of tourists, and young men busk by the fountain. The hub of the town is surrounded by a circle of small museums and churches, but the most interesting place is the house in which the potter Margit Kovács (1902–77) lived and worked; it is now a museum dedicated entirely to her pottery, ceramics and sculpture.

The human figures with which her sculpture is almost entirely concerned reflect the central European naïve art which has also been the parent of the Czech, Hungarian and Russian tradition of cartoon film-making. In the religious work there is more than a hint of Byzantine influence here and of medieval woodcarving there, but the bland expressions and the wide-apart, baby-blue eyes tend to pall after a while; are these clay people telling you anything, or are they merely decorative? Even in depictions of grief there is more emotion in the figures' hands than in their faces, which remain detached, cartoon-like. It is interesting that this potter can express feeling more cogently through hands than a face. I was happier with her glorious, impractical, huge jugs with their wild decoration, and with the birds and horses gambolling across her bowls, than with her Walt Disney people.

I timed things badly, and headed into Budapest from here just in time to catch the Friday rush-hour. I was armed with a good map but I had to cross the city and deliver the Lada on the other side. The approach is through dismal high-rise suburbs, a uniform grey, and, despite the sunshine, under a pall of smoke. After the Árpád Bridge, the city begins properly. The traffic was as heavy as in any western town at this time of day, but the stop-and-go helped me, since it gave me time to find out where I was. Apart from falling foul of an inexorable one-way system which forced me to cross the Danube when I didn't want to, I found the car-hire company without difficulty, and bade my by now travel-stained Lada farewell.

A taxi took me to the modest hotel I'd selected, another Art Nouveau building, rather Parisian in atmosphere, and I dumped my stuff, gratefully ordering a beer and leafing through the English-language copy of the *Daily News* (it is also published in German). Hungarian papers generally pay more attention to what is going on outside their country and even outside the Bloc than their eastern neighbours', and *Newsweek* is freely available. Samantha Fox, the London blonde already mentioned, grinned perkily from most news-stands. She was the cover-girl of the initial issue of Hungary's first home-produced girlie magazine, which had just made its appearance. I learned from the *Daily News* that some of its profits will be donated to AIDS research. A more important new publication, also a reflection of more relaxed times, is *Hitel*, a name which has the double meaning of 'credit' and 'credibility'. It is the newspaper of the Democratic Forum Association, an organi-zation of liberals which is the foundation of an actual opposition party. Events in Hungary are moving fast.

Budapest has a population of two million people, one-fifth of the population. Two towns grew up in parallel, on opposite sides of the Danube. The first settlement, Pest, was on the flatlands on the right bank, but the hill of Buda opposite provided an ideal location for a castle, and, in later years, protection from the depredations of the Turks, who destroyed the town of Pest time and again. They only succeeded in taking the castle in the sixteenth century, when it was incorporated into their own trans-European defence system. Thus it is that Buda is now the Old Town, and Pest the New. Divided by the Danube for centuries, their only contact with each other by ferry-boat, flimsy pontoon bridges, or, in cold winters, across the ice of the frozen river, the names and the cities did not join together until the nineteenth century when, in 1839, the Scotsman William Tierney Clark designed a chain bridge. It was completed by his brother Adam ten years later. Adam also drove a tunnel through Buda hill to connect it with the flat land beyond, where the town was spreading. The square between bridge and tunnel bears Adam's name. In 1944, the retreating Germans destroyed all of Budapest's bridges (they blew up the Margaret Bridge at a time when it was crowded with traffic). The chain bridge was the first to be rebuilt, and was reopened in its centenary year.

Six road and two rail bridges now link the two halves of the town, but they are still distinct from each other. Pest today is the child of Hungary's recognition as a state independent of Austria. Though the Dual Monarchy of 1867 was a compromise solution, since the two countries still shared the same emperor and the same ministers for foreign affairs and war, it was a major step forward in the struggle for autonomy which had first found true expression in the voices of Kossuth and Petőfi, and in the revolution of 1848. Hungarians celebrated by changing Pest from a provincial city into a capital to rival Vienna. Great boulevards were planned and laid out; Britain, the world's greatest power, was friendly, and invested; and large, confident Jugendstil buildings in grey stone sprang up everywhere to establish the city which exists today.

On the Buda side, Pest flung its influence as far as to erect a palace on the site of the former castle to rival and indeed outstrip the Hofburg, while on its own bank of the Danube a vast Parliament House was built by the river. Although it is frequently compared with the London Houses of Parliament, it is a lighter, airier building altogether, and its river façade with its half-egg green dome made me think of Italy rather than northern Europe. Facing away from the river on the other side of the building is the main entrance, guarded by two bronze lions which might have escaped from Landseer's studios, except that their expressions have an element of sardonic humour missing in those of their more ponderous cousins in Trafalgar Square: 'It's a job,' they seem to be saying; 'but there's no need to take it *that* seriously!'

Pest is where the action is. There is a vigorous, frenzied energy in the city. Shops in the centre are elegant, varied and well-stocked. In record stores, all the music of western pop singers is available. In chemists' it is easy, or at any rate easier, to buy things westerners would take for granted, such as talcum powder or toothbrushes. The town, however, was as dirty as London or New York, and an air of decay hung over many buildings. I could not help getting the impression that the energy of Pest is the energy of an animal struggling in a net.

Comparisons with Vienna spring to mind. In Budapest there is none of the old-fashioned stuffiness which I find infects the Austrian capital, making it claustrophobic and provincial. Budapest is forward-looking, longing to be part of a larger world than it can be at the moment. It strives towards that world through its development as an international conference centre, a position it has achieved and is consolidating because for the west European it is remarkably cheap; and standards of service, food and accommodation are high. For the east European it provides a window on the West; Budapest is the closest to a west European capital most east

Europeans will get. 'Rich Russians love to come here and load up with western goods,' one local told me.

Conversely, the Russian soldiers stationed here are not made to feel welcome. In general, one does not see them, except in bewildered huddles at railway stations, and as Hungarians tend to regard them as an army of occupation and treat them with according discourtesy, tensions have arisen akin to those between British soldiers and West German civilians in the Fifties and Sixties. There has been talk, at least, of a withdrawal of the four divisions, and as Russian troops have already withdrawn in part from East Germany such a move seems likely across the east European board.

My hotel was on Rakóczi útja, and taking a wrong turning out of it, I ended up at what I took to be a cathedral. It was in fact the Eastern Station. Buildings in Pest tend to be large and grandiose – some are pretentious, but all reflect a flamboyant optimism. I turned round and headed south-west towards the river. It was a little early for dinner so I made for Váci útja. Between Vörösmarty Square and Párizsi útja, it is a pedestrian street containing shops of Fifth Avenue elegance. Here were the only queues I saw in Hungary; they were outside the Adidas shop, and just round the corner at McDonald's. The river is only one block south-west, but the bank is marred by a number of ugly, modern luxury hotels, and the promenade, the Korzó which leads north to Roosevelt Square, is a bleak and windswept place.

I retreated into town and found the Kárpátia restaurant in Károlyi Mihály útja. I settled down in its dark pre-Raphaelite interior and ordered duck. In most east European restaurants there is no written menu: you either have to ask the price of things or trust the waiter. And if there is a bill of fare there will certainly be no wine list, so anyway you end up by paying for something or other blind, because often if you ask the price you will either get a vague answer like 'not expensive', or you are made in subtle ways to feel cheapskate or vulgar, or both. At the Kárpátia there was no such problem, but in any case it wouldn't have mattered, so relaxed and well looked after was I made to feel. A note on the menu read: 'If we've left something off your bill, don't tell us. It's our mistake, not yours.'

Another man was dining alone at a table near mine. From a distant part of the restaurant a Gypsy orchestra struck up with a vigorous allegro version of 'Solvejg's Song', and we shot each other sympathetic glances. Across the gap between the tables we struck up a conversation. He was from Munich and had been visiting Budapest regularly every year since 1973. 'It's got everything we have and more at a fraction of the price, and there are *real* Turkish baths. There's a good one just by the Elizabeth Bridge – it's the one all the professional sportsmen use, and if you have time you must try the Király.' He regretted that over the years the town had been growing steadily seedier. 'It's because of Communism,' he said. 'It simply doesn't work; not like this, kept static. But then, look how we abuse democracy. People have learned a lot since they climbed down from the trees, but not how to run themselves, even though they've developed some interesting blueprints.'

A downpour which had been threatening since late afternoon now started, so we dawdled over cognac, watching the water pitch down. I finally decided that it was not going to let up, and resigning myself to getting drenched, set off; but as soon as I did the rain stopped as abruptly as if someone had turned off a tap. The grey streets had turned to iron in the wet, and the brightly-lit shop-fronts reflected dazzlingly in the pavements.

The following day I made my way down to the Elizabeth Bridge, Budapest's newest, to book a table at the Mátyás Pince restaurant nearby. The Town Church at the Pest end of the bridge is a disappointing, mainly early eighteenth-century building, now shouldered aside by the bridge's feeder road in much the same way as St Martin's is in Bratislava. From here I wandered over to the National Museum, and made my way to the suite of rooms covering the social history of Hungary. The contents of these rooms cover a thousand years, and two items illustrate the breadth of the range: an opulent Turkish officer's tent captured in the fighting in the second half of the seventeenth century when the Ottomans were finally driven out for good, and a Biedermeier black piano surmounted by an obelisk. Where had it come from? A chapel of rest?

Across a landing you find the crown jewels of Hungary. Dramatically lit in two glass cases in a darkened room lie the iron sword, the crystal orb, the sceptre, and the crown. A suitably dignified and reverent usher supervises you as you file past, but the policeman on duty was slouched dozing on a plastic chair in a corner. Nothing can detract from the crown. Its age, its owners and its history command awe. It doesn't matter that experts now believe that it is 200 years too young to be the crown which Pope Sylvester II presented for the coronation of Saint Stephen, and its bent cross, like an honourable battle-scar, gives it a distinct personality – all this apart from the fact that it is a masterpiece of Byzantine art.

I wanted to get away from the traffic. The evening before, the chirrupy German-language local station, Radio Danubius, had informed me that traffic on the Árpád Bridge had been brought to a standstill again as 'yet another car has driven into the Danube'. I retraced my steps and made my way up Váci útja to Vörösmarty Square, a large and attractive space given over to pedestrians. Dominated by a large statue of the nineteenth-century poet and nationalist after whom the square is named, it is sprinkled with exponents of modest free enterprise. The first thing to greet the eye is a rank of about fifteen portrait artists, sitting in a row, each on a camping chair with a vacant one opposite him ready for the punter. None was occupied, though a knot of people was hovering on the off-chance of something interesting to watch. Beyond them, oblivious of the handful of delighted tourists snapping him with little whirring Japanese cameras or shouldering intrusive camcorders, a little, shabby old man with a faraway expression was playing an endless tune on a glass xylophone. He didn't seem to be begging, he seemed to be playing for himself alone. Only those standing closest could hear him, as the noise of his dainty instrument was drowned by the slightly-too-wholesome group of young people at the foot of the statue singing pop songs with a Christian bent. The girl singers, who doubled as modest go-go dancers, were all tan and teeth, and could have been imported from California. I retreated to Gerbéaud's.

Gerbéaud's runs along the north side of Vörösmarty. This Art Nouveau café knocks spots off anything similar in Vienna – the coffee and the cakes are better, the service is friendlier, and there is room to move. The only thing that jars is the customers' clothes – jeans and T-shirts just don't go with Jugendstil. I had a sweet Tokay and a coffee with my burnt-caramel-topped *dobostorta*, thinking about some nineteenth-century *Doppelgänger* who might have sat here smoking good Havanas and making notes with a fountain pen on India paper. But the only people who looked remotely in keeping with the place were a small family of Gypsy women, healthy and radiant in bright dresses, clutching grubby infants to them and moving among the tables begging, stroking the shoulders of embarrassed tourists who stiffened at the contact and would not look at them. Soon after their arrival a couple of waitresses gently shooed them away and they left without fuss.

From here, Vigadó tér is a minute away by the river, a breath of decent nineteenth-century romanticism among the hotelier concrete; but sadly I was still too early for the concert hall to be open for the autumn season. I walked north along the Korzó to Roosevelt tér and the Chain Bridge, which crosses the river from it. Roosevelt Square itself is as solidly Victorian as anything around Westminster, and a Chinese restaurant on the eastern side incongruously occupies the ground floor of the Gresham Building, originally built to house a British insurance company with interests here in the nineteenth century. A plaque in the entrance commemorates the businessmen involved and the British names are at once out-of-place and reassuring. Later, in the cashier's office of the completely alien state travel agency in Bucharest, I was to see a huge and ancient safe which had been built in Bolton. The effect it had on me was the same.

I drifted north to the Parliament and then west along the lovely, residential Alkotmány útja, with its equally attractive Biedermeier side-streets, to the Western Station to pick up my ticket for Romania. There was virtually no queue for international tickets, but when my Hungarian failed me while negotiating the purchase with the clerk, my few fellow-queuers all chipped in with helpful advice in German and English. A first-class ticket all the way to Cluj, a good 200 miles, cost the equivalent of £2. Walking back through the station I realized that it, in common with all the other railway stations I had encountered so far in eastern Europe, was almost devoid of the population of down-and-outs and drunks who hover around the stations of the West. In Budapest in general, however, there were more of such people than I had seen elsewhere on my travels.

From here a short walk took me past the enormous, pompous St Stephen's Cathedral. I turned left into Népköztársaság útja. The name, People's Republic Avenue, is the latest of many. It started life as Andrássy útja, and in its time has also been Stalin útja. It is probably the city's most outstanding street, containing the highest peaks of Jugendstil architecture. It runs north-east all the way to the Town Park, but the buildings of most interest lie between the cathedral and November 7th Square. Dominating them is Miklós Ybl's neo-Renaissance opera house, built between 1878 and 1884 and badly damaged in the street fighting towards the end of the Second World War. Restoration was completed in 1984, and it is quite simply superb, outside and in. Tickets were almost impossible to obtain, however. I had to resort to heavy dollops of charm and a discreet bribe.

Budapest has three metro lines. Numbers 2 and 3 are perfectly good, run identical trains to those in Prague, but are otherwise unexciting. Number 1 is the oldest in Europe and, with Oslo's, the most delightful Underground in existence. Oslo has little wooden carriages, and is run by charming Indians. Here you ride at alarming speed in diminutive yellow tramcars, through little white-tiled stations with their names in whirly Art Nouveau writing. I got on at November 7th Square and off at Heroes' Square (Hősök tér), which abuts the Town Park.

Heroes' Square is dominated by a large semicircular colonnade reminiscent of a Greek temple. Between the columns stand statues of Magyar heroes from the distant past, and at the centre is a large equestrian figure of Prince Árpád, the great-grand-father of Saint Stephen and the founder of the nation. The whole monument was built to commemorate Hungary's millennium. It tends to overshadow the memorial to the dead of this century's two world wars, which is a far more modest structure.

On either side stand two large neo-Classical buildings, almost twins. To the left is the Museum of Fine Arts, and to the right, its portal topped by a semicircular pre-Raphaelite mosaic, the Art Gallery. This, when I visited it, contained a large, striking exhibition of contemporary textile sculpture, notably by Zsuza Szenes and Judit Droppa. As in Czechoslovakia, I was impressed by the vigour of modern art, but was left wondering what direction it was taking. The Fine Arts Museum has a permanent collection housed in a bewildering and seemingly endless series of rooms. The paintings are well kept and displayed, and the museum has one of the best collections of seventeenth-century Dutch landscapes and still-lifes anywhere. Vying with this is the Spanish collection. I have never warmed to El Greco, who is well represented; but there are also two or three superb Velásquez portraits and a series of what looked like early Goyas. One room is given over entirely to the English School; there is at least one painting each by Reynolds, Gainsborough, Kneller, Lely and Zoffany. The one item I would have liked to steal, however, was a small portrait of a young man, Antonio Broccardo, by Giorgione.

The park beyond is large, containing a zoo, Gundel's restaurant, and an artificial lake for boating and swimming. On an island in its centre is a piece of pure Disneyland – a fake Transylvanian castle built around 1900. It is a reminder, too, that Transylvania was until recently a part of Hungary, for the castle is a copy of Hunedoara, one of Hunyadi's castles, now in south-western Romania.

By the bridge that crosses to the castle, a woman was settling down with a large wooden box containing six ginger bloodhound puppies. She put the box with the sleepy dogs in the sun, erected a fishing-stool, parked herself on it and took out her knitting. I had seen quite a few 'status' dogs being walked here – Afghans, Springers, and one Saluki. By the time I passed her again half an hour later, three of the puppies had already been sold and the rest were surrounded by an admiring crowd of children. In Czechoslovakia pet dogs are subject to a luxury tax, but I was unable to discover whether similar laws apply in Hungary.

The castle houses an agricultural museum. I particularly liked the steam tractors of the 1870s. It also has two excellent exhibitions, on conservation and on hunting. The latter activity is still much pursued in eastern Europe and sold heavily as a tourist attraction both in Hungary and Bulgaria. A Bulgarian tourist brochure reads insouciantly: 'The shooting of wolves, jackals, wild cats, foxes and other vermin is allowed all the year round.' Bear, deer, chamois and wildfowl escape slaughter for six months of the twelve.

I bought a beer in the park from a man with an old ice-cream freezer in which the bottles were packed, sitting on a crate under an umbrella. When he heard my accent he asked if I was Czech or from the DDR, as people often did, simply because western tourists, especially travelling alone, are very rare. He was astonished and pleased to hear that I was English. Walking back to Heroes' Square I passed a small yellow bridge, built in memory of an eminent cement manufacturer who lived in the early part of this century. On it, someone had aerosolled the words 'Punk Is Not Dead' in English. Grafitti is something else which reappears in Hungary. I was able to identify the correct subway exit when arriving back at my 'home' stop not by the vague official signs but by the name 'Tony Montana' written in bold felt-tip next to it.

The next port of call had to be the Café Hungária, conveniently just round the corner from my hotel, in Lenin körút. By local standards it is expensive; I drank two large Tokays and bought a packet of cigarettes, all of which cost the equivalent of £3.50, including free pretzels. It was worth it, though I was told that the restaurant, which I didn't use, could be better. I sat at the bar, a piece of modern sacrilege in upholstered red vinyl, for the Hungária is a high temple to Art Nouveau. Originally called the New York by its founder, who had made his money in that city, it transcends the wildest dreams one might have of a coupling of Jugendstil with Baroque. Satyrs leer from columns above the bar, busty nymphs blush, shepherds pipe, barleysugar columns crowd – all in dark, highly-polished wood. Above the hanging globes which light the place, paintings on the ceilings depict risqué episodes from the lives of the gods. Somehow completely consistent with the atmosphere, the barmaid was a glorious blonde in a white blouse and a tight leather mini-skirt wrapped round with a broad studded-leather belt, her hair held up by a strawberry-pink gauze bow, and a black velvet choker with a cameo brooch round her neck. Her face was exactly that of the girl in Manet's *A Bar at the Folies-Bergère*.

Apart from two Libyans cheerfully drinking Tokay with Coca-Cola chasers, I was alone at the bar. At nearby tables a handful of Hungarian men lingered over minute glasses of liqueur, reading newspapers in wooden holders. Periodically a troop of tourists dressed in their best would be ushered in to eat. They were overawed by the place, as who would not be. The astonishing thing is that this temple to privilege was lovingly restored under the auspices of the new communist government after the war – it had been destroyed in the fighting. Reborn, it was renamed the Hungária. Perhaps it is a sign of the times that today it is called the Hungária-New York.

The way to go from Pest to Buda is to cross the Chain Bridge, which spans 600 metres of sluggishly-flowing Danube to take you to Clark Adam tér. It was early morning, and still cool enough to make bearable the steep climb via Hunyadi János útja up the system of steps which bring you to the Mátyás church. The church is dedicated to the Virgin, but its popular name derives from Matthias Corvinus, who established a great court at Buda during his reign, and who married here. His emblem decorates the interior.

Buda's own history begins with the fortification of the hill in the wake of Pest's destruction by the Mongols in 1241. After the Turks took over in the 1520s the church, a yardstick of the citadel's history, was converted into a mosque. When the Habsburgs drove the Turks out 160 years later, the building was damaged by Christian bombardment. Later, Baroque and most recently neo-Gothic styles were imposed on it. The atmosphere and look of the place today is Victorian, though the lavishly-painted interior gives it a William Morris medieval aspect. It was as well that I had arrived early for Mass – early enough for the communion which preceded it. Though it was full, I nevertheless found a seat; but by the time Mass started the church was overflowing. A gentle bishop conducted the service, an attendant removing and replacing his shimmering white mitre, deftly snapping it open and arranging the lappets on his shoulders as the rite dictated. The organ thundered, the unseen choir – which most of us foreigners had come to hear – was duly magnificent, and in the course of his sermon the bishop addressed a few words of welcome to those of us from abroad in shy German.

The sky had turned grey when I emerged, and by the time I reached the Fishermen's Bastion, a nineteenth-century neo-Romanesque attempt to give the church a backdrop in white stone, a steady drizzle had begun to fall. The bastion gives wonderful views over the river across Pest, but is in itself a piece of kitsch. Many tourists wandered around it, including a bunch of young Russian soldiers, eating strawberry ice-creams and taking photos of each other. As the rain intensified, I made my way down Fortuna útja – having failed to find even the smallest corner to sit in the Ruszwurm Café. Here are two hotels, almost opposite each other. The first is the relatively recent Hilton, which from the opposite bank seems to blend in quite sympathetically. Close up, one sees what a monstrosity it is. Umber-tinted windows have been set in an eighteenth-century façade, and a medieval tower incorporated into the building has been capped by a stumpy modern spire in sludge green. Inside, the place is comfortable and bland, though cramped. The consensus among Hungarian friends I asked about it was: 'We hate it but it brings in the money.' People who live in Buda express themselves more strongly. A little way along, the older Fortuna is pleasanter architecturally, but at least the staff in the Hilton are friendly: When I asked a starched maître d' in the deserted Fortuna restaurant if I might lunch there, he informed me in an icicle voice that they were fully booked, and did not deign to look at me as he did so.

Buda today is a pretty Baroque town, and its main streets, especially those linking the church with the palace (now a museum), are packed with tourists. Having explored in that direction, taking in a dramatic statue of an immense eagle clutching a sword, and listening to a talented busker playing the hurdy-gurdy, I walked back north-west along the hill. On the Fortuna útja again, I stumbled by chance on two small museums – of Catering and of Commerce. They sounded dull, but to escape the rain I dived in. Catering was a delight – a cluttered exhibition of nineteenth-century culinary extravagance, supervised by donnish old ladies. There was complex kitchen equipment looking like instruments of torture, butter-churns worn and dark with age, slim blue-glass wine bottles, and foxed bills of fare in blue and cream listing choices of food and wine which today one would need a mortgage to afford. Commerce was even better. It covered Hungarian advertising from about 1880 to 1940. Posters, tins, bottles, packets of every description were crowded together. A glass case displays pengö notes – the unit of currency which preceded the forint – of vast denominations, and a 1946 photograph shows a man lighting a cigar with a bundle of them, each worth ten million. In the next room, there is a reconstruction of a turn-of-the-century grocer's shop. My favourite item, however, was a poster-advertisement for a brewery from about 1916. It shows two handsome, masculine troopers, one in German field-grey, the other in Austro-Hungarian sky-blue. They are leaning on a beer barrel, jovially toasting each other in huge 'Steins'. Beyond them in a corner, English, Scottish, Indian and French soldiers are cravenly surrendering. Alone in the museum, I asked the ladies in charge if I could take photographs. They looked doubtful, then decided: 'You can take *some*, but not *many*,' then smiled disarmingly, and went back to their conversation.

I came out into sunshine and, round the corner in Kapisztrán tér, on a temporary stage erected below the melancholy tower which is all that remains of the church of St Mary Magdalene, young people were performing folk dances for a small group of contented Hungarian spectators – at the far end of the hill from the tourists, I noticed. The men's costumes were particularly splendid – cream felt jackets and trousers with black frogging.

I'd despaired of finding anywhere to eat on the hill, but descending on the north side by way of Ostrom útja I found the Vörös Kaviár, where I was ushered without fuss to a table and given a good white wine, *debrői hárslevelü*, and a solid, meaty fish called *fogasch*. An invitation to tea detained me in Buda after lunch, so to fill in the time I strolled down to the Danube and along Bem rakpart, via Fő útja where the Király Baths are situated. The Király is a medieval Turkish building, low green domes hunched over its rugged walls, constructed over a deep artesian well. The minerals in the water are said to be very good for you. Female emancipation is not yet far advanced in eastern Europe, and these baths are not open to women, though others, such as the Gellert, are.

Bem rakpart must be one of the most desirable residential streets in the city, right on the river with a view of the parliament building opposite. It was becoming a heavy autumn afternoon, saturated with sunlight, and the benches on the embankment were filled with elderly couples sleeping off their lunch under the trees.

I climbed back up the hill and crossed to its western side, taking the opportunity to walk down Úri útja, with its crowded Baroque gables and façades hiding lovely secret courtyards. Beyond it, heavier, more serious buildings still bear the scars of bullets and bombs from the fighting of 1944–5, for the Germans staged a desperate last stand here. 'You won't find our house very good to look at from the outside, but at least it's easy to recognize,' I had been warned, and indeed as I approached it I saw that it was certainly the most war-battered of the terrace. The hall and the stairs to the flats had the pleasantly crumbling quality one finds in similar old blocks in Rome and Venice, and reaching the first floor I saw that the flats which looked out from the back of the house, and therefore faced the rising wall of the hill, had little courtyards built out to join that wall, full of tubs of bright flowers. Virginia creeper and ivy tangled over the wall itself.

My hostess was eighty, looked sixty, and had always lived 'in the castle' as she said, though there had been periods early in her life when she had lived in what is now Czechoslovakia, and later in Transylvania near Cluj. She showed me photographs of the country manor houses which had been her homes. One had been torn down long ago; when last heard of, the other was being used as a squat by Gypsies. 'The Treaty of Trianon was a disaster for Hungary,' she said. 'It was the beginning of the end.'

Since 1945, times had become hard for the family. Her husband, a career officer born in the region of the 'Sieben Burgen' – the seven towns in Transylvania originally settled by German colonists under the supervision of Géza II in the twelfth century – had returned from the war a broken man, mentally and physically, and was never able to work again. The situation was exacerbated by the fact that they were a blue-blooded family. 'All odds were automatically stacked against us,' she explained sadly, but also rather proudly, tapping her signet ring. She supported her family on her salary as a nurse, teaching English, French and German, all of which she had learned thoroughly as part of her education, to fill out the money.

She had baked little cheese savouries for me, and minute sausage rolls in flaky pastry. We drank coffee as thick as soup from thimble-cups, and Tokay of enormous age and impossible sweetness from glasses barely bigger than buttercups. The flat was a comfortable chaos of books, old newspapers, squashy chairs and sofas, and Turkish rugs.

She worried about her son, a graphic artist. 'He can't be much older than you, but he's got such a beer-gut ...' He was happy in his work, she explained, but his original ambition had been the stage. He had passed three of the four auditions to qualify for drama school with flying colours, but the fourth had been held by a woman Party member, and he had been rejected. My hostess was convinced that this was because he came from aristocratic stock.

'But it's all one now. Today, everyone has problems. I can remember a time when people actually smiled. Now, everyone's too worried to smile. Too worried about making money.' She was particularly distressed that her grandson and his wife, who had shared the flat with her until they'd been able to get one of their own, never came to see her now. 'He's a taxi-driver; he works every hour God sends to make money, and still there never seems to be enough. But he's obsessed by it.' The worst thing, she said, was that her four-year-old great-grandson no longer recognized her when she met him in the street.

Speaking of the past, she cheered up, though there was a dark story of a distant cousin, a governor in some remote province, who had been taken by two Jews and tortured and blinded. This kind of story is typical of those upon which Hitler fed, told against the Jews in the anti-Semitic atmosphere of central Europe in the early days of this century.

Her own childhood had been happy and privileged; there had been horses, ballet classes, travel to France and Italy. After the hurried departure from Kolozsvár (Cluj in Romanian, Klausenburg in German) in 1920, an officer friend of her parents had managed to salvage most of their possessions and sent them on to Hungary; but the crates had taken three years to arrive. Much of the furniture in her flat was from that time. Back in Budapest life had resumed an even tenor, only to be disrupted again by the Second World War, this time for good. She still worked part-time at a medical museum. 'But my colleagues envy me because I can speak foreign languages.' Nevertheless she talked of her work with enthusiasm, and after tea we visited the museum together. It was full of horrific Victorian surgical instruments, but among more interesting articles was a sixteenth-century anatomical model of a woman, made of wax.

Bidding me farewell she asked me to greet the mutual friend in England who had introduced us. 'He is my son, Hungary's son,' she said. She added: 'I have been very gloomy about my country. Perhaps I would have been less so if it were not for my leg.' A few weeks earlier she had sprained her ankle in a fall. It was not right yet and she was impatient. 'For the first time in my life I feel old. I've always been athletic – I was a good tennis player all my life – and I hate having to move slowly, like an old woman. Which I am, but God, how I hate to admit it.'

That evening, the Mátyás Pince restaurant was full, hot, friendly, and cosmopolitan. At a table near me, four Japanese businessmen were drinking their way through endless bottles of Tokay with a seriousness that only began to curl at the edges towards the end of the evening. On the other side, two gigantic, blond, middle-aged Swedes sat down with a couple of suitably statuesque and expensive-looking Budapest pickups. Across the room a brittle US couple with loud voices offered stilted sympathy to their much older, low-voiced Hungarian Jewish dining partners when the talk turned embarrassingly to the Holocaust. The American wife was dressed in expensive green leather, and dripped gold. I overheard that the couple's next port of call was Romania, and wonder how they fared there. A Gypsy orchestra churned out the usual numbers.

After a morning at the Art Nouveau Museum of Applied Arts, I made my way across town to the large cemetery on Mező Imre útja to look at the Pantheon of the Workers' Movement and the Kossuth Mausoleum, but all the gates were closed. Here, the centre of Budapest is already beginning to blend into the first suburbs, and the sooty buildings have a run-down look, which is emphasized by their battle-scarred appearance, for here, too, fierce street fighting went on at the end of the war. Eleven years later there was more, as the 1956 uprising was crushed.

I turned up at the wrong part of the university for my meeting, and consequently was a good fifteen minutes late. Hot and apologetic, I was calmed down by my host, who sat me at a low table in his large office and asked me to wait. He disappeared through some double doors beyond which I could hear a meeting coming to an end. I leafed through a medical magazine and admired the array of massive pot plants guarding the window. Everything in the office was green, I suddenly realized, from the leaves to the leather upholstery and the carpet.

Tibor soon returned. Dressed in the academic 'uniform' of a white overall coat, he was neat and precise – a plump Hungarian Wilfred Hyde-White. We drank apricot juice and talked about his medical laboratories.

'One of the main problems is equipment – it's the old story of earning enough hard currency to afford to buy up-to-date stuff, and we haven't yet the resources to develop our own technology. So we have a mishmash of Japanese, American, British and Russian stuff, some of which is over twenty years old. But it still works, so what the hell?' He sipped his apricot juice and broadened the base of the argument. Hungary would slowly have to phase out the old, Russian-inspired heavy industries and develop lighter projects and competitive products.

'The problem is breaking into your markets. We can't compete with any of the stuff you already have – yet.' Electrical goods, light bulbs and pharmaceutical products are potential front-runners, but Hungary is still caught in a cleft stick. 'Here, we've also started taking on fee-paying students from abroad who've failed to get on to medical courses in their own countries simply because they are over-subscribed, or reduced because of government cuts.'

Recently courses have been inaugurated in German and English. Students come from East Germany, Algeria and Iran; but also from Scandinavia, the USA and West Germany, among others, and associations have been formed between Hungarian academic faculties and sister faculties abroad. 'At present we have only one lecture theatre with audio-visual facilities. This we share with other departments. At this moment, there are some English Literature students being taught in there.'

We talked for half an hour, and towards the end we were joined by a slim, serious man of about fifty in a white hospital T-shirt, jeans and sneakers – Professor Rényi.

'I have to go to a meeting now – they never stop – but János will show you round if you like.'

János and I set off. I wasn't quite sure what I was going to be shown, but as we made our way round a number of laboratories, and he pointed out the equipment, accompanying the tour with a great deal of technical detail, I realized too late to put things right without embarrassment that he had taken it for granted that I was a fellow research scientist. Luckily there was time for more general conversation.

'It's certainly true that we all do as many jobs as we can,' he said with a grin. 'But they are nearly all extensions of existing skills. Now, I'm a pathologist. There isn't a lot of part-time work for people like me.'

'Isn't it exhausting for people to do two or three jobs? When do they see their families?'

'Not often. It's very depressing. The worst aspect is that your whole attitude to work is dulled. You plod through every job as best you can, unstimulated by any of it, and so numbed that you're unable to enjoy what little free time you have. I think a lot more marriages would break up than actually do, simply because people survive better economically if they stay together. But you can imagine the extra tensions that introduces.'

I was silent. I had been thinking, through my contact with Hungarians, how much less stress there seemed to be here than in London. I decided to admit this.

'I can't comment on London, but we certainly have our fair share of stress. I might add that we have one of the highest suicide rates in Europe; but that's more a reflection of our temperament than our present situation, I think. The suicide rate has always been high – even in the days of Austria-Hungary.'

'What about drug abuse?'

'No. That's a luxury few people here can afford. But it's not a problem I'd rule out for the future. We may seem to envy how you live; but it's really the freedom of your economy we admire; and we know that every Eden has its serpent.' He smiled again.

'Who uses all the private services then – the expensive hairdressers, for example? Someone must have money.'

'Oh yes. The *rich* have money. People who are able to do business abroad.' He paused with his hand on another door. 'This is the path. lab. Would you like to see it?'

Unthinkingly I said yes. We entered and I saw a room with three red marble dissecting tables in the middle. A technician with a hose was cleaning up. 'The tables are originals,' János was saying. 'They've been here a hundred years. We're getting metal ones soon.'

I was about to say that marble seemed a perfectly good material to me – I was embarrassed by my evident inability to make any intelligent technical comment – when I noticed three familiar shapes lying on one table. They were dead babies, and one of them had its skull and abdomen opened up. János, naturally assuming I would have seen such things a dozen times before, continued to talk.

'I have a friend who, I think, has had enough,' he told me as we parted. 'He is able to travel out of the country quite frequently, and he has been setting something up. Now, at home, he and his wife speak only English, and the children have been brought up to speak it too. I know he means to take his family on holiday and not return. But despite all our problems I do not envy him. I think we will sort things out, and I want to be here when we do. It's sad that all of us behind the Iron Curtain have got cast in the role of second-class citizens, the "other" Europeans, call it what you will. The more we believe that, the harder it'll be for us to pull ourselves up by the bootstraps. The simple truth is that we're in a hole, and you have too many problems of your own to pull us out. Never mind. One day perhaps we'll be able to do something together.'

On my way through town up to Margaret Island, I passed three wedding-parties. Flower-bedecked cars, and the bride in white – something else which has recently reappeared, and was to be seen everywhere I went that summer and autumn.

Margaret Island is a large park. There is a ruined nunnery, and an open-air theatre famous for operetta – but I had missed the season, and its only occupant, fortunately behind locked gates, was a very large guard dog, big as a Great Dane, with an Alsatian's looks and a boxer's colouring. It didn't need to bark; it just glared at you. The island is also full of flowers and lovers, and families trundle about on four-wheeled cycles with fringed canopies that look like very early horseless carriages. It is a good place to escape from the rush-hour.

I had someone else to meet. Large, jolly and bearded, Béla had survived Auschwitz as a boy and returned to Budapest after liberation to see if any of his family were still alive. He ran into his father by chance in the street, and together they discovered that his mother had also survived. 'There was talk of going to Israel, but somehow we never had the time to get things organized.' In the Sixties he had taught medicine for three years at Algiers University, and later in Tunis, but returned home to nurse his mother, who was a widow by then.

All this he told me as we sat over a drink in the hotel's *Bierstube*. He had been reserved at first, almost frosty, but as soon as we stopped fencing in German and switched to French the atmosphere relaxed. After an hour he suggested I might like to return to his flat for some dinner.

'I apologize for the smell of fish,' he said as we climbed into his car, a new Volkswagen. 'A friend of mine from the Algerian Embassy brought back some prawns, and some red mullet and parrotfish for me today. He bought it this morning in the Port d'Alger.' Mediterranean fish is a rare treat for landlocked Hungary, so the dinner his assistant was cooking him the following evening was something keenly looked forward to.

We arrived at his large and untidy flat quickly because once the rush-hour is over the streets are deserted except for the buses, trams and taxis. Bustling, he dumped his medical bag, roughly tidied the coffee table, and fetched a bottle of William pear brandy. 'Pour us a couple of glasses and come into the kitchen. I'll see what I can rustle up. Forgive the mess,' he added over his shoulder. 'The wife's away so I'm leading a bit of a bachelor existence.'

'Is she away for long?'

'Three years – she's teaching in Africa. But don't worry,' he laughed, seeing my expression. 'It's not the Foreign Legion. We can get together in the vacations.' In the kitchen he sorted out some crispbread and found a packet of frankfurters which he deposited in the Russian microwave. From the refrigerator he pulled a nearly-full bottle of dry Tokay and some mustard. 'Our simple supper is coming together. Not quite the Alabárdos, but it'll do!' (the Alabárdos being one of Budapest's best restaurants). While I ate I told him where I was going next, and he expressed concern. 'Eat as much as you can before Romania. And watch your wallet. But don't worry. Most of the people are fine.'

After dinner, he switched on a massive Japanese television with a built-in video and fired a remote controller at it. *News at Ten* unexpectedly appeared. 'This will pick up all the Czech, Austrian and Hungarian stations, and Sky and Superchannel,' he told me. 'Soon we'll be able to get even more satellite stations.' He uncorked a bottle of tequila. 'Let me know what you think of Romanian television if you get a chance to watch it – I think you'll find there's quite a difference.'

The conversation turned to Béla's work. He had just developed a yes-or-no questionnaire, the responses to which when run through a computer program would give an accurate indication of the subject's susceptibility to heart disease. By the end of the evening, and several tequilas later, I'd accepted a warmly-pressed invitation to meet again the following evening to help eat the fish.

On the tram there the next day a sad-looking man sat opposite me. He looked as if he might have been recovering from a stroke. When he started to talk and I explained my lack of Hungarian, he switched to flawless English, explained that he had lived in London for ten years, displayed a detailed knowledge of Chelsea pubs, and told me that his mother still lived there – in Flood Street, no less. He added that he was a keen stamp collector and asked me to send him an Olympic Games First Day Cover when I got back.

The dinner – at Béla's assistant's flat – was excellent. There was too much of it even for the four of us who sat down; we were joined by his assistant's daughter. A plate of fish was taken down to the concierge, whose first reaction was deep suspicion at something so unfamiliar. The family's small dog was more enthusiastic and devoured heads and tails as fast as you could throw them. I didn't want the evening to end; my last day had been spent dawdling about quite agreeably, but now I had been in one place for longer than anywhere since Prague, and the idea of packing and travelling to somewhere new and unfamiliar was as unpleasant as the idea of Monday is when it starts to get dark on Sunday. Once I was alone again, there would be nothing between me and the journey to Romania, and to make matters worse I would have to get up at 3 a.m. to catch the only reasonable train, which left from a station some way from the centre of town.

I consoled myself with the thought that I was going to a relatively unknown country, one which until recently had been a prosperous agricultural nation, looking West rather than East, but which since the war had virtually disappeared from view, tucked away between Russia and the Black Sea. Above all, a country which since the mid-Sixties had become a dictatorship under a leader who had plunged it into economic disaster, but who hadn't been toppled. It would at least be interesting.

PART THREE

EAST:
Romania
and Bulgaria

17

'YOU ARE MY FIRST ENGLISHMAN'

The first meeting for eleven years between the Romanian and Hungarian heads of state had drawn to an unsuccessful close a few days before I boarded the train for Cluj in the late summer of 1988. Ideologically, the two countries are growing further and further apart, and that summer tens of thousands of people in Budapest had demonstrated in support of the threatened Hungarian villages of Transylvania. There has been tension between the two neighbours for a long time. This century it has been fuelled by Hungary's loss of Transylvania to Romania at the end of the First World War, and it is unlikely to be eased by the Romanian president's plan to destroy up to 8000 villages, mostly in this region and largely occupied by the Magyar ethnic minority of two million people. The official reason for this extra-ordinary scheme, involving the death of over half of Romania's villages, is that with the increasing industrialization of agriculture, village life is becoming outmoded. The villages will be replaced by so-called agro-economic complexes – large, modern, tower-block communities. To Romania's president, the tower-block symbolizes an advanced society.

What may be closer to the truth is that not only will villagers' independence be undermined, thus reducing the risk to Ceauşescu of any organized underground opposition, but the Romanian authorities will have fewer mouths to feed. This conveniently ties up with the policy of 'Romanization' (difficult to pursue in a country which because of its history and geographical position is in any case a racial melting-pot), because it means Ceauşescu can slough off the ethnic minorities. Magyars can be sent to Hungary, Germans to the Federal Republic. It doesn't matter that these minorities' roots here go back several centuries. Jews and Gypsies do not fare better. Meanwhile, in speeches like the one he gave to the Joint Meeting of Magyar and German Nationality Working-People's Councils in Bucharest on 27 February 1987, the president said:

We took and take action for village development, construction and reorganization. True, we have only made a beginning, but we plan that the centres of the 558 joint agro-industrial councils should take shape before this five-year period ends, and that some should even be declared agro-industrial towns ... Our entire activity should be grounded on the revolutionary conceptions of scientific socialism, historical and dialectical materialism, on the latest achievements in science and technology, in human knowledge in general. We should never forget even for a moment, that the huge transformations that have developed and are occurring in the general development of society, in science, in deepening man's knowledge, impose a new approach to the problems.

There is economic method in Ceauşescu's policy, for Bonn is prepared to pay about 8000 marks 'compensation' for every ethnic German released under the terms of a little-publicized agreement of ten years' standing. Under this, 120,000 so-called 'Saxons' have already gone, making Romania about a billion Deutschmarks; there remain another 280,000 such people in Transylvania – descendants of the original settlers of the 'Sieben Burgen' – who may not be reluctant to leave this benighted country. Ceauşescu once said in an unguarded moment that oil, Jews and Germans were his best exports. Now, the oilfields of the north-east are drying up, and all but a tiny group of Jews have gone. He is turning his attention to other sources of income; and if Hungary cannot afford to redeem her Magyars, increasingly intolerable conditions have encouraged many of them, and indeed many Romanians, to flee. But while Hungary has set up refugee camps to cope with the influx of Magyar Transylvanians, Romania does not seem eager to let them go. The reason for this is simply that the government does not want word of how harsh conditions are in the country to get out – though this is now a case of shutting the stable door after the horse has bolted. 'Ceauşescu would like to get rid of the Magyars, sure,' one Romanian dissident now in exile in Hungary told me. 'But he doesn't want to see them go to Hungary. He'd rather see them dead.' In 1989, Hungary reported that the Romanians were actually erecting a fence along the common frontier – this at a time when elsewhere the talk was turning to dismantling the Berlin Wall. Work on this fence has since ceased; Romania simply lacks the resources to build it. By the same token, there are neither the manpower nor the resources to implement Ceauşescu's plan to destroy the villages – at least, not nearly as quickly as the *Conducator* would like. If, in the midst of all this, ethnic village Romanians also suffer, it does not seem to matter.

It doesn't matter what the people think, either, for *Conducator* Nicolae Ceauşescu is a dictator in all but name, and has entrenched his position through nepotism. At least forty members of his family hold key government and military positions, and he hopes to assure a dynastic succession through his wife Elena and their son, Nicu. Nicu, currently in charge of the relatively prosperous Sibiu district, is a playboy, and unlikely to be a solid successor; and the current world political climate makes Ceauşescu look more and more like a Canute.

For the time being, however, the Romanian people are crushed. As the president has been immoderately keen to pay off his country's foreign debt, a system of rigorous internal economies has been imposed. Food rationing, introduced in 1981, now severely limits supplies of cooking oil, bread, milk, sugar and meat; eggs, butter and coffee are rarely available. Most of the agricultural produce, and all of the good stuff, is sold abroad – to Russia in particular, to help repay the debts to that country. Electricity and fuel for domestic lighting and heating are restricted so that factories can have the lion's share, even in winter, and this affects hospitals as well as private homes. Car owners are limited to thirty litres of petrol a month in summer and ten in winter. Ambulances are not exempt from this, and calls concerning patients over sixty are refused. Even ordinary everyday medicines like aspirin are almost impossible to come by.

By dint of this stringency ('Our Mr Ceauşescu is your Mrs Thatcher writ large,' one Romanian Communist Party member told me proudly), the country reduced its foreign debt astonishingly fast. However, even that is a source of fear for some people: 'What's he going to do when it's all paid off?' a man in Braşov asked me. 'Once he's cleared the debt, people outside will care even less than they do now about what's going on here. And what if he seals the frontiers?' The cost of the achievement is widespread human misery and oppression. In the middle of April 1989, six months after my visit, Romania announced that the entire foreign debt had been repaid. Exact figures are hard to come by, and the truth of the announcement is impossible to assess. But, ominously, the president has now said that 'we have decided not to depend on anyone any more, either economically or politically.' It may be noted, however, that Romania continues to export to the EC.

Responsibility for the accumulation of the debt in the first place lies at the door of the president himself. He came to power in the mid-Sixties and within a very short time embarked on a programme of massive industrialization, his ambition being to make his country an economic power in the world as fast as possible. There was nothing wrong with that, but he sought to realize it both ruthlessly and foolishly, and he was dogged by bad luck. He built expensive refineries to process Iranian oil, but the deal was made with the Shah; soon after, the Shah fell. Then the price of oil plummeted. An over-optimistic expansion of the steel industry was implemented, which coincided with that product becoming a drag on the market. Added to which, a whole series of factories were opened to produce finished goods which Romanians couldn't afford and nobody else wanted. In the mid-Sixties the president inherited a relatively stable and prosperous agriculturally-based country. In a quarter of a century he has made certain innovations, but in the process brought it to its knees.

Why? He didn't do it on purpose; but he is an old-fashioned Stalinist technocrat, and he wanted to change Romania at full speed from an agricultural rural land to an industrial urban one. Unlike his predecessor, Gheorghe Gheorghiu-Dej, who pursued a cautious and gradual transition from one to the other, Ceauşescu, obsessed with self-aggrandizement, went at it like a bull at a gate. He courted the West in successful pursuit of massive loans which he spent on industrial expansion. From the mid-Sixties on, peasants in a land which up to then had been eighty-five per cent agriculturally based, were herded into factories, uprooted from traditions and a mode of life ingrained in them by centuries of use. 'I can remember in 1969 markets overflowing with fresh vegetables, cheese, wine,' one exile in Paris told me very recently. 'The peasants brought their produce to market to sell. The tobacconists were full of every kind of western cigarettes, and there were wonderful Austrian cake-shops. Within five years I was to see the same peasants transformed into factory-workers, living in cement blocks of flats. You would see them sitting on their balconies, bereft of everything which had given their existence meaning, staring into space for hours on end or playing endless games of backgammon, and, of course, drinking. They had been wrenched away from their culture for no reason that they could see, and there was no psychological help for them to bridge the gap between living in the country, close to the seasons, to animals, to the extended family, and living in concrete prisons out of sight of the sky. You can't just turn a peasant into a blue-collar worker overnight.'

Another exile told me that seeing his plans falter only made Ceauşescu the more determined to force them through. 'He has the desperation of a man who cannot afford to lose his illusions. He has no formal education or training to fall back on, no trade or craft. He's simply been a political agitator since he was a teenager.' Born to humble parents in a village in the southern Olt district in 1918, the *Conducator* did in fact work as a shoemaker for a short time before being sucked into politics. 'Now,' I was told by the Parisian exile, 'he considers that the Romanian people have failed him, and thus it is that he is punishing them. If you're unemployed for any reason that isn't satisfactory to the state, you can be imprisoned for "parasitism", which is a criminal offence. To pay off the nation's debt, everyone except the élite must suffer want. And my guess is that even when the debt *is* repaid, there will still be no food in the shops, because the government will sell all it can to Russia – all the meat, and the fresh vegetables.' His words have so far turned out to be true. The only meat freely available (*when* available) in Romania is pigs' trotters, nicknamed 'patriots' – because they are not exported, i.e. they do not leave the country.

Exiled Romanians have been encouraged by persistent rumours – the only way any real news circulates in and about Romania – that Ceauşescu has cancer of the prostate. He has been to China and North Korea for treatment. 'But the rumours have been going round for years, and he's still there. He lives frugally, and he has the best doctors. Don't forget that we lead the world on cures for old age. Look at *Gerovital*,' the Parisian exile told me wrily, mentioning a patent medicine developed by Dr Ana Aslan, whose powers are regarded with cynicism by every Romanian I met, but which is sold in the West in the never-ending pursuit of hard currency.

Ceauşescu wants to leave his mark on Romania, and he thinks that by doing so he will get himself a chapter in the history books. To this end, a personality cult is pursued of such dimensions that it would be absurd if it were not so serious and so sad. The man's name is everywhere: on books, on hoardings, on every third line of the newspapers, and recited like a mantra on television. He wants the words 'Romania' and 'Ceauşescu' to become one, and he wants the Romania he leaves behind to bear the physical stamp of his taste and preoccupations. Meanwhile, ordinary Romanians have to supplement their meagre supplies by using the black market; people die for lack of heating or hospital treatment; criticism is stamped on; nationals are not supposed to talk to *any* foreigners without reporting the encounter to the police. Small wonder that people despair. Only days after I left Bucharest, I heard that a man had immolated himself outside the Canadian Embassy after having been refused a visa. 'The wonder is that he got hold of enough petrol to do it,' was the black joke my informant made when he told me.

But apart from the all-too-visible destruction of Bucharest's old quarter in the south of the city centre, and appreciating that the president's name is impossible to avoid, you could travel everywhere you're allowed to and have very little inkling of any of this; and you would see a beautiful country and meet a kind and charming people. One hopes that both will survive the 'Ceauşescu Epoch', as the president likes his reign to be known.

The train had started its journey as far away as Prague, but arrived exactly on time. Few other passengers were waiting for it in Budapest, and I found a compartment with two elderly Hungarians who were bound for Oradea, the first major town across the frontier. Our route lay over flatlands, and the sun rose over scattered farms and tiny villages as we rushed eastwards. Towards the frontier, a great line of poplars appeared, stretching from north to south, and, beyond them, the first hills of Transylvania rose. We stopped at the Hungarian frontier for a long time, but the customs and passport officers let us through without formality. Only a young man in a boiler suit, with a gun strapped to his waist, checked under the seats and under the carriage itself with a certain thoroughness. Then the train moved slowly forward through a grey no-man's-land of goods-wagon sidings towards the Romanian frontier-post at Episcopia Bihorului.

It had begun to rain, and the greyness of the day may have exaggerated my impression that the station here was crumbling. The only brightness came from the well-tended flowerbeds and the flags. A man in a crumpled grey suit came into the compartment to effect the obligatory currency exchange of ten dollars a day. The unit of currency here is the leu, and at the time the official rate of exchange gave you nine of them to the dollar. This rate was a little meaner even than Poland's. It is designed to maximize foreign currency income, and it makes Romania an expensive country for western tourists. The same is true of Burma, and it was often of Burma that I thought when seeking parallels for Romania in my mind.

The exchange clerk was courteous and spoke impeccable English. He borrowed my good ballpoint to fill in the exchange form, counted out a pile of notes so ancient and worn that one could hardly read them, wished me a pleasant stay, and departed. He was followed by a young sandy-haired man in a khaki uniform with red shoulder-boards, which looked to be of turn-of-the-century design. The officer took my passport, scrutinized it, and disappeared with it, not returning until just before the train left. In the meantime a customs officer in blue, equally courteous, was searching the Hungarians' luggage. He confiscated two magazines with covers about as risqué as the old *Tit-Bits*, and turned to me. Everything was inspected, including the metal back-support struts of my pack, which he pulled out. I think he suspected a concealed radio. To my disappointment, the strategically-placed copy of *Dracula* failed to elicit the smallest response, but I was probably far from the first western tourist who had tried to ingratiate himself in this way.

It was only after the train was moving again that I realized the exchange clerk had neglected to return my ballpoint.

Approaching Oradea we passed what was to be the first of many enormously long goods trains. There is little containerization in eastern Europe yet, and these trains carry the old-fashioned type of rust-red truck remembered from childhood. I counted fifty wagons at least. Progress on trains in Romania is slow, but Oradea is not far from the frontier, and we must have reached it within twenty minutes. At its outskirts, ragged and dirty small boys wearing woollen hats with high crowns reminiscent of those worn in Scandinavia appeared by the side of the train, either to wave, yell, or throw stones. Such children would accompany my progress by train in and out of every city in the country, and they provided an interesting contrast to the happy, well-scrubbed, red-neckscarved little Pioneers who present flowers to Nicolae and Elena at Party rallies, and who hold joyous rallies themselves of a quasi-military nature. As we arrived, I noticed just before the station an elephants' graveyard of large black steam locomotives. There must have been forty or fifty of them, all drawn up in a great pack. Later I was to see similar groups of apparently abandoned steam-engines, and as I only rarely saw them in operation I assume that they were redundant, though they looked in good repair. They would have been a railway-enthusiast's dream.

At Oradea my Hungarians were replaced by a middle-aged Romanian couple who looked extremely well-to-do and had a silky chestnut-coloured Pekinese dog with them, to which they fed the occasional chocolate drop. The husband had black, thinning, brilliantined hair, and wore a formal grey double-breasted suit. His wife was a large redhead with thick black eyebrows, baby-blue eyes behind flyaway spectacle frames, and pillar-box-red lipstick. We got as far as saying hello, and I learned that they were travelling back to their home in Sighişoara before my Romanian foundered. We had no other language in common, but in any case the revelation that I was not only a foreigner but a westerner seemed to have unsettled them. They remained friendly, however, and later offered me some very good orange-flavoured chocolate.

The third new passenger was in his early twenties. He was fashionably dressed in a casual white shirt, jeans, and real Puma trainers, bought on the black market in Timişoara, near the Yugoslavian frontier, where he was a medical student – in itself a mark of his high social status. He had a narrow, aquiline face topped by curly blond hair. For quite some time he chatted with the couple, and I thought he was in some way attached to them, but after about half an hour he turned to me.

'I couldn't help noticing your book,' he said in English. 'Where are you from?'

I told him, and he was delighted. 'You are my first Englishman! I was sure you must be a Czech or a Hungarian who just happened to have an English guide-book.' He apologized for the rain, which was still coming down fitfully. We were travelling through downland, dotted with the occasional flock of sheep. Here and there by the track there was a small field of maize, somebody's private supply.

We discussed Romanian food and the ease of getting about the country by train. He told me he had learned English by himself, through watching videos ('but this is a great secret'), and through talking to fellow-students from Libya and Iran. Then he said, 'I invite you for a cigarette.'

We were in a smoking compartment, but out of deference to the couple we went into the corridor, which had the advantage of being empty and noisy, so that one could not be overheard. He had a packet of Yugoslavian cigarettes which he told me a friend had procured for him – 'our own are awful' – but refused a Marlboro on the grounds that he didn't like Virginia tobacco. Armed with advice from home, I had brought packets of Kent cigarettes and Wrigley's chewing-gum to use as presents and bribes, so I stored this information away. Later, I was to discover that although Kent seemed to be virtually the only brand of western cigarette on sale in Romania, packets of them were by no means the universal currency they had been cracked up to be, though in lieu of tips they were welcome, along with the gum. A packet of western cigarettes cost about 120 lei – quite a sum, translated into the official rate of exchange, but given the vast wads of lei black marketeers carried about with them, perhaps not as much as it appeared.

My new friend had only been out of the country once, on a day trip to Yugoslavia, but he looked forward to the time when he could travel properly. His ambition was to become a plastic surgeon. The status would be helpful, he told me. 'It's not always easy here. Food tends to be a bit hard to come by, but you shouldn't have any difficulty with our national dishes. Anyway, with dollars, your way will be as smooth as silk. That's another little secret.' I couldn't be sure if he was sounding me out, or just being ironic. Even so I was sorry to say goodbye to him when I left the train. He was travelling on to Braşov: 'Though the speed this train's going, I'll be lucky to get there by tomorrow morning!'

I was grateful for his help when we arrived at Cluj, for as there was no station name-board, I had no way of identifying the stop. This turned out to be the case at a number of major Romanian stations, none of which, however, neglected to have large red-and-white signs exhorting loyalty to the president, linking his name with Romania and peace, for it is as a fighter for international nuclear disarmament that the president currently sees himself. Small stations, on the other hand, are invariably clearly marked, and few carry any reference to Ceauşescu. To make quite sure of where they are, Romanian travellers carry copies of the timetable, and tick off the stations as they pass.

Stumbling as I had on a group of well-to-do Romanians – people who could afford western clothes, to eat chocolate and keep pets – I did not really enter the country until I got off the train. It was still raining, a thin but persistent drizzle which managed to permeate everything. The hall of the station was crowded; huge queues stood at the antique ticket counters, and hand-painted boards gave arrival and departure times, occasionally amended with strips of paper glued on them. Because petrol is so strictly rationed, the train is a vital and much-used form of transport. This is true throughout eastern Europe, where private ownership of cars is far less common than at home; but in Romania it is particularly remarkable. The railway network is much better than the road system, too – roads are modest and frequently in a poor state of repair. Farm carts and, at the other end of the scale, huge agricultural machines often clog them, making progress slow. The advantage of this for a tourist is that vast areas of Romania are unspoilt and breathtakingly beautiful, especially in the heart of the Carpathians in the north of the country and around the painted monasteries of Bukovina (which are preserved as national monuments).

Cluj-Napoca (Napoca is its ancient Roman name, recently resurrected) is the 'Klausenbergh' where Jonathan Harker changes trains for Bistritz at the beginning of *Dracula*. The Romanians have a castle, Bran, which is popularly known as Dracula's; but it is to the south of Braşov. The Count's abode in the book must be far away from there, to the north of Bistriţa. His historical antecedent perpetrated his bloody deeds somewhere else again. The only bloodsuckers I encountered in Transylvania were mosquitoes, and they were vicious.

My first impression was that I had left Europe. The people are so mixed racially that set down from the sky at Cluj station you'd be hard put to it to say where you were. Dark skin and fair. Aquiline noses and snub noses, Russian button noses and Semitic noses. Sleek black hair and tousled blond hair. Narrow eyes and Mongol cheekbones; fierce Turkish moustaches and smooth French jawlines. Something nudged my legs, and looking down I saw a beggar-boy so monstrously deformed that it was impossible to distinguish arms and legs among the four stumps on which his twisted torso scuttled. In his teeth he held a smeared polythene bag in which he collected coins and notes. I'd become used to seeing a greater incidence of mild deformity and eye complaints in eastern Europe than encountered in the West – bandiness, squints and even rickets, though not common, I saw often enough. Equally, I saw a number of men with an arm or leg missing – the result of industrial accidents, for these people were too young to have been in the war. Prostheses in such cases were very rare. Nothing, though, had prepared me for this boy, nor would I have expected to see such deformity outside Africa or Asia. I did not encounter anyone quite so physically wretched in Romania again, though the number of amputees, struggling on ancient, even home-made wooden crutches and in one case a peg-leg, and of appalling wounds and scars, was higher in this country of expensive spas and clinics than anywhere else in eastern Europe.

I had no map of the town, and only a general idea of the location of the hotel I intended to try for. Emerging from the station and pausing in the rain, I was in for another shock – that of the familiar. The station and the high street leading off it, Baroque and Jugendstil with modern additions, were typical of any south central European town. Architecturally, I hadn't budged from Austria-Hungary. I asked the way of a man in a leather trilby and plastic jerkin. He was grizzled, and looked about fifty. I had just about enough Romanian to follow his directions, but even if I'd been fluent my clothes and luggage would have bellowed 'foreigner'. He drew me a little map on the back of a tattered notebook whose pages had been used again and again (paper is not something to be used extravagantly here either), then looked at me shrewdly.

'Where are you from?'

He couldn't believe it. 'Do you speak German?'

'Yes.'

He looked over his shoulder rather theatrically. Several Romanians I spoke to did this, if they were not drunk. I wondered if it might have attracted too much attention, but I do not live there, so I cannot judge what precautions must be taken. 'Why have you come here? Everything's to shit and buggery here. There's nothing. Nothing to eat, nothing to drink, and all because of that shit, Ceauşescu.'

I called to mind a joke which an East German student had told me on a café terrace in Prague, a world away now. 'We have this story about Romania,' he said: 'Radio Bucharest comes on the air at 6.30, and everyone has to switch on: "Good morning. This is Radio Bucharest. Now the president is waking up, and we are waking up . . ." And at 6.45: "Now the president is brushing his teeth, and we are brushing our teeth . . ." And at 7.00: "Now the president is pulling on his trousers, and we are pulling on our trousers . . ." And at 7.15: "Now the president is sitting down to breakfast and we are wishing him *bon appetit!*"'

I walked down the soaking strada Horea, barely taking it in. There were buildings of beige stone, by no means unattractive (though Cluj has a high-rise hinterland as unpleasant as those riding on the backs of so many other old towns throughout eastern Europe), large grocery stores which seemed to sell nothing but thinly-spaced jars of conserve, banks, shoe-shops, a chemist's with bare shelves, and a green-grocer's with surprisingly abundant goods for sale and a knot of people outside, though I never saw such a place again. In alleyways smallholders sold green grapes, and apricots, and maize. Long queues ending at tiny open doors in walls or set in large wooden double courtyard gates indicated where bread or milk was available.

I didn't discover why the queues formed at these tiny openings until much later: all staple foods, milk, bread, butter and so on, are difficult to obtain. To queue for these, you have to go round to the rear of the shops in the back-streets, out of sight. The president doesn't want unsightly queues, which are also bad propaganda, on view along the main streets and boulevards. 'We have a joke,' a nameless woman I met in a bookshop in Cluj told me in English as we walked from the shop down a deserted alley. 'The president and his wife are flying home to Romania after one of their many state visits. "Ah," says Nicolae to Elena as Bucharest emerges beneath the clouds, "look at all our wonderful Romanian rivers." Elena looks, and purses her lips. "My dear, look again. I am afraid those are not rivers; those are queues."'

As elsewhere in eastern Europe, queuing is done where possible by the old people, to enable the younger ones to work. The burden here, though, falls on women. Under the constitution they have equal rights; in practice and by tradition, they have no rights at all. 'We are a Latin race with a Turkish tradition,' a woman doctor in Bucharest told me. 'What do you expect?'

Crossing the busy little River Someșol brings one into the Baroque town, and the street changes its name to Gheorghe Doja. One or two restaurants appear, discreetly veiled from the street by thick net curtains, yet revealing glimpses of privileged interiors through their glass doors. It was past 2 p.m., too late for lunch, and here as elsewhere in eastern Europe a chair placed in the entrance indicated that an establishment was closed. The street finally debouched, under a canopy of trolley-bus wires, at piața Libertăţi. How familiar the language of this remote land was. The square is dominated by the great Gothic bulk of St Michael's Cathedral, the town's Roman Catholic foundation, guarded by the turn-of-the-century statue of Matthias Corvinus, known as Matei Corvin in his birthplace; and claimed by the Romanians as their own.

Skirting the dark church, and avoiding a lurching drunk with dramatic, saturnine features offset by a large, bleeding gash on his forehead, I made my way across the perfect flower-garden in the centre of the square to the Hotel Continental, another Art Nouveau wedding-cake. No room was available, but the receptionist, who might have been Parisian, told me in perfect French that she would find me another hotel, which she did, two minutes' walk away. I would take breakfast at the Continental, for which vouchers would be issued.

The street might have been in a southern Italian town. Inside, the Hotel Siesta was panelled in dark stained wood, and finished in a style fashionable in the Fifties. The rain had made interiors prematurely dark, and a solitary bulb was lit over the reception desk. Hot water would be available between eight and ten, I was told by the receptionist, a girl in heathery tweeds and spectacles. She was heavily pregnant – one of the very few pregnant women I saw during my whole time in Romania, which made me wonder. In order to boost the size of the population, the authorities had made abortions next-to-impossible to obtain, expected families to produce at least four children, and even policed the incidence of pregnancy among factory workers. (The president has said: 'A certain drop in the birth-rate ... is a question that concerns us very much and we took steps to ensure as good as possible a birth-rate, of about eighteen to twenty in one thousand inhabitants, because this is the only way to ensure the growth of the people.') Any woman who seeks a back-street abortion, often undertaken by nurses or medical assistants using home-made equipment, and finds herself thereafter with an infection requiring hospitalization, will not be treated until she discloses the name of the child's father and the name of the abortionist. There is at least one *Securitate* (secret police) official in every department of every hospital, as indeed there is in every institution and hotel; and in gynaecology departments the *Securitate* officer must have a record of all admissions and discharges. One horrific allegation I heard from exiles in Hungary was that in a small and unnamed town in the Bukovina an autopsy on a woman who had died as a result of trying to induce her own miscarriage was performed, as a deterrent, by police doctors in *public* in the market square. But there is little government support for the parents of large families, only a notional benefit (called *alocatie*) to parents of more than three children. Couples with no children, however, have to pay an extra tax.

The pretty receptionist's gentle face was wrapped nearly all the time in an ironic smile. ('You'd go quite mad here if you didn't have a sense of irony and hope for a better future,' a student I met in Braşov told me later.) On a green cushion on a chair at the reception desk a beautiful grey kitten dozed. It was a stray which she had rescued.

The wall of the building opposite was so close that my twin-bedded room was almost dark. At least the electricity was working. The chandelier had one low-watt bulb in it and the bedside lamps both worked, but the bathroom neon had to be coaxed into operation and even then whirred alarmingly. The hand-washed sheets were dank and grey. Outside, between dawn and dusk, an electric town clock blared out a wobbly tape which played what I think was a section of the national anthem every half hour, together with the appropriate chimes. There were no curtains.

The room was dominated by an enormous 'Diana' valve television, which didn't work. The television here transmitted on one channel, on weekdays in the evenings between eight and ten, at weekends for most of the day. The programmes, when I finally saw them, blurred and undulating on the screen in black-and-white, were mainly concerned with three connected themes. The first, using selected newsreel film, showed miserable West German workers on strike, wretched French students demonstrating, and dismal British unemployed at Job Centres. The commentary gave the impression that the whole of the western world was in starving capitalist-imperialist misery. The scene would then change to show beautiful young Roman-ians wandering through cornfields with the wind in their hair, passionately reciting poems in praise of the president – or we would see workers with noble faces describing the output of a certain factory or the success of this year's harvest. The third theme was connected with the president himself – his life and achievements. Often shots would be shown of him on a podium with his wife, giving a curiously truncated two-handed wave, his small hands to-and-froing in staccato rhythm close to his face. Then little children would present flowers and be kissed. Elena put her bouquets down elegantly; Nicolae, his public image still needing a final polish, dumped his immediately and unceremoniously.

Big valve televisions presided in every hotel room I used, but only two worked, and the one in Braşov only deigned to show me a glimmer of an Italian movie in which Fernando Rey starred as a corrupt capitalist politician, before going off into a buzzing snowstorm.

Venturing out, I found that the rain had once again obligingly abated. I went along to the tourist office, where a shy woman explained how to use the train timetable and left me to it, apologizing for her halting English, 'but it is so long since I've used it.' Having noted my trains, I then went to the *Agenţia de Voiaj*. This was a dark Art Nouveau cave lit by three or four yellow bulbs, which revealed queues of no more than twenty or thirty people each at tiny frosted-glass *guichets*, above which were circular boards with the numbers of trains on little metal plaques hung on them. I was given three cardboard tickets – one for my seat, one for first-class supplement, and one for my reservation, all punched in a system of intricate metal machines. I was treated with the usual calm courtesy and began to feel ashamed of having expected Romanians to be irritable, or at the very least resentful of westerners. 'Some of them will think you have just come to laugh at them,' a Czech friend had warned me, but I never found this to be the case.

I had ended up at Liberty Square again, and crossed the corner of it to the café-restaurant of the Continental, where I'd had a beer earlier. Now only wine was available. Two youths at a table near me asked for western cigarettes, but turned down chewing-gum. An elderly beggar was moving among the tables. After me, he descended on two Libyans sharing a bottle of wine with a Romanian friend. There are many Libyans in Romania; President Ceauşescu and Colonel Gaddafi are close friends.

'Your Princess Dee very beautiful,' one of the Libyans told me, ordering another bottle. They had both spent five years as students here, and now they were back on holiday. 'After Transylvania, we go to Constanţa – the coast is the best place in this country.' All the time as we chatted the lofty, sad room, with its still lovely though faded blue, white and gold decoration, was getting darker and darker. The waiters in their threadbare dinner jackets had to go to the tall, net-curtained windows to see well enough to sort out change. The place was full, though the only food available seemed to be overblown cream doughnuts, and only a handful of people were eating them. Suddenly, a clutch of bracket-lamps were switched on – maybe a quarter of those available – and everyone clapped and cheered ironically.

I went in search of dinner. At my hotel, the pregnant receptionist had been replaced by a cheerful blonde who had torn herself away from the football on television – Romania versus Italy – for long enough to advise me to try the Central-Melody restaurant. By now it was dark. Few cars were around, and street lights were only on at occasional corners. The quiet, the wet streets, and the darkness in a sizeable town struck an odd note. Under one light at a corner of the square, a gathering of perhaps thirty or forty men stood, all dressed in trilbys and shabby suits, all silent. One or two smoked. From behind the dimly-lit, yellowing curtains of one restaurant the languid sounds of a Palm Court orchestra drifted on to the square.

The Central-Melody had closed at 7.30, and I remembered too late that energy-saving also meant restricted opening hours. I turned along December 30th Street (I could never fathom the significance of all the different dates east European streets are named after) and found a small restaurant which still had a light on. Penetrating its depth, I became aware as my eyes accustomed themselves to the gloom that no one was there, but at the back I found a middle-aged woman counting wads of lei at a table spread with a blood-red cloth. She was on the verge of closing, but she told me she could offer me chicken and took me to a table, pouring me a glass of delicious apple-juice – something I was offered automatically at every restaurant in Cluj, but not elsewhere. She went away, to return with two rock-hard grey rolls and a plate with a leg of chicken and three small dollops, as from an ice-cream scoop, of potato, a kind of coleslaw, and *mamaliga*, the Romanian staple, a distant relative of polenta.

The food was lukewarm-to-cold, and the chicken barely more than skin and bone. I felt ashamed that I found it all so poor, ate it double-quick, paid my twenty-six lei, and left.

I got back to my room to find that it had been searched, and that a packet of chewing-gum had been stolen.

After so long in eastern Europe, I was used to seeing plenty of people in uniforms, with guns, wandering around the streets. Here, the variety and smartness of the uniforms provided a contrast with the dowdy clothes of the civilians. Lots of bright colour – pale blue and red and bright green – mingled with gold at the throat, on the shoulders and at the cuff as well as on peaks of caps and capbands. Women soldiers wore forage caps jauntily on top of clouds of bouffant red and blond hair, and did not carry guns at their belts.

There were plenty of soldiers and *militia* (police) on the streets of Cluj – but no Russians. Though a member of the Warsaw Pact, Romania has not participated in Warsaw Pact manoeuvres and exercises since 1968, when Ceauşescu denounced Russia's invasion of Czechoslovakia. The cheering for him in the West was genuine then, and the British gave him the Order of the Bath.

After breakfast at the Continental – black tea with salty soft cheese and some

above: Modern East German architecture in New Dresden: the 'Centrum' department store

below: Old Dresden. Semper's Opera House, built in the nineteenth century but totally destroyed by Allied bombing in February 1945. After painstaking restoration of both the exterior and the interior, it reopened in 1985. Semper also designed the Victoria and Albert Museum, London, having fled to Britain after taking part in the revolution of 1848

Right: Beach chairs at
Warnemünde, on the coast just
north of Rostock

Below: The town centre of
Rostock, East Germany's
principal port and home of one
of Europe's oldest universities

Below: Goethe's town house in
Weimar, from the garden

Right: The Great Crane at
Gdańsk – restored after the
war. Ninety per cent of
Gdańsk was destroyed during
the conflict

Below: The Palace of Culture in
Warsaw – an unsolicited gift
from Russia in the mid-fifties

Left: The Mariacka Church in Cracow. The most famous of Cracow's many hundreds of churches, it contains a magnificent carved wooden altarpiece by Veit Stoss. From its taller tower a melancholy trumpet call is played every hour, in memory of a medieval bugler killed by a Tartar arrow in the midst of raising the alarm

Right: Auschwitz-Birkenau: the broken back of Crematorium II

Below: Southern Bohemia: the main square of České Budějovice, which is a masterpiece of domestic Renaissance architecture

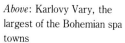

Above: Karlovy Vary, the
largest of the Bohemian spa
towns

Above: Grey longhorn cattle on the *puszta*.
Originally bred for their beef, these charming and docile creatures divide their time between browsing and sleeping

Left: In Slovakia: the ruins of Spišský hrad. This castle, now partially restored, is one of a series built in the Middle Ages to guard against invasion from the north. Slovakia is littered with their highly picturesque ruins

Above: A *csiko*, or horse-herdsman, on the *puszta* near Hortobagý

Left: The church of St Anthony in Eger. This magnificent baroque church, built between 1728 and 1730, is believed to be the work of Kilian Dietzenhofer

Above: Cars decked out for a
wedding in typical East
European fashion – these were
in Debrecen

Top: Still bearing its red star in
1988 – the House of Parliament
in Budapest

Left: In the German cemetery at Sighişoara: a First World War memorial from the lost days of the Austro-Hungarian Empire

Below: Sighişoara – perhaps the most beautiful town in Transylvania, and the former seat of Vlad Dracul

Below: Bucharest – the Triumphal Arch, built in 1922 in imitation of the Arc de Triomphe. It is a memorial in celebration of the Allied victory in the First World War, and in honour of Romania's war dead

Left: The Village Museum in
Bucharest. Here, examples of
village architecture from all over
Romania have been collected
since the thirties.

Right: Old Plovdiv – the
quintessence of Bulgarian
'National Revival' architecture,
which was introduced after
liberation from the Turks

Below: The monastery at Rilski
– perhaps the most famous of
the fortified mountain
monasteries which were the
guardians of Bulgarian culture
during the centuries of Turkish
occupation

Above: The Church of St
Dimiter of Salonika, in Veliko
Târnovo. Here it was that the
brothers Peter and Asen
proclaimed the liberation of
Bulgaria from Byzantine
domination in 1185. The church
has been completely restored,
after falling into ruin under the
Turks

Right: The Turkish single-span
bridge which crosses the River
Neretva at Mostar. It was built
in 1566

Left: Fortification at Budva. This tiny fortified Venetian town was virtually destroyed by an earthquake in 1979. It is now restored, and will soon be entirely taken over by tourists

Left: Space-age shopping centre at Bar. Lying far to the south, on the coast almost at the Albanian frontier, Bar is being developed as a major port, and there is a direct rail-link with the capital

Below: The monument to Enver Hoxha erected in his birthplace, Gjirokastër, in 1988

Above: Street scene in Gjirokastër. The news had just come through that Albania had lost 2:0 to England at home. Some soldiers crept into this photograph, making it illegal

Above: One of the diverse capitals on the
Byzantine monastery church at Apollonia

Right: One of the last full-figure statues of
Stalin on ordinary public display anywhere
in the world. It is to be found in Tiranë, the
capital of Albania

Below: Tiranë: Socialist Realism is still *de
rigueur* in Albania. This is the façade of the
new National Museum

smoked pork, eaten with grey German bread – I crossed the street to the university bookshop. All the books in the window were by, or about, the president. *Man of Destiny* was a typical title. Within, a bank of the same books greeted my eye, and only beyond them were other subjects more quietly ranked. I left, and joined the throngs of people in the streets; it seems, looking back, that every street in Romania was full of people of all ages during the daytime, weekdays and weekends alike.

I walked along the strada Dr Petru Groza, the broad boulevard lined with attractive houses which links the two main squares. I was on my way to piaţa Victoriei, but dropped off down a side-street when I noticed the Tailors' Bastion at the end of it. This is all that remains of the medieval town walls, and its name indicates that the various guilds were each responsible for sections of the town's fortification. There are bastions in Braşov named after the weavers and ironsmiths who paid for them. The side-streets in themselves were interesting – quiet, prosperous reminders of a sedate, bourgeois age, now lined with parked Dacia cars, the Dacia 1300 being almost the only model you will see in Romania, although the slightly smarter Oltcit sometimes puts in an appearance. The Dacia is reminiscent of the Renault 12 – hardly surprising since, under an agreement with France made several years ago, Romania took over the old French model for development in her own factories. Ceauşescu's plan was to develop the Dacia to outstrip its rivals in eastern Europe, and then market it within the Eastern Bloc and possibly even in the West. 'He entirely failed to grasp that in the West this was already an old car,' I was told by Ioan, an engineer in Cluj. 'Such is the extent of his self-delusion, and his total lack of understanding of what it's like on the other side of the Curtain.' Incongruously, he laughed merrily.

'How do you stay so cheerful?'

'We have a saying: *haz de necaz*. It means, "to make fun of trouble". It's in our blood. It must be something to do with being stamped on by the Turks and overrun by everybody else for seven hundred years. After all, our ancestors probably saw far worse than the *Conducator*, and Romania will survive him.' But his expression clouded. 'It will be at a cost, though,' he added. 'What has been destroyed in our culture already will remain dead.'

The bulk of traffic on Petru Groza was pedestrian. Large peasant women in bright dresses and headscarves sell flowers on every corner, but not from stalls; they simply stand with three or four bunches in either hand. There are queues outside scattered food-stores, the women in midi-skirted suits, or smarter, younger ones in jeans and red leather jackets; the men in trilbys, stubble on their faces, imitation leather jackets buckling across their backs, shapeless suits trailing trouser bottoms on the wet pavement. My beard attracted a few stares, but so did my belt-pouch; it looks like a holster.

There was a small mob outside the cinema. Most films are Romanian-made, about the freedom-fighters of the liberation from Nazism, or about the doings of Matei Corvin, Decebalus, and heroes of ancient Dacia – though I noticed that a play by Woody Allen was advertised on hoardings and his film *Hannah and her Sisters* was playing in Bucharest. Cinemas are well patronized, and always prominently marked on maps. They still run serial films here (you come back next week to see the next episode). 'I'd stay home and watch TV if I had one, and if there was anything worth watching,' a girl in Sighişoara told me, laughing.

I walked on, past the usual shops – an optician, a tailor, a haberdasher – all narrow-fronted places with twilight interiors and a counter with shelves behind it. Self-service is unheard-of in eastern Europe outside a handful of supermarkets in the main towns. But there is something missing here: there is no gaiety. The only advertisements are for the president, and there are not even coloured-paper decor-ations in shop windows to entice you into their unlit depths. I stopped outside a florist's in surprise. Inside and out it was as elegant and as well-stocked as any flower shop in Paris, Hamburg or Amsterdam. It seemed out of place here, unnatu-rally, unfairly prosperous.

The answer to why this was may lie in the Romanian love of flowers. Victory Square in Cluj is a large public garden, alive with flowers planted in intricate patterns, colours blending and clashing like the patterns on peasants' skirts and tunics, whirling round the bases of tall conifers in kaleidoscopic pools and eddies. Is it too much to suspect that Romanians express the colour that is in their souls, the colour that has been taken out of their lives by their government, through flowers? Is it because flowers are one of the few things they are allowed to enjoy without restriction? But there is a yearning in their music so wild and free that it suggests a spirit longing for far greater outlets than municipal flowerbeds and domestic window-boxes, however much ordinary Romanians may attempt to crowd these with at least a little of the brightness of life. A friend of the prominent and courageous dissident Doina Cornea told me drily that the expression 'half a loaf is better than no bread' would have an extraordinarily concrete currency in Romania – 'not least, of course, because of the bread ration'. Doina Cornea herself has not been seen since April 1989.

Two majestic buildings face each other across the square, drawing attention away from the fine terrace that runs between them on the far side. The Romanian Orthodox church is built in such close imitation of a Byzantine basilica that one might not immediately guess it was only completed sixty years ago. The interior is dark, and heavy with the smells of incense and tallow. A service was in progress when I visited, strong baritone voices soaring confidently upwards to God. The congregation all but overflowed onto the steps outside, and so many thin, honey-coloured candles were being sold and lit that two church staff – a headscarved crone straight out of Grimm and a portly official in a brown caretaker's coat – were permanently employed clearing space among the clusters of iron spikes for new ones to be placed. A small man in a brown suit a size too large wandered like a lost child among the devout as they constantly genuflected and crossed themselves. He must have been at least forty-five, as tiny lines had etched themselves all over his moon-like face despite the absence of thought reflected there. His young-old eyes caught mine for a moment, suspicion mingling with curiosity at this sight of a stranger, then darted back to familiar faces.

Confronting the church is the Teatrul National, yet another neo-Baroque effort by

Helmer and Fellner. This is a beautiful building with a complex façade featuring three tiers of columns flanked by church-like spires surmounted by wild charioteers with, I think, lions in their shafts. *Don Carlo* and *The Merry Wives of Windsor* were playing. I was shortly to meet one of the cast.

I had found a restaurant for lunch in strada Gh. Doja. It was decorated in pale wood, and some lights were on despite the fact that it was midday. There was, as usual, no menu, but the waitress ran through what was available in German, and I ordered. Along with the apple-juice came what appeared to be gammon steak with the same trimmings as I'd had the night before. It was almost cold, but very good. To drink I had *ţuica*, the Romanian schnapps. This came in large glasses with dangerously chipped rims, and was overpoweringly alcoholic.

I was joined at my table by three individual diners, all male. Two had a clerical look about them, and ordered drinks which looked identical but which came in different glasses – one in a balloon, the other in a flute. I asked about this. The man drinking from the flute smiled and said, 'We're both drinking brandy. It's just that mine has come in a thin communist flute, and his has come in a fat capitalist balloon.'

Also drinking brandy was a large middle-aged man dressed in denims, his hair curly and tinted chestnut. He had a handsome, florid face with a big broken nose. He also spoke some German, and after asking whether I had any unopened packets of cigarettes, or dollars that I wanted to change, we settled down to a more general conversation. Had I been to New York? Or Los Angeles? We talked about Italy, where he'd been as a young man. 'Before all this ...' There was something familiar about this man, with his open-necked shirt and neckscarf, his rings and his too-good-to-be-true tan.

'You're an actor,' I said.

He was delighted. 'Yes! At the theatre up the road.' We talked theatre as best we could for a while. Later, I changed ten dollars with him, in the doorway to a courtyard down a back-street, with much furtive whispering and backward glances. The transaction over, he kissed me on both cheeks, delighted beyond measure, and scurried off. He didn't want to be in my company for too long, since we'd been seen leaving the restaurant together.

I made my way through a web of little yellow back-streets where Gypsies had set up an impromptu market, selling hard plums and half-rotten pears from plastic buckets, to emerge finally at the strada Universităţii. Heading uphill, I crossed strada Avram Iancu and continued up past elegant villas set well back from the road in leafy gardens; some of them announced themselves by plaques as university departments; others might still have been private houses.

My goal was the Botanical Gardens, for which Cluj is famous. Unable to slow my pace from its natural London speed, I found myself overtaking dark-haired girls ambling back to the office from lunch. They gazed at me in astonishment: who could have anything so pressing to do that it required such fast walking?

The gardens were not disappointing. Little paths ran down to algae-covered ponds under dripping branches, and timber-baulked earth steps led up to tiny alpine clearings under fir boughs. Chinese bridges spanned ornamental lakes, and everywhere labels told in Romanian and Latin of comfortingly familiar roses, clematis, berberis and pyracantha; bright pentstemon, pale yellow inula, and vulgar red hot poker. Not far from the gate, presiding over this autumnal and solitary retreat, was a bust of what appeared to be a particularly benign Lenin; but closer inspection revealed him to be Florian Dorcus, a botanist who died in 1906.

I returned to the town centre and the Ethnographic Museum. I was the only visitor to this rich collection, which ranged from folk costume to fishermen's dugouts and the carved wooden tridents used to spear sterlet and trout up until a decade or two ago. An elderly woman in a headscarf accompanied me silently, to turn lights on and off as I wandered through, and she and her three colleagues seemed reluctant for me to leave when the visit was over. The museum is housed in an Empire palace which almost within living memory belonged to a now vanished Hungarian nobleman. I wondered how Romania could so lovingly collect and seemingly revere a culture which she is systematically destroying where it still lives. Regretting that I had arrived here perhaps only a decade too late to see country people wearing the garments and special embroidery of their village as everyday clothing, I wondered too whether official thinking in Romania considers that the only place for folk culture and architecture is in museums – tidied up.

I stopped off at the second-hand bookshop, packed with people, opposite the main entrance to St Michael's, and found a foreign-language section. Dozens of decaying French paperbacks – beige covers, and uncut pages of Proust, Mauriac and Pagnol. In English, I found a 1937 engineering manual and a 1967 Civil Defence booklet on what to do in the event of a nuclear war. Another shelf contained far more volumes in Hungarian and German, Serbian and Russian, and a handful of religious works printed in beautiful Slavic script.

Strada Corvin leads away from the church, at its end the heavy and modest medieval building where the great king was born. Turning left, I wandered happily over cobbles through fifteenth-century back-streets whose charm had not been self-consciously turned on for tourists. A mother with two smart young daughters with red ribbons in their hair turned to let her family into their house, putting the key into the lock of an ancient green door set anonymously into the wall. The little girls waited under the ornate gables and wrought-iron brackets which had perhaps once carried shop-boards.

I continued on to the Parcul Central, where another bust of Florian Dorcus awaited me, except that it wasn't him at all, but one more Lenin lookalike. I walked down the central avenue, along with a handful of other early evening strollers, pairs of lovers, and a group of little boys throwing sticks into the branches of the horse-chestnuts to get conkers down. I reached the smart, modern, ugly Hotel Sport, glanced into its tenebrous, unlit interior, and walked back towards town. Earlier, I had noticed long queues at small kiosks or dark open doorways, from which some kind of hot food was being dispensed. Now I joined one of the queues and bought myself, for two lei, a *gogoși*. In colour and taste it was like a doughnut; in shape it was like a *nan*. Quite delicious, and a cheap way of filling your stomach, I guessed. Most people walked away with two or three. I never saw them again after Cluj.

It was dusk, and the streets were emptying after the brief flurry of rush-hour. Dacias stood in a silent row along one side of the cathedral. I made my way to the Continental for a glass of wine. The price had changed from last night, but I grew used to these fluctuations, not always to one's disadvantage, from waiter to waiter, everywhere between Czechoslovakia and Bulgaria. From somewhere in the depths of the hotel a combo was playing 'mood music', which was interrupted now and then by mysterious loud bursts of Dire Straits numbers from another hidden enclave. I was halfway through my second glass when a drunk approached my table and asked for a cigarette. Then he sat down and started to chat.

'*Sprechen Sie Deutsch?*'

'*Ja.*'

He nodded sagely, and continued in Romanian, now peppered with the odd German word. He was a lecturer in psychology at the university. 'I apologize for being drunk,' he said. 'But sometimes that is the only way to be. And I must ask you not to be offended if people here seem stand-offish. It's because we're not supposed to talk to you, you know.'

I said that I knew about that, and was sorry, but understood and wasn't offended.

'Don't be offended,' he insisted. 'Actually, we love meeting foreigners – we meet so few, and we can't go abroad.' He finished his cigarette. 'The people at the next table are looking at me,' he said. 'I must go.' And he did, without another word or a backward glance.

I watched a couple of young men, one calm and reasonable, the other drunk and spoiling for a fight with an unassuming waiter who may have suggested that he'd had enough. The drunk kept standing up and making threatening remarks and gestures, before subsiding onto a stool in an attitude of maudlin dejection. His friend managed to get him out of the bar at one point, but back they came a few minutes later. Finally peace was declared, and the two men settled down to more drinks in minuscule glasses.

By then a chestnut-haired man of perhaps thirty-five had joined me. After introducing himself, he ordered a bottle of wine, which he drank with great rapidity. We established a common language which was a mixture of Romanian, Italian and French. 'I'm a truck-driver so I mustn't get drunk or the cops'll get me,' he said, ordering another bottle and filling my glass when it came. He would only accept cigarettes as a swap, my Kents for his Snagovs. 'These are the only Romanian cigarettes that aren't full of sawdust,' he told me. 'I think. But then, they put sawdust in everything, even the bread.' After the second bottle, we split the cost of another; I was not allowed to treat him.

'It's a bugger here,' he told me cheerfully. By now they had switched the lamps on and his eyes danced in the dim light. The place had emptied and there was no one sitting near us. In any case, he was too tight to notice. I was certain that he was not a security policeman, but remained as non-committal as I could. He told me that he was relatively well off, as a bachelor, but that friends of his with two or three children could barely make do on the rations, which had dropped to under a litre of cooking oil per month and only a kilo of flour per family. 'And that's not all – you'll be lucky to get a litre of milk a week, and maybe three loaves.'

'Can you afford to drink?' A bottle of the rough white Tirnave cost twenty-five lei.

'I can't afford not to!' He dropped his voice. 'You know what's going on here. And it's not just happening to the Hungarians and the Germans. He wants the rural life of this country to go altogether. I think he hates it because it's successful, and because it was here before he was.'

'But can anyone do anything?'

He shrugged. 'Some of us wrote a letter to him, just pointing out that he's getting rid of a central slice of our culture. And villagers forced to move away are being cut off from roots that go back generations. It'll kill them.'

'What'll happen to the letter-writers?'

'God knows. But you've got to do something. You can't just sit and take this kind of treatment forever. I think they got a copy of the letter out to the West. Someone's got to know what's going on here.'

He didn't pursue the subject after that, turning to everyday things. Did I enjoy fishing? What about football? What team did I support? Where was I off to next in Romania? We finished the bottle, and when we shook hands at parting I felt that his hand was as hard as wood. It was another friendship that I was sorry had no future. 'But perhaps if you come back one day you'll be able to stay at my house and we'll go fishing,' he said. There was not much hope in his voice.

18

VLAD'S SEAT

The weather had finally changed for the better, and I walked back up the strada Horea in blazing sunshine. The streets were already dry, though pools of water remained in potholes and dips in the road. An occasional car or small lorry trundled past; men stood on street corners chatting, the bread queues which had formed before dawn were still patiently waiting for the dark, secretive little doors to open and distribute loaves from the depths behind them. Two rookies ahead of me saluted a corpulent officer in a uniform which owed something to the British and something to the Italian army in its design.

I was early, but it was easier to find the correct platform than I'd expected, and I settled down on a bench close to the electric train indicator. I'd booked on a *rapid* to Sighişoara. There are three kinds of train in Romania – the *rapid*, which only stops at major stations, and is quite slow; the *accelerat*, which stops more frequently, and is slower; and the *personaua*, which stops everywhere but generally arrives on time and has the most interesting passengers. Romanians assumed that as a westerner I would always want to travel first-class on the *rapid*, and sometimes it was difficult to persuade them otherwise.

It was while waiting on the stations among one's fellow-travellers that one got a sense of being at the confluence of Europe and Asia; but this had as much to do with Romania's primitive nature and the apparent poverty of the people as anything. Guide-books suggest that in Romania the tourist has a last chance to see rural Europe as it was fifty years ago. In terms of seeing lots of horse-drawn hay-wagons with wooden wheels, that is true; but the people who live here would like to benefit from some of the advantages technological progress has put within the reach of most westerners and other east Europeans. 'It will come when we have paid off our debt; then Romania will enter a truly brave new world,' the Romanian Communist Party member in Bucharest told me – I hope that he is wrong, in the sense that he means. I wondered for a moment if he was being ironical, then realized that he could not have read Huxley's book.

Weatherbeaten faces, black walrus moustaches, battered trilbys and ancient double-breasted suits suggest Turkey. Older peasant women have impossibly wide hips, and wear their black headscarves and dark clothes sprinkled with tiny white floral designs into which women in these parts still seem to grow with age. By the time the huge train with its antiquated carriages arrived, the platform was crowded. East Europeans like to travel heavy, and in an attempt to find my appointed carriage

I had to struggle through a milling throng of people toting huge bundles, vast cardboard boxes and string bags lopsided with wretched chickens darting their inverted heads from side to side in panic. No one thought to move along the train on the other side of the platform, which was empty, but even doing this myself I failed to find my carriage, and I was not alone, since several fellow-travellers asked me if I knew where *their* carriage might be. The problem was that no one had numbered the wagons. I decided to get on anyway or lose all hope of a seat for the 200-odd-kilometre journey, which even on paper was going to last three hours.

I found a free seat by a window. The reason it was free was that it half-collapsed under me as I sat down, but it held, and was a small price to pay for the views I would get as we moved into the heart of Transylvania. If only the railway companies of eastern Europe would clean the carriage windows from time to time.

My travelling companions included a portly man in a leather jerkin and collar-and-tie opposite; next to him a cadaverous old man in a chocolate brown suit and lime-green socks, asleep; a tall, thin young man in a sports jacket who blushed and buried his head in his magazine when he overheard me say where I was from; an artistic-looking man with blond curly hair; and a plain girl in a demure blue suit with lace at the collar and cuffs. She was sitting next to me, and clearly wished she wasn't once she learned I was from the West. Since the question I was generally asked in Romania was not 'Where are you from?' but 'Are you from East Germany?' I took to saying yes. It put people more at ease.

No one talked to me, or to each other, for the entire journey, which ran through peaceful, lush, rolling countryside which gave no hint of the turmoil of its history – Transylvania has been one of the most fought-over areas in the world – or of the painful processes it was experiencing now. Cushioned from Russia to the north and the Regat – Old Romania – to the east by the snaking Carpathians, it was part of Hungary until the Treaty of Trianon ceded it to Romania in 1920 and rang the death knell of the provincial Hungarian aristocracy which held on here until the Second World War ended all.

We followed the River Nadaşul due south to Turda and then on to Ocna Mureş, where the river joins with and is taken over by the Mureşul. At Teiuş we turned east, and a slow ascent began, through Blaj and the black industrial town of Copşa Mică, on past vineyards to prosperous and soulless Mediaş, with a 'Saxon' village at its core. From there we climbed more steeply, and, after long waits occasioned by work on the lines, I was deposited at Sighişoara – my travelling companions, consulting their timetables, told me I'd arrived, and said goodbye with shy smiles. We were only an hour-and-a-half late.

The little station with its flower-clad courtyard is on a slight rise beyond the town and commands a good view of the fortified old city on its steep rock. In the valley of the Tîrnava Mare immediately below it stands the large neo-Byzantine black-and-white Orthodox basilica. There is only one hotel, the Steaua. After getting directions from a friendly policeman I set off down the little hill and then up the strada Gării to the town.

Because of its river, fertile land and an easily-fortifiable rock, the area has been settled since at least the Bronze Age. In the third century BC the Dacian fortress of Sandova stood here, and four hundred years later a *castrum* was established of the Thirteenth Legion *Gemina* – the Roman force which brought down Decebalus in AD 89. German settlers came here in the twelfth century; and in the thirteenth and fourteenth, as a result of Turkish attack, the settlement grew into a heavily fortified township. Fourteen towers were erected, each named after a guild, of which nine remain. By the high Middle Ages there were twenty-five guilds in Sighişoara, which had become the major trade centre of the Sieben Burgen, attracting business from as far away as Moldavia and Wallachia on the other side of the Carpathians. And much later, in July 1849, just upriver at Albeşti, the battle took place at which the Austrians crushed the revolutionary army of General Bem. Among the fallen was the twenty-six-year-old Sándor Pétőfi.

At the top of strada Gării a paved square opens out, flanked on one side by the basilica and on the other by a cluster of attractive modern flats with wooden gables. At the corner of the street is a modest memorial to the Russian troops who fell liberating Romania from Germany in 1944, and beyond it a brightly-painted loco-motive stands in front of a restaurant or club called the Sauna. Children play on the engine. I crossed the river by the road bridge and found myself at the top of the town's main street, named after the first of Romania's two post-war presidents, Gheorghe Gheorghiu-Dej.

There was the usual crowd outside the little Lumina cinema at the corner of the wide street, and across the road a greengrocer's stall offered peppers for sale, as well as half a bucket of bruised pears and a handful of paprikas and sorry-looking tomatoes. The pavements were crowded with people who looked much more countrified than the citizens of Cluj, dressed in mud-stained suits and high-crowned caps. Many looked completely Turkish, and there were dirty Gypsy families in ragged, once gaudy pullovers and grimy flared trousers. Leaning on a thin bolster set across his window-sill, an elderly, heavy-jowled Jew surveyed the scene.

I passed an old woman sitting by a half-bucket of hard lilac plums for sale, and checked my directions with a smart auburn-haired man in a beige pullover and slacks, who answered me in English. English and French are taught in Romanian schools, and in Sighişoara German is widely spoken, but of the Germans who settled here eight centuries ago I could find little trace yet. A red Lada covered with fir branches was clearly bound for a funeral, and I noticed that the inscription on the wreath which a black-clad man and woman were loading onto the back seat was in German Gothic script. At a street corner I overheard two elderly women in suits and smart coats talking to each other in German, but that seemed to be all.

The houses were early nineteenth-century, brightly painted, jauntily gabled. Some, especially two on the corner of strada Avram Iancu and Şoseaua Mihai Viteazul, were overgrown with Virginia creeper. The road was dotted with horse-droppings, and the organic smells were those of my childhood. It was hard to believe that half a mile behind me was the New Town, a modern industrial complex based on textiles and glass. It did not intrude, it wasn't enormous, and what I saw of it did not seem unpleasant; there were sports facilities including a football stadium, and the blocks were broken up by trees.

The only sign of decay here was in some of the back-streets, where children played hide-and-seek among the crumbling ruins of what were once pretty Baroque houses, and at the corner of strada Morii, by the footbridge near the basilica, there was an ominous building site.

The hotel was a cheerful early twentieth-century building, decorated with concrete cherubs painted grey. Inside, large windows ensured plenty of light, and its brasserie was packed with beer-drinking locals. Immediately beyond the Steaua, Lenin Square opened out. A large restaurant, the Perla, stood at one corner, and beyond it, surrounding a flower-filled garden, ran a handful of open-air beer-halls which I would see fully occupied throughout the ensuing weekend. From here, two narrow cobbled streets ran up to the Old Town.

Rearing above one of them is the fourteenth-century clock tower. One street goes under the arch it stands on, the other close by it. The tower easily dominates the other pinnacles and turrets of the Old Town, which from a distance has the romantic appeal of a fairy-tale castle. You would not be surprised to see Rupert of Hentzau ride out to greet you on a palomino stallion.

But it is another figure, far from romantic, whose memory dominates the castle hill. Vlad Dracul of the Basarabs, Prince of Wallachia, lived here for four years in the fifteenth century. 'Dracul' means 'dragon', and Vlad took the title after his emperor, Sigismond, had awarded him the Order of the same name. But warlike and bloodthirsty as Dracul may have been, it is his son, Vlad Ţepeş, who casts his shadow over the history of these hills. He exposes Count Dracula for the pallid figure of late Victorian fiction that he is, though Bram Stoker got the physical features right. Vlad Ţepeş stares at you from his portrait with hyperthyroid, intelligent, half-mad eyes above a long nose and vast, sloping moustaches. His nickname was Vlad the Impaler. He did not drink the blood of his Turkish and Bulgarian enemies; he stripped them and impaled them in their thousands on sharp wooden pikes embedded in the ground. The pointed tip was inserted in the anus, and the victim's own weight and gravity allowed the stake, if its progress was tidy, to slide through the bowels and gut to emerge at the throat or through the mouth. All who displeased him could expect this treatment.

It is hard, standing in the peaceful, cobbled piaţa Muzeului today, watching the old men sitting with their pipes on blue benches under the spreading tree which dominates it, to acknowledge that this was one of the scenes of those executions. Perhaps it was here that he ate his alfresco breakfast, surrounded by a writhing, screaming forest of victims, as depicted in a famous contemporary woodcut. If so, then it is to the rock of Sighişoara, not Bran, that tourists should be directed if they are to see Dracula's real castle.

Prince Dracul's former house on this square is now a very good wine bar and restaurant. A lower room painted buttery yellow contains wooden benches and tables at which men sit in their caps or *berets basques* drinking Romanian cognac, *ţuica*, or the watery red Carnaca wine. Upstairs is the small restaurant, where you can follow the Romanian habit of ordering a bottle of wine (it isn't often served in smaller quantities anyway) and a litre of mineral water with whatever's on the menu. This is usually limited to two or three dishes anywhere you go. Here I had a pork cutlet, which was delicious and almost hot, with chips and some tasty but unidentifiable pale vegetable which may have been related to sauerkraut. Although the price was reasonable, I was well aware, sometimes uncomfortably, of how luxuriously I was living compared with most of the local population, though equally I was almost always the only westerner.

The clock tower, also on this square, houses the town museum. Floorboards creak and crack alarmingly under you as you wander round the dull exhibits with a handful of other tourists, some from other parts of Romania, a handful from East Germany. Things get better as you ascend from floor to floor. There is a magnificent painted Baroque wardrobe in blue and gold, and at the top you can see the exposed workings of the Renaissance clock itself. A glass panel lets you see the otherwise hidden wooden figures who emerge and parade outside when the clock strikes the hour.

The view from the red wooden gallery under the roof encompasses the valley. Arrows fixed to the balustrade point in the direction of major cities, including *Londra*, and give the distances to them. On a wall, a fading chart in German gives details of mean rainfall here between 1888 and 1938.

The Old Town is very small, and here, finally, greeting older people, you hear the *Grüss Gott* of southern Germany, not the *bună ziua* of Romania, and walking past lovely, buckling green and yellow houses down narrow cobbled lanes you hear voices inside speaking the German of the Transylvanian 'Saxons'. The streets, where much restoration work is in progress, are like coloured gullies; behind wooden fences pigs grunt, and along the cobbles chickens bob and dip after food. On one barn door a rare piece of graffiti celebrated the pop group Queen.

Each street ends at a section of the city walls, beyond which thick woods conceal views of the town, except on that side which looks west across the valley. The walls are punctuated with towers – the leatherworkers', the pewterers', the ropemakers', the butchers', the furriers', the tailors' (a splendid twin-arched building on the opposite side of the Old Town to the clock tower), the cobblers' and the locksmiths'. All are square or rectangular except the polygonal cobblers', all are of sandy-coloured stone, and all have the high, red-tiled gables and little square windows like eyes under the eaves which mark them indelibly as Transylvanian.

In the centre of the Old Town is piaţa Cetaţii, on one corner of which is 'the house with antlers'. A stag's skull with full antlers, painted red, is set at the corner of the building. Pigeons scavenge and children play. A cat, appalling with mange, skirts a house in shadow. Green, yellow and pink buildings nudge one another along strada Şcolii, the broad central street which leads away from this square to the wooden, covered steps which climb straight up to the church under their roof of mossy slates. The church is fifteenth-century, badly weathered, and locked. Nearby a neo-Gothic building is similarly deserted. Once a seminary, it is now a 'school for industry'. Some brightly coloured washing hung on a line in a corner of the churchyard and a little cottage nearby showed signs of life, but no one was about so I had to content myself with looking at the stout, plain exterior of the church, relieved by two statues either side of the main door, too worn by time to recognize. The church seems little used. There is another down by the clock tower where the Lutheran Germans worship.

In front of the main door was a gate in a grey stone wall. The gate itself was freshly painted black and swung silently on its hinges. Next to it, a sign in German admonished: 'Whoever you are, do not forget that you are about to enter a cemetery.' I passed through it and immediately entered a hall whose columns were tall grey trees, and whose roof and vaulting were branches bearing dark green leaves. Below, tumbling down the hill, were the graves, hundreds and hundreds of them, the oldest too worn and covered with moss to read properly, the newest, bright black marble obelisks with the names cut in deep and coloured gold, dating from 1981, 1985, 1987 ... All were in German, and all gave the name of the town in its German form, Schässburg. Passing through that gate I had been transported from Romania to a German Highgate. Whole families of Müllers, Fassbinders and Heims, Bauers and Heiters, lie buried here. Two white-haired gardeners who looked like brothers were at work on the lower slopes, clearing fallen branches. They greeted me with a dignified *bună ziua*, in response to mine, and I regretted not having used the German greeting. Further down the hill, a stone eagle as tall as a man presided over the fifty or sixty half-overgrown identical graves of Schässburgers who fell in the First World War.

Climbing back, I noticed late swifts and martins darting and diving to and from holes and crevices in the town walls. There were plum trees, and I saw with surprise that some fallen fruit lay ungathered on the ground. On benches under the bastions, lovers had begun to cluster. I started to make my way back to the piața Lenin, but it seemed an unnecessary return to the real world, and I walked once more around the Burg, so that there was not a street I hadn't trodden.

Saturday was a day of weddings, with much music and dancing. All three restaurants in town were occupied by large crowds. Battered cars were brightened with carnations sellotaped to their bonnets and boots, and men and women wore formal black, the women with lace frills, the men in grey ties, with little gauze lily buttonholes. They danced, ate and drank all afternoon and long into the night. The Dracul restaurant had the up-market crowd, while my hotel restaurant catered for the middle-class, and the Perla had the workers' wedding. At the Dracul wedding, they sang 'Gaudeamus igitur' right the way through in Latin. The brides wore clouds of chiffony white and their young waxy grooms, hair and moustache plastered into position, were rigid with nerves but wore shy smiles of pleasure as they posed in satin-edged jackets for the photographer.

I went for a walk in the country, heading out west in the direction of Şaraşu, a 'Saxon' village about ten miles down the road. I paused to help a girl who was steering an old man – her grandfather? – towards home. He was staggering along, one hand dripping blood from a fall, the red garish against his gnarled, dusty knuckles, and he moved with the quiet concentration of the seriously drunk. The town straggles for a long distance. You pass pretty red houses bright with flowers, and cross a little tributary of the Tîrnava before reaching open country. There was a large farmstead on the left – a long, low building with barns into which men were unloading hay with pitchforks from long, low horse-drawn carts. To the right, on the slope of the hill above, a small, immaculate graveyard stood pale grey against the lush grass.

There was little traffic – the occasional tractor, more frequent horse-drawn wagons and traps carrying weatherbeaten peasant families about their business; two old men on foot. No one passed without a greeting. Once alone among the green hills, scarcely disturbed by a house and dotted with poplars of an even deeper green, I paused to watch an old man in the valley below scything grass to make hay, the timeless, inexorable movement he made lulling my senses. I have read somewhere that we in the West are never free of noise any more – it is even present in the form of low-level traffic hum when we believe there is silence. Our tired senses have tried to shut it out. Here, I believe the silence was absolute. I put my foot on the low balustrade of a bridge over a brook, rested my arms on my knee, and enjoyed it. The sunlight penetrated me. Crickets carelessly basked in it on the road, and large dragonflies darted by and hovered on a quiet blur of wings.

To cool off I turned into a wood. A sign announced it to be part of a nature reserve, and nearby in a natural alcove of trees stood a roadside crucifix of painted tin, flowers at its foot. The canopy of leaves was so thick that it was almost cold here, and I followed a path blindly and happily into the unvarying depths until I realized that I was lost. I turned in what I hoped was a curve back to the road. The feeling of isolation in the forest-tracks where I found myself was complete, and I felt a sense of urban panic steal over me – as detestable as it was irresistible, because a large part of me loved it here, alone among trees, walking along dusty paths.

After half an hour I discerned the line of the road breaking through the verticals of the treetrunks. I was almost on it when an unearthly wailing started from a thicket not far to my right, and the bush began to vibrate. I stopped in my tracks. If it was a bird, it must be a very big one, and I had never heard a bird make such a noise. An animal then? But what? Hardly had these questions formed than a beast the size of a goat erupted from the leaves, dark brown and shaggy, with a red mouth and yellow eyes. It bounded towards me, still emitting the curious shrieks I had heard a moment before. There was no time to be frightened. It veered slightly to avoid actual collision, stopped on the path a few yards ahead of me, and gazed in my direction. Then I saw that it was cowering; it was as scared of me as (I now realized) I was of it. This confrontation lasted for no more than ten seconds; then the animal scampered away, tail between legs, with an anxious backward glance. Pausing again at a safe distance, it cocked an ear and barked bravely. Just a dog after all.

On the road again, I fell in with Rainer. We introduced ourselves and spoke in German from the outset.

'But you are not from around here,' he said. 'You don't have the right accent. And your clothes ... '

We discovered that we both owed our Christian names to German forebears, from roughly the same part of Germany, too; but our present nationalities put us far apart, though he was amused when I told him that within the Common Market, Britain was regarded as the 'Romania of western Europe'.

'Hardly a compliment. Still, I wish I had your luck.'

'It isn't all as free as you might think.'

'It can't be as bad as here. Most of the pure Germans want to get out. Others are arguing that they have a right to be here, where they've always lived, and Bonn should support that right.'

'And you?'

'Well, I'm a half-caste. I feel Romanian. This is my country. I'm not proud of what we're doing at the moment. What do you think of us in the West?'

I mentioned what had been attracting the attention of the press.

'I think it's even worse for the Hungarians here. A friend in Cluj told me there were rumours that the border guards were shooting at people trying to get into Hungary near Satu-Mare.'

'What about the villages?'

'There are the usual delays. But once they've got themselves organized, got enough petrol for the bulldozers, enough dynamite . . . it's only a question of time. If the villages can survive this government, they will be saved. But most of us think that nothing will survive this government.'

'What do they do?'

'To the villages? The plan is to do it quickly: people will be evacuated at a month's notice, their village will be bulldozed, and they will be given temporary accommodation until the blocks of flats are ready. The whole scheme is crazy, and unworkable, but he'll do it if he can. He equates housing development with progress. The new flats are not as good as the old houses, and no one in them has even a scrap of private land to grow a bit of food or rear chickens, so that there's nothing extra to eat to supplement the rations, and no eggs to use for barter on the black market.'

I thought of Britain's own domestic architectural disasters of the Sixties and Seventies, and the vandalism and misery they bred. We too knocked down good modest housing to make room for them; now we were knocking the tower-blocks down.

Rainer went on: 'You won't see anything like that happening round here, or anywhere near the tourist resorts, or the spas – that would be noticed. Ceauşescu's no fool. He doesn't want too much international pressure to build up against him, at least until Romania's debts are paid and he can afford to stick up two fingers to the rest of the world.'

'Will he ever be able to do that?'

'I think he'll have a go. He can't last forever, of course, but what worries us is that what follows could be along the same lines.'

'What do you think will happen?'

He gave me the Romanian ironic smile: 'You're not with the *Securitate*, are you, by any chance? No – come back in ten years – maybe five – and find out for yourself.'

19

THE LAST OF TRANSYLVANIA

Passing black-suited worshippers on their way to the basilica, I arrived at the station in time for the slow train to Braşov. The ticket inspector was a dignified elderly man in the universal European blue uniform with red cap. His teeth were quite black, edged with gold, and he had a quick, captivating smile in which his whole face took part.

We stopped everywhere, and as it was a Sunday many of the passengers were fishermen, for the route follows the River Oltul closely and fishing is a passion in this area. The others were a mixed bunch: there was a sophisticated lady with short grey hair who was travelling back to Bucharest with her daughter, and there was a very large number of peasants, mainly stout women in brown cardigans, headscarves and heavy boots, who joined and left the train at each of the tiny stations we stopped at. Often these would be no more than stone huts in the middle of fields, which those disembarking would cross to some hidden village. The hills beyond the farmland were densely wooded, and occasionally the tower of a Transylvanian castle or the bulk of a fortified church would rise above the trees, the architecture of war reflecting the battles and incursions of the centuries.

The scenes at the stations, or glimpsed in villages near the track as we passed, might have come from a nineteenth-century album. Women in long skirts hauling water from a well. An old, weatherbeaten man, his face half-hidden by his Balkan moustache, a tall cap on his head, sitting on a bench smoking a long-stemmed pipe. A carter mending a wheel, crouched down by the axle of his vehicle, while his horses, still in their traces, patiently cropped grass, and two rare pigs rootled in a ditch nearby. The heavy ploughlands were re-emerging as crops had been gathered, and when clouds scudded across the sun, sending their shadows sailing over the land, one could imagine oneself in Suffolk.

I liked the pace of this train. It didn't pretend to be anything but slow (we took about four hours to cover 120 kilometres), and the changing cast of passengers and the scenery gently passing banished even the slightest threat of boredom. A man of about thirty on crutches, one leg amputated below the knee, came through the compartment begging. The stump where the leg bent below the knee was bound with rags to a hand-carved wooden cradle, below which a home-made peg-leg projected to the ground. Everyone gave him something. Huddles of peasants, standing for lack of space in the carriage entrance-way (these are not corridor trains), peered in at us. Although the little stations all bear clear name-plates, everyone had a timetable which was constantly consulted. An elderly couple behind me – he a nut-brown dwarf in knickerbockers, Norfolk jacket and straw trilby, his stubbly jaw in constant motion as he chewed tobacco, and she a black-clad, black-headscarved creature with translucent white skin and thick spectacles with tiny lenses set in heavy round black frames – kept us all informed of where we were as they sustained a duologue which struck up every time we arrived somewhere. It appeared that he was guessing the name of the station, and she confirming it from the timetable. He was always right.

'Caţa?'

'*Da*, Caţa.'

'Homorod?'

'*Da*, Homorod.'

. . . and so on.

Braşov, formerly Kronstadt and once, briefly, Stalin, is the most easterly of the 'Sieben Burgen', and the most prosperous. Settled on the very edge of the Carpathians, the town has two distinct halves, old and new. The station, smart and modern, is in the New Town, at the head of the broad Bulvard dul Victoriei – a tree-lined street flanked by towering grey blocks of flats. They are set well apart from each other and the breadth of the boulevard prevents them from being too overpowering. The shops in their ground floors looked brighter than any I had seen before in Romania.

All the countries I had passed through ran national lotteries. In Romania tickets are frequently sold in little envelopes – a kind of instant prize draw – which are threaded on to steel rings, carried by the seller. I asked a girl presiding over a deskload of these how to get to the hotel I was aiming for, and was told it was too far to walk, I'd have to take a number 4 trolley-bus. Obstinately, for I had no map yet and none was on view at the station, I started to walk anyway, but Braşov is a substantial town, and it soon became clear that she had been right. At the next bus-stop I checked with a man who answered me in English, and put me on the right bus. Another man on board saw that I got off at the right place, with the same friendly, shy courtesy which I encountered everywhere, though Romanians could also be extremely volatile. Hotel staff would fly off the handle at each other at the slightest provocation; but I could only guess at the stress under which these people lived.

At the edge of the Old Town and across the road from the two expensive modern hotels is the Parcul Central, a rectangle surrounded by large, crumbling nineteenth-century houses of dressed stone. In the park, which was crowded, a band played German marches and dance music of the Thirties. The players were all middle-aged men, belting out the rhythms on elderly instruments – battered drums, tarnished saxophones, and trumpets. I wondered if this was the same band I had seen at dusk the night before, walking up the main road to the station after playing at one of the Sighişoara weddings. At tables under trees nearby, men in straw hats and dun windcheaters were playing chess.

I walked through the trees and made my way up Citadel Hill. The castle was built in the Middle Ages to protect the town against the depredations of the Turks. It has now been completely restored and reconstructed to house a complex of restaurants and a discothèque. It costs a few lei to get in, paid to a man at the gate dressed very roughly like Robin Hood, and each of the restaurants has a medieval theme, with waiters and waitresses dressed in appropriate costumes. The place was packed, for Braşov is not far from the summer and winter holiday resort of Poiana Braşov. I wandered around the whitewashed buildings for a while, but all trace of the original castle had been buried under tourism, and although the transformation was very tastefully carried out this was not a place for me. I returned to the park via a pleasing maze of cobbled streets. Everywhere one looked, one could see the louring hills which surround the town.

On the other side of the road from the hotel, I noticed what looked like a large glass museum case. It was filled with a display of photographs of the president: here wearing a hard hat as he inspected a factory; there formally greeting the representative of an African republic; here again kissing children and receiving flowers. The photographs, not all of them recent, seemed, with their typed commentary, to constitute a newspaper. Later I saw similar displays at railway stations. Further on from this was the stop for the bus to Poiana Braşov. I waited in the patient and orderly queue, which only lost its temper when the bus arrived and two peasant women tried to elbow their way on first. In the end we all crammed aboard, and the bus toiled up the hill away from the town, passing children tending goats by the roadside.

The resort is about ten kilometres to the south of the town. A green valley from which the mountains rise steeply now contains nearly twenty hotels and restaurants, attractively designed (most of them look like giant chalets) but bunched together. It was hard to judge what the runs would be like in winter, but I rode a ski lift up one which looked narrow and tough, with one or two unpleasant pieces of scrap iron and broken concrete on its floor which would have to be well covered by snow. In summer this is a walking and riding centre. The visitors were mainly well-to-do Romanian families, though I was aware of one or two Italian voices and met a group of three elderly British communists from Burnley, who told me they were here simply 'to get some sun and mountain air'. They had not visited Braşov, and showed no interest in the rest of Romania. 'It's a communist country, and it's warm and it's reasonable,' they said.

Once away from the neutral resort, you can let the gaunt mountains seduce you. Less dramatic than the Alps, bald crops of grey rock only just jutting beyond the tree-line at first, the Carpathians soon reveal themselves as lonely, high and wild; and although here at least they cannot honestly be called as beautiful as the mountains of Austria, Italy and Germany, the knowledge that they are so empty gives them an attractiveness that their brothers in the West do not have.

That Braşov is a more opulent town than either Cluj or Sighişoara is immediately apparent in the density and smartness of the shops which line the strada Republicii, the main pedestrian street which links the park with the hub of the Old Town, the piaţa 23 August. The people are more smartly dressed too; but there is scant trace of the original German inhabitants.

Something else distinguishes Braşov: there are virtually no medieval domestic buildings, for most of the city was destroyed in an earthquake in the eighteenth century. The architecture here is grand and the accent is once again on the Baroque. It is a lovely place. In the centre there is a medieval Town Hall, much restored in Baroque style in the 1770s, and the terrace on the north-eastern side contains a Greek Catholic church and a Renaissance market hall with a striking colonnade. The Town Hall has a dull museum; there is, apparently, a better one in the *Bastionul Ţesătorilor* (Weavers' Bastion) in the south-west wall of the town, but when I was there it was closed for restoration. The square itself is paved in pale stone and dazzles in the sun.

All the restaurants in town were again taken over for weddings, and everywhere through net-curtained windows one could see people, hot in formal clothes, drinking and dancing, first to young pop musicians in white shirts and black trousers hammering out 'Poetry in Motion', 'Dream Lover', 'Sweet Little Sixteen', 'Devil Woman', and 'Twist and Shout'; then, as the day wore on and the guests became less inclined to be athletic, 'Yesterday', and 'Memory'. In the evening the pop groups gave way to oompah bands.

Heading south through cobbled back-streets ornate with decorated sandstone *Bürger* houses, turning golden in the late afternoon sun, I caught hints of German ghosts. On a wall by an entrance a faded epigram delivered as a couplet was painted in Gothic script:

> *Während des Lebens, Sorg' und Muh';*
> *Nach dem Leben, Gottes Ruh'.**

A battered enamel plaque might announce a lawyer's or a dentist's business in German, rather than Romanian. Three old men in Homburgs, with arms linked, wearing overcoats and neat scarves despite the heat, might have turned the corner from a side-street in Vienna. Walking on, I arrived at the foot of the Tîmpa, the little mountain which overlooks the town. A beech wood climbs it and so does a winding path, but I lazily took the Italian-made cable car. At the elegant Panorama restaurant at the top, prices reflect the cost of getting the food up the hill, but from here footpaths fan out across the surrounding hills, which are a nature reserve. A mouldering stuffed bear stands guard over a signpost which indicates walks, climbs, and the distances involved. I stayed and admired the view across Braşov, the Old Town spreading out under its neat red roofs like an accurate model – and beyond it, under a slight haze, the grey buildings of the New Town. Dominating the view was the mass of the Black Church.

I walked down through the beech wood, only meeting a group of small boys knocking conkers from some horse-chestnuts near the bottom, and found myself finally on a long promenade, the Aleea Filimon Sirbu. Several beer-gardens spread out along it from the cable car station, and this early Sunday evening they were filled

---

* *During life, there's toil and care;*
  After life's end, the peace of God.

with drinkers. One man in an untidy lightweight suit had already had more than enough, and he was staggering down the Aleea, shouting what were clearly imprecations, though only one word was recognizable to me: Ceaușescu. I felt nervous on the man's behalf; surely this was courting disaster. The people at tables within earshot glanced at each other anxiously, and then down at their drinks as he passed.

The only place I could find to eat that night was in the hotel, in a corner of the restaurant curtained off from another wedding reception. All the guests seemed enormously fat – few Romanians look very fit – but they were dancing with gusto to 'The Dashing White Sergeant'. Service was not fast, but I was adapting myself to a more Balkan pace by now, and nowhere was I irritated by slowness, except when it came to paying the bill. After East Germany I learned to tack half an hour on to the time allowed for a meal just to settle up. Ordering food could take a while, too – though once ordered, the dish would make a fairly speedy appearance.

Sharing my table was a young, dark-haired Romanian who was finding it even harder to get served than I had.

'Have you been to Bucharest yet?' he asked me.

'No. What's it like?'

He grinned. 'You'll see. It's a big, modern, communist city.'

'I've heard there's a lot of new building going on there.'

'Oh yes. They've been knocking down some of the state-owned houses in Ghermanesti too. Nice houses ...' Ghermanesti, he explained, was a village some distance north of the capital. 'I live in Bucharest, and by the time I get back there in three days I expect I'll already see more changes. But it's happening everywhere. I heard that they were going to move in on Bodoc, which is only a few miles north of here; but I don't see how they could; there's a spa there.'

I poured out wine for both of us. Once a waitress came within hailing distance and he waved at her, but she was distracted by a couple dancing across her path and didn't see him. He waited another ten minutes, getting increasingly angry, and then excused himself and left. A handful of times in Czechoslovakia and Romania earnest young men had got me into conversation apparently by chance, but they had always led off in English and left abruptly when I failed to rise to the various baits they offered me: 'What do you think of our country?' 'Our leader is a very bad man, don't you think?' 'Do you think that western criticism of the Czechoslovak/Romanian way of life is justified?' and so on. I wondered about this evening's encounter, but I don't believe my would-be dining companion was a policeman. I think he left simply because he was fed up that he couldn't get served.

I went to my room. The night before, in Sighișoara, I had for some unaccountable reason been able to get the BBC's World Service loud and clear on my little radio, which didn't even have short wave. For about an hour I had listened to domestic news, and then a Mozart symphony relayed from the Proms, before it was blotted out by Radio Tiranë – the familiar call-sign recognized from its medium-wave intrusion on Radio Three towards evening in Britain. Radio Tiranë featured two lugubriously voiced women dispensing news about the Deputy Chief Associate Party Secretary of

This and the Consultant Administrative Party Sub-Committee Chairman of That in heavy, nasal English, so I switched off. Tonight, I tried to fine-tune my radio again, but could get nothing apart from blurred noises and, once, the wild untamed music of Romania.

I'd had the Cerbul Carpatin in Braşov recommended to me as the best restaurant in the country, but the advice came from a source a few years out of date, and times seemed to have changed. The barn of a place, in a restored sixteenth-century merchants' hall on 23 August Square, was packed, but the only food to be had was rissoles in a kind of dour stew. Still, I was hungry, and it wasn't bad, and everyone else was eating it quite happily, so who was I to complain? Afterwards I drank a beer and my table filled up with four students, who ordered beer and cognacs, so I joined them in another round. The only way we could communicate was by toasting each other. 'We get very lazy about foreign languages,' one of them told me in Romano-French. 'Because we can't travel, there's no incentive to keep them up.'

The Lutheran Black Church, St Mary's, gets its nickname from the smoke-stained walls it acquired when the Austrians set fire to the city in 1689. No trace of the soot remains today, though along the west side of the central nave a number of blackened figures of saints, brought in from outside, stand guard above box pews decorated with late medieval German paintings of personified virtues. The massive building is said to be the largest church between Vienna and Constantinople, though I wonder if the cathedral at Košiče in Czechoslovakia isn't a rival. Building began in 1383, but the nearly-completed structure was all but destroyed in the Turkish invasion of 1421, and another fifty-six years passed before it was completely rebuilt. Even then, only the south tower was constructed. There are three naves of equal height, and the interior is unusually light for a church of its size, thanks to high, broad windows; but in the course of the hundred years of restoration which followed the fire of 1689 much of the original Gothic design was adapted to Baroque taste, or lost. There remain two great medieval works of art: the bronze font of 1472 which somehow survived the fire, and a fresco in the south portal showing the Virgin flanked by Saint Barbara and Saint Catherine.

A restoration programme instigated by UNESCO in 1970 was completed in 1984, despite the interruption of a major earthquake in 1977, which also affected Bucharest. I wonder if they haven't overdone it, though the church has other treasures to overcome any misgivings. It has one of the best organs in Europe, and a superb collection of seventeenth- and eighteenth-century Anatolian carpets, which hang from the galleries and pews, glowing and glorious in the sunlight (the windowpanes are made of glass which filters ultra-violet light to protect the colours). The carpets come from Ladik, Brussa, Giordes and Ushak, the gifts of merchants and town guildsmen travelling back from the East. There are about a hundred of them, and each is a masterpiece; they form the best such collection in Europe, and one of the best in the world.

I dragged myself away unwillingly, but I had to find the *Agentia de Voiaj* and get a ticket for the capital.

20

CITY IN TEARS

There was a handful of other tourists on the crowded train, including two black ladies from Chicago with a mountain of luggage and a Jackie Collins novel apiece. I never found out quite why they had decided to holiday here, beyond 'We came over to do Europe, so we thought, why not do the lot?' I was sorry not be able to sit with them, but their compartment was full. 'Is this *really* first class?' they asked doubtfully when they saw it.

My compartment already contained two other tourists. The first was an Italian engineer who had just spent two weeks at Poiana Braşov and was going to Bucharest to catch a plane home. The other foreigner was a young fair-haired New York Ivy Leaguer who was coming to the end of a course of study in International Relations in Vienna, and had decided to 'do' Hungary, Romania and Yugoslavia before going home. This was his last stop.

'Romania's very pretty. But it's nothing like Austria. How do you find the people?'

'Very nice.'

'Really? The only decent people I've met have been the doctors. They've been great.'

'Are you ill?'

'Something I ate here, they tell me. They call it seminal poisoning. So I'm on a diet of mineral water and I go to the can about every five minutes.'

Our route lay due south across the curve of the Carpathians, passing through the ski resorts of Predeal, the highest town in Romania (the *Pas Predeal* is the border between Transylvania and Wallachia), and Sinaia – the latter so named because a Romanian prince, Cantacuzino, founded a monastery here in the seventeenth century and named it in memory of his pilgrimage to Mount Sinai. The monastery still exists, with Victorian additions, and near it grand villas in what I can only call Transylvanian Tudor built for the Romanian aristocracy, which are now converted into holiday accommodation. But even the wildly ornate neo-Baroque Peleş Castle is dwarfed by the threatening majesty of the mountains which tower above.

The River Prahova has its source near Predeal and snakes along the side of the tracks until a few miles north of Ploieşti. This is the larger of Romania's two major southern oil towns, at the beginning of the plain which runs from the foot of the Carpathians down to the Danube. Ugly and sprawling, but with a brash energy of its own, it belches clouds of black smoke, and spurts flame into the sky. Its skyline from a distance could be the background of a Bosch painting.

Sixty kilometres of plain lie between here and the capital. My opposite neighbour, a serious bald man of about fifty in a grey-green suit, produced a greaseproof bag and laid it on a newspaper. From it he then drew several slices of grey bread and several slices of greasy red sausage. Holding a slice of each in either hand, he ponderously proceeded to eat, chewing with inexorable thoroughness. My American friend turned green, said 'Excuse me,' and left. I stayed and watched the lot go down – the man timed it perfectly and was applying a large check handkerchief to his lips as we drew into the Gara de Nord.

The terminus on that hot Wednesday afternoon was a seething, confused inferno and I passed through it to the square beyond with relief. But the heat and the confusion there were, if anything, worse. A ragged army of people flung themselves on the occasional taxi, but the drivers all seemed to pick the passengers they best liked the look of, regardless of others who, believing they had a prior right to their services, would bang on their bonnets and roofs and shout half angrily and half despairingly. After about fifteen minutes of this, I decided to cut my losses and walk. Taking out my map (bought in London), I set off down the Calea Griviţei.

The road was hot and dusty and filled with exhaust fumes. The exhaust was nothing new: but the dust seemed to fill all the volume of the air. The road was uneven, the pavement narrow and broken. I passed clusters of broken-down shops and a couple of seedy hotels. There were a few once-handsome Victorian houses which looked on the verge of collapse. At one road junction a car sped across my path and stopped; an enormously fat man in a vest clambered out and imperiously suggested changing dollars. When I declined he shouted at me. This was not an auspicious beginning.

But soon the road became quieter, shaking off the ugly area around the station. A well-trimmed privet hedge defined the grounds of a small museum, and ahead of me on the corner of strada Nuferlior was the Catedrala Sfîntu Iosif. A few yards further on brought me to calea Victoriei, the city's main street, which divides it from north to south and has at its centre piaţa Gheorghe Gheorghiu-Dej, where the main government buildings are housed in the former royal palace. Here are also the university library, the headquarters of the Romanian Communist Party, and the neo-Classical Atheneul Roman (Athenaeum) – the country's principal concert-hall.

The chief impression this part of town gives is of large, pompous but not unpleasant grey nineteenth-century building, mainly neo-Classical. If it reminds you of anywhere, it is Washington. The side-streets behind the centre are immediately residential, and some of them, with their decorated façades and wrought-iron balconies, still show why Bucharest was once known as the Paris of eastern Europe.

I tumbled into the third hotel I tried, an early nineteenth-century building, recently restored. My room overlooked an opulent courtyard with a massive swimming pool, a relic of better days, which was empty and disused. The room itself, as if to make up for this, was stuffed with as much furniture as possible.

I thought I'd have a beer, but the hotel couldn't sell me one because it was stocktaking, so I set off for the Bulgarian Tourist Office to see about my onward journey to Sofia. There I met Tyrone Shaw, a jazz saxophonist from Vermont. He'd flown in via Frankfurt two days earlier and, finding Romania twice as expensive as he'd thought, was trying to get to Bulgaria instead. But he hadn't got a visa. There would be no problem, but it would take eleven days.

'And I only have a fortnight's vacation.'

He had to book a phone call home and we crossed the road to the Hotel Intercontinental, which had facilities for this. The hotel is a dark, overheated pastiche of its American and west European counterparts, and equally soulless. We had a beer in the 'Genuine German' *Bierstube* while we waited for the call, paying the sullen waitress in dollars. The beer cost as much as it would in a London nightclub.

'I think she's beautiful,' Tyrone told me. 'But that's because she's got Slav blood. My own Ukrainian genes are responding.'

After the phone call we had another beer. Over it, we compiled a list of famous Romanians and got as far as Ilie Nastase, Radu Lupu, Brancusi, Ionesco, Tristan Tzara and Saul Steinberg. Tyrone indicated two girls in tight pullovers and miniskirts at one end of the bar. They'd looked across at us and smiled as we sat down.

'Hookers,' he said. 'I met them last night. I didn't realize they were professionals at first, and I was looking at one of them a bit too closely. The other one speaks English. She came over to me and said, "Do you like my friend?" in that unmistakable way. I made a joke of it. "I think you're very beautiful too," I said. She said, "The more the merrier." It made me quite depressed. Especially as the only thing hard they're interested in is your currency.'

There was a sad side to this too, as I discovered later from a Romanian friend. 'Along with the professional girls,' she said, 'there are the amateurs – the opportunists, if you like, who might go to bed with a westerner on the off-chance of being given some make-up, or a few dollars, or a packet of decent condoms, or, in the old days, a pair of jeans. But now, more and more, girls want to get to know westerners, or anybody from any non-communist state, with a view to getting married and getting out. The problem for westerners is that there are at least half-a-dozen chambermaids in any big hotel who are policewomen, who'll simply go to bed with you to pump you for information, see if you say anything useful to the *Securitate*.' She grinned. *Haz de necaz*, I thought.

I looked across at the girls again. One dark and dramatic, the other plump and motherly. Shortly afterwards, they left with two of the many Africans who were staying at the hotel.

'I wouldn't have minded,' said Tyrone. 'But for AIDS.'

We left and crossed University Square, passing the new National Theatre which stands next to the Intercontinental and is also a modern building, of equal hideousness, and continued on down Bulvard dul 1848, a broad street of imposing, soulless buildings. We made forays from it down dusty side-streets, where enclaves of pretty little houses still remained. Approaching the Old Town district of Lippscani, we turned right and were soon in a maze of busy side-streets which were a cross between Paris and Istanbul in atmosphere. The dust caught in one's throat. As dusk approached, lights were turned on in a manner I found dazzling after the provinces.

Politely turning down a student on a street corner who wanted us to change $1000 dollars' worth of lei with him the next morning at an inordinately high rate ('I am going to Austria so I will offer you 150 lei to the dollar if you will change $1000') we walked down strada Şelari – a street that reminded me of the rue Mouffetard in Paris, full of bustling market life and small shops – to the hotel-restaurant Hanul lui Manuc. Built by a millionaire Armenian as a town house in the early 1800s, this was where Russia and Turkey signed a peace treaty in 1812. It is constructed in the style of a medieval inn, four galleried walls surrounding a large courtyard. We found a table on the first gallery; a waiter had spotted us in the courtyard and beckoned us up. Pork and *mamaliga* was preceded by a delicious tomato and salami salad, and one paid accordingly, though the waiter told us we could pay in dollars. 'But be discreet – slip the money under the bill,' he said, leaving his pad on the table. *Mamaliga* looks like overcooked rice which has stuck together, has a mushy texture, is beige in colour, entirely without flavour, and usually stone cold.

The table was set for four and we were joined shortly after our arrival by two other men. Jim and Chris were Pan-Am flight crew, based respectively in Berlin and Warsaw. Chris, whose parents were born in Delhi, told me cheerfully that Warsaw was a punishment posting. As I chatted to them Tyrone wandered off in response to frantic beckoning from two Romanians at a table nearby, and started to haggle over the best prices for the Camel cigarettes he had brought with him. He told me he wished he had brought more low denomination dollar bills and disposable goods. It is true that in Bucharest at least the distribution of these ensures a lei income on which you can live like a king.

Before we left, Jim and Chris gave us a tip: 'Go to the twenty-first floor of the Intercontinental – there's a small bar there, and some lavatories. In the vestibule outside there're always a few Somalis who run a money-changing racket. It's perfectly safe – the police turn a blind eye to it. They must get a rake-off.'

Tyrone had lost his alarm-clock and on the way back through the dark street, pleasantly and dramatically lit by low-level electric streetlamps at the occasional corner, we stopped at a clockmaker's which was still open and I helped him buy a replacement for the price of a packet of Camels. Outside again, we passed a cinema which was discharging a crowd onto the pavement. The illuminated yellow-brown dust, which still hung in the air like a portent, shrouded them. They were mainly young, in jeans and white shirts, laughing and hugging.

'In the parks, the lovers are positively Parisian,' Tyrone told me. 'Especially in the evenings. I guess it's because it's so dark!' I told him that to my eye the city was positively ablaze with light, and he looked nervous. He intended to hire a car the following day and head into the interior. 'I've got to get out of Bucharest,' he said.

We found the twenty-first floor of the Intercontinental. The men's lavatory was buzzing with furtive transactions.

'You have made me a very rich man,' giggled a drunken Korean businessman to a solemn waiter as he stuffed a monstrous bundle of fragile, elderly Romanian banknotes into a jacket pocket. The waiter riffled the slim wad of crisp Deutsch-marks he'd received and slipped out of the room.

One of the Somalis, a serious, handsome man of perhaps twenty-five, had been in the city for four years and had another two to go.

'It's a stupid place, really. They've just decreased the meat ration again. I eat rice, mainly, when I can get that. But this job ensures that I don't starve.'

'How long have you been changing money here?'

'Since I arrived. I do evenings now. The beginners have the daytime shifts.'

He told me he was a student at Bucharest University.

'What are you reading?'

'Journalism.'

When I left, I said goodbye to Tyrone too. The two of them were getting a taxi to his hotel in order for him to dig out some more cash to exchange.

The following day I set off early for the state air and rail travel bureau to buy my train ticket for Sofia. This operation took three hours, in an atmosphere which appeared chaotic but was in fact very orderly. The only problem to begin with was that the queue for tickets intersected with another for information, but the man in front of me and I managed to reorganize the two so that they ran parallel to one another. The only other vexation was the constant jostling by hard-elbowed old women who were in a permanent state of irritable anxiety and fought an unremitting campaign to queue-jump. Otherwise, everyone was patient and good-tempered, treating the whole experience with the slightly amused, detached sense of irony I had found everywhere. Only one fat blonde caused a near riot when her turn came: she wanted a ticket to a town in northern Siberia; it took half-an-hour to sort her route out.

The women clerks were indomitably good-tempered (though elsewhere I'd seen Romanians display signs of extreme volatility) and sustained themselves by chewing sticks of dry bread. The man in front of me in the queue was travelling to Italy with his wife and two children. It had taken him three months to set the trip up.

The whole huge, sepulchral room was surrounded by counters dispensing various services, and was finished in polished granite reminiscent of prewar school halls. The central area was a seething scrum of people, variously waving money, passports and tickets. As time passed, one's emotions progressed from mild irritation to anger, to panic, to a stubborn determination to see the thing out, to blank resignation.

'We're lucky,' the man in front of me said. 'It's moving quickly today.'

Finally my turn arrived and I ordered my ticket. I then had to join another queue for the cashier, a severe, matronly woman in a large glass box, who nevertheless looked lovely when she chose to smile. She took my money (dollars only), stamped my various pieces of paper, took one, inspected my passport, filled in another form, and sent me back to my ticket clerk. In the meantime, as the by now static queue informed me, she had gone to lunch.

Luckily it was a quick lunch and only thirty minutes later I was out in the street, grasping my precious ticket in its raspberry-coloured paper folder. Little did I know then that the whole exercise had been in vain.

I walked back north along calea Victoriei. After the government buildings and the Athenaeum have been left behind, the street changes character. The public buildings, the museums, and the dress shops with their faded, rather self-conscious chic, are left behind. Green hedges begin to appear, and small churches with twin onion-domes, and large houses set well back from the road, along with massive, stuccoed buildings which may once have been banks but now house various archives, libraries, and ministerial departments. A building site at piaţa Victoriei marked where a new hotel will rise – bigger and better even than the Bucharest itself, which is currently the newest and the largest in town. Opposite, a neo-Classical building houses the foreign ministry, while across the huge circus of the square at the beginning of the broad, tree-lined Şoseaua Kiseleff, there is a dignified red-brick Victorian pile which is the Natural History Museum.

I continued north under the trees. There were few pedestrians, but traffic was relatively busy. I noticed however that cars invariably stopped for pedestrians at zebra crossings. Several people were jogging, and two were training seriously, sprinting up and down a marked distance, timed by a man with a stopwatch.

The exhaust fumes and the dust were left behind, and I found myself in elegant suburbs. There is a large grey Triumphal Arch in the middle of the next circus, and beyond that Şoseaua Kiseleff penetrates the large Herăstrău Park which stretches across the north of the city in a succession of lakes, linked by the River Colentina. Along here is the Muzeul Satului.

If the administration is engaged upon 'rationalizing' village life, this museum stands in ironic contrast to that programme. It is an open-air museum, in which over the past fifty or sixty years examples of village architecture from all over the country have been collected and most beautifully and generously set out over many acres. There are now seventy-one buildings or groups of farmyard structures, water-mills, woven wattle grain-stores, wooden-slatted kennels, stone-and-wood houses with deep eaves and wide first-floor verandas, and highly decorated wooden churches. Of course it is dead here; while everything is scrupulously maintained there are no villagers. But although the argument exists that Romania is mummifying that part of her cultural heritage which she is destroying where it is still alive – and Romania's is very much a folk-culture – it is hard to believe that there is no hope for a country which so obviously cares for its past.

As far as the state is concerned, everything is fine. Or at least, that is how things have been since the war. The changes in Russia are causing panic in her more conservative satellites; and in times of change and uncertainty instinct makes leaderships cling to conservative forms of government, provided that those forms can sustain themselves convincingly enough, or by force. One of the difficulties confronting change in the Eastern Bloc is that a whole generation has now grown up without the benefit of the traditions of free thought; but against that may be set the fact that the instinctive desire to think for oneself is inherent in human nature, and however much it may be suppressed, it cannot be destroyed.

But although we may sacrifice on different altars ideologically, the effect of our actions is sometimes the same. Ceauşescu is conservative and stubborn; he is also of a generation which still thinks that a technocracy is the ideal form of state. In the West we made the same mistakes two or three decades ago, and only now, only partially, are we beginning to learn from them. Great Britain's thinking still falls behind that of the other advanced countries of western Europe. Here too, in a diminished democracy, the aims of the state are set above the wishes and needs of the people. Ours is not a country which can afford to feel too self-righteous about what is going on in Romania.

North through the park, and skirting the lake with its banks of riotous flowerbeds, its rowing boats and its stand-up snack bars where people lean on tall metal pedestal tables drinking sweet beer and eating a derivative of the hamburger, when available, you come to piaţa Scînteii. Even the statue of Lenin here is dominated by the building behind him – the state publishing house, Casa Scînteii, with its uncompromising high Stalinist façade, its eleven arched entrances in line abreast and its fat, square-spired tower. This marked the northernmost limit of my exploration. Later I was to meet a journalist who had spent most of his working life here, for not only books but newspapers and periodicals are produced from this building.

I walked back through the park and reached piaţa Aviatorilor. I was now some way from the centre and cast my eyes around for a metro station or a taxi, but found neither as I wearily began to tramp south along Bulvardul Aviatorilor, passing elegant houses, largely divided into flats. A young man stood near his gate resting on a garden fork, smoking his pipe, while a little dog and two small children gambolled round him. This was a far cry from the ragged little country boys who threw stones at trains, or the leprous old woman begging at the University metro station, or the thin blind man hovering at the entrance to the Art Deco Palatul Telefoanelor downtown. At the aviators' monument I turned off to cut through some quiet suburban streets, all elegant yellow houses hiding behind trees, with shining cars parked outside them. Men in suits carrying briefcases were returning home from work; an old woman stopped on a corner and stared at me long and hard.

I worked my way back to the centre via the dreary grey concrete canyon of calea Dobranţilor. Even at the hotel food was hard to find on this particular evening, for I had arrived rather late, so I contented myself with a snack and a bottle of the heavy white Murfatlar, taken by the empty pool. A violinist and a clarinettist serenaded us, but in particular two pretty girls at a table alone. Most of the other people were young, well-dressed, happy-looking. But this was an enclave of the rich.

After a good deal of shouting at each other down the telephone, the hotel clerk and the switchboard operator got me a local line and I rang my Romanian acquaintance. We arranged to meet the following day.

'I'm sorry I'm late. Parking's hell,' he said as we shook hands. I suggested coffee, but he preferred to go for a walk in a nearby park. 'The town's getting too crowded,' he said as we nudged our way across it in his Dacia. 'Everyone wants to live in Bucharest. But they've pegged the population now; and you can't move here unless you have to on account of a state appointment.'

'Why is there so much dust?'

'That? Oh, that's from the building sites. There's a lot going on down south of the river. You ought to go and have a look. This is rapidly becoming our showcase city.'

The smile belied his words, or at least gave me the chance to place my own interpretation on them.

He had been born in the 'Sieben Burgen'; during the war the Jews of this area had fallen under the jurisdiction of Hungary and he had shared the fate of his race in the concentration camps. He'd returned to Romania afterwards to try and find his father and mother, in the event without success. But he had become a convinced communist in the camps, and now threw himself body and soul into the reconstruction of his country. Later he had joined the army as a career soldier and had risen to the rank of colonel before turning to journalism.

'There's only a tiny Jewish community in Romania now. And most of the Jewish quarter here in Bucharest has gone.'

'Do you ever regret coming back?'

'No, but I've had a good life. I've been able to earn my living by my pen since I left the army.'

He talked about his war experiences freely, but resolutely turned aside any attempt to discuss the present, which was a pity, as I had no intention of trying to dig hard luck stories out of him. But I understood his position, just as I understood why he had chosen a park for our conversation, and in it a bench with its back to dense shrubbery, facing a commanding view of the area round us. I gave him a package of cigars and chewing-gum as I left – all I had. I wished it could have been more.

'I doubt if we'll meet again,' he said as we parted. 'But if you do ever come back here in my lifetime, get in touch.'

I had to return to Balkantourist to find out about accommodation in Sofia. They greeted me with long faces and said that as two international conferences were going on in the capital, every single hotel was full. I could get private accommodation, but I'd have to go to the bureau responsible before it closed for the weekend on Friday evening. This left me in a quandary. The train I'd booked took all day to reach Sofia and would arrive late at night; if I didn't have accommodation I wouldn't be registered with the Bulgarian police, and further complications would ensue. There was a way out: to fly; but there were only two flights a week, and these were booked solid, except first class, for the next month. Nevertheless it would be cheaper to take such a flight than to spend longer in Bucharest.

Of course there would have been other ways of solving the problem; but my judgement let me down at this point because it was overridden by mild panic, born of an instinct that had been growing in me since my arrival in Romania: I wanted to get out. I cannot attribute this feeling to anything specific. I am sure I was watched and that my room was searched once at least. But all that was more or less to be expected, and ordinary people here had been invariably charming. Nevertheless, the instinct won. I bought an air ticket.

'You can get a refund on your train fare.'

'I don't think I can face the travel bureau again.'

The Bulgarians smiled sympathetically. In fact I did go back to the travel bureau. Getting a refund was easy and took about three minutes. The matronly cashier and her immediate boss, a young woman in a grey suit, her hair piled in a heavy bun on top of her head, were delighted at my blundering Romanian. They both spoke good English. The queues for tickets were as long as ever, and I noticed some of the same anxious faces that I had seen when I was here first. What could have been holding them up, that they had to return to this grim hall to queue, day after day?

My visit to the travel bureau had brought me downtown again, and I wandered back through Lipscani to look at the Curtea Veche, the ruins of the Ducal Court. A palace built first by Vlad Ţepeş, and extended by a later prince, Constantin Brâncoveanu, in the seventeenth century, this is now a museum. A few walls of fifteenth-century brickwork, a row or two of delicate columns, and earlier foundations of large stones rounded by the river from which they came, are all that remain. Hemmed in by other buildings, in the shadow of a modern high-rise, and held together by concrete slabs, the Ducal Court is a sad ghost of what it must once have been. Of its former glories as a palace of the capital of Wallachia, nothing remains.

There are treasures of another kind not far away in the Muzeul de Istorie al Republicii Socialiste România. Housed in a massive neo-Classical pile, which was built as the central post office at the turn of the century, the history museum is a dark cathedral inside. Many sections were closed, but armed soldiers lurked in corners, and a fixed route had to be followed, shadowy attendants switching lights on and off before and behind you as you progressed through the galleries. Vast, sombre collections stretch into the twilight; in the treasury priceless gold and silver artefacts glint dully in glass cases. Among these are famous pieces: a neolithic seated figure, elbows on knees, head cupped in hands – nicknamed appropriately 'The Thinker' – and the great Thracian treasure of Hinova.

But there is more. An entire upper floor of the museum comprises a suite of gloomy rooms filled with high glass cases among which attendants sit like lost souls. The cases are filled with a bizarre collection: a stuffed African elephant's head, tilted so that it looks skywards; metal precision models of railway locomotives, or machine tools from Moldavian factories; dolls in national costume, sets of cut-glass goblets, even a furry mascot from the Los Angeles Olympics, which Romania attended in defiance of Moscow. A whole room is given over to cases of academic dress, and the stars and sashes of the Orders of many countries are laid out in their scores. Honours from Iran, Libya, Mexico; the Gold Coast, Uruguay, Honduras. The walls are spread with tapestries and rugs, paintings on velvet, wood-inlays, and etchings on glass, whose subject is always the same: smiling, healthy people, factories in the background, greeting a smiling, healthy couple, depicted somewhat larger than the rest. The couple are Nicolae and Elena Ceauşescu, and these rooms house the permanent exhibition entitled 'Homage to the President'. Such a collection is not unique, but for sheer eclecticism this one must be. A large portrait of the president – it is the official one which shows him as he must have looked twenty or thirty years ago, with brown hair and a vigorous, warm smile – presides.

In contrast to this, the National Gallery, behind the present Palace of the Republic, is astonishing. The ground floor contains a rich collection of Romanian craftsmanship, from delicately carved wooden panels of the sixteenth and seventeenth centuries to medieval goldsmithery and Renaissance tapestry. The floors above contain the paintings, and although the rooms themselves are dingy and grey, with cracking walls, the well-lit pictures are a revelation. In the foreign collections I remember particularly a fine Jan van Eyck flanked by two superb Memling portraits. But the Romanian nineteenth-century rooms show what has been lost by forcing art into the service of political ideology; there are painters here to stand beside Turner, Ingres and Renoir. One above all, Nicolae Grigorescu (1838–1907), remains in my mind, principally because of a sleeping nude: her supple body, and one sure dab of white on her lips to make them glossy, turns this into one of the most erotically charged pictures I have seen. In another room, a large canvas by Constantin Aviazowski (1817–1900) is called *Shipwreck*. A mariner clings to the top of the mast of a sunken ship. He is about to be engulfed by a wall of translucent turquoise water, though to call it turquoise barely does the colour justice. The wave is alive, and the sense of light in it is unsurpassed. On a lower floor, the modern art collection is just a series of Socialist-Realist canvases, almost all of which show the president surrounded by smiling Romanians. In one, a smiling little girl holds a *whole* loaf of bread. I didn't see a whole loaf anywhere in the country. People buy them in rationed halves.

I made my way back south through the city, through the crumbling back-streets, down to where the dust thickens the atmosphere and the exhaust fumes bite the back of the throat. I reached the little River Dîmboviţa, contained at a regular width in a concrete channel, its banks edged with grass grey with dust and neat iron railings.

Beyond it to the south lies a vast building site – or rather, as things were then, a great cleared wasteland. A monastery marked on my three-year-old map has gone. This area is part of the site that will include the new Palace of the Republic and Boulevard of the Victory of Socialism. The drive forward on this massive new development began in 1984. Since then, a score of churches and monasteries, a hospital, and close to twenty per cent of the old town have been destroyed, and in this part of the town you can practically see the buildings fall under the bulldozer and the steel ball as you watch. Armies of construction workers swarm, and the skyline is a forest of tall cranes. The quiet little sandstone streets just to the north of the Dîmboviţa, with their vine-clad iron balconies, tremble. The old town around the Hanul Manuc is dusty and run-down. The past is being ruthlessly swept aside, sacrificed to one man's idiosyncratic taste and vision. Here, money is evidently no object. As no one can stop him, the irregular streets of the district of Uranus will soon be gone, and more will follow. The excuse sometimes given is that many of the older buildings in Bucharest were so damaged by the earthquake of 1977 that they have to be pulled down in the interests of public safety. We commit enough architectural atrocities ourselves, but this is wholesale destruction. There will soon be no room for people.

After dinner, I gave my map of Bucharest to one of the young waiters who had admired it. He and a colleague had had the difficult job of tactfully ejecting three very drunken businessmen who'd come in in the hope of a table but weren't about to be offered one. As it was my last evening, I'd treated myself to a meal in the Casa Lido. There were few other people eating, and I'd taken my time.

On the way back to my room, I almost collided with a blonde girl in a green top I'd noticed in the restaurant. I apologized, she smiled, I collected my key and went upstairs.

The knock at my door came half an hour later, when I was running a bath. It was the young desk clerk who'd checked me in on my first day.

'Excuse me, sir, but there is a girl here who would like to talk to you,' he said in perfect English.

I was nonplussed, but on the face of it this seemed like a pleasant surprise. 'What girl?'

'The girl in green.'

'?'

'From the restaurant. Didn't you see her?'

'Yes, but . . . ' The penny still hadn't dropped.

'She is here now. She would like to talk to you.'

'Can she wait until I get some clothes on?'

He looked straight at me. 'That wouldn't matter, sir.'

At last light dawned. 'Ah.' Temptations and reservations hurried through my mind. Finally I said, 'No. But thank her for me.'

He smiled. 'I will, sir. Forgive me for bothering you; but I have to do my duty. And if I may say so, sir, you have made a wise choice. She is not of the first quality.'

The flight was at 1.30 p.m., but although it only lasted half an hour I had to check in by noon at the latest. A taxi took me to Otopeni, where the small international airport sits just outside a new town development. It was strange to see advertisements for Pan-Am along the road to the airport. I began to relax, but I wasn't out of the woods yet.

At the entrance to the shabby concrete airport building I handed my passport to an official for the first check. Then two people, a man and a woman in a different uniform, put my luggage through an X-ray machine; the man searched me, and went briefly through my bags. I then mounted the stairs to a waiting hall where a worn tape played elderly pop music very loudly. I bought a bottle of fizzy lemonade, a great mistake.

As soon as I could, I checked my bags through and then opened them for the customs search, which was, as I had hoped, briefer than they had been on the trains. The officer was a plump woman of about my age, who untypically smiled at me when she was through. My main bag went down the chute to the plane. I swung the other bag onto my shoulder and took my passport out for its final scrutiny. All I needed now was the exit stamp on the visa.

At the passport counter, the large moustachioed official in his glass box was shouting at an old man who appeared to be both drunk and in some confusion about his flight. Having banished this unfortunate, he turned to me. I hoped that in his irritation he would be brief, but as soon as he saw my blue-and-gold passport a new light crept into his eyes and I knew that something bad was going to happen.

The official glanced at me imperiously and disappeared with my passport and boarding card. There weren't many other passengers about and I waited under the wall-like gaze of other uniformed men until a small, wiry officer of about thirty-five with olive skin and a broken nose appeared. He was in yet another uniform. In between his large finger and thumb he held my passport.

'Mr Geel?'

I said yes, and watched disbelievingly as he undid the flap of his holster.

For the next hour or so, which seemed like several lifetimes, I was aware of nothing but my immediate surroundings and this broken-nosed security policeman. I will never forget his neatly cut straight brown hair, his almond eyes in a Calabrian face. He was unfailingly polite, but I knew he would have snapped my spine, had occasion demanded, as easily and as carelessly as he would have cracked a nut.

My bag was summoned back from the loading bay. The porter who got it stared at me in a way I never want to experience again. He was looking at a condemned man. Meanwhile Broken-Nose was speaking sharply and rapidly to the plump customs officer. Then he began his search. Virtually everything came out, but I couldn't help noticing that he didn't look as thoroughly as he might have. What he was interested in was written materials and film. Throughout, he questioned me in harsh tones, though never raising his voice, in Romanian. When I told him I didn't speak his language, he merely repeated the question with more edge a couple of times before moving on. His eyes were almost black; you could see very little white around the iris.

He had collected a pile which included all my money and traveller's cheques, my notebooks and all my exposed film, some postcards I'd bought in Budapest, a Penguin novel, a couple of books of poetry by Donne and Marvell, and a photograph of my wife. He had by now allowed himself two jokes. One was when he noticed my copy of *Dracula*, and the other was when I had shown him my remaining lei. There were twenty of them.

'Suveneer,' he grinned with his mouth. He was not amused at the paper toy my wife had given me which opened up from its flat pack to become a potted plant. The customs officer laughed aloud with pleasure when she saw it, but he took out a pencil and poked among its folds and crevices, no doubt looking for microfilm.

He picked up his haul and motioned me to follow him, after allowing me to repack my main bag and send it back down the chute. The porter helped me with surprising deftness. During the whole episode my keyed-up senses were conscious of waves of sympathy coming from the other porters and the customs officer. I sat in an indicated corner of the departure lounge and Broken-Nose disappeared down a short corridor into an office with a varnished door. From time to time similarly uniformed officers would emerge and pull on cigarettes, glaring at me as if they'd like nothing better than to stamp me underfoot. I forced myself to leaf through *Dracula*, which for some reason had not been taken away.

I have rarely been more frightened, because I knew that if they decided to arrest me for spying there would be nothing anyone could do about it. At that stage no one even knew exactly where I was. My mind raced with contingency plans, and cursed itself for not having hidden my notebooks and film, though I knew that if they had been deliberately concealed my situation would be even worse. I thought of compatriots imprisoned in Beirut and Tehran; nothing had been done for them. My blood ran cold. The irony was that ninety per cent of the film and notes concerned other countries than Romania: the names of Czech and Hungarian artists and architects, and the dates of churches and palaces. As for my pictures, what would the *Securitate* make of my photographs of Rostock? Of the Teyn Church? Of *puszta* cattle?

After close on an hour, Broken-Nose re-emerged and untidily restored to me my books, my money and my traveller's cheques. But still no passport, boarding-card, film or notes. It took another fifteen minutes (by now I had of course given up hope of catching the plane) before he came out again. Was there a half-smile on his face? He adjusted the cap on his round head, delivered my passport and boarding-card, and . . .

'This is a receipt for four notebooks and seven films. We have taken the film out of your camera also. You may redeem your material upon presentation of this to the proper authority when you next come to Romania. It is valid for ninety days. Your other bag has now been loaded onto the aeroplane.' Though he was speaking Romanian, I understood every word. I glanced round, away from his retreating back. Relief was predominant, anger came later. Meanwhile, I was still not off Romanian soil, and if they should change their minds . . . I looked at the posters on the walls. Pictures of the Carpathians. Pictures of beaches. 'Why not come to Sunny Romania?' 'Romantic Romania, Land of Sun and Fun.' And so on. Another sign innocently wished one a pleasant flight.

'So they let you go,' said a friendly voice in English.

I turned to see two Polish businessmen, immaculate in blazers, whom I'd noticed earlier checking in for the flight to Warsaw.

'Would you like a cigarette?'

I accepted one gratefully.

'We have been watching you. We thought they were going to keep you.'

'Really?' I said. Keep me? I tried to sound calm.

'Oh yes. What did they take?'

I told them.

'It isn't unusual. They are completely paranoid about their image abroad. I should say they were having a slack morning and just picked on you because you're a westerner. Though of course if you've met any Romanians while you've been over here, they'll know about it. But you're lucky they didn't detain you until they'd developed the film,' said the one who'd given me the cigarette. 'That happened to a friend of mine. He had to stay here an extra fifteen days. But then he'd tried to hide his stuff. They don't like that.'

'Anyway,' said the other, 'at least they've given you an open invitation to come back to Romania!'

I said that, this experience apart, I would like to return one day. They looked at me and shook their heads. 'You can say that after what they've just done to you? You just don't know these people. Was your stuff valuable to you?'

'Yes. But I'll see what my embassy can do when I get home.'

'We wish you luck; but I think your material is as good as at the bottom of the sea.'

At that moment I hardly cared. I had at least taken precautions against this happening, and all I wanted now was to be safely airborne, safely past Bulgarian immigration. On the flight, in almost solitary state in the first-class section of the cramped little Balkanair Tupolev, I exploited the privilege of my ticket and downed two enormous vodkas. They had no effect on me at all. Beneath me, the flat brown land of southern Romania swept away.

21

RUMELIA'S CHILD

'You look as if you'd seen a ghost,' said the cashier at the airport. There is no obligatory currency exchange in Bulgaria; but it's necessary to have official receipts if you want to pay hotel phone bills and so on in leva, let alone buy train tickets – perversely, here you also pay international fares in the national currency. There is, however, a thriving black market, and nearly every Bulgarian I met asked if I wanted to change money as a sequel to 'How do you do?'

I told the cashier what had happened. Having got through passport and customs control without a hitch I was already feeling better, though the meaning of the loss of all my film and notes was beginning to sink in too.

The girl laughed sympathetically.

'It happens all the time,' she said. 'They're crazy in Romania. I feel sorry for the people who have to live there.'

A man appeared at my elbow and asked if I needed a taxi. To be offered a taxi rather than have to search for one was another shock, and my relief cast any reservation aside; I didn't care if this was a rogue cab. I gave him Balkantourist's address and followed him out to an unmarked car.

'Where's your sign?'

He opened the boot. Lying in it was a Cooptaxi roof-light. 'Today I am working privately,' he said.

Once on our way, he asked me what I'd got for my dollars. When I told him, he offered double. Then he added a menu: 'I can do you Russian caviar for ten dollars a tin, attar of roses, fifteen dollars a bottle . . . ' the list went on. When we arrived at my destination, he shook hands and said, 'My name's Kostadin. I'm at the Bulgaria Hotel every evening between five and six, so if you want anything just drop by. There's no charge for the ride, by the way.'

I was in good time for my appointment with Mrs Georgieva but she appeared immediately and went through the accommodation vouchers I had booked in Bucharest. Because Sofia was packed with conferenciers – the city hopes to rival Budapest as an international conference venue and already regularly plays host to several per year – I was lodging privately here. Cars were at a premium for the same reason, but I'd managed to reserve a Fiat Uno for as long as I wanted it, essential for getting to some of the more isolated places I wanted to visit without joining a tour group. I expect that in due time both Hungary and Bulgaria will dispense with the irritating police 'statistics' forms, which have to be stamped everywhere you stay as proof that you have toed the line. The paperwork can even confuse the Bulgarians, as I was to discover almost to my cost.

Months earlier I had been to a concert of Bulgarian folk music at the Royal Festival Hall in London. The small but wildly enthusiastic audience had been made up almost exclusively of Britain's Bulgarian community. The culture of this country has been fiercely guarded down long centuries of foreign domination, and the music has a wild defiance, a lonely sonorousness that is quite distinct from the plaintive, poignant notes of Romania or the sugary tunes of Greece. Unaccompanied singing is a tradition which belongs to the women, and the harmonies achieved by it at its best are unearthly. Listen, if ever you have a chance, to the Trio Bulgarka, and you will see what I mean; but it is best to hear them live.

As a state in its own right, disregarding the long periods of occupation, Bulgaria has existed for 1300 years – since its foundation by Khan Asparoukh in 681. Bulgaria also claims to be the birthplace, two hundred years later, of the Cyrillic alphabet. The brothers Cyril and Methodius were sent to what was then the north-western extremity of the Byzantine Empire by the Patriarch of Constantinople to convert the tribes living on the borders of the Bulgar Khanate, and as a means of so doing invented an alphabet which draws on those of Greece and Rome. They were among the first clerics to use the vernacular in the liturgy, which attracted the usual reaction from conservative representatives of Church and State, but they were highly successful; and in the years following Cyril's death Methodius translated the Bible into Slavonic, a mighty undertaking. Bulgaria still uses the Cyrillic alphabet, the only country apart from Russia to do so, though it is also employed in Serbia.

Bulgaria as a cradle of *Homo sapiens* goes back a long way. There is evidence here of a sophisticated culture existing in 6000 BC, and the traditional patterns of Bulgarian pottery and weaving extend well before our era. The original, shadowy occupants of the Balkans were the Thracians, famous for their horses and their cavalry, notorious for the orgiastic ritual surrounding the god who became the Greek Dionysos and the Roman Bacchus. It was the Macedonians under Philip and Alexander who absorbed Thrace first, to be followed by the Romans. Plovdiv is the site of Philippopolis, which under the Romans was to become Trimontium; under the Romans Vidin was Bonnonia; Silistra, Durostorum; Sofia, Serdica. Ovid ended his days in desolate exile in Tomis, which is now Constanţa in Romania.

The Slavs gradually filtered in from the north-east in the shadowy centuries which followed the departure of the Romans, as their empire decayed and shrank, though the country remained part of the Eastern Roman, and later the Byzantine, Empire. After the disastrous fall of Constantinople to the Fourth Crusade in 1204, it formed the northern part of the so-called Latin Empire, one of the small states carved out of western Byzantium by the crusaders. This short-lived country was soon washed away and the area reverted to the name of Byzantine Empire, but at the end it covered little more than what is Bulgaria today. To the north-east, the Khanate of the Golden Horde threatened all of northern and central Europe. To the south-east, the Ottoman Sultanate was making conquest after conquest, would soon become an empire and in its turn threaten Europe. Had it not been for the interruption of Timur, successfully attacking the Turks in the east, the history of Europe from about 1400 might have been very different, though in its western reaches clerical and temporal bickering continued in apparently total ignorance of the vast threat not five hundred miles to the east.

With the eventual disintegration of the Mongols, the Ottomans pressed forward into Europe. Nothing could stop them. On 29 May 1453, the Byzantine Empire finally fell to the greatest Ottoman emperor, Mehmet II, but by then it had shrunk to a rotting, emasculated city abandoned (except in theory) by the west, with a tenth of the population of the prosperous trading capital of 250 years earlier. Upon seeing what he had taken, palaces and churches ruined by centuries of neglect rather than by the eight-week siege, Mehmet quoted lines by a lost Persian poet: '*The spider weaves the curtains in the palace of the Caesars; the owl calls the watches in Afrasiab's towers.*'

But long before this the Turks had swept around and beyond the beleaguered city. Bulgaria was occupied in 1396, and was to remain in Turkish hands for five hundred years. Apparently quiescent, in remote fortified monasteries and villages lost in the high, bare mountains, the Bulgarians kept their language and culture alive. As the centuries passed, art and literature became expressions of the fight for freedom. The people had a long wait, but by the nineteenth century the Turkish grip finally began to weaken and rebellions started. The men who led them, among whom the most famous are Vassil Levsky and Hristo Botev, died in the fight for liberty, but are remembered in street-names in every Bulgarian town.

The Turks put down these rebellions with the utmost severity, but they overstepped the mark when they crushed the April Uprising of 1876 at Koprivštica, with such savagery as to turn world opinion against them. The Turkish spread westwards had long since been halted; but they were still in Europe, and still had Christian Europeans under their sway. It may have been, too, that other uprisings in Bosnia, Hercegovina, Montenegro (which had in any case maintained its independence) and elsewhere indicated to the other European powers that there might be gains to be made, both in influence and territory, when the Ottoman Empire collapsed. The closest of these powers to Turkey was Russia, which, after haggling with Austria over future spheres of influence in eastern Europe, moved its armies south. Russian forces took Sofia early in 1878. Associated exclusively with eastern Europe throughout her history except for the brief period of vassaldom to petty crusader monarchs, Bulgaria now began her long relationship with Russia.

At first grateful to their liberators, the Bulgarians quickly saw that Tsar Alexander had it in mind to run their country from St Petersburg. They countered by electing as their king Alexander of Battenberg, who was a nephew of the Tsarina, but also German enough to have inherited a mistrust of Russia. His successful policies confirmed Bulgarian independence and attracted British support, since Britain was seeking fresh buttresses against Russian expansion to replace the deteriorating empire of the Turks. Alexander's successor was another German prince. Ferdinand of Saxe-Coburg was related to Queen Victoria and descended from Louis Philippe of France, and thus seemed to be the ideal man to keep Bulgaria in the western camp; but he was aware of Bulgaria's geographical remoteness from allies there, and in 1896, two years after the fall (caused by overreaching himself) of his famous minister Stambulov, Ferdinand signed a pact of friendship with Russia. Apart from the few years of the Second World War, when Bulgaria allied herself to Germany, her close association with her huge neighbour (with whom, however, she shares no frontier) has continued ever since.

From a Russian point of view, Bulgaria has been the loyallest and most stable of her client states. Her tiny population of nine million live in what was once the market garden of Europe, and now, although there is much heavy industry, fruit, wine, rose and tobacco products are still important, and are largely exported to earn hard currency. In the last few years tourism has increased to an extraordinary extent, and now provides the country with her principal source of foreign income. Like Romania, she offers skiing and a lovely coastline at much cheaper prices than the West; but since she is free of the difficulties which beset her northern neighbour, she attracts six million tourists a year.

There's still plenty of paperwork, however. Once I'd collected my vouchers, I had to go to a different office round the corner and exchange a voucher for another one, which then had to be stamped by a cashier. This had to be handed in to my 'house-keeper' when I arrived at my private accommodation. I was lucky to get somewhere within walking distance of the centre; others in the queue were despatched to the outer reaches of town.

The flat I was staying at was in Car Asen Street, just behind the southern end of Vitoša, Sofia's main north-south boulevard. I found that the house faced a grey nineteenth-century courtyard, reminiscent of those you find in the suburbs just north of Paris. The flat was composed of a large central hall, off which was a small kitchen, a shower room, and the guest room, with two beds, a wardrobe, an armchair and a bookshelf. Finally glass doors opened onto a living room in which a large mahogany table fought for space with a vast dark sideboard in highly polished wood, and a brown sofa-bed which loomed along one wall. This was the nerve-centre of the flat, in which my hostess, Mrs M., lived, moved, and had her being.

In my limited experience of private accommodation, you invariably get a clean room in a more or less shabby flat occupied by an elderly widow. Mrs M. was perfectly pleasant, talked to me incessantly and volubly in Bulgarian, unconcerned by the fact that I understood barely a word, unless she wanted to make an especially important point, when she would fix me with her eyes and spell out the words loudly and slowly, with additional hand gestures for emphasis. We got along quite well, and on the second morning she even gave me breakfast, which was not in the contract. It consisted of a kind of Madeira cake, though it was closer to the German *Gesundheitskuchen*, and a large cup of very treacly coffee. When she had drunk hers, Mrs M. inverted her cup on her saucer, telling me by operatic gesture that it was done in order to 'read the coffee grounds'. She laughed when I followed suit.

The Grand Hotel Balkan, now refurbished and wordily renamed the Sheraton Sofia Hotel Balkan, is one of Europe's greatest, and as it is absolutely central, on

Lenin Square, I made it my headquarters, even eating there once or twice when my wallet would stretch to its prices, which were at least three times above the average. It was full of government officials from all over the world, and of every imaginable shape and size, attending an international conference.

Vitoša is the main shopping and restaurant street. It is broad and tree-lined, and after Romania the brightness of its lights at night seemed dazzling. What was available in the shops also seemed overwhelming; even without the contrast to Romania there appeared to be more than enough. The Central Department Store is as good as its counterparts in Hungary, and young Bulgarians dress with a flair and a sense of fashion to rival their peers anywhere.

The day I arrived had been hot and unpleasantly humid, but rain and a fresh wind had cleared the air soon afterwards, and now the weather was perfect for walking. Sofia has sprawling modern suburbs, but the core is small. There is very little earlier than the 1880s, but when wandering along the boulevards of this imposing city, past its elegant grey and yellow turn-of-the-century buildings, it is as well to remember that a century ago it was a run-down provincial town in what was then Rumelia – the northernmost region of the Ottoman Empire. Then it had barely 15,000 inhabitants, and its buildings crouched close to the ground, half built under it, for the Turks had decreed that roofs must not reach higher than a mounted rider. Two mosques from the period of Turkish rule remain, but otherwise they might never have been here.

Sofia is squarely on the ancient trade route through Europe to Istanbul, and the area has been settled for at least 5000 years. During the massive building programme of the late nineteenth and early twentieth centuries, buildings and the sites of buildings of great age were rediscovered. In the courtyard – one could say in the embrace – of the Hotel Balkan is the recently restored little church of St George. It is the oldest ecclesiastical building in the town, and has had a chequered history. Originally built in the fourth century as a Roman temple, it was destroyed when the Huns overran Sofia in 447. A hundred years later it was rebuilt as a church by Justinian, under the Turks it was used as a mosque. Dwarfed by the massive hotel building, the little red-brick church transmits an unexpectedly powerful impression of the scale of life when it was built. Looking at it, modern Sofia seems to melt away; one can imagine the town in its glory days as a trading centre, smell the spice markets and see the travel-stained merchants and businessmen from Dalmatia, Florence, Venice, and Nuremberg in their long felt coats, brushing against the silk or fur-decked shoulders of their counterparts from the Crimea, the Caucasus and Turkey. It is sad that Marco Polo left us such a prosaic account, though perhaps we should also be grateful that he did not embellish.

Restoring the town after the ravages of Attila, Justinian also built the Church of St Sophia, set in its own garden on the north-west corner of Alexander Nevsky Square and dominated by the almost flashy 1903 cathedral. The city derived its present name from the 'saint' to whom this simple, cruciform, red-brick basilica was dedicated. Its atmosphere rivals that of the much older St Irene in Istanbul. Though there is a Saint Sophia, and a number of other minor saints of the same name, the name of the church does not refer to her: like the basilica of the same name in Istanbul, it is dedicated to the Holy Wisdom (*he haghia sophia*) – that is, Christ as the Incarnate Word of God.

The town was much more sophisticated than I remembered it. Twenty-five years ago it had had an almost rural air, and the only things you could get to eat were green apples and rock-hard bagels sold from little glass boxes at street corners. But away from Vitoša and the ring-roads there is still little traffic, especially in this quarter, which contains the principal buildings of Church and State.

In the centre of the circus towers the overdone Cathedral of Alexander Nevsky. The thirteenth-century prince of Novgorod was Alexander II's patron saint; a further compliment to the tsar is his equestrian statue, dominating the Liberators' Monument in National Assembly Square, just to the south of the cathedral.

I was hoping to attend a service here, for the choir is legendary, but on most occasions that I visited it the church was shut, and the first time I succeeded in entering a small group of tourists and I were almost immediately chased out by a warty janitor in a vest who shouted at us vigorously despite the presence of an academic-looking priest with a white goatee, who smiled apologetically from behind tinted glasses. When I returned to Sofia a few weeks later I was finally able to see the interior. Every surface is painted; large, rigid saints stare fixedly at you with round, flat, dead eyes. Whirls of colour carry your eye upwards to the dome where Christ sits in impartial majesty. It is an imposing place, but it lacks warmth.

The crypt has been turned into a large museum of icons, covering work from the thirteenth to the nineteenth century. Iconography was considered a rebel art form during the centuries of Turkish domination; and no doubt as an expression of Bulgarian belief and culture, it was. But I am not impressed by rigid naïve forms which allow little development.

Many hundreds of icons are displayed here, some of great size and opulence: gold leaf darkened and enriched by time. The most popular saints are George and Dimitri – the one piercing a variety of serpentine dragons with his lance; the other impaling a Turk through the neck. Saint Demetrius may in fact have been an early deacon of the church who was martyred in Serbia, though his cultus was centred in Salonika. In time, as in the case of Saint George, the soldier of Christ of history was transformed by legend into a noble warrior, an armed knight. George and Dimitri protect Bulgaria from the forces of evil and the infidel respectively. Sometimes they are displayed side by side, gazing coldly at you as they carry out their ritual slaughter.

I walked back west across town and found myself in an area behind the main streets where a fruit and vegetable market was taking place along Georgi Kirkov street. Here almost exclusively tomatoes and peppers were on sale, though I had seen a greater variety of other vegetables in Sofia than anywhere else. There was even a certain amount of fruit – though still no oranges or bananas. I bought some tomatoes and ate them. Though good, they were not quite on the same level as Romanian tomatoes, which, when available and fresh, are excellent.

I found myself outside the Vietnam Restaurant, and, thinking that a change of diet would be welcome, went in. It was deserted except for two Vietnamese or possibly

Lao diners in a far corner, drinking soup. Conversation with the pretty waitress was hard, since she only spoke Bulgarian and Vietnamese, and deciphering Cyrillic transliterations of Vietnamese dishes from the menu wasn't easy; but finally we thrashed out what I hoped would be a suitably varied lunch. The names were certainly exotic enough. I waited in eager anticipation and ordered a beer.

What arrived was roast chicken, a plump leg reposing on a bed of greasy, stone-cold chips. The other dish was a rissole, almost warm and deliciously spicy, surrounded by prawn crackers flavoured with, as far as I could tell, soap. However the cost was a quarter of that charged in the Hotel Balkan, and the waitress offered me an extraordinarily good exchange rate for dollars.

I set out for the National History Museum, housed in the vast neo-Classical former law courts just to the south of Lenin Square. The collection is exhaustive; miles of sombre halls display artefacts and treasure from remote Thracian times (especially a superb nine-piece set of gold plate and drinking horns, the closed ends exquisitely formed as rearing horses and goats – the Panagjurište Treasure), through the period of Roman occupation (how like old friends the familiar statuettes, the pottery vessels and mosaics became as I met them again and again in every country), to the Turkish overlordship, when the monasteries became the custodians and guardians of every indigenous art and craft. Upstairs there was a small exhibition celebrating east European and Soviet space exploration, and an almost endless series of rooms laying out the history of Bulgaria's struggle for freedom in the greatest possible detail, with photographs, documents, uniforms, weapons, paintings and maps. The principal characters stare passionately out at you from sepia prints; pale brown parchments lie in glass cases, heavy with seals. A dark-blue uniform jacket in moth-eaten felt with yellow piping, a hole ripped in its shoulder by a bullet. Home-made banners. Rusty, impossibly cumbersome revolvers. Bloody cavalry clashes commemorated in naïve paint, the Turks with great sweeps of black moustache like wings under their noses. Pictures of prisoners, manacled hand, foot and neck, glumly confronting the camera lens, the end of the chain which links them held by a Turkish soldier standing proud and stiff, nervous of being photographed.

All explained in great detail, but only in Bulgarian.

A thunderstorm broke abruptly at dusk, and blew and raged all night, banishing the last traces of humidity from the high basin where Sofia sits. The town is surrounded, loosely, by mountains: to the north, the Balkan Range rises from the plateau; to the south-east, part of the Sredna Gora range; to the west, the Ljulins, and, dominating the southern part of the city, right on the doorstep, Mount Vitoša.

I set off towards it early the next day. Like all mountains it looked far closer than it was, but the first half of the walk was easy and pleasant, lying past the new National Palace of Culture, an attractive polygonal giant at the northern end of Južen Park. It is named after the wife of Todor Zhivkov, then Bulgaria's president, but otherwise there are very few public indications of the leadership.

Bulgaria's last king was Simeon II, swept away along with the last monarchs of Romania and Yugoslavia in the wake of the Second World War. Zhivkov has been chairman of the Bulgarian Communist Party since 1954, when he was 43. Since 1971 he has also been chairman of the Council of State, under a new constitution, though he was prime minister from 1962 to 1971. He was a partisan leader during the war and led the communist overthrow of the monarchy. One of the oldest of the Eastern Bloc leaders, he has always been interested in promoting friendly relations between Balkan countries, and he has firmly supported Bulgaria's traditional relationship with Russia. Under him, a conventional east European centrally planned economy has been developed, concentrating on heavy industry. Coal and iron ore are mined, and there are Black Sea oil rigs. By way of successful innovation, her telecommunications industry supplies the USSR.

The stability of the country since the war has led to what appears to be a certain dour prosperity. Južen Park sweeps generously south from the Palace of Culture, and on the Sunday morning I was there it was full of strollers, joggers, fathers (wearing the ubiquitous east European mauve tracksuit) playing football with their sons, and people walking their dogs – expensive-looking and well cared-for pets, reminiscent of those in Hungary. I saw an Afghan hound and an Irish setter, and one or two Giant Schnauzers. Crossing the park by following the bank of the little Perlovska Reka (the only thing Sofia lacks is a decent river), I emerged at the southern suburb of Emil Markov. The road named after this nationalist is a broad boulevard, on either side of which untidy clusters of high-rises, some painted in pastel colours to relieve the concrete, rear up from scruffy hillocks of grass, waving row upon row of washing and dotted with the bright red of geraniums in thousands of window-boxes.

I joined Bâlgarija, the main road which cuts through the edge of town from north-east to south-west, and followed it out to Bojana, the suburb which was my goal. I met almost no one on my walk, and few cars passed me, though the motorway is new and broad.

The little church I wanted to visit here contains some early frescoes, but when I arrived it was to find the place closed for renovation – an 'air-acclimatizer plant' was being installed. Still, I was not sorry for the walk. Bojana is full of pretty new houses on the slopes of Mount Vitoša, and on this fine day people were out mowing their lawns and cleaning their cars – new Wartburgs, but also several Fiats. I saw not a few Mercedes in Bulgaria and, deep in the countryside, one elderly Daimler. I found a Greek 'picnic' (open-air) restaurant and had *kebapčeta*, enormously spicy veal rissoles, followed by a Greco-Bulgarian version of kleftiko. Many traditional Greek dishes have a Bulgarian counterpart, the most delicious of which was moussaka. The Turkish *imam bayildi* – stuffed aubergines – is also represented as *imam bajalda*. The restaurant's terrace overlooked the city on its broad plateau just below us. It came as a mild shock to see that the skyline was almost entirely modern, as you don't get such a strong impression of newness when you are actually in the town, but it was still possible to pick out the bulk of the cathedral, its golden dome and tower burning in the sun.

Once back in the centre, I visited the dark, crowded nineteenth-century Church of Holy Sunday (*Sveta Nedelja*), aglow with the beeswax-coloured candles which the faithful burn in their millions in churches all over eastern Europe. A little further north, the Mosque of Banja-Baschi was closed and had a look of neglect as the Sunday crowds swarmed around it, shopping in the clothes market, buying spicy sausages in bread rolls or toffee apples from little stalls, or being weighed on bathroom scales supervised by elderly men squatting on the pavement.

Over a drink I met Gavril ('Call me Gary') and Colette. They lived in Philadelphia, where he was a banker; but he'd been born here, in Sliven. Thirty years ago, when he was twenty, he had got out. Somewhere along the coast between Sinemorec and Rezovo he had plunged into the sea one summer night and swum to Turkey. 'Eleven miles. It took me eight hours.'

'He wanted to show me the spot he took off from,' said Colette; 'but it's a border zone now – you can't get into it without special permission.'

'To tell you the truth, I was nervous of coming back at all, but then I figured, I've got a US passport, and I've anglicized my name, they can't touch me. Still I didn't like to let it out that I could speak Bulgarian.'

'Have you kept it up?'

'It's pretty rusty, but yes, somehow I have. This is still home.'

'How can you say that?' interrupted Colette. Turning to me, she said: 'Normally he won't poke his nose out of Pennsylvania. Hasn't been back here since he left. Wouldn't have, either, if I hadn't insisted.'

'She's been wanting to see Bulgaria practically since we met. Finally I thought, well, it's now or never. I never realized the country could still have such a strong pull on me.' Even so, he added, he'd be glad when the holiday was over. 'It's entirely irrational, but while I'm here I can't shake the feeling that they might decide to keep me.'

After a vain search among the restaurants for one which was neither closed nor full, I cravenly returned to the Hotel Balkan, now filling up with delegates for the conference of the following week. The cashier told me all the rooms were fully booked until the spring. As a centre for international meetings, Sofia is putting itself on the map with great determination. At the same time, unwelcome elements are kept at bay. A fortnight before my arrival, Bulgaria deported 56 foreigners who were found to be carrying the AIDS virus.

22

MONKS, MOUNTAINS AND WINE

I'd equipped myself with diesel vouchers, picked up my car, and finally located the main road south. It lay through a plain between mountains – green to the east, brown to the west. On the plain maize fields stretched far and wide, but at least in Bulgaria there was obvious evidence of its consumption, since at every street corner in Sofia a figure sitting or squatting by a brazier would be selling roasted corncobs. As I progressed southwards, maize began to be replaced by tobacco, yellow as old gold and hanging out to dry on racks made of branches under polythene tents. There were no more sunflowers now.

The mountains keep their distance until you turn left towards Rilski Manastir. Then they rush to greet you, almost as soon as you have passed the little town of Kočerinovo. Rila comes next, with its red roofs and its elevated untidy forest of storks' nests. The way lies on through gorges and past brown hills scrambling up into the sky. Great monolithic slabs like the towers of gigantic Indian temples sun themselves by the side of the road, dwarfing peasants with faces like walnuts pulling handcarts full of kindling. Then thick woods turn the hills dark green, and they close in on either side of you as you begin the long beautiful climb up the cul-de-sac which ends at the most splendid of Bulgaria's fortified monasteries.

To get to the hotel beyond, you skirt the massive grey walls of the place, following a road just wide enough for your car, and pass through the little village – two houses, a restaurant and a shop. The hotel itself is modern and spartan, like a ski-hotel; but in the autumn there are few guests – a handful of tough hikers in plaid shirts. There is nothing else. All around the mountains soar fantastically, protecting and concealing the fortress of the Christian god.

A chapel, barely more than a hermit's cell, was first set up here long before the coming of the Turks by Ivan of Rilski in the tenth century. A monastery grew up around it, but was destroyed by fire, after which a devout local baron called Hrelju caused a new house to be built on a site not far away. This was in the fourteenth century, and the monastery continued its existence as a centre for prayer, the arts and printing for five hundred years, barely disturbed by the Turks. It was ironic that the great house, which in its solitude had avoided the ravages of war, should be destroyed when independence was almost restored to its country, by a great fire in 1833, which wrecked all but Hrelju's sturdy Byzantine tower. It gives an inkling of what the old monastery must have been like. It was more austere than what can be seen today.

The third monastery is constructed in the National Revival style, in which architecture celebrated Bulgaria's independence. It is a blend of traditional building design and elements incorporated later from abroad; it was developed towards the end of the eighteenth and throughout the nineteenth centuries. Its effect is pleasingly medieval, though it is a style in its own right and not a reconstruction of medieval design.

Rilski Monastery faces inwards, presenting only sheer grey stone walls to the outside world, and access is only through the low arches of two gates, to the east and the west. Inside, however, four storeys of highly decorated galleries face the church which stands in the centre of the grey-flagged compound. An unsuccessful attempt has been made to incorporate Hrelju's tower by adding a gaudy arched kiosk to its lower half, which contains a clock and belfry.

The galleries are picked out in black and white. Low broad arches on squat columns run along the outer side of the wooden walkways which continue around the four sides of the almost perfect square formed by the walls. Around some of the arches and at the corners, elements of rust red are introduced, and these are taken up in the red and white decoration of the basilica, with its cluster of low domed towers. Looping curves define its upper façade, while below, protected by an arched and columned arcade also decorated in black and white, a mass of bright paintings cover walls and ceiling. They represent Biblical scenes, and confrontations between angels and devils, but their style and colouring is such that they wouldn't seem out of place on a Burmese temple. The lowest frieze carries the theme of the Last Judgement. These are faithful recreations of medieval style from the National Revival schools of Bansko and Debar, and fittingly restore to the monastery those traditions of Bulgarian Christian art which it has spent all its working life protecting and nurturing.

The massive complex of buildings is given over now to two museums – of church history and of ethnography. There is still a small community of monks, and the call to prayer is given by one of their number walking round the compound banging a resonant plank of wood with a mallet, very vigorously. Within the twilit church there is only a small congregation – half a dozen black-clad women from the village, a plump-cheeked priest of perhaps thirty with a thin brown beard and rich chestnut hair, its length tucked under the black collar of his soutane; one or two others, a handful of tourists. An officiating priest walks round briskly, swinging his censer so vigorously that it sparks and glows, spitting. His face is carved out of some dark hardwood – a beaked nose, fierce, defiant eyes, beard growing almost up to meet them over high cheekbones. And from behind the iconostasis, pellucid baritone voices echo out to us.

The next morning I left early after a horrible breakfast of goat's cheese, bread and jam and one cup of luke-warm herb tea. The night before I had indulged in generous helpings from a bottle of Scotch bought at a hard-currency shop, so to clear my head I went for a brisk early walk in the surrounding hills, meeting no one except a curious lady who seemed bent on selling me something mysterious from one of two heavy plastic bags she was carrying. The air was keen and smelt of pine needles.

The head of the mountain above me was bathed in primrose sunshine while I walked below trees in cool shadow. A few lines of Marvell came into my head:

> Meanwhile the mind, from pleasure less,
> Withdraws into its happiness:
> The mind, that ocean where each kind
> Does straight its own resemblance find;
> Yet it creates, transcending these,
> Far other worlds, and other seas;
> Annihilating all that's made
> To a green thought in a green shade.

I cannot explain better how that morning walk made me feel.

I checked out, got my passport back – it is the custom of most east European hotels to keep your passport until you leave – said goodbye to the receptionist, who spoke fluent French, and drove back the way I'd come to pick up the E79 and head south again – this time almost to the Greek frontier. There were even signposts to Athens. The road by-passes one major industrial town, Blagoevgrad, and a handful of anonymous smaller ones, though Sandanski is reputed to be the birthplace of the gladiator-turned-revolutionary, Spartacus. The scenery increases in beauty as the Rila mountains give way to the more austere Pirin range. Now the countryside is, not surprisingly, very like that of inland Greece: rolling brown hills disappear in the haze; sharp peaks pierce the clouds.

Within a few miles of the frontier I turned left again down another cul-de-sac to Melnik. As you approach the little town – the smallest in Bulgaria – the gentle hills, on which the vineyards have begun to appear, undergo a bizarre and abrupt transformation. They become more compact and steeper, and finally break up altogether into a series of giant stalagmites, quarry-like gashes and cliffs of what looks like compacted sand. Erosion and the action of the wind on this soft stone has created a landscape which is as unique as the grape which grows here. Tucked into the middle of it is Melnik.

The town lies a short way down the valley of the River Melniška from the monastery of Rozhen, high up in this strange land of giant's teeth at the end of the road. I had seen fewer and fewer tourists – it was late in the year and I was moving further away from their routes – but here there were some, and the time to come is after the coachloads (mainly of East Germans and Russians) have gone. Houses in the village below are decked with necklaces of red chillies, drying in the sun, or yellow ones of maize. The monastery is a far more modest affair than Rilski, but it must have been even more remote. Today it sits surrounded by a haphazard disposition of faded metal signs telling you in Bulgarian and German that this is a frontier zone and that you may not pass into it without special authorization. However, in this area I saw no soldiers or policemen for once. After so long in eastern Europe it was a rest for the eyes.

'Mel' means friable stone. But despite its apparently uncompromising location, until quite recently the town was large and flourishing, with more than 3600 buildings – a trade centre for silk, wine and tobacco. Its decline was due to three main causes: it was badly affected by the Balkan War of 1912–13; a large proportion of its Greek inhabitants returned to their homeland; and finally a new through road was built along the River Struma, several miles to the west – the road I had been using. Melnik was left off the beaten track. It dwindled. Houses fell and their stones were taken away to build barns and pigsties. Only now is a programme of restoration in progress, and some of the ruined houses are being rebuilt, but, as everywhere in eastern Europe, this is a question of great lengths of time. 'Five years,' people say; time east of the Iron Curtain seems divided as if by common consent into units of this length.

What remains, built either side of a little brook which feeds into the Melniška, is a pretty, sleepy little town of about 300 people. One bank is dominated by a disproportionately large primary school, the other by the hotel: both are modern, but built in the National Revival style of the rest of the buildings. Typically, the ground floor is cellar or storage space; the projecting upper floor, with windows under generous eaves and red-tiled roofs, is where one lives. Most buildings were painted white against the sun, which here has a Mediterranean quality – it is hard to accept that one is so far from the sea. Buildings are loaded with swags of bright flowers, pink, red and white, which cascade down to street level from balconies or drape themselves under eaves, while bright green creepers romp across façades. Here, the temperature is in the twenties and thirties in summer, and never drops below ten in winter, though as we are in the mountains the nights then are cold.

Paperwork struck when I came to check in and realized that at Rilski they had forgotten both to take my hotel voucher and – more importantly – to stamp my 'statistics' card. I needed no telling to know that this could mean endless delays and explanations later if I didn't return and sort things out – it was lucky that my route doubled back on itself, since the cross-country mountain road was impassable due to landslip at the time. I dumped my bag in a cell-like room, and set off in search of a restaurant and what I had come for: the wine.

I'd discovered Melnik red wine by chance in London a few months earlier. The grape is indigenous to the area and the taste, dry with a hint of blackcurrant, is unlike that of any other wine I know. I imagined that the wine *in situ*, made from grapes not of the general region but grown on the slopes within sight of the town, would be even better.

There was a restaurant a short walk from the hotel, and in it one or two people were finishing their lunches. I sat down, and finally the waiters gravitated towards me. One of them, a lean man with a silvery-grey Beatles haircut, a Zapata moustache and very serious, watchful brown eyes, could speak some German. Lunch, he told me with friendly regret, was over.

'Can I have a glass of wine?'

He gave an apologetic shrug. 'Not when the restaurant is closed. You can have an apple-juice.'

It was 2 p.m. I was thirsty. I settled for the apple-juice. It was delicious, but not what I was after.

When he brought it the waiter told me that there was some moussaka left. 'It's cold. But it's very delicious cold. In fact the flavour's better. Can I bring you that?'

'Yes please.' At the only other table still occupied three stout old men were draining their orange-and-black clay tumblers. What had they been drinking? I ordered another apple-juice.

He brought the food and sat down at my table while I ate. The moussaka was cooked in the Bulgarian way, with more potatoes than the Greek version and a cooked yogurt top. It was as good as he'd promised, and I decided to try more yogurt while I was here since it was 'invented' in Bulgaria.

While I ate we chatted about this and that, once the initial formalities about changing money had been dealt with. Hristo had been born here, he told me, and had worked in this restaurant for the past eight years. I told him a little about London in response to his questions, but I didn't get the impression that they were in the nature of more than a polite enquiry. All the time he stared at me with his candid, dark brown eyes. I found this discomfiting. I hurried my meal anyway, since they were clearly going to close; but there was no question of my being hurried. As I liked the place I was sorry to hear that they would be closed all the next day – 'our day off'. It would be, I thought irritably; but the offers to change money had been very pressing and I was disinclined to come back for more. I had in any case invented a travelling companion, at present resting a stomach-ache in the hotel. This mythical figure came under the heading of Insurance in Tight Corners; there was somebody else around who would miss me and raise the alarm. But he was also useful at times like this: 'I'll have to ask Charles about it – I don't know if we need any more leva.' It gave me breathing space.

We'd started to talk about the wine, and the conversation became more lively. The vineyards yielding the true grape – that is, from those vines grown in the right soil – stretch only for two kilometres either side of the town. Hristo had a small private vineyard, inherited from his father, which he tended with love and great care. Once I'd eaten he took me off to see it. The valley was so loud with crickets that before I'd identified them I looked round for a waterfall. They stopped abruptly at sunset, as if someone had pressed a switch.

The vines (as they all did) looked scruffy and dusty, but the bright green grapes below the leaves were perfect.

'They will be ready for picking on 10 October. The first wine will be ready to drink forty days later. And there is a schnapps we make from the crushed grape pulp when the fermentation is over.'

It seemed a very fast process to me, but I was sorry I couldn't stay until 19 November. We walked back to his house to try some of this year's stock. On the way back into the town we passed much evidence of rebuilding, though no actual activity. It was, to be fair, the hour of the siesta, and the afternoon sun was soporific.

'It takes us so long to rebuild because there's no labour. Usually it's the materials which are lacking; but we don't have that problem here.' He added that there had been a sizeable Greek population as recently as twenty years ago. 'The vast majority of people were Greek – maybe 15,000 out of a total population of 20,000. But then there was an exodus . . . After that, the town died. The 5000 Bulgarians who were left soon dwindled; most drifted off soon after in search of work elsewhere. The houses that had belonged to the Greeks were pulled down or pillaged for building materials.'

I tried hard to get more details of this, it was so unlike anything I'd read; but it was impossible. We reached his house. It was still a little way from the town centre, and stood apart. Down in the centre the buildings are so close together that the edges of their roofs touch. We smoked a Balkan cigarette each and ate fresh figs pulled from the stumpy trees in his garden. Then he ushered me through a large wooden double door into the ground floor.

It was a sizeable cellar, containing nothing but a washbasin in one corner and about a dozen barrels, two of them enormous, the others smaller, man-handleable. The tuns lurked at the back. In front of them, a hogshead had been upended to form a table, on which two pottery beakers and two bottles of wine stood. Along the wall by the door smaller casks were ranked.

'They're nearly all empty now,' he said ruefully. 'But I've enough to last me until this year's vintage is ready.' I noticed that two or three of the smaller casks were still bunged and caulked with clay. Hristo poured from one of the bottles, and we toasted each other, 'To life!'

The wine was cold, which accentuated its dryness and freshness. It burst invigoratingly on the palate – unmistakably the wine I'd drunk at home, but drier, less obviously fruity and lighter. We stood in the grateful cool of his cellar, looking out through the open double doors at the sun-whitened street outside. A number of plump people in holiday clothes, the women in brightly-patterned sun-dresses, were walking down the street.

'Russian tourists,' said Hristo with a polite lack of enthusiasm. 'We have very many such. These will leave first thing in the morning.'

When I said goodbye he gave me a full bottle and said it was for me to share with my friend Charles. 'This wine, if you just drink one glass after a meal, will stop any stomach-pains,' he told me solicitously. This made me feel guilty but I was not going to refuse the gift.

That was incomparably the best Melnik I had in the town. The wine both in the taverna and in the hotel restaurant was tired. I was driven to dine in the hotel restaurant because everywhere else was closed, the town fast asleep by seven. Even the folkloristic cellar was shut. Perhaps they only open it for large groups. The small restaurant was full of locals, but I found a table and ordered *sarmi* – cabbage leaves stuffed with meat – and a cheese pie called, pleasingly, *sirene po šopski*. The only drawback at dinner was the four- or five-man pop band; guitars, drums, keyboard, singer. Huge speakers shook the room as the group hammered out 'Volare' and 'When a Man Loves a Woman' – both sung in their original languages. The latter, a Percy Sledge hit from 1965, must have been very popular in Bulgaria when I was there as I heard it three or four times. The only folk music I could find was on the radio, where several channels play it constantly.

After dinner I walked the length of the deserted dark little town – the only pedestrian around. A cat loped across my path ahead and a late lizard scuttled away to avoid me.

23

BULGARIA IN THE RAIN

It was an uneventful drive to Pazardzik. I'd chosen a route which would take me past the ski resort of Borovec, which is a sprawling place, littered with complicated roadsigns directing you to the various slopes, hotels and restaurants, all of which are shrouded in a thick forest of pine which hugs the road. It was misty up in the mountains, and suddenly cold – the first real suggestion of winter I had had. Among the trees there were glimpses of hardy walkers in shorts, red socks and stout boots.

I had left Melnik after a resistible breakfast of salami, tomatoes, dry white bread, espresso coffee (one cup), and a glass of water. I had wanted mineral water but was told it couldn't be served until the restaurant opened for lunch at noon. I retraced my route, making a detour to Rilski to sort out my vouchers and passport stamps, all of which was done with much charm and no apology. Turning east again a few miles north, the route passed through another broad valley flanked by brown hills. In the countryside tobacco hung out to dry in golden swags, and shepherds as brown as the mountains tended large flocks of lolloping, gangly sheep with beige fleece and the solemn faces of unintelligent senators. But the bucolic scenes gave way abruptly at the edges of towns to bustle and industry. The road was a busy one; lorries pounded along it, rushing past horse-carts and tractors. The towns themselves passed by indifferently: lovely names on the map, anonymous provincial centres in reality, though not without a certain charm given to them by the autumn sunshine.

Pazardzik had started off by merely being a place to spend the night. I'd intended to get as far as Plovdiv, but my visit coincided with the autumn international trade fair and every square inch of accommodation had long since been taken up. I knew nothing about the town, where I had booked a room, and no guide-book that I could find mentioned it. It was a pleasant surprise.

I found the Hotel Elbrus by my usual technique of aiming for the centre as well as I could and then asking (in delighted astonishment, people would dredge up scraps of German to talk to me). I don't think the town had seen many tourists before, certainly not from the West, and I was greeted with shy friendliness mingled with bemusement by most. Only one elderly waiter at the hotel, with a grey beard and thundery looks, seemed to think that foreign guests had no right to be in his bar. As usual in Bulgaria, the hotel bar and café were packed solid with locals, and even the foyer was full of people glued to the Seoul Olympics on television, so I skipped any refreshment before setting off on my tour of the city centre.

As was so often the case, it had been turned into a pedestrian precinct. There was a park, a large open square, and ornamental fountains in profusion, as well as a number of monumental 1950s sculptures, either embodying general concepts of peasant/worker happiness or portraying heroes of the Bulgarian struggle for independence in the nineteenth century. Monumental affirmations of friendship with Russia also reappeared. The impression was of a bustling, prosperous town. Almost inevitably, the hotel overlooked a large building site, on which a vast yellow supermarket had been constructed already. It was spartan in its decor, and no attempt had been made to gloss over the simplicity of its layout – concrete floors and bare bulbs – but it was well stocked. Fruit and vegetables are canned or bottled rather than fresh or frozen.

The streets teemed with people, for this was late afternoon – about the rush-hour. There was little evidence of any truly old building – Bulgaria's pre-nineteenth century architecture suffered virtual extinction at the hands of the Turks, and on account of natural disasters such as earthquakes – but a dusty mosque remained at the corner of a busy cobbled road a short way from the centre, and a sort of Victorian Tudor clock tower overlooked the main square. Modern architecture was low-rise, grey, and vaguely neo-Classical where it was not plain and functional.

The soul of any town lies in its people and in the ways they either overcome, or come to terms with, the places they are given to live in. The atmosphere of Pazardzik was friendly and relaxed. There were hideous concrete blocks of flats, cement-grey and overlarded with the dust thrown up by the traffic. But there were vines growing defiantly on every balcony, forcing beauty out of deadliness, disguising and softening the uncompromising straight lines that everywhere constrain and beleaguer the mind. The smell of exhaust almost made me, a hardened Londoner, gag; but some of the side-streets still had red-brick walls, steeply gabled rooftops, bright windowboxes untidy with rebelliously healthy geraniums and petunias. And in the very centre of the town was a market, entirely oriental in its appearance and its odours, selling fresh flowers, fruit and spices. It might have been in a suburb of Ankara. The influence of five hundred years of Turkish rule cannot, after all, be thrown off in a century, though in all that time the conquerors did not commingle with the conquered to any significant extent. Today, the Turkish frontier is only 120 miles away.

On the other hand, the cinema is showing a Woody Allen film, *Hannah and her Sisters*; and at the theatre the repertoire is *Caesar and Cleopatra*, *Tartuffe*, and *The House of Bernarda Alba*. A man pushing his bicycle passes me, his scythe strapped to it, reminding me of the incursions the countryside makes into towns in eastern Europe; I remember two sicklemen cutting grass on the hill of Buda, and goatherds on the edge of Braşov.

I walk back from the main square to the park by the busy shopping street which connects them. People sit for hours on benches, alone, doing nothing. Old men play chess and drink wine over endless discussions involving some slow gesticulation but never raised voices or hasty speech. I arouse no curiosity. Beards are quite common, and clothing is noticeably better here than in Romania, even away from Sofia. A group of youngsters are sketching, their paper held on clipboards. I have seen similar groups in Melnik and Rilski. They are not old enough to be art students; nor is their work that good; but they have the confident insouciance of adolescence; they slouch and pout, and angle their shoulders.

At the hotel I am treated like royalty. A table is found for me, mercifully far from the band, and I order veal wrapped in mushrooms and melted cheese, accompanied by delicious salty tomato and sheep's cheese salad and wonderful yogurt, unexpectedly quite unlike Greek yogurt, and a dry white wine akin to Muscadet. The food is nearly warm, and by now I can at least identify dishes and ask for things politely in Bulgarian, which delights the waitress. The band is grander than the one in Melnik, and the singer, a young baritone, delivers standards originally from Sinatra, Lloyd Webber and Tom Jones with operatic gusto; in fact his voice is too full for the kind of music he's singing. Later he joins friends at a nearby table where they are drinking the standard Bulgarian tipple – Coca-Cola with a cognac chaser.

As I finish my meal I am asked if I mind sharing my table. A man joins me – a tobacco exporter based in Varna; beyond telling me that, he is not communicative.

The road which links Pazardzik and Plovdiv gives up any pretence at being attractive and becomes simply arterial. Even the countryside, sensing the approach of Bulgaria's second city, retreats. It is no distance between the two cities and I arrived relatively early in the morning, having by now learned enough Bulgarian to order myself a proper breakfast – the Elbrus at my behest came up with scrambled eggs, toast and jam, coffee and hot milk.

The outskirts of Plovdiv are interesting. Trees line the road and there is a hard shoulder on which you are not allowed to park unless you have broken down; your attention is drawn to this in French, German and English as well as Bulgarian. In English the instruction is: 'Flawless Parking Prohibited'. After this promising start Moskva, the main east–west road north of the River Marica, becomes a dull urban six-laner between dirty, untidy high-rises. Finding a parking space after a couple of kilometres' drive through a sad industrial landscape, I walked back towards the Old Town.

North of the river is solid industrial sprawl of the ugliest kind, though no doubt it all functions to Bulgaria's material benefit. There is no cosmetic treatment, and nothing to lift the soul. The only patch of brightness in a sea of grey or muddy terra-cotta was a long bridge over railway tracks and the kind of blasted wasteland which surrounds factory sites everywhere in this part of the world. Two men were patiently engaged in painting its simple but extensive ironwork pale green and white.

Further down the road, pavement-laying was in frantic spate, and I trod a precarious path either on ankle-twisting scrubland to one side or along the edge of the road on the other. This was metalled, but thunderous with traffic whose fumes turned my throat to dust. Once these hurdles had been overcome, however, it was possible to cut through side-streets which were suddenly quiet and beautiful, tree-lined, with luxuriant creepers thrown over mellow stone walls. These brought me back out to another main road, which in turn led to a bridge guarded by lazy stone deities. Across it and immediately to the left was the high, sudden rock on which the Old Town was built, originally Thracian, then the site of Philip of Macedon's capital in the fourth century BC, and of the later fortress outpost of the Roman Empire, almost as remote to them, except in climate, as Hadrian's Wall.

At the northern end of the hill are the faint remains of the Thracian settlement of Pulpudeva, foundations superimposed by the ruins of Roman building. To the south, more substantial Roman ruins stand – a theatre which is still used in summer, and to the west the ancient stadium of Philippopolis is half-buried in the embrace of concrete reconstruction which also includes a sunken open-air café and various small shops. Of the ancient settlement this is all that remains, and of Turkish Filibé there is less still. Only in the overgrown and surly fortification walls and gatehouses does some faint whisper of past overlords linger.

This quarter of town, however, retains the pattern of its medieval streets, narrow and cobbled, running along and around the contours of the hill. The houses to be seen today are almost all National Revival. The more opulent houses are set back in their own gardens, and their typical façade is a bowed middle section, where the first floor is supported on columns over a portico, flanked by flat-fronted wings which may also have first floors supported on columns over a recessed lower storey. The roofs have elegantly curved gables, and above the windows and on the gable ends elaborate foliate decoration is painted. The most beautiful is the villa of the goldsmith, Arghir Kouyoumidjioglu, set back in a walled garden, its façade finished in black and gold. Inside, it now houses a modest ethnographic museum, but it is the rooms themselves that attract. On each floor there is a central area, gloomy but huge, and oval in shape, its walls and ceiling of wood, Turkish rugs on the floor, a complex lozenge carving decorating the ceiling. From these splendid and darkly affluent halls with their lavish plasterwork other rooms lead off, and from them further rooms still. Wall hangings and carpets may have Bulgarian patterns, but the traditions and culture they point to lie further east than anything one would normally associate with Europe.

The day was humid and dull. A bad autumn day, slightly relieved by a steady drizzle which set in towards noon as I tramped the steep cobbled streets. Groups of teenage sketchers had arrayed themselves in front of the more attractive buildings and were doggedly working away under golf umbrellas. Beyond the Old Town to the south, Plovdiv has developed a sprawling, wealthy city – unappealing, and too big to explore. I regained the Fiat and headed north through the Sredna Gora range to Karlovo.

As I reached the hills, the countryside re-established itself, and for part of the way I was kept company by the River Sirjama, a tributary of the Marica. There were several motorcyclists on this road. Most wore an intricate helmet of padded leather, a cross between a rugby player's protective headgear and a First World War fighter pilot's cap.

Karlovo is much larger than it should be, to judge by the size of its name on the map. My first impression was of the usual line of high-rises, ribboning along the valley between the Sredna Gora range and the Balkans to the north, and immediately dominated by the great crag of Mount Botev. The almost threatening proximity of the mountains dilutes the urban ugliness here, and the centre of town is a pleasant pedestrian precinct centring on a large, open square dominated by the town theatre at one end and an unpromising monument whose dedication I failed to discover. The town is the birthplace of the freedom fighter Vassil Levsky (1837–73); he has his monument here, too, where he stands accompanied by a lion – an animal which figures largely in monumental sculpture here.

The one hotel also faces the square. It is entirely functional and had on duty a most glacial receptionist, but I think the arrival of a solitary westerner was on a par with that of a mammoth. I checked in quickly, then walked the streets. Not unfamiliar. Girls queued to get into a small boutique opposite the crowded town cinema (which was showing *The Name of the Rose*). Shops stay open late, and because, unlike in Romania, they turn their lights on at dusk I was made aware for the first time of the shortening of the days. Beyond the square the town simply spread out to east and west in modern development, while to the south pretty, older, suburban streets ran in a grid pattern. To the north, man's progress was bounded by the mountain, which, though not all that high – trees reach almost to the fawn rocks at its summit – loomed over the square impressively enough.

As the sun set, an ornamental fountain at one end of the square started to play, and from loudspeakers nearby came rousing music, to be followed by a news bulletin – I think they were relaying the radio. The hotel's 'tavern' was packed by now. I noticed that far fewer people in this crowd sported Balkan moustaches or twirled worry-beads than I'd seen further south. The consciously modish amongst them wore stone-washed denims.

The restaurant was equally packed, but I found a table where I was soon joined by four men of about my age who ordered plates of ham and salami and three bottles of Russian champagne in succession. The champagne isn't cheap but it is very good. We toasted each other and crept towards understanding via French, a language which is much in use here, especially on official notices which it's important for foreigners to understand. They were all machine tool operators, and they were celebrating the engagement of one of them, Petâr, to be married. He was round-faced and chestnut-haired, not unlike Mario Lanza, and flushed with nervous enthusiasm. He got the standard international ribbing for throwing himself away on matrimony.

Karlovo lies more or less exactly between Klisura to the west and Kazanlâk to the east, in the middle of the Valley of Roses. The rose industry was begun under the Turks in the 1830s. Attar of Roses is its most famous product, but there are also jam, sweets, a liqueur and some dermatological medicines. It is an old industry, and involves many people, at least in the picking season in early summer, since it can take 5000 petals to make a litre of attar, and the blooms must be picked before the sun is high since it can draw off half the oil in a flower.

I had been tempted to journey west from here, just to see the little town beyond Klisura called Anton; but resisting such frivolous reasons for travel I made my way east again, towards Kazanlâk, and then north to the former capital, Veliko Târnovo. I had chosen, I hoped, a particularly attractive route.

The day dawned dull and sluggish. Mount Botev had disappeared under a fat-bellied grey cloud, the roads were slick, and the blocks of flats rose like gravestones out of a dirty mist. I left as late as I dared, hoping the weather would clear with full morning, but if anything it closed in. I could hardly see the mountain as I drove off, and almost as soon as I was out of Karlovo the rain slapped down. The clouds had descended over the hills on either side of the road and all I could see from time to time were sodden shepherds in pacamacs tending equally sodden, dark grey sheep. There were vineyards, fields of maize, sunflowers, and even a few orchards, but I saw no rosebushes at all. I hadn't expected to see blooms, and the weather blanketed much from view, but this was not the Valley of Roses I had anticipated. Perhaps it is better towards Klisura. Perhaps the industry itself is becoming a thing of the past.

I'd ignored turnoff signs to the left in order to drive through Kazanlâk, but the rain precluded a stop, and in any case I needed all the time available to feel my way through the centre of this grisly industrial town, for roadsigns quickly petered out in the centre. After half an hour of driving in what I divined was the right direction, I was deposited on a ring road which brought me back to the motorway I'd come in on. Abandoning Kazanlâk to its fate, I drove back to the Gabrovo road. Behind me, I caught a final glimpse of a dark-grey mass clamped to the land, sulkily belching black smoke from twenty or thirty tall chimneys.

Gabrovo is another industrial town, but to reach it you have to cross the Šipka Pass. The town of Šipka itself is a pleasant little place, with a disproportionately large memorial church to the Russians and Bulgarians who died in the war of liberation against the Turks. It was strange to see several red-and-white buses here, disgorging hundreds of Russian tourists swathed in plastic macs.

Otherwise the place seemed too remote for tourism, even on a fine day. But the pass was the scene of much fighting as it lies on a key north–south route. Serene and densely wooded today, it is punctuated with memorials to the fallen. Bulgaria fought for her liberty hard enough and recently enough still to take nationalism very seriously indeed.

I climbed up the pass into total cloud. I could just see the woods on either side of the road, the red lights of the bus ahead of me and the headlamps of the lorry behind. I moved in wreaths of exhaust fumes which I could neither escape nor dispel. As I drove higher, so the mist became denser and the crawling convoy longer. Still, I was grateful for the filthy bus in front because at least it showed the way. Then, in what seemed to be the middle of nowhere, but which must have been the site of one of the monuments along the pass, the bus turned off to a carpark and I found that I was at the head of the queue. I could see nothing at all.

Gingerly I followed the curves of the road as vegetation loomed up at me, and then quite suddenly the cloud retreated a few yards. Birds flew across the road – bright jays, and magpies, and a little pinky-beige collared dove which seems to be everywhere in Bulgaria. For a short time I had hints through the broken cloud of how lovely the densely-wooded hills must be, but then the fog closed in once more.

Soon, however, we were descending, and in no time were approaching the outskirts of Gabrovo by a road which hugged the mountainside. The mist had been left behind, but the rain continued to drive down with unrelenting ferocity. The town lies on the Jantra river, which now loosely accompanies the road to Veliko Târnovo and rejoins it there. How hard it is to judge a place when it is flattened by rain, all colour washed away, the people hurrying hunched and soaking, shoes trailing sprays, cars bucking and tipping in potholes filled with water like pools of oil.

Gabrovo is twinned with Aberdeen. I had been told that the citizens of Gabrovo are famous for their sense of humour, but they had little cause to display it on this rainlashed Friday. I was unable to find out the date of their annual Festival of Humour, and all attempts to locate the Museum of Humour ('110,000 humorous items from all over the world' says a guide-book – surely not to be missed) sadly foundered. At least Veliko Târnovo was by now clearly signposted.

On my way out of town I passed three covered wagons carrying families of Gypsies. Pots and pans, bottles and ropes of onions and garlic, swung and rattled against the sides as the wagons lurched along over the uneven road. The driver of the lead cart cast me a glance. He had an old tweed jacket on, which was soaking, and his long black moustache was waterlogged. I considered how romantic his little horse-drawn convoy would have looked on a sunny day, and felt ashamed.

After Gabrovo the weather eased and I took advantage of this to make a detour to the village of Boženci. It lies a few miles to the east of the main road along a country lane which dips and weaves through secret woods and fields reminiscent of northern Essex. The village itself is tiny, its protected houses all of a piece, with whitewashed walls and heavy split-stone roofs. In the green, dripping aftermath of the rain it was deserted. At its entrance is a sign in Bulgarian and English. In English it admonishes:

'*Keep the area from fire, pollution and damages! Keep the river clean! Use only cameras! Don't spoil the buildings, the signboards and inscriptions! Switch off the radios! You can find here the silence and beauty which you lack in town! No noise! No shouts! No buzzing of engines! Listen to the song of nature! Don't leave any traces of disorder.*'

I was led to the inn by the loud sounds of Bulgarian pop music emanating from it. These proved to be coming from a large television set with headache-inducing wobbly colour. Some kind of talent competition seemed to be in progress which was won by a bubbly blonde singing a song about her sexy skintight slacks. Everyone in the bar clapped. There were two old men bent over coffee and brandy, and an old lady who in England would certainly have been sitting in a corner over a bottle of Guinness but here had a glass of wine and a cake. The bar was run by a pleasant girl and an operatic waiter with a dramatic sweep of black hair and huge sideburns. He brought me a bottle of white wine. There ought to have been an open fire, for the place was low-roofed with heavy wooden beams and had wooden furniture covered with rugs and cushions in bright Bulgarian red, black and white patterned material. Otherwise, I might almost have wandered onto the tavern set for *Moonfleet* or *Jamaica Inn*.

It was warm. I eased my stiff neck and sipped my cold wine gratefully. Even the awful music didn't seem too terrible. At least it was home-grown. I was lulled by it. The people were friendly, the wine good. It was tempting to stay longer, but I was eager to get to my next goal – Veliko Târnovo, the greatest and best-preserved of Bulgaria's ancient cities. Outside, in the glittering, empty streets, the rain had stopped and the birds, tentatively, had begun to sing again.

24

HOMELAND OF THE ASENS

The River Yantra arrives at a group of three hills – though hill is a misnomer, for they are gargantuan rocks, set close together. The river, in finding a path through them, has had to carve a great loop, doubling almost completely back on itself, creating of one rock a peninsula joined to the 'mainland' by an isthmus. This is Tsarevec. Immediately to the west, a sister rock, Trapezica, has also been turned into a peninsula by the action of the Yantra. To the south lies the largest hill of all, Sveta Gora, which has no natural moat.

Perhaps it is a wonder, given its huge natural advantages, that Great Târnovo was not fortified earlier; but its foundation dates from about 1185, when two noblemen, the brothers Peter and Asen, led a successful uprising against the Byzantine Empire and as a result founded the Second Bulgarian State, which was to last until the Turkish invasion. (Previously, before the coming of the Byzantines a Bulgar Khanate had emerged in the ninth and tenth centuries from the Danube Bulgars who settled along the river in the seventh and eighth centuries.) For just over two hundred years Târnovo was the centre of Bulgarian culture and rule. From here issued the dynasties of the Asens, the Terters and the Shishmans. On Tsarevec a mighty fortress town was erected; as the new kingdom gained stability and confidence, the boyars built themselves palaces on Trapezica to rival those of the ousted Byzantines. For two hundred years the kingdom flourished. Then, in 1393, Târnovo fell to the Ottomans of Bayazet.

Nine years later the great Turkish conqueror was to be humbled by Timur (Marlowe's Tamburlaine) at Ankara, but Bulgaria would not regain her independence for five centuries. Târnovo itself was razed to the ground. What was built subsequently suffered great damage in an appalling earthquake in 1913, but the cultural lamp which had burned between 1185 and 1393 was extinguished for ever; only fragments remained from the school of letters of the Patriarch Euthymius, or of frescoes and miniatures. What is left is widely scattered: examples can be seen in London, in the Vatican, and Moscow.

My hotel was friendly but seedy; it served the best beer in the Eastern Bloc since Krumlov, and its great advantage was to be at the gates of Tsarevec. I did not start with the sprawling ruin of what, had it survived, would surely be one of the wonders of the world today, but followed the banks of the Yantra – here a sluggish dark green river in a deep gully – to the north of the medieval city, and so on to the district of Asenov. This was the craftsmen's quarter in the Middle Ages, and though little of it now remains, the National Revival building which has replaced the medieval work-shops and cottages is a fitting successor. Even new buildings in this area are built in Revival style, for Târnovo, given its historical importance to Bulgaria, was among the first towns to be restored, on independence, as a symbol of national crafts-manship.

Asenov straddles the river between the northern ends of Tsarevec and Trapezica. On what is now the west bank of the abruptly twisting river lies the city's oldest church, the twelfth-century basilica of St Dimiter of Salonika. The building which now stands is a complete restoration of the original, which was destroyed to its foundations, but its simple interior, traces of once magnificent frescoes restored to its walls, still has the power to move. In this small, modest church, Peter and Asen declared the new kingdom. It was a misty morning when I visited and no one was about, even in the village, though one or two small yellow dogs loped by on business of their own and cats roamed a rooftop world of rust-coloured tiles. But as I turned to go, a man appeared. He introduced himself in German as the caretaker, took me back into the church, switched on lights, pointed out saints among the faded faces of the frescoes. He was about sixty, tall and stooped, his wavy hair still yellowy-brown and swept back from his temples with so much brilliantine that it looked sculpted or painted on. He had a pencil-line moustache and wore a sports jacket in loud hound's-tooth check.

He didn't follow me when I wandered off to look at the outside of the church, with its complicated geometric patterns of red brick and dark green tilework, its low recess-work and blind arches. When I left I offered him a tip, which he politely declined.

There are two other churches of note here: but the one dedicated to SS Peter and Paul was closed, and the Church of the Forty Martyrs was entirely cloaked in a green tarpaulin, covering a shed which had been built over the just-discernible Byzantine walls. I turned back to begin my tour of Tsarevec.

The fortress complex is dominated by the Patriarchate Church, the only complete standing building on the hill, apart from the towers along the outer curtain walls. Like them, it is entirely restored, and its interior has been covered with awful modern murals; but it provides a focal point and from a distance sets off a dramatic skyline. The other landmark of the complex apart from the gatehouses in Baldwin's Tower at the southernmost tip – so named because Baldwin of Flanders, one of the leaders of the Fourth Crusade which took Constantinople so shamefully at the behest of Venice in 1204, is reputed to have been imprisoned here during the messy years that followed the sacking of that great city. His ultimate fate may have been less romantic: one version has it that King Johanitza of Bulgaria, having made Baldwin his captive, had his hands and feet cut off and threw him into a gully, where it took him three days to die.

Lengths of the curtain wall have been restored in pink and beige stone, which may be accurate but gives it the look of a modern fireplace. Following it north, I came to the isolated Judgement Rock – once a tower, now marked by a platform. This was the place of execution for condemned prisoners, and it was from here that the Patriarch

Jikasim III, found guilty of high treason, was thrown into the Yantra in 1300. Death would be certain before hitting the river two hundred feet below. It is not hard, looking down, to imagine a body dashed onto rocks and bouncing off them again several times before disappearing into the turgid water

Two coachloads of Russian tourists and one of Chinese had disembarked by now and were scrambling about the ruins in the mist. The entire area had been cleared, and the walls of houses and shops and several churches identified and reconstructed to a height of two to three feet. Some small low buildings remain, and are currently used to keep the restorers' equipment, as this symbol of the Bulgarian nation emerges once again from the anonymous rocks which surround it.

The town perches on the steep sides of its hills, but never climbs to their tops, never dominates them. Nor do the few modern buildings on this side of the town intrude. The rocks and the trees are omnipresent and ineradicable, limiting and protecting.

On the slip of steep land which forms the isthmus between Tsarevec and Trapezica is the quarter settled by the Turks, brushed aside in their turn to make room for a 'new town' constructed in National Revival style. Steep cobbled streets weave narrowly between wooden balconied houses of whitewashed stone, half hidden behind rampant columbine with vivid blue flowers. One of the greatest exponents of National Revival, Nikola Fičev (Kolya Fičeto), worked here, and his larger buildings are now museums filling the small squares into which the narrow streets open.

I cannot imagine where everybody is. Apart from a religious procession, led by a young priest with a vigorous brown beard and made up for the most part of elderly women carrying icons and singing, snapped by two eager long-haired and bejeaned local press photographers, I am alone. I wander through the archaeological museum. Two middle-aged ladies are in attendance and one follows me, switching lights on and off as I walk through rooms full of arrow-heads and broken beakers, and then on to jewellery and ironwork showing strong Celtic influence and teaching me how far east the La Tène Celts spread in the third century BC. A great emphasis is laid here on early Bulgarian culture; the people are keen to stress that the period of Turkish domination was an interlude during which they were not swamped by the culture of the intruders. Had the two nations shared the same religion the story might have been different

Above this part of town, and before reaching the flat land where the new town stretches modestly westwards, first nineteenth-century and then twentieth along Dimitâr Ivanov, there is another pocket of National Revival: Rakovski Street is delightfully crowded with craftsmen's shops – coopers, gunsmiths, potters and coppersmiths. I contented myself with what most of the locals were eating and joined a queue for hot-dogs. Eating mine, I set off for the New Town through the broad, crowded weekend streets. There were dozens and dozens of national servicemen, ceremonial daggers dangling at their thighs, bright red caps on their freshly-shorn heads. Many were making for the red-brick cinema near the Mother Bulgaria monument, where *Crocodile Dundee* was showing.

The Mother Bulgaria monument is a memorial to the dead of this century's world wars. Close to it, on a lean spit of land created by yet another twist in the Yantra, is the great monument to the Asen Dynasty. Erected in 1985 it shows four horsemen in black metal – the boyars Peter, Asen, Kaloyan, and Ivan Asen II guarding a black spire which is a bronze sword. It is a superb, romantic piece of work, full of free and wild movement, and a relief after the stolid Socialist Realism nearly everywhere else. On its brick base someone had aerosolled in English, in large capitals, 'Make love, not war'. In front of it is the modern Byzantine-style building which houses the 'Veliko Târnovo through the Eyes of the Artists' permanent exhibition, which was closed. The building was being drawn by another group of schoolchildren, casual in jeans and anoraks, with long untidy hair and bright scarves, grasping clipboards and pencils. One of them had an anti-smoking T-shirt on.

It was dusk by the time I reached the hotel, and from my window I could see that as the sun set so the hill of Tsarevec was floodlit, isolated from the present by the gathering dark and returned to the past by the light.

I'd decided to make an early start, but unknown to me Bulgaria had gone on to winter time during the night and when I descended no one was up, let alone ready to check me out. The day had decided to be fine, although there were still some slight swathes of mist across the lower parts of the road, which ran west straight through the middle of the rugged brown slopes of the Balkan Range. There are no major towns between Târnovo and Sofia on this road, and soon after dawn was a good time to be driving. The countryside was sun-splashed and empty apart from the occasional shepherd tending his small flock. White farmhouses with red roofs slept on in the early yellow light; ochre villages might have been ghost towns. There was one exception to this. On a lonely stretch I suddenly saw several cars and small lorries parked. Their owners were in the fields by the roadside, piling a red fruit into shallow wooden crates which were then stacked together ready to be loaded. They were picking paprikas, and they must have been at it since well before dawn for several dozen crates were already filled.

As the sun rose, a few other cars joined me on the road – an oncoming car flashing me at one point to warn, as it turned out, of an impending police speed trap. A policeman stands concealed behind a bend with a red 'lollipop'; if you come round the bend too fast, he nabs you. In Bulgaria, speed limits are not only imposed in towns and villages but at bends, near factories, and at crossroads as well.

A motorway bores its way by means of tunnels through the hills for the last few miles before tarmac is replaced by cobbles, buildings crowd, trolley-buses and trams finally appear, and you know you are back in the capital. After wrestling with an unexpected one-way system which seemed to have come into force simply to define a temporary pedestrian precinct around the town centre, I returned the Fiat to Balkantourist. The girl who had hired it to me arrived exactly on time to pick it up, took the keys and my money, gave me a dazzling smile and said 'Have a nice day'. I shouldered my pack and set off down sunny back-streets for my overnight digs near the station.

The flat I'd been assigned to showed no sign of life when, after ringing the doorbell in vain, I let myself in with the keys supplied. It was in a modern block, part of a group built around a shabby but sunny courtyard. I left a note for my landlady, deposited my things, changed out of by now very travel-stained clothes, and set off.

On the way back into town I passed the tents of the visiting 'Circus Bucharest', but there was no sign of life so I walked on, for the sake of walking in the sunshine, until I found myself again at the cathedral. The warty concierge was there, more composed this time, and wearing a jacket and shirt. He smiled benignly at the tourists who milled around him. In the square outside, a wedding party was posing for photographs. 'Here, we have a long wedding season, from August right through September,' I had been told. These must have been the very last, but plenty were still taking place. At the modern Hotel Sofia the sounds of a folk orchestra drummed and wailed into Narodna Sâbranie Square; I blundered into a wedding in the tiny Russian Orthodox Church along Ruski Boulevard. Outside the Hotel Bulgaria, a group of flushed people had come up for air from the old-fashioned brown-varnished-wood barn of a restaurant where, through the dusty net curtains, could be seen acres of dishevelled white tablecloth bearing the remains of the banquet. People danced fitfully to the encouragement of *gadulka* and *gaida*, but they could not keep up with the zest of the music. The men in the group outside tugged at their collars. They wore shiny light suits of brown and beige, whose jackets barely met over barrel chests. In the place of buttonholes, decoratively folded lilac handkerchiefs were pinned to their lapels.

Completing my circuit, I arrived at 9 Septemvri Square, coming to a halt in front of the plain, dignified Mausoleum of Georgi Dimitrov. A permanent guard of two young soldiers stands either side of the doors to this marble monument. They are dressed in a ceremonial uniform of black trousers and white jackets with red frogging. On their heads they wear a white fur shako with a tall feather at the front.

I noticed that today the doors stood open, and saw that people were coming and going. A small sign I hadn't seen before told me that the mausoleum was open every afternoon, without exception, to allow people to pay their respects to the 'father of modern Bulgaria'. Georgi Dimitrov died in 1949 at the age of 67. He became a member of the Comintern's executive committee in 1921, but was exiled in 1923. In 1929 he moved to Berlin, but four years later he was arrested and accused with others of complicity in the Reichstag Fire, which provided Hitler with the excuse to abolish parliament. However, he was acquitted, and travelled to Russia, becoming a naturalized citizen of that country and secretary-general of the Comintern. He returned to Bulgaria when the country was liberated in 1946, and became its first communist prime minister that year. He is universally revered; there is not a town that does not have a street named after him, and I had driven beside the River Georgi Dimitrov when approaching Kazanlâk.

I wasn't sure what to expect. Entering, you turn right and then proceed around the inner perimeter of the rectangular mausoleum by way of a narrow marble corridor. At each corner stands a soldier in dress uniform, who snaps to attention as you pass. I was beginning to think that this was all one did, contemplating as one walked the great man on the other side of the inner wall, but just before the circuit is completed a narrow door opens to the left. Darkness lies beyond it.

I entered a hall – the centre of the mausoleum. I took in, first, a policeman and four more guardsmen, all in dress uniform. One of the guardsmen doubled up with an irrepressible sneeze as I entered, blushing deeply with embarrassment as we caught each other's eye. There was a religious solemnity about the hall. In the dramatic darkness the huge glass coffin, with its curlicued wooden frame and decorations, is brightly lit, as if from within. In it, Dimitrov lies, his head on cream pillows, the brown hair receding from the brow swept back, the drooping full moustache giving the same air of sadness to the face in death as it did in life. He is dressed in a black formal suit, his hands clasped, fresh flowers at his feet.

Standing in this secular church, I wondered about this curiously old-fashioned custom of preserving a leader's body and leaving it open to view, as if itself alone could impart some mystic inspiration which the writings and achievements left behind by the dead man could not. There was something akin to the preservation and exposure of relics of saints. Do we anywhere in the West still retain this direct reverence for corpses – except, of course, for the corpse of Christ, symbolically adored?

Leaving the mausoleum – one may not linger, and the visit cannot have taken more than two or three minutes in all – I felt strangely exhilarated. I walked into the city park towards the theatre. There was a Charles Bridge atmosphere here, as traders with portable stalls sold chunky jewellery, hand-printed T-shirts, motif'd pullovers and clumsy paintings of the town. At least this felt more familiar. A small, dark man whom I'd met three times already through his unsuccessful bids to change money gave me a friendly wave. I had too many leva left, and no faith in anyone's offering to change them at the frontier, so I wandered off to the Hotel Balkan to indulge myself before returning to my digs.

Perhaps it was the grape brandy, perhaps the rich lamb *Vrtena*; but I passed the worst night of my journey. There was still no sign of my landlady, though I had heard muted signs of life as I lay half-asleep late at night, and again in the early morning. But we would have to meet, for I had to give her her voucher.

Finally I ran into a timid woman in the corridor, who was much younger than I had expected from the shuffling sounds and the coughing. She was pleasant, shy, and spoke hesitant German, but by now there was no time to talk. I set off into the early-morning streets, passing office workers queuing for hot snacks from booths before settling down for the day, and made my way to the long grey marble modern block of the station.

I was catching the Istanbul Express, which plies between that city and Munich. The train was a motley of carriages – Turkish, Austrian and West German, together with one or two others I couldn't identify. My reservation was in a German carriage. It was too comfortable, not foreign enough.

The train was by no means full, and the only delay was caused by the unloading and loading of a large motorbike which some intrepid West German was taking home, having spent a fortnight touring Turkey on it. The motorbike blocked one entrance completely, and was at once a source of irritation and a cause for admiration among the guards and porters.

I was alone all the way to Dimitrovgrad, the first town on the Yugoslav side of the frontier. We travelled out of Sofia through flat, scrubby farmland for some time until hills began to rise as at an unseen signal, and massive craggy mountains, larger than anything I had seen since the Carpathians, loomed ahead. After my recent experience, I was becoming nervous of Customs at Dragoman on the Bulgarian side of the frontier – my new notes were discreetly packed away; and my films back in their original cartons, masquerading as unexposed, but nevertheless ... In fact, long before we reached the frontier town a diffident young man in a dark blue windcheater wandered into my compartment. I took him to be a fellow-passenger at first, and only realized that he was the customs officer after our conversation had taken a very definite turn towards the contents of my bags. I told him I had nothing to declare and he didn't even ask me to take the small bag down.

'Got any levas left over?' he asked.

I showed him the ten that remained.

'That's all right. Souvenir,' he grinned. Then I asked him about the diesel coupons I had left over, in the faint hope that the guide-books might be right and I could get their dollar value back.

His brow furrowed. 'But they are valid until the end of December.'

'I'm afraid I may not be back within the next two months.'

'Ah ...'

We had reached an impasse. I couldn't insist, and we'd had a good chat. Anyway I was full of fellow-feeling for him. He didn't even wear a peaked cap, and I realized how abraded I was feeling after so many uniforms for so long.

'Would you like them?'

He smiled: 'Sure?'

'They're no good to me.'

He pocketed them and clapped me on the shoulder. '*Gute Reise*,' he said.

At Dragoman two passport officers came to see me. They too were capless, and their uniforms were simple grey suits. They both spoke English.

'British!' said the one wearing glasses with real pleasure as he saw my passport. At least he scrutinized my 'statistics' form fairly thoroughly. After all my efforts to ensure that it was in order, I couldn't have borne it if he'd just glanced at it. He stamped my visa and handed me back my passport. 'Come back soon,' he said, and sounded as if he meant it.

His colleague lingered, his eyes on the novel I was reading. 'Have you got any other English books?' he asked.

There was nothing in his voice, but I was on guard immediately. 'Only one other novel,' I said, guardedly, thinking of *Dracula*.

'Have you read it?'

'Yes.'

'Um, I don't suppose you'd let me have it, would you? You see, we can't get anything much in English here, except for the *Morning Star*, and that's usually weeks old. Reading's a good way to stop going rusty.'

I dug out *Dracula*, riffled through it quickly to see that I'd left no notes looseleafed inside it – an action which did not escape him – and gave him the book. He beamed. 'When you next come, bring plenty of magazines and newspapers – anything,' he said. 'The Yugoslavs are so lucky. Have you been there before?'

'Many years ago.'

'They can get anything they want from the West. Oh well . . .' a look at his watch. 'I'd better get off; goodbye.'

The train rolled slowly out of Dragoman towards the frontier. Soon I would be, if not in western Europe, at least back on my side of the Iron Curtain. A sense of anti-climax filled me. I thought wryly of all the currency exchange papers from every country, which I had religiously kept and never been asked for once.

The journey continued through little villages that looked more cheerful somehow, and on through dramatic rocky gorges. The engine began to blow its whistle. Quite irrationally, though it must have just been relief at having got through another frontier, I interpreted its sound as whoops of joy.

At Dimitrovgrad the officials were pleasant and informal. It felt odd not to need a visa, not to be issued with a form, not to have one's luggage searched or be confronted with a string of suspicious questions. I was joined in my compartment by a burly man laden with carrier bags and a large enamel bucket, which I helped him stow on the luggage rack. He was a bank manager from Belgrade, returning from a friend's wedding in Gradina. His bags contained farm produce – plums, pears, apples – which he was taking home to the city. He shared some of the fruit with me and it was delicious – how quickly we learn to appreciate what we take for granted, as soon as we are deprived of it. My thoughts flicked back to Romania, with which this country also shares a frontier.

The banker told me of his admiration for Mr Gorbachev and Mrs Thatcher – 'a strong, principled woman' – but in the case of the British prime minister his praise was based solely on the fact that so far – this was the autumn of 1988 – she had been able to control inflation, which at the time was one of Yugoslavia's two major problems.

The great mountains which separate Yugoslavia and Bulgaria continued to rear up round us but gradually distanced themselves from the track, giving way to maize fields, brown and wrinkled by this time of year. In the course of my journey I had seen the green crop turn golden, be harvested, and wither. Now the brown stalks that remained were being gathered and stacked. After an hour's stop at Niš we were joined by the Morava, an idyllic, dark, slow-flowing river, like black mercury, hugged by shrubs and overhanging trees. A secret, magic stream. Passing one particular curve, the banker leaned over and pointed. 'Train crash there a few years ago. 141 dead.'

Later he slept, explaining that he had danced late the night before. I watched the countryside turn black as the sun set. The train was running late; I would have been on it eleven hours by the time we reached Belgrade. The banker woke shortly before we arrived, and pointed out lights on the horizon. The first fortifications of the old citadel, isolated watch-towers, came into view, then the exhibition halls of the Belgrade trade fair, cold with neon light and deserted. Skirting the confluence of the giant rivers Sava and Danube, a geophysical feature which has ensured that settlements have been here since man first learned the words trade and war, we passed the Nebojša kula and rounded the walls of Kalemegdan. Five minutes later the train pulled into the unexpectedly pretty little central station.

It was a kind of homecoming for me – familiar and yet not so, for memory barely holds over twenty-five years. I had last been in Yugoslavia as a fifteen-year-old schoolboy, the guest of a family who lived in Subotica, some distance to the north, but I remembered parts of Belgrade – the zoo and the castle – vividly and with affection.

PART FOUR

SOUTH:
Yugoslavia
and Albania

25

TITO'S LEGACY

The ancestors of the Yugoslavs (the Southern Slavs) were the tribes which settled in the Balkans during the sixth and seventh centuries and spread to the Alps in the west. For the most part these peoples were settled and converted to Eastern Orthodox Christianity by the ninth century, and the area covered by Yugoslavia today began, very slowly, to be defined. Towards the end of the ninth century the bulk of it was controlled by the Kingdom of Great Moravia, that shadowy empire which stretched up to the Baltic and reached the frontiers of Germany and Russia. The Dalmatian coastline, however, was still in the hands of Byzantium. By the mid-tenth century Croats and Serbs had emerged as distinct, dominant tribes in approximately the same areas that they occupy today, and the Principality of Serbia had appeared by 1090.

In the centuries following the collapse of Constantinople and the western Byzantine Empire, the eastern half of Yugoslavia fell under Turkish dominion, while the western half was absorbed by the Kingdom of Hungary. Venice controlled the coast. The only stable area was the maritime city-state of Ragusa-Dubrovnik, which achieved independence following the Fourth Crusade in 1205, and retained it, partly because of its importance as a port, partly by shifting allegiance to the ascendant power, be it Austria, Hungary, Venice or the Sultan, until it was taken by Napoleon early in the nineteenth century. Since Venice clung to control of the Dalmatian coast until late in the eighteenth century, it is not surprising that the little fortified cities along it show the influence of the Italian republic. After the fall of the French dictator, what was later to be Yugoslavia became the southern part of the Austro-Hungarian Empire, to emerge as a country, or rather a federation, in its own right, in 1918.

There are six members of the Socialist Federal Republic of Yugoslavia: the republics of Bosnia-Hercegovina, Croatia, Macedonia, Montenegro, Serbia, and Slovenia. Serbia has – at the time of writing – two autonomous provinces, Voivodina and Kosovo. It is by far the largest republic, both numerically and (if you count the two provinces) geographically. Macedonia and Montenegro are the poorest, and a world away from Slovenia, which is far closer in culture and religion (Roman Catholicism) to Austria than to her fellows. Slovenia has the lion's share of successful industry, and resents Serbia's power-mongering. It also has its own language; the other two languages of the Federal Republic are Macedonian and Serbo-Croat, which last is to all intents and purposes the official language of the country, though all three are treated as equal in theory. There are two alphabets: roughly speaking, the Roman is used in the west, and the Cyrillic in the east.

The disparities of language, culture and religion as well as racial differences have until now been held together by two forces – a strong sense of national (or supra-national) unity, and a unique interpretation of Socialism whose elements feature mutual help, from inter-republican to personal levels, and self-management. Workers, in every field from factories to hotels, manage the means of production and decide on the terms and results of their labour, thereby avoiding monopoly. Similarly, all workers are directly involved in making decisions on public and state affairs. In addition to this, private enterprise is increasingly permitted and encouraged, though on a limited level, the idea being that socialist principles should not be compromised.

All this is good theory, and so far it has been good practice. That it was developed and sustained at all is partly due to the consistent rule of the country by Josip Broz Tito between 1945 and his death in 1980. He kept Stalin and Russia at bay, asserted Yugoslavia's independence and non-aligned status, and unified the country under him. Ruthless as he may have been to achieve this, he was, and still is, regarded as a benign father-figure.

His death left a vacuum which no one has yet been able to fill. No one has tried. Such was his impact that since his death presidents have been rotated annually, Tito's mantle being considered too big for anyone else to don. He was eighty-eight when he died, but had trained no successor; it was almost as if he could not bear the thought of Yugoslavia without him. His lack of foresight has now placed his country at risk, one which is exacerbated by two major problems – inflation, and ethnic unrest.

Standards of living in Yugoslavia are generally high for the Eastern Bloc, and overall records of consumption are impressive. Between 1947 and 1975 incomes rose by 500%, personal expenditure by 400%, and social and housing expenditure by 600%. Between 1955 and 1983 electric power consumption rose by 1200%. The consumption of goods of all kinds increased very fast; cars, television sets, washing machines and so forth were rare in the late Sixties, common by the mid-Eighties. Western consumerism is running athwart socialist administration.

The economy was developing too, but Yugoslavia had borrowed heavily to achieve this. When international economic growth began to falter in the West, the effects in the East were soon felt. More money had to be borrowed to cover Yugoslavia's mounting balance of payments deficit. By the early Eighties, Yugoslavia owed $20 billion – a sum which reflected the increasing costs of imports, from oil to technology. Production began to slow down, inflation to increase. There was no Tito to rally round. By the time I arrived in Belgrade, inflation stood at 217 per cent. There had been 800 strikes in the country in the past nine months.

In addition, national unity is threatened by increasing tensions between Serbians and ethnic Albanians, who outnumber them by eight to one in the province of Kosovo.

This problem is not helped by the fact that the Albanians are also increasing in population at a far faster rate than the already outnumbered Serbs. There is a movement among them to establish a separate Albanian republic in Kosovo (though integration with Albania itself seems less likely or desirable). However, Kosovo is also the cradle of Serbian culture, as important to the Serbs as Masada is to the Jews or Zimbabwe to the Bantus. The area was settled by Slavs in the sixth century, and by the end of the twelfth Kosovo had become the centre of the medieval Serbian state. Many monuments of great significance have survived from that time, but in 1389 the area was overrun by the Turks, who remained in power for 450 years. The original Serbian population maintained a resistance, but many were forced to migrate northwards out of the Turkish sphere of influence, while to replace them Albanians moved up from the south. These came to be co-religionists and allies of the Turks, who recruited them to put down Christian rebellions and then settled them on vacated farms and in abandoned villages. As recently as the Second World War, Serbs have blamed Albanians in this region for collaboration with the pro-Nazi Croatian corps, the *Ustashe*. Now the Serbian minority is diminishing as people leave in the face of Albanian harassment: 30,000 have gone over the past seven years, out of a population of about 210,000. The Albanians number roughly 1.25 million. They say they are tired of being treated as second-class citizens without adequate representation in the province's administration. Albania, which shares a stretch of frontier with Kosovo, supports them.

Kosovo is rich in minerals, the known deposits of lead and zinc alone accounting for over 50 per cent of Yugoslavia's reserves; but it is also the least developed region in the whole country. The crisis has thrown a tough new Serbian leader called Slobodan Milosevic into prominence. Serbs see him as a saviour, even as a new Tito, and interpret his desire to bring Kosovo under Serbian control as the only way to police it properly. Members of the other republics take a more cynical view – that Serbia is using Kosovo as an excuse for empire-building. 'They will annexe Kosovo and Voivodina, and then what? Already the majority of the police and army are Serbians,' one Croatian told me in Dubrovnik. But I am getting ahead of myself.

None of this had impinged on me yet, as I climbed the steep hill away from the station into the friendly, quasi-western city of Belgrade. The centre was in massive disarray, for it was being converted into a pedestrian precinct. Cars were already banished, but walkers had to pick their way over the most treacherously uneven terrain, littered with potholes, sandbanks, ditches bridged by unstable planks, and twists of rusty wire which would ensnare your ankles, ladder stockings, and trip you up.

Yugoslavia had gone on to winter time, too, and it was appropriately cold and dark. A sharp wind flicked around the right-angles of the modern streets, and the open-air cafés were deserted. Later, I picked my way past the clumps of trees waiting to be planted and the stacks of lamp-posts waiting to be erected and crossed Trg Republike, making my way to Francuska and the Writers' Club, where I hoped there might still be a table for dinner. The inside is shabby but the food is good, and the people who eat here are better. Going downstairs to the restaurant from the faded yellow hall, reminiscent of a decaying London gentlemen's club, one enters a new and irresistibly attractive world, for Belgrade is still small enough for people to know each other well, and those involved in the arts still gather to exchange ideas.

Belgrade, like Edinburgh, is predominantly grey. With one or two exceptions the nineteenth-century buildings are the oldest, for the city's strategic and commercial importance has ensured a succession of sackings down the centuries. Belgrade suffered at the hands of the Turks for the insurrection of its inhabitants in the early nineteenth century – it was not liberated from Turkish rule until 1867 – and the Germans sent 300 bombers over the city in 1941, killing 25,000 people on Palm Sunday morning. Much of the town is therefore modern, but it is not soulless.

The next day, my onward travel arrangements dealt with, I headed south through the artisans' quarter beyond the station towards the Tito Memorial Park, passing the little booth-like shops of watch-repairers, cobblers, metalworkers and cabinet-makers. Soon, I had left the homicidal traffic behind and was walking beneath the trees of Hajd Park towards the complex of buildings where Tito lived and worked, and which are now his memorial. The first building I came to was his resting-place in the so-called 'House of Flowers', part garden-room, part conservatory, in which he spent his last days. The tomb is a plain slab of pink-grey marble, his name in plain gold. At each corner of the massive rectangle stands a soldier in the bright blue uniform of his Special Guard. I was alone here, and it is a mystery that I was allowed to go this far unchallenged, since a visit to the memorial is strictly in groups only. It wasn't long before an official caught me and sent me back to the Museum of 25 May, where one buys a ticket and wanders through a large photographic exhibition covering the history of the country since 1945. A side hall contains a collection of models of ships, railway carriages and field guns made by workers' co-operatives and presented to the Marshal. One entire wall contains a collection of ceremonial batons.

Then you wait in a vestibule until a group of ten people has collected, whereupon you set off under the guidance of a taciturn, uniformed attendant, who will occasionally tell a member of the group to hurry up or, if he is going disrespectfully fast, to slow down.

After the museum, the first stop is the Presentation Collection. In the entrance hall, a severe full-size bronze of the Marshal in a windswept greatcoat confronts you. His image is still to be seen everywhere in Yugoslavia, in the most homely and informal surroundings as well as the most august. 'A loved and respected leader, whose place is still to be filled,' one Serb told me. Another said that Tito had made Yugoslavians so dependent on him that they were still looking for a new father-figure. 'In the meantime, we cling to the image of the one we remember.'

The collection is vast – far too big, far bigger even than that of presentations to President Ceauşescu, but of greater interest and quality. Naturally, there is a room dedicated to Tito's uniforms and another to the academic honours which were conferred upon him. Among the diplomas is one from London, dated 1955, from the Institute of Naval Architects, conferring Honorary Membership upon the Marshal. Room upon room opens out, displaying coin collections, art collections and presents from every corner of the world, from a silver decanter and beakers from Finland to

woodcarvings from Nepal. One room touchingly displays Tito's personal belongings. From them you quickly gain the impression of a man who liked his pleasure
and his comfort – a potentate, not a socialist leader. Gold cigarette-cases and
pipe-style holders, amber fobs, gold wristwatches, gold travelling alarm-clocks. His
famous spectacles. In other cases lie similar, more modest artefacts from earlier in his
career. Every watch and clock (except for one we saw later in the Residence) was
stopped at five mintes past three on the fourth of the month, Tito having died at that
time on 4 May 1980.

Among our group (two Israelis, two West Germans, three soldiers, and an elderly
couple) were an old Macedonian peasant and his son, whom he was visiting in
Belgrade. His traditional costume was battered and worn, and his son was slightly
embarrassed by him as he limped through the rooms on bandy legs, loudly
expressing his awe at every new expression of Tito's wealth. I began to perceive the
Marshal as a Hemingway figure – either a character the novelist might have
invented or the kind of man he would have liked to be. His hunting lodge is packed
with mounted horns from a hundred slaughtered deer, and the stuffed heads of boar,
wolf, and moose stare down from sad glass eyes. Bearskins are draped across walls,
and a rhino horn projects from a wooden shield. In cases in the centre of the room are
the Marshal's guns – twenty sporting rifles and shotguns – two of them by Holland
and Holland.

A small annexe to the Billiard Room (another separate building) displays his
cameras. He was a keen photographer: two Nikons, one or two examples of his work,
and even a Kodak carton on which he had scribbled a note. The Billiard Room also
contains his workshop; he had trained as a machine tool operator and maintained his
skill as a hobby well into political life. Large grey lathes stand ready by tables laden
with machined engine parts. Beyond a wooden screen the main room gives the
impression of a public lounge in a good seaside pension. There is a bar, Turkish
carpets on the floor, overstuffed armchairs drawn up around circular coffee tables
with glass tops, and a small billiard table with no pockets, orange and red balls, and
three little wooden skittles arranged along the centre of the baize.

Our walk continued through the fastidiously landscaped park, across whose
manicured lawns black squirrels skip and dart, to the Residence itself, an impressive
but impersonal building erected in the early Thirties. Large, light and airy, with a
great, open, galleried hall. Its furniture suggested an uneasy mixture of Versailles
and a country house hotel. The 'workroom' with its boardroom table and massive
desk still holds the man's presence; of the entire complex, this room most vividly
reflects the taste and personality of Marshal Tito.

Back in the city, I had a BIP beer at a terrace café. Heads turned as three
black-leathered punks ambled self-consciously by, but otherwise nothing disturbed
the evening homeward rush of office workers. Impending economies and the threat
of civil war in Kosovo seemed far away. The shops were full and the town bathed in
electric light.

26

FEZZES FOR THE TOURISTS

The train to Sarajevo left early, and as I sat in my compartment waiting for it to start I watched a family of Gypsies on the platform – a mother, grandmother and three small children – get up and with lazy dignity fold their clothes and collect belongings which were hanging from the concrete railings. One of the children was a tiny baby, entirely swathed in woollen rags. The family seemed to be treated with friendly tolerance by the railway officials, but their life must have been dismal.

Pale sunshine brought intense light but as yet no heat. It was a fast train, painted red and silver, and all the carriages were plush first class. We were even provided with a complimentary lunch in a small plastic carrier bag.

West of Belgrade the countryside stretched away as a level, maize-bearing plain; but once we had turned south and crossed the Drina, the plain gave way to hills hispid with trees, and these in turn grew to be mountains as we ascended, passing through Croatia into Bosnia. Small private farms dotted the landscape, and orchards – among the first I had seen anywhere in any quantity – began to appear.

Sarajevo is a Turkish name and the town owed the best of its building to the governor Gazi Husref Bey. His appointment lasted from 1521 to 1541, but the inspiration he provided carried momentum long after his departure. By the middle of the seventeenth century there was a large number of public buildings and baths, and seventy-three mosques. Little remains, for at the end of that century the city was taken by Eugene of Savoy, whose troops vandalized it to such an extent that it did not re-emerge as a town of importance for almost 200 years. But a number of mosques remain, and there is a rather self-consciously 'eastern' old town, which is sanitized and touristic.

The old town lies along the River Miljacka, in October barely a stream feeling its way along the middle of a rocky bed. On its north side, by the bridge which bears his name, a plaque marks the spot where Gavrilo Princip shot and fatally wounded the Archduke Franz-Ferdinand, thereby providing Austria, encouraged by Germany, with the excuse it needed for attacking Serbia and precipitating the First World War. It is hard to imagine so momentous an event happening in such a small town, among such narrow streets.

The nineteenth-century part of the old town is dignified and residential, containing a number of cumbersome Austrian buildings, some of which attempt to meet the Orient halfway but which nevertheless sit oddly only yards from the central mosques, which are close to the river on both banks. Chief among them is the Begova

Džamila, built by Gazi Husref in 1530. The call to prayer is still performed by a muezzin, and the number of the faithful who answer it reminds one vividly of how long the Turks were here, and how recently they departed. The population of Bosnia-Hercegovina is still 40 per cent Muslim. Thinking of Bulgaria, I considered how differently people react to colonizing powers.

Continuing west from Vojvode Putnika you eventually come to the station and the new town, where the real centre of the Bosnian capital now lies. There is heavy industry here, and as Sarajevo lies in a basin surrounded by mountains there is nowhere for the smoke to escape. It hangs over the city like a pall. Sarajevo is Yugoslavia's most polluted town, and alarms are fitted in the streets to warn children and elderly people with pulmonary complaints to keep off the streets at times of especially high density. Approaching the city by train from Belgrade you are confronted not by dreaming minarets but by a daunting grey forest of sky-scrapers.

I ran into Jovanka at the station, trying to find my way to the hotel. She was going in the same direction and said she would show me. She had an hour or two to kill before catching her bus to Igman, where she was attending a symposium. Igman is the site of the 1984 Winter Olympics, which are still remembered assiduously by the local tourist board; out of season the hotels there play host to conferences.

Jovanka was a psychologist, specializing in the problems of physically and mentally underdeveloped children. We wandered through the streets and ended up at a coffee shop in Vase Miskina. By then I had learned that she lived in Loznica and was married to a transport manager. They had two children. She was nervous about the symposium, where she was to deliver a paper. It emerged that she is in the forefront of a movement among clinical psychologists to unite the research and experience of the several republics under a federal umbrella: 'We are all going off in our own directions at the moment and wasting a lot of energy, instead of helping each other by pooling what we've learned.'

She was equipped with a video demonstrating her work methods, and carried a Walkman with her speech notes on a cassette. We spoke in English, and whenever the conversation faltered we had recourse to a little English–Serbo-Croat dictionary which I had providentially bought in Belgrade a couple of days earlier.

'You are the first person I've ever had a really long conversation with in English,' she told me. She had a candid face and an infectious smile. She'd been born in Zagreb.

'We have a very good flat; it's a little small with the children, so we are looking for something bigger, but there is the question of getting a bank loan to pay for it. Do you have a flat?'

'A house.'

'Is it very big?'

'Not specially.'

'Do you have children?'

'No.'

'Perhaps you are wise.'

She explained that when she had started work her job carried a lot of status. 'But that was seventeen years ago. Now I'm nearly forty, and I have to face the fact that the government no longer regards this kind of work as highly as it once did. I'm not going to give it up. I was offered a job by the hospital in Loznica but I turned it down because it meant giving up working with children. I couldn't do that. But it's frustrating, because our department is silted up with underqualified social workers and they give our work a bad name. It's a vicious circle: our status declines, and our resources are cut, and so our status declines even more.'

Travel was her unfulfilled ambition. 'You live in London? That is the one place I am determined to visit before I die.' She told me that her thirteen-year-old son was learning English and German, and that she herself had recently started to learn German too. 'I am determined that my children should have as western-oriented an education as possible. The future for us must lie to the west, not to the east, if we ever get out of our present mess.'

I had noticed a large number of sizeable villas along the railway in the country-side. In some cases the ground floor was completed and inhabited, while the upper storeys were still to be finished. Jovanka explained that as private enterprise was increasingly encouraged, people were getting grants to build their own homes. 'They build them big because the extra rooms are for paying guests – some people think that tourism is the only hope for us. And if the money runs out before they're finished they put the work into abeyance for a while and expand their houses as and when they can. But the people who are best-off are the little farmers. They have a steady market for their produce and can keep prices in line with inflation. That's something. For those of us who are buyers, not suppliers, it's a problem, because things go up by several hundred dinars overnight at the moment. But it's not that easy for self-employed people either. Taxation is punitive.'

She added that nevertheless people maintained a good standard of living.

'Those that can afford to, obviously. You wouldn't think this was a socialist country any more. Some people really are having to tighten their belts, even cut down on expensive food like meat. But those who are earning well, especially in Slovenia, are spending to match, because with inflation so high there's not much point in saving. The Slovenians are spending it as fast as they can make it, and what they can't spend on themselves they spend on their kids. Lambrettas with lots of lights are the latest toy ... Actually it's faintly disgusting, but they say they're the nation's breadwinners, and they're fed up with the Serbs trying to lord it over every-body else.'

Talk turned to Kosovo. The Yugoslavian papers carried nothing but reports of the problem there. Jovanka, as a Croatian, was sceptical. 'Most of us are worried that the Federal Government will play into Serbia's hands and use Kosovo as an excuse for tightening up internal security generally. The fact that we're in the middle of a financial crisis makes a conservative reaction all the more likely.' She glanced around the room. It was late afternoon, and only a handful of kids in jeans sat around over Cokes. From time to time a shopkeeper might wander in, wearing a fez for the sake of the tourists but clearly owing nothing to Turkey in his own ancestry. Outside the sun bathed wooden shops and cobbled streets in deep yellow light.

Jovanka switched the conversation back to domestic matters. Did we have a dishwasher? She hadn't yet, but most of her friends had and she was thinking about getting one, especially as it was becoming increasingly difficult to get hold of a 'daily'. Did we have the same problem in England? Did I help with housework myself? 'I think we have a long way to go in Yugoslavia when it comes to equality of the sexes, on any level.'

I wasn't equipped to comment on this, though the long-established existence of female engineers, train and bus drivers and manual and road workers in eastern Europe hasn't automatically set them on an equal footing with men. Jovanka was looking at her watch with increasing nervousness.

'When are you giving your paper?'

'The day after tomorrow. But I must catch the next bus out to Igman or I'll miss the official meeting and greeting. That would never do. Anyway, I've got to go over my notes and tomorrow I'll be sitting listening to other people's speeches all day, so there won't be an opportunity.'

I walked her to the bus-stop and waited with her. She looked in her bag and produced two large green apples. 'It is traditional here to welcome strangers with the gift of an apple. Luckily I have two. Have them both. It shows how glad I am to have met you.'

A minute later the bus arrived. She kissed me and was gone.

Continuing south, the mountains as one enters Hercegovina pile up on each other like monolithic sand-grey citadels, to whose flanks tiny white villages cling. Descending on the other side, the railway is joined by the River Neretva, whose course to the Adriatic at Kardeljevo is interrupted by a series of hydro-electric plants, as a result of which lakes have been formed. At first the dark turquoise river plunges deep in a cleft below but then, tamed by the barrages, becomes broader and slower, even boasting a beach here and there. The countryside becomes gentler and takes on a more Mediterranean aspect, and the weather has a profounder quality of heat.

On the train to Mostar I met Marija, a dignified lady of seventy, a retired chest-specialist from Tuzla.

'My daughter lives in London, in Bayswater. She's a doctor too – a neuropathologist – and her husband's a lawyer.'

I made suitably impressed noises. Marija smiled. She had the careful, gentle movements of someone who was very ill. 'I have a heart condition, which meant that I had to retire early, and I cannot travel often. But I have spent all this summer in London. Your weather has become appalling again, hasn't it?'

After our cautious opening gambits the conversation relaxed. Marija was also from Croatia, born in Karlovac of a Yugoslavian father and a French mother. 'She could never get used to living here, and our house was a little shrine to France. At home she would only speak French. I think something of that has rubbed off on me. I don't consider myself Yugoslavian, which means that I look dispassionately at what is happening here. If you want my candid opinion, things are going downhill fast. Only one thing can save us, and that is tourism, but the government must spend more on developing it.'

'Do you think the federation might split up?'

'Most Yugoslavs will tell you that that is the last thing which is likely to happen, whatever our problems. I am not so sure. But we will have to compromise socialist principles if we are to survive economically. That is the very simple truth. Macedonia and Montenegro are bankrupt. They've never been developed industrially and their soil is poor. Of course they are helped by levies on the other republics, but I don't know how long Slovenia, for example, will be prepared to go on bailing out her fellow-states. There's the question of personalities, too. We're an attenuated country. At one end the frontier's with Austria, at the other with Greece. Now, consider the difference between the Austrians and the Greeks. And you don't even have to go as far as Macedonia. The Slovenians are serious, hard-working people. The Bosnians are open-hearted and lazy. On the other hand, there's no way Slovenia would want to associate herself with Austria after the centuries she had under Austro-Hungary, fighting to preserve her language and her culture.'

Her son has stayed in Yugoslavia and works as an engineer for Yugo cars. Cars and footwear are two of the country's principal exports, but it is difficult for them to compete in quality or even price with what is already available on western markets. I talked about this over beers at a café table under a roof of thick vine in Mostar with a Yugoslav called Stane, who had lived in California for thirty years (so he said) and had now returned to settle near Dubrovnik. At present he was in the middle of negotiations to buy some land on which he hoped to establish a nutria farm.

'When the deal's completed, I'll come back for good and end my days here,' he said sentimentally through mouthfuls of the cold chicken we were sharing. He was more nationalistic than his fellow-countrymen, and much more confident about Yugoslavia's future than Marija had been. However, I was not at all sure about Stane. He was a jolly, bulky man in the most extraordinary suit I had ever seen, though it may have grown that way through the influence of its wearer. Everything about him defied grooming. His shirt would not remain tucked into his trousers, his hair stuck out obstinately in all directions; his glasses would not sit straight on his nose, nor his socks stay up. He talked with conviction, but not always convincingly, in English which simply didn't reflect thirty years spent in a country where it was the native tongue. There was no reason for me not to trust him; it was just that there was something curiously insubstantial about him. When I asked what he did in America, he told me that he was 'an economist'; when I asked where he lived, he said 'on the West Coast', but wouldn't be specific. It was less his answers than his manner which gave me pause.

Nevertheless he was good company – eccentric, hearty, and a great talker. He took me through the history of the country from its formation in 1918 to Tito's declaration of independence from Russia in 1948, and went over Princip's assassination of Franz-Ferdinand in great and sometimes bizarre detail. 'After he had fired the shot, he leapt into the Miljacka. He had a suicide pill, but there was no water in the river for him to swallow it with, so they arrested him. As he was under 18, he couldn't be executed. They imprisoned him in Terezín. He died of TB.'

He was more optimistic about industry than Marija was, but deplored the way the country's finances were run. 'Do you know that in 1950 Yugoslavia and Japan were *on a par* economically? Communism and commerce just don't mix. People don't *care* if they don't *own*. We export to COMECON countries and to the EC, though we belong to neither; and we should be proud of our independence; but we do some remarkably stupid things. We import wheat, which is ridiculous as we produce more than enough, and there's an enormously high percentage of private ownership in our agriculture. Private smallholdings produce 75 per cent of all our agricultural output.'

'How big are the smallholdings?'

'You're allowed up to ten hectares; twenty if you live in the mountains. But most smallholdings are about half that size, or less.'

'There must be a lot of them.'

'About two and a half million, I think.' He brushed this topic aside impatiently. 'But we need to get in there with foreign trade. At the moment it's a shambles. There's no state-run foreign trade system and anyone who is equipped and authorized can import and export off his own bat. But we need more foreign investment in general. Not that that's likely at the moment. No one in his right mind would invest in us, given our inflation and a goddam' civil war brewing in Kosovo. It's all *Politika* [a Serbian newspaper] talks about. Kosovo, Kosovo, Kosovo. I'm sick to death of it!'

I suggested ordering some more beer but he stopped me and had a bottle of the local white wine brought. This is Žilavka Mostar, a magnificent, crisp drink made from a grape, Žilavka, cultivated only in Hercegovina since Roman times. Stane clinked glasses with me and then drank, pausing afterwards to contemplate the yellow-green liquid.

'How do you like it?'

'It's good.'

'It's first mentioned in a charter of King Tvrtko of Bosnia in 1353. But it was the Viennese Court that really developed it. They had the vineyards around here planted in 1886.'

As we drank the wine, he discussed Kosovo, much along lines I had already heard. 'I haven't got too much sympathy for the Serbs in Belgrade,' he concluded; 'but I'm damned sorry for the Serbs in Kosovo. The Albanians are Muslims, so there's no abortion, no contraception, and on top of that there's a tradition of large families – most of them have nine or ten kids. Now Serbs who've lived there all their lives and for generations before them are having to sell cheap in order to sell at all, and get out. Their children are harassed at school, they get beaten up on the streets. The Albanians have smelt blood. But they're capitalizing on it in Serbia – they'll let things get so bad that the army'll have to go in, and then Kosovo will be annexed. Don't think Serbia hasn't got its eye on taking Voivodina's autonomy away either. It's the richest region of the entire country, and culturally the most advanced, and Belgrade's on its southern border.'

'On what grounds?'

'National security? They'll find something. Milosevic's a rabble-rouser.'

Shortly afterwards Stane took his leave of me, announcing that he had an appointment concerning his nutria project. I hope he managed to conclude the deal. I like to imagine him down near that hot, rocky coast, surrounded by his coypus.

Mostar, though even this late in the year fairly dense with tourists, was one of the prettiest towns I had yet seen. It was at its best at dusk, by which time the gaudy souvenir shops of Kujundžiluk were closed and the tourists had all been tidied away into the hotels. Then one could imagine the town as it must have been in its Turkish heyday, and people it with characters from Ivo Andrić's stories. The name of the town means 'old bridge'; the single-span, hump-backed bridge, its narrow white footway worn dangerously slippery, and marble smooth with over four hundred years of passing feet, is still the centrepiece of the town. Although the streets either side of it have lost most of their original character and are given over to souvenir shops and pop-belching, neon-lit cafés, nothing can detract from the architectural dignity of the bridge and the Tab'ana and Tara towers which flank it, nor do the shops spoil the low wood-and-stone buildings with heavy stone slab roofs which house them.

Below the bridge, the Neretva idles through the town. In summer, local youths prove themselves by jumping from the highest point on the hump into the water. Cliffs rise to three thousand feet on either side, but Mostar seems free of the pollution which besets Sarajevo. A walk north and west takes you to the pleasant, uncrowded modern town, passing through time as you do so, for the transition from medieval Turkish to modern Yugoslav is made via a touch of fin-de-siècle Habsburg.

The Turks were here until 1878, and the skyline is still speared by the minarets of many mosques. Chief among them are the simple and dignified Karadjozbegova and the Koski Mehmet Pašina. The Muslim attendants were amused and pleased when I made to take off my shoes before entering: shod tourists are allowed into a small area fenced off from the main mosque and covered in straw matting. The foliate murals in the Karadjozbegova are exquisite. Though both mosques were neglected, the Turkish cultural element is made much of here. At the Turkish town houses open to tourists, young guides in fezzes, looking hopelessly European, conducted gangs of babbling and gasping elderly Americans through the low, carpet-clad rooms.

I wandered out towards the New Town, passing the Medresa which still stands, flanking one side of the fruit and vegetable market (for the first time since London I saw oranges and bananas for sale), and continuing via the Art Nouveau Hotel Neretva, whose interior, as far as I could see, has been a victim of Sixties renovation. I recrossed the river and walked on along the Šetalište Lenina to the new Catholic cathedral, built in 1980, a clean white building, Scandinavian in style and inspiration.

I returned via the east bank of the Neretva, climbing steeply through the residential quarter to see the two Orthodox churches, old and new; they were both built in the nineteenth century, within fifty years of each other. Sultan Abdul-Aziz contributed funds towards the building of the new church. Both are impressive buildings from the outside, particularly the neo-Baroque new church; but both were closed, so I returned through the baking afternoon town to the centre.

The streets had gradually emptied, and I walked slowly across the polished cobbles of Brassworkers' Street back over the bridge and along Oneščukova. The tourists had gone, but the evening *korzo* was beginning; the walkers were all young, in their late teens and early twenties, and dressed up to the nines. The girls were beautiful, though so much more westernized than the girls in Bulgaria, or indeed anywhere else that I had been, that somehow a veil seemed to be thrown over their true selves.

I went back to my room. Its balcony was shaded by an enormous fig tree, and beyond it rose a high bald hill. Now in the evening it stood like a hunched ghost tinged with silver in the beginning of the moonlight, silent and lonely, above the garrulous self-absorption of the town. To my left I could hear the bustling dappled rush of the little green river as it was forced through a gully. Two cautious, friendly cats leapt onto the wall of the balcony from nowhere and observed me solemnly. They were white and ginger, and had the lean bodies, small heads and large ears of their Egyptian cousins.

Downstairs, in the spacious wooden open-plan restaurants and bars, the hotel was thronged with more of the young of Mostar. This was obviously the place to come at night. Chairs in the vast lobby, arranged in the style of an airport waiting-hall, were filled with boys and girls in suits, wing collars and bow-ties, skin-tight jeans and high-heeled slingbacks, black sweaters sewn with gold sequins, all drinking Coke. They had come to listen to a local group.

I walked back towards the bridge. The *korzo* route only led up to it; beyond was silence. Now the Old Town was deserted, and something of what it must have once been like could be felt, though one needed the babble and smells of any Turkish or Indian town from Samsun to Madurai to invigorate it. I found a café, drank some wine, and watched a scorpion engage in an epic battle with a monstrous horned beetle among the crevices of the wall near my terrace table. The outcome was lost to me in darkness.

THE LITTLE REPUBLIC

Taxi-drivers in Yugoslavia are terrible sharks. I had already paid prohibitive prices in Mostar, and the sum demanded in Dubrovnik was laughable. I gave up taxis after that. I had arrived there after travelling by train from Mostar and then by bus along the rocky, beachless coast. I hadn't been to this part of the Adriatic coast for twenty-five years, and I was curious to see how much had changed. I was both disappointed and relieved: disappointed because the great influx of tourists to Dubrovnik, mainly in packaged planeloads which fly into and out of the resort, has bred in the locals the cold insouciance which one finds in all such overexploited places. On the other hand, I was relieved that hotel development had not dominated and crushed the town.

In the early Sixties the little fortified town on the rock projecting into the sea was pleasantly tumbledown, weeds grew between the paving stones, ancient towers mouldered into the sea. The physical appearance of the place, which has been much restored since the glancing blows it received from the 1979 earthquake in Monte-negro, is too squeaky-clean for my taste, but it has neither lost nor compromised its atmosphere, which remains solidly Venetian.

It is built of white marble, and the classical severity of its original plan is softened by its superb Gothic and Renaissance buildings, their appearance confused where additions have been made following the ruin brought about by fire or earthquake. The cathedral, St Blaise's Church, the Rector's Palace and the Sponza Palace spring to mind, as does the clock tower, into whose base an 'antique-style' digital clock has been bizarrely inserted. But the city underwent its most dramatic change with the introduction of Baroque façades to replace those destroyed along the Placa in the terrible earthquake of 1667.

The town was originally settled by refugees from Epidaurus, now Cavtat, a few miles down the coast, who moved here in the seventh century after their town was taken by encroaching Slav and Avar tribesmen. The island rock they found, with its natural harbour, gave them a defensible position with easy access to the sea. The new settlement ultimately took the name Ragusa (a corruption of the original Greek name based on *laos* – a rock), while on the mainland close by a Slav settlement grew up, taking its name of Dubrovnik from the oak forests in the immediate hinterland on the slopes of Mount Srdj.

By the twelfth century the strait separating the two communities was filled up and they were united. Intermarriage soon took care of remaining racial differences, though the integrated inhabitants stood aloof from the surrounding population. Because its position was unfavourable in terms of defence, it enclosed itself in deep curtain walls. Realizing that it could only maintain its independence through diplomacy and changing sides where necessary, the emerging little city-state paid lip-service to whatever neighbouring nation happened to be in control at the time, while carefully maintaining its mighty defences, especially its corner-forts of Sveti Ivan, Revelin, Minčeta and Lovrijenac.

After the Fourth Crusade, Dubrovnik transferred its allegiance from collapsed Byzantium to ascendant Venice. When the Hungaro-Venetian war ended in defeat for Venice in 1358, Dubrovnik found itself under the lighter yoke of Croato-Hungary, which contented itself with an annual tribute. Dubrovnik, entirely mercantile, was far from poor and welcomed this opportunity to consolidate real independence, which it achieved to such an extent that when Venetian rule in Dalmatia was reasserted in the early fifteenth century it hung on as an independent republic. The town even staved off the Turks, propitiating the Porte with tribute, banking (literally) on her importance as a trading centre. Venetian competition was effectively stifled in this part of the Adriatic during the latter half of the fifteenth and the sixteenth centuries because of rivalry with Constantinople, and as a broker between east and west Dubrovnik thrived.

Wealth encouraged liberalism and an enlightened government. Dubrovnik had an old people's home by 1347, and abolished slavery by 1416. Torture was made illegal the same century. Education and the arts were encouraged by generous subsidy. The Golden Age lasted as long as the Turks held sway over half of Europe. The Ragusan Peter Bošković translated Molière and Corneille in Paris; in London, his brother Roger, a distinguished astronomer and mathematician, was elected to the Royal Society.

But at about the same time the emphasis of trade was shifting westwards, and the Mediterranean now began its decline as the centre of the world. At dawn on 6 April 1667, the people of Ragusa awoke to the tremors of an earthquake which shook the ancient city for hours, destroying most of the older buildings. The citizens rebuilt their town, and in the eighteenth century the republic experienced a resurgence of trade; but it was the last flickering of a candle. After the defeat of Austria at the hands of Napoleon, the entire Dalmatian coast was ceded to France. Dubrovnik tried to stave off the inevitable by asserting its independence, but it could do nothing against the Corsican dictator. The city-state was occupied, and on 31 January 1808 its freedom was brought to an end forever.

It's pleasant to walk from the Old Town along Maršala Tita to the new harbour, Luka Gruž, which is almost as full of flashy yachts as the Hamble in Hampshire. Most have Yugoslav names and flags, so it is clear that not everyone is suffering because of the recession.

Maršala Tita itself skirts the metallic, torpid sea high above, before turning to cross the neck of the Lapad peninsula. It is a pleasant street, lined with lovely, crumbling, pale yellow stucco villas. One breathes more easily away from the Old Town, encased in its walls, and it is a relief to get away from the press of people. The town has spread along the lower slopes of the great wedge of rock which hems it in to the sea, not always attractively, but more or less bearably.

At Gruž there is a vegetable market round the corner from the bus station. I found a café nearby and sat down to read my map. I didn't want to take another taxi, and I wanted to avoid the ugly streets to the north of the town. In contrast to other places I had been, the sight of a camera and a map deters rather than attracts locals, but over my coffee I talked to a couple of students catching a late week's break before returning to Novi Sad.

'We've got to get Tito out of our system,' Beroslav told me. Tito, he said, had become a paradoxical figure in the Yugoslav consciousness. 'He's like a kind of god who won't go away. Sooner or later we've got to grow up and learn to do without him, but ...'

'He stayed too long and he buggered things up,' said Milanko, a physics student, stocky, fair and intense. 'He was out of touch long before the end. He must have been, or he wouldn't have run up such debts. Okay, he stood up to Russia, but he still went along with heavy industry policies of the same sort that Russia imposed on the Eastern Bloc countries. Madness, really. We could have built up service industries and stolen a march on our neighbours. But now we're so far into the shit we're going to use up all our energy digging ourselves out.'

'The problem was that he saw himself as a king, so that he came to surround himself only with people who'd agree with him. There was no debate any more, no criticism,' said Bero. 'And yet we still need him, because it's only the common memory of Dad that keeps the family together.'

My own impression as I travelled through Yugoslavia was that people were less apt to smile and dance than when I was last there. I told them so.

'That's for sure. Those were really happy-go-lucky days, and the dollars were pouring in,' grinned Milanko. 'At least Tito wasn't a Serbian. Now they seem to think they're the only ones who can save the country.

'We had a big demo in Novi Sad a few months ago. Big Serbian protest on behalf of Milosevic. Condemned by our leadership in Voivodina. Good for them; we don't really want to become part of Greater Serbia. But then what happens? A week ago, another big demo, but not a couple of thousand people this time – oh no, tens of thousands.'

'A hundred thousand,' put in Bero.

'What was the protest about?'

'They think the Voivodina leadership is corrupt, which is probably true to a certain extent, but no more than elsewhere; and they say that they are blocking reforms, which is always a good catch-all, and that they are siding with the Albanians in Kosovo, which is daft. But the result of all that was that the Praesidium resigned to a man.'

'Thus paving the way for Serbia to annexe Voivodina.'

'That's partly why we came down here.'

'A quick relax in Disneyland before going back to the real world.'

I looked across the café to where a waiter, who'd clearly been told once that he bore a passing resemblance to Sylvester Stallone, was chatting up a handful of girls: two leathery Americans and two pink Englishwomen.

The driver of the bus which took me back to the Old Town had a profile which would not have looked out of place on a Greek frieze, and Grecian looks were not unusual among the people of the town. There is a brief period of twilight when no one is on the streets. Even the scruffy pigeons which infest the squares have retired, though a skinny cat darting from shadow to shadow managed to unsettle a handful of last-minute strutters.

Then, as darkness falls, which it does with southern abruptness, thousands of young Ragusans take to the Placa for the *korzo*. They are got up with conscious trendiness, but none of the cocktail over-dressiness which I'd seen elsewhere, especially in Dresden and Mostar. They were far smarter than English or American youth, more like Italians or French. Muted pop music wafted from bars – everything from Abba to Dire Straits. Some people wore T-shirts with *Nema Problema* written across them.

I walked up and down myself for a while, and then found a small restaurant where I sat with a book and a bottle of local white wine called Dingač. I watched a pair of elderly English ladies in Canary Island sunhats being mothered by a large-bellied waiter of their own age. 'We were wondering if we might have a nice pot of tea ...' wandered across the balmy air.

I dined on orado (gilthead bream), and then took myself to a concert at the Rector's Palace.

When it was an independent republic, Dubrovnik's administration was the collective concern of its nobility. The state was formally headed by a Rector, who was elected for a period of one month, during which time he was not allowed to leave the palace except on state business, the idea being that he would consecrate all his time to the Republic. However, he had no actual power. That lay with the Great Council, upon which every noble took his place when he reached the age of twenty. The Rector was elected from their number.

The palace is the best building on the rock. It was originally built as a fort in the twelfth century, but this was destroyed by the accidental explosion of a gunpowder dump in 1435. Reconstruction was placed in the hands of one of Dubrovnik's principal architects, Onofrio della Cava, and the Renaissance façade was later added by Salvi di Michieli. Damaged again in 1667, it was restored by Jeronim Scarpa of Korčula, who completed the work in 1739.

The concert was held in the atrium of the palace, delicate columns supporting the roof around the upper gallery, a sweeping staircase framed by an asymmetrical arch. The music itself – Albinoni, Bach, and Mozart – beckoned me back ironically to my own world, the Europe I had left a long time ago, which now seemed unfamiliar and even unwelcome.

In the early morning the Old Town is at its most beautiful, as the sunshine flirts with the tops of the pearl-grey bastions and slips along the marble-smooth streets to glance off Baroque churches and plain medieval façades. At the Pile gate I chatted briefly with an Indian street artist who spent his winters at home in New York and his summers working the Yugoslav and Greek coasts. 'You can't imagine the number of broads I used to pull,' he told me. 'But what with AIDS and all nowadays I'm just as happy to go to bed with a copy of Vasari.' He produced a battered copy of *Lives of the Artists* from a back pocket. 'I'm never without it,' he said.

The present walls are late; on the landward side they date from the fifteenth century, and on the seaward from the seventeenth. Together they form a girdle almost two kilometres long. From the sentryways along their tops, the red roofs of the town spread out below as a scattering of terra-cotta tiles, above which rise the towers and domes of the churches and the huge Baroque façade of the Jesuit Church. The streets behind the great church, on the seaward side of the town, are still as they were – quiet, lived in, hung with washing. Tourists do not penetrate this far, and I felt like an intruder.

Across the walled town at Luža Square is the eighteenth-century Church of St Blaise, a Baroque jewel containing a silver-gilt statuette of the city's patron saint. As in all representations of him, he holds a model of the city in his left hand, and it is recognizably the town of today. The statuette is kept behind glass above the high altar, and is the only surviving relic of an earlier medieval church which was destroyed by fire. All the fortress-cities of this coast have their own protector saint, whose image is frequently embossed on the outer walls. Across from this church stands the Sponza Palace, built early in the sixteenth century in Gothic-Renaissance style by Paskoje Miličević. The airy inner courtyard is surrounded on the first floor by a columned and arcaded gallery. It was sad to see it hosting an exhibition by an appalling folk-artist given to painting jolly fat men with twirling moustaches getting into various risqué scrapes.

At the southern end of the long square is the dull Baroque cathedral. Upon payment of a fee you can visit a side chapel near the high altar which has been converted into a small, untidy treasury, which is made up in the main of a vast collection of relics, chiefly saints' forearms sheathed in reliquaries of varying quality ranked in a jumble on shelves. In a crowded case near the front there is, however, a real treasure: the reliquary of the skull of Saint Blaise. Made in the form of a Byzantine crown, it dates from the twelfth century and properly displayed would reveal qualities to rival Saint Stephen's crown.

Beyond Dubrovnik and a short way from it by boat is the island of Lokrum, a dull place which in the sixteenth century served as a place of quarantine for the port, and which now functions as a park. There is a nudist beach at one end, which I stumbled upon by accident. It contained a number of extremely fat pink men perched on various rocks. One or two were playing chess.

As we sailed around, passing the afternoon idly exploring the pellucid waters of the broad bay, I chatted in a fractured mixture of German, Serbo-Croat and English to the crew – a pitch-black, gnarled Montenegrin of about thirty-five and his bumptious adolescent son. Lists of local fish grew out of our conversation, and we caught a few. I saw no octopus, except a few dead ones strung out on a pole in the Old Harbour, but we did see huge amberjack – fat, silver-grey and about a yard long – as well as orada, grouper and red mullet. They told me that occasionally there were loggerhead turtles, and that they frequently caught moray and conger eel.

Back at Dubrovnik, I found a place on Gundulićeva poljana which fed me gritty local oysters and a tangy, urine-yellow wine which I drank as the brief dusk stalked across the square, drawing the night behind it like a curtain.

The bus next day was so full that it was only by luck that I secured a seat near the back. Two German tourists who had told me while we were waiting for its arrival that they wanted to have an adventure by travelling with the locals for once instead of on an organized tour, now promptly had a row and gave up the project. Half a dozen young men with black bomber jackets and designer stubble clambered aboard at the last minute and clung to the luggage racks as the battered old coach lurched and shoved its way out of town. I looked back once. The city seemed even less real, viewed from the outside at a distance. One expected to hear the yell 'Cut!', and to see Charlton Heston doffing armour at the side of a costume caravan.

We climbed steeply away from the town and joined the Magistrala, the coast road which runs all the way down to Ada on the Albanian frontier, where it abruptly stops at the banks of the River Bojana. It was not long before we left Croatia and entered Montenegro – Crna Gora – the desolate mountain country which fought fiercely for its independence against the Turks for five hundred years. It was ruled by bishop-princes, notably those of the Petrović clan. Its reward was independence, achieved at last through the Congress of Berlin in 1878; but at the end of the First World War it was united with Serbia, and although it is now the smallest independent republic of Federal Yugoslavia it remains closely allied to its large northern neighbour.

The twentieth century has not been kind to Montenegro. It was undeveloped in the years between the wars, and relied on primitive smallholder farming. Economically things were so bad that per capita income was only a third of the Yugoslavian national average. What few minor cottage industries existed were destroyed during the National War of Liberation in 1941–5. Since the war, industry has been developed, and there are two hydro-electric power plants, but the disastrous earthquake in 1979 meant an enormous setback. A Montenegrin sitting next to me on the bus told me that the future of his state really lay in its coastline. 'The soil's too poor to farm, and we're too small to compete in industry. But we can make something out of tourism and trade by sea.' Reflecting this, a railway link has been built recently between Belgrade and Bar, a developing port near the Albanian border. Montenegro has traditionally provided Yugoslavia with her best sailors. Peter the Great of Russia sent sixty of his nobles to study shipbuilding at Perast, and Ivo Visin, the first 'Yugoslav' to circumnavigate the world, in the *Splendido* between 1552 and 1559, is celebrated in the maritime museum at Kotor.

The coast road is tortuous and carves its way between the sea and the grey rocky hills that monotonously flank the coast, following a route defined by intricate peninsulas which embrace enormous protected inlets with narrow mouths across which in earlier centuries chains were drawn to protect the shipping within from Turkish and Levantine pirates.

The major town of this stretch of coastline is Herzeg-Novi, which is uninspiring to drive through but which contains the remains of fortifications reflecting its chequered past: Venetian, Turkish and Austrian. Soon after, the road descends into Risan, where Teuta, the last queen of Illyria, took refuge from the Romans and drowned herself rather than fall into their victorious hands. She is also an Albanian heroine.

Risan stands at the beginning of the great bay of Kotor, which must be one of the biggest natural harbours in the world. The town of Kotor, set at its farthest point from the open sea, presides over a dull blue millpond. From the road, close to the shore, two islands can be seen, each surmounted by a church. The first is St George, the site of a ruined Benedictine monastery and a sailors' graveyard. It is now abandoned except in the summer when theology courses are held here. It looked familiar and later I discovered that it had served as the model for Böcklin's romantic painting *The Isle of the Dead* – perhaps when he saw it, in the late nineteenth century, it was more remote and mysterious than it seems today. The artificial island nearby carries the church of the Virgin of Škrpjelo on its back. A local legend tells how fishermen discovered an icon on a rocky crag and brought it to the mainland church; the next day the icon had miraculously returned to the crag. God's will seemed to be that a church be built here, and so an island was constructed. The church is picturesque in a conventional way. One can imagine endless reproductions of it hanging in dull hotel rooms.

Kotor, unfortunately set about with a clutter of hideous modern buildings, sits at the end of the bay with its back to the bleak grey bulk of Mount Lovčen, up whose slopes the medieval city walls still incomprehensibly scramble towards a church. The old port is tiny: a main square surrounded by Venetian-Baroque houses of great beauty sits at the edge of a web of narrow vine-clad streets through which posses of tourists are led by girls from Atlas Tours in blue-and-white striped dresses. Nothing, however, can detract from the Italian elegance of this little town, although it was severely damaged during the 1979 earthquake, and it is clear that the wounds will take a long time to heal. By a miracle the 700-year-old cathedral of St Tryphon, the city's protector, did not fall, but it has sustained severe structural damage, and its magnificent twin towers looked appallingly fragile. Inside there is a low relief silver panel by one John of Basle, an artist who fled here to escape charges of bigamy in his strait-laced native land.

On the main square, beneath the clock tower, a television film was being made. Actors looking like characters from a Marcel Pagnol novel sat in the sun while minions ran around at a florid director's bidding. Two men and two girls were dressed up as Gypsy musicians and made an interesting contrast with the real Gypsy family begging just the other side of the city gate.

From Kotor, I couldn't resist a detour to Lepetane simply because I had been told that the name derived from the Italian *le putane*; but I could never discover when it had been brothel town – presumably during the long Venetian possession of this coast. Now it is little more than a row of attractive Italianate houses. A ferry plies across the mouth of the bay between here and Igalo, cutting out the long road loop around the bay. When the shipping traffic was at its height the girls must have been worked hard. As there were none left now to detain me, I turned eastwards again and made my way to Budva. This fortified medieval town on the coast is a mini-Dubrovnik; it was all but destroyed in 1979, and has since been rebuilt. Though people are moving back in, there is still a raw newness about it. A large hotel threatens nearby, and one can only bow one's head to the inevitability of Budva's future as another resort.

At least Budva will escape the fate of Sveti Stefan. Beautiful from a distance, this little fortified village on a coastal islet halfway between Budva and Bar had fallen into total decay by 1945. At the time one could have bought the whole place for less than the cost of a modest London flat. The Montenegro Tourist Authority have recently developed the whole village as a luxury hotel. A causeway links the little island to the shore, and separates two slips of shingle beach – one public, one private – beyond which an unpleasant restaurant caters for day-trippers. The 'hotel' itself, perfectly restored, is a rich man's ghetto, without soul or character. Brochures boast of the number of popular film stars who stay here.

A bus took me via the hidden and delightful resort of Čanj to Bar, past fields, wedged in between the unforgiving mountains and the sea, which looked like slices of Surrey. Beyond Sveti Stefan, the mountains rise higher, and there is drama in their lines as they crash down sheer to the sea. We passed a number of small seaside towns with minute beaches crammed between the bullying hills before suddenly in the dusk Bar spread along the coast before us, still some distance away, its lights twinkling like those of a liner.

It was dark and raining steadily when I arrived, and I had to walk miles back to the centre of town and the Hotel Topolice, the one place to stay. The Topolice has been built in the manner of an expensive international hotel, with prices to match and glacial receptionists. At the moment it is an anomaly, because it has been built in anticipation of what Bar will become. It is not the only building of this type in the town, which is as far from the tourism of Dubrovnik as you could hope to get. But soon it will be the biggest port on the Yugoslav Adriatic coast.

When I was there it consisted of one main street and some goodish modern blocks of flats in the hinterland. Its backdrop is provided by the grey mountains which rise immediately behind it and at present give the eerie impression of sealing it off from the rest of the world. The moon-landscape provided by the mountains reinforces the impression that this might be some future city built on another planet, or another kind of film set: a city of the future conceived by a Fifties imagination, a city for Dan Dare or Robbie the Robot.

Even the enormous department store is built in the shape of three flying saucers, parked side by side. It sits in the centre of town, a huge white temple. White is the predominant colour. I visited the store in rainy darkness and found it full of goods and customers. Lost in space, Bar is a boom town. I wondered what all the people did until in the morning I saw the shining cylinders of oil tanks across the bay, where the harbour was already receiving a stately procession of mighty ships.

I was tempted to find out if I could persuade anyone to take me clandestinely by boat to Albania, which is only about thirty kilometres down the coast from here. My attempts to arrange such a foray met with a variety of reactions, astonishment and ridicule being high on the list, suspicion and concern following close behind. One fisherman said I was mad to consider it. 'They're the most trigger-happy bunch I've ever come across, and if they caught you you could kiss the world goodbye for twenty-five years,' he told me.

I decided to resign myself to the only way I could legitimately enter Albania, as a member of a group tour. But to have come so close to the frontier, and then to have to make a detour via London to get to Tiranë was galling.

28

OVER THE BLACK MOUNTAINS

Bar didn't look as attractive in daylight. As in many new towns, there is a lot of scrubland around, despoiled countryside that would be better off built on – unloved and dirty, with a few stubborn, doomed plants growing on it. I made the trek to the station accompanied in the last stage by a sad-eyed pi-dog, alive with fleas, which longed to be adopted but parted company with me philosophically when we reached the railway. The station is a modest, attractive country building with a busy café, and a surprisingly large number of people were waiting for the up train to Belgrade in the morning sunshine. It wasn't yet nine, but already it was cruelly hot.

My companions for the journey were all Serbians. They were teachers and physiotherapists accompanying a group of disabled people back to Valjevo after a fortnight's 'rehabilitation – but we've been swimming, painting, drinking most of the time'. Jak had injured his legs in a lift accident in 1972, and Slobodan had been paraplegic since the age of fifteen. Both men were in their mid-forties now, and worked as clerks. With them was their art teacher, a fat, jolly man whose name I never caught, and a bearded social worker called Dusan. Typically, once we had introduced ourselves and they discovered where I was from, I was given the window seat, and we shared bread, cigarettes and water, chocolate, *slivovice* and fruit.

The train quickly climbed into the grim mountains. Once among them the scenery is transformed. The views are of secret valleys, green splashes of mountain meadows on the harsh slopes, rivers plunging through vertiginous clefts, and bright, huddled villages so remote that one wonders how anyone can ever reach them. On a ten-hour journey through a landscape which would change frequently and radically, these first few miles were the most spectacular.

Bar was soon left behind, gleaming white next to the painted, glittering sea as we headed up to the Sutorman Pass. Beyond it, after the rural alpine world, we descended rapidly towards Titograd, a modern city baking on a flat plain. The first impression is of great bleakness. In an attempt to alleviate this, some of the concrete high-rises had been painted in pastel shades.

My travelling companions had inevitably broached the problem of Kosovo, close to whose borders we were now travelling. Their view of the problem was much more direct than what I had heard from members of other republics.

'The Albanians are fomenting revolution to destabilize the whole country,' one of them maintained. 'They've been put up to it by the Albanian government.' Everyone held the view that the Albanians were at fault, and said that they had collaborated with the Germans during the war. 'It was hellish throughout Yugoslavia during the Liberation War, but nowhere worse than here,' said the art teacher. 'I know, because I was a little boy growing up in Priština at the time.'

'Tito wouldn't have let them get away with this,' someone else said. 'But what is that expression you have in English? When the cat's away . . .'

'They have always been a thorn in our side. We ought to have driven them back across the mountains long ago. Now they are breeding like rabbits. There's a whole power-structure organized. If we don't move soon there'll be no Serbians left in Kosovo – they'll all have been driven out.'

'We ought to have sent the army in by now. I only hope it's not too late.'

The discussion had been overheard in the neighbouring compartments and others from the same group now joined us. Feelings were running high. The country was affected by a rash of demonstrations, which had increased in size as the year wore on, both in Belgrade and in towns within or near the affected province – in the busy, ugly, modern town of Kraljevo to the north, for example, and in the provincial capital, Priština.

Priština was in the hands of the Turkish Empire until 1912, and although much of the town is modern now – a kind of papering over the oriental cracks – the atmosphere is more eastern than western. The dominant building is the Emperor Mosque, built by Mehmet II in 1461, and the central market is entirely oriental. It isn't a much visited place, but at the time I was there it was full of western journalists. You don't have to have many conversations with the locals on either side to get a graphic impression of the anxiety of the Serbians and the determination of the Albanians. 'We stick together, and we have money,' one said to me simply. The clan and the extended family are of central significance.

Outwardly the streets are calm. But there is a palpable tension in the atmosphere and there is no doubt that both sides are hoarding weapons. 'It's the only insurance we've got until the government stops shilly-shallying and does something to help us,' the Serbians say. 'This is our homeland, not theirs.' Not far from Priština is the site of the largest battle fought in medieval Europe, between the Serbs and the Turks at Kosovo Polje in 1389. The town of Peć, not fifteen miles from the Albanian frontier, was the seat of the Patriarchs of the Serbian Church throughout the Middle Ages. But the problem is that Kosovo is both people's homeland, for the Albanians are no newcomers.

Titograd is built on the site of the town of Podgorica, originally a Roman settlement but totally destroyed in the fighting in 1944. Some relics of the old town have remained, especially the medieval fortress of the Nemanjić kings of Serbia and the ruins of the original Roman town of Dioclea. But it is an ugly place now, and the kind which bakes in summer and freezes in winter.

Beyond Titograd the ascent begins again, skirting the Sinjavina Range, the mountains proud and hard against the flat blue sky. Descending from them beyond Prijeploje, subtle changes begin to take place with the progression north. The weather becomes cooler, the farms larger and greener. Clouds break up the unvaried blue, and hints of the orient in architecture and in the faces of the people disappear. The hills become softer, rounder. They are covered with grass, and take on the appearance of Austrian farmland. This mellowing after the proud harshness of Montenegro continues, along a very gradual descent, until a suburban sprawl heralds Belgrade.

Work on the pedestrian precinct had progressed dramatically since I'd been away; the trees were planted and most of the lamp-posts were up, though less had been done about the paving stones and the crowds still had to pick their way over the obstacle course. Workmen ambled among them, sucking pungent Balkan cigarettes. I started my day in the bookshops of the Terazije. I found a three-day-old *Daily Telegraph*, but it cost the equivalent of £3. It was something of a shock to see west European newspapers, magazines and books freely available again. In decadent Dubrovnik even *Playboy* was displayed at kiosks (prohibitively priced), alongside home-produced pin-up magazines.

I walked up Kneza Mihaila, the part of the pedestrian precinct which had been completed. It is a street of smart cafés and shops and there is no hint at all of the predicted social and economic collapse. Only a few days earlier, however, there had been a major demonstration in front of the Parliament by several thousand workers demanding higher wages. One man alone could appease them: Slobodan Milosevic.

Mihaila leads directly to Kalemegdan Park, the area covered by the fortress which formed the original town. Built at the confluence of the Sava and the Danube, the surviving buildings are scattered and broken up by trees and grassy squares, so that it is difficult to get an impression of unity. What remains, in red brick, mostly dates from the period of Turkish dominion. Gornji Grad, the citadel, sits at the top of the hill, still commanding the rivers and the city; it is a haunt now of lovers and old men, who sit gazing at nothing in the autumn sun.

One of the best museums in Europe is here. It is simply called the Military Museum (*Vojni Muzej*), but it is more than just that. Tracing martial development from 1800 BC, social, demographic and political history is just as important here. The most moving and well-documented series of rooms covers the fight for liberation from the Germans between 1941 and 1945. The primitive weapons with which the partisans fought – pikes and guns made from pitchforks, bits of piping and driftwood – make it hard to understand how they could possibly have withstood the German army at all, until one becomes acquainted with the terrain over which they fought. Knowledge of the mountains was the ultimate weapon.

There is little left of the Turkish occupation. Not far from Kalemegdan is the only surviving mosque, the Bajrakli Džamija. The Mosque of the Flag is dusty, shuttered and sad, crowded by later, larger buildings in a prosperous *fin-de-siècle* suburb reminiscent of Paris. The sight depressed me as I made my way back to the city centre in the fading light. I had a final BIP beer at a chilly terrace café with red plastic chairs and blue plastic tablecloths. The place was crowded and I was joined at my table by a man of about thirty in a blue suit and bow-tie who presently asked me if I was English. He had noticed my guide-book. He turned out to be a West German businessman with diplomatic connections who was here to explore the possibility of exporting bottled water. I asked him how he found living in Belgrade.

'I can imagine better places. But you know the old Chinese curse, "May you live in interesting times." I think Communism is doomed here. We've got masses of Yugoslavian guest-workers in the Federal Republic, about a million of them, and they see a better standard of living under a system that works pretty well.'

'But they've managed all right here.'

'Not so well since Tito. And they want more *things*. People always do. Look at the Slovenes, they live right next door to Austria, and if the Austrians weren't the traditional oppressors and they had a free hand they'd secede overnight!'

We talked about Slovenia. Just as I was setting out on my journey, three journalists and a soldier had been arrested in Ljubljana and shortly afterwards given heavy sentences, the soldier for leaking, the journalists for publishing, secret military police plans to contain any revolutionary element in Slovenia. The documents also postulated the arrest of 500 known leading Slovenian dissidents. This Federal initiative, added to the fact that all court proceedings were conducted in Serbian and not in Slovenian, caused an uproar in the republic. The convicted men were granted the right of appeal, and any possible attempt by Serbia to destabilize Slovenia was thwarted. But however firmly Serbian expansion would be counteracted by Croatia and Slovenia, the writing is on the wall for Titoism. People want to decide for themselves. They have seen their economies, not just in Yugoslavia but throughout the Eastern Bloc, either falter or fail to get off the ground altogether. They are also tired of being locked away from the rest of the world. No system which depends on force for its survival can last forever. Repression can only work in the short term; though it may take centuries, the pressure from inside will invariably become irresistible.

I flew out of Belgrade on the first leg of my journey to Albania via London the following day.

29

LAND OF THE EAGLE

The name of the country derives from one of its tribes, the Albanoi, but the Albanians' own name for their homeland is Shqipëtarë, a word which is said to be derived from *shqipe*, an eagle, and therefore signifying a mountain race. Albania has had a bad press in the West. This is partly its own fault, because of the secretive and isolationist policy instituted and carried out by its only post-war leader until recently. Enver Hoxha formally took power in 1944 and did not relinquish it until his death in 1985. His successor and near contemporary, Ramiz Alia, continues to pursue Albania's stringent political line.

The first trickle of tourists arrived in 1962. Though strictly controlled, tourism is increasing, and it may be that within the next twenty years the last remaining miles of unspoilt northern Mediterranean coastline will have been swallowed up in the same development that has engulfed the rest. ('We have many tourists from France and Italy; but the most from West Germany,' one of our guides told me unsurprisingly.) Citizens of the USA are not allowed in under any circumstances, and nor, at least in theory, are journalists. Another banned profession is the priesthood – of any religion. Foreign soldiers and policemen are equally unwelcome.

Contact with outsiders will eventually erode the one-sidedness of thought in Albania, inculcated in the people through the media. This single-mindedness had its advantages when the country was struggling to rise to its feet after five hundred years of Turkish rule and the Dark Ages of King Zog's feudal reign between the wars; but nowadays its effect is stultifying. Though there have been extended periods of practical support from Russia and China, Albania is substantially a self-made country, and its people and administration are proud of it. But the signs are that, since the death of Hoxha, Alia is cautiously opening doors to the West. Diplomatic relations have been established with 100 countries, and trade relations exceed that number. Only certain powers, notably the Soviet Union, the United Kingdom and the USA, remain beyond the Albanian diplomatic Pale.

Various western journalists have visited the country briefly and written articles which describe the sensation of travelling back in time, bad plumbing, bad food and surly people, while quoting generous dollops of Byron. There is some truth in what is said, but not much, and little attempt is made to give the Albanians a chance. But one is hampered, because it is still impossible to travel in Albania except as part of a group, and it is almost impossible to make direct contact with people. Although French and English are taught as the first foreign languages in schools, having supplanted Russian, not many Albanians speak them readily; and Albanian, though of Indo-Aryan derivation, constitutes a side-branch of its own which is pretty impenetrable. Very few westerners learn it, and there are only three million Albanians to speak it with, though another five million live outside the little country (which is about the size of Wales), principally in Yugoslavia and the USA.

Albanians are also famous for their love of secrecy. Tour guides promote the best aspects of their country, and fail to mention the worst. While that may be true of tour guides anywhere, as one drives through fat farmland in a comfortable West German bus one feels twinges of conscience on account of vaguely-formed impressions from Amnesty International reports of the horrors of, for example, Spac Labour Camp in the district of Mirdite. But it is easy to cast the first stone, and easy to forget that a country which has been running itself for less than a century should not be judged by the standards of one which has been doing so for a millennium.

Questions are welcomed and answered on any topic, including ones like religion and political imprisonment, though one is left to use one's own judgement on the quality of the replies. One of our two guides was a Party member. He had achieved the status symbol of having two smart suits and a good overcoat, all in shades of brown. He had also travelled abroad, and a little coaxing revealed that this was on Party business. In a land where all men are equal, no car is in private ownership. Nevertheless, the 'higher-ups' are driven about in Volvos and Mercedes limousines.

The stock impression is of a poor country rooted in the Fifties, with a secret policeman on every corner, grim prisons full of wretched dissidents, and the people who are at liberty bent under the yoke of an iron-handed Stalinist dictatorship. The other thing I thought I knew about Albania is that men with beards are obliged to shave them off at the frontier.

It is true that Albania is poor, but it is developing, not declining. It is barely rooted in the Fifties at all. It is also true that political dissent is severely flattened: Albania cannot yet afford it. The *Sigurimi*, the secret police, is certainly a sinister force, and other sinister aspects of Albanian society are the system of voluntary part-time police information service, and the People's Courts.

There are still a few statues of Stalin in evidence. Most have been supplanted by the crop of busts and statues of Hoxha which have sprung up since his death. Hoxha was fiercely, even slavishly, loyal to Stalin's memory, but it would be a mistake to attribute to the Albanian leader all the evils of his mentor. He was ruthless; many dissidents were imprisoned and killed during his regime. Albania's record on human rights makes grim reading, and Hoxha himself is credited by some with having personally shot his prime minister and close associate of forty years, Mehmet Shehu, when Shehu began to deviate too much from the Party line. Hoxha's writings, collected in sixty-odd volumes and in many bookshops virtually the only works on sale, seem turgid, hectoring and dated. But there is equally no doubt that he pulled the Albanian people together, and brought about extraordinary changes for the better in agriculture, industry, and social welfare.

When we were there, England was playing Albania at football. Those British fans who had beards religiously shaved them off before going, but it's a long time since the ban on beards was lifted. They were discouraged because they were associated with priests. The profession of religion was declared illegal in the late Sixties, and the reason why priests were forbidden will become clear, as will Albania's determination to do without anyone else's help.

Albania is a very ancient country. Set in the warm Mediterranean belt which was the cradle of several ancient cultures, its first identifiable occupants were the Illyrians, who may have sprung from intermarriage between an autochthonous Eneolithic race and Indo-European immigrants in the late Bronze Age. Herodotus describes them as tall and well-built, and good fighters, but fond of drinking and not much concerned with cleanliness. Albania's frontiers have always been loosely described by the mountains which cover two-thirds of it and the western plain bordered by the sea. For many centuries it was the domain of feudal, warring lords who divided the country into great estates. The people were tribal, the social unit was the extended family under a patriarch. This system survived the five centuries of Turkish rule, and remained strong up to the Second World War.

No more graphic descriptions of tribal life in Albania exist than those written at the beginning of this century by the British traveller Edith Durham. But Byron had been there a hundred years earlier and wrote of it in *Childe Harold's Pilgrimage*; and in the middle of the nineteenth century Edward Lear went there to sketch. Drawing was regarded with suspicion by the Muslim population, and Lear was frequently stoned by small children, when he wasn't in trouble with the Turks who took him for a Russian spy. At the same time he seems to have been under constant threat of attack by ferocious dogs, and the hotels of the time – the *khans* – depressed him thoroughly:

Midnight – O khans of Albania! Alas! the night is not yet worn through! I lie, barricaded by boxes and bundles from the vicinity of the stable and enduring with patience the fierce attacks of numberless fleas. All the khan sleeps, save two cats which indulge in festive boundings, and save a sleepless donkey which rolls too contiguously to my head. The wood fire, blazing up, throws red gleams on discoloured arches within whose far gloom the eye catches the form of sleeping Albanian groups. Bulky spiders, allured by the warmth, fall thick and frequent from the raftered ceiling. All is still, except the horses champing straw within and the gurgle of the rapid river chafing without.

For centuries the people lived in fortified houses, in small communities of blood relations. Beyond belatedly converting the bulk of the population from Catholicism (in the north) and Orthodoxy (in the south) to Islam, the Turks did nothing to disturb this system, which did not interfere with their main business of demanding tax and allegiance. Political disunity was, in any case, in the Turkish interest. Originally nomadic herdsmen and hunters, the Albanians were more given to war than to the plough. They were fierce individualists, had no deeply implanted religious sense or even, for a long time, any feeling of nationhood. It was not until 1908 that a unified alphabet was adopted, and phonetic rules of spelling were only formally introduced after a congress in Tiranë in 1972.

The Turks were first significantly victorious in Albania at the Battle of Krujë in 1378. Eleven years later, the decisive Battle of Kosovo brought Serbia, Albania and Bulgaria definitively under Turkish rule. During the subsequent period many thousands of Albanians converted and enlisted in the Turkish armed forces. Twenty-seven Albanians rose to become Grand Vizier in Constantinople, and Mohammed Ali, Viceroy of Egypt from 1805 to 1848 and founder of the dynasty which ended with King Farouk in the 1950s, was one of Albania's most famous pre-revolutionary sons. Landowning families were obliged to give over their children to the Turks in order to maintain their own local ruling rights. The children were converted to Islam, and enlisted as Janissaries, soldiers in the Turkish army recruited mainly from tributary Christian children. Until 1826 they formed the backbone both of the infantry and the Sultan's Guard. Out of their ranks, ironically, arose Albania's hero Skënderbeg, the first man to unite the tribes and organize a resistance to the Turks which was truly national.

Gjerj Kastrioti belonged to one of the dominant tribes of northern Albania. He was born in 1405 and taken to the court of Murad II at the age of seven. After conversion, he took the name Iskender, after Alexander the Great, whom the Turks greatly admired. There followed twenty years of military training, and he distinguished himself in the Turkish army so greatly that he was granted the honorific title of *beg*.

At this time the Turks were failing to protect the interests of their Albanian vassals against incursions from their Serbian neighbours. In 1430 Isak of Skopje seized a part of the Kastrioti possessions and the Turks did nothing. Local uprisings followed. Then, in the early 1440s, while taking part in an action against the Hungarians at Niš, Skënderbeg suddenly withdrew from the Turkish army and returned home with 300 Albanian cavalry. On 28 November 1442, an important date in the Albanian calendar, he entered Krujë and proclaimed the independence of the principality of Kastrioti. The clan flag – red, with a black double-headed eagle – became the national flag, and still is, with the addition, since 1944, of a red star above the eagle.

Skënderbeg waged successful war on the Turks for the rest of his life, forming diplomatic links and alliances abroad and coming within an ace of forging a Balkan–West European alliance against them. But he had no worthy successor, and with his death in 1468 organized resistance crumbled. The idea of national identity, however, did not die, and Skënderbeg himself was long after mourned and celebrated at home and abroad. Vivaldi wrote an opera about him, and Longfellow a poem.

Not until the seventeenth century did the Turks begin a serious programme of proselytization, and then they conducted it in their usual pragmatic way: if you converted, you received benefits and tax relief. The campaign of conversion was successful, though perhaps not entirely so; for what took root in Albania, and indeed became a focus for later nationalism, was the Bektashi sect of Islam.

Bektashism is fundamentally Shi'a in doctrine, but it also includes pagan and Christian elements. Confession and absolution from sin form part of the rite; women do not wear the veil; alcohol is allowed, and formal prayer is of small importance. New adherents are welcomed in a ritual which involves the sharing of wine, bread and cheese. No importance is attached to Mecca. Like all religions, the sect is forbidden by law in Albania today; but it survives. At Krujë, within the museum-and-castle complex, there are two little chapels, formerly centres of the Bektashi sect. One is accessible, but in a sorry state of neglect. The other, larger one is sealed off with metal doors and brand new galvanized metal shutters. Even the upper windows have wire mesh over them. And yet, in the niches of the outer walls, candles burn in Turkish coffee cups.

The dominant rule of life in Albania down the centuries was the Canon of Lek. This tribal rule-book was allegedly the work of one of Skënderbeg's lieutenants, Lekë Dukagjini. Its cornerstone was the blood feud ('a head for a head' as the Albanian saying goes). Natural justice was the order of the day, and the rifle the means of its dispensation. Any insult was rewarded by death, and that death had to be avenged by a member of the murdered man's family – quickly, or he would become an object of his community's contempt. The vendetta would continue indefinitely thereafter, unless resolved by a Council of Elders, who might impose such penalties as exile or the burning of the latest 'criminal's' house and property. The blood feud, according to the Canon and the society for which it was introduced, must have been crudely effective, in a land whose topography forbade any central or unified administration of justice; but its ultimate effect on agriculture and society was disastrous, as Edith Durham reports and as the modern Albanian novelist, Ismail Kadare, poignantly describes in his otherwise grimly Socialist-Realist book *The Wedding*.

Although officially eradicated since 1955, the blood feud survives, just, despite all the efforts of the post-war government – and not only in the northern mountains, the stronghold of Albanian conservatism. The clan to which Mehmet Shehu belonged has sworn vengeance on Hoxha's successor, Ramiz Alia, and *his* clan; and the son of King Zog, Leka, who was born in 1939, has long since declared a blood-feud against the family of Hoxha himself. Women and children are excluded from the feud, and at any time a truce, established by a word-bond called a *besa*, can be called. It is inviolable; anyone breaking it forfeits all rights.

As the Turkish grip gradually weakened, power passed into the hands of the pashas, the most powerful local landowners who by the end of the eighteenth century were in a position to acquire vast tracts of the country and rule them with almost complete autonomy. The most notorious of these was Ali Pasha, a strong leader and vicious autocrat who won Byron's admiration when the Englishman was his guest at Tepelenë.

The large areas ruled by such men as Ali were known as *pashaluks*, and they served as a unifying factor in Albanian thinking in the nineteenth century. Already, in the early decades of the century, a desire for independence was forming, though it was not until 1912 that Albania formally emerged as an independent sovereign state. The nineteenth century saw increasing bickering between Serbia, Italy and Greece over Albania. The grasping territorial ambitions of her near neighbours, which the great powers did little to discourage and which continued well into the twentieth century, go some way towards explaining her mistrust of outsiders.

Albania was declared an independent sovereign state on 28 November 1912, four hundred and seventy years to the day after Skënderbeg's own declaration. Its first leader was Ismail Qemal, and its first king a minor German aristocrat. Something of the Ruritanian nature of those days, or an indication of how flippantly Albania's future was regarded by the great powers, is suggested by the fact that one of the other candidates for the throne was the English cricketer C. B. Fry. The First World War saw Albania carved up again, with Italy leading the field. In 1920, however, the Albanians managed to eject an Italian invasion force from Vlorë (abetted by Italian workers who threatened a general strike unless Mussolini withdrew), and for a time Albanian independence was re-established.

Two figures entered the political arena at this time. One was an intellectual liberal, an Orthodox bishop and man of letters called Fan Noli, already famous for his impeccable translations of Shakespeare and Edgar Allan Poe. The other was the young son of a landowning family, called Ahmet beg Zogu. Zogu had served with distinction in the Turkish and the Austro-Hungarian armies, and was originally a member of Noli's Democratic Party, but later he switched to the Progressive Party, which represented the interests of the landowners. Zogu became prime minister in 1922, at the age of 27, but his hold on power was not yet absolute, and a struggle between the two parties and the two men continued over the next two years. At the end of 1924 Noli, after briefly enjoying the premiership himself, finally lost the battle. He subsequently went into exile, and died in Boston in the Sixties.

Zogu became president, with Yugoslav and, later, Italian support. In 1928 he proclaimed Albania a 'parliamentary and hereditary monarchy', and transformed himself into King Zog I.

Attempts have been made to apologize for this man, and those who do so point to the eleven years of stability enjoyed during his reign; but that stability was achieved through as brutal a suppression of opposition as anything perpetrated by Hoxha. The economy was conducted purely for the benefit of the landed classes, and funded by selling vast concessions in Albania's rich oil and mineral resources to Italy. In 1938 there were only 32 tractors in the entire country; only 39,000 tons of wheat were harvested (in a country where agriculture accounted for ninety per cent of the Gross National Product); eighty per cent of the population were illiterate. There were very few doctors, and malaria raged in the undrained marshes which covered much of the western plain.

In March 1939 the Italians put forward a proposal to King Zog that Albania should become an Italian protectorate. Zog's answer to this was to flee, allegedly helping himself liberally from the exchequer before he did so. Never allowed to return to Albania, he lived in exile in Greece, England, and Egypt; he died in Paris in 1961. The Italians occupied Albania and a puppet government offered the crown to Victor Emmanuel III; but most Albanians refused to collaborate with the invaders. Three main focuses of resistance grew up, which represented Nationalism, the Monarchy (for Zog had never abdicated or been legally removed from office), and Communism. The communists were the strongest faction, especially after the fusion of their own three groups in 1941. The leader of their united resistance group, the National Liberation Front, was Enver Hoxha.

Hoxha was born into a middle-class Muslim family at Gjirokastër in 1908. He joined the workers' movement at an early age, while receiving a French education at the Lycée in Korçë. He subsequently went on to study in France, where he joined the Communist Party. This resulted in the withdrawal of his grant, and he abandoned his studies to work as a journalist on the left-wing newspaper *L'Humanité* in Paris. He returned to Albania at the outbreak of war and taught in a high school before joining the Resistance, where he immediately became a dominating figure. His range of activity was wide, embracing the military, political and journalistic fields. He was the founder in 1942 of *Zëri i Popullit*, still Albania's major national newspaper. Under him, the National Liberation Front became the National Liberation Army, which with minimal Allied help won Albania back from the Germans, freeing Tiranë on 17 November and Shkodër on 29 November 1944.

Initially disposed to be friendly towards the West, Hoxha was treated with suspicion by the Allies, and any early hopes of amity on either side soon disintegrated. The situation was not eased by Hoxha's aid to the Greek communists or by the rather half-hearted Anglo-American attempts to bring down the communist government of Albania by a series of secret missions composed of Albanian Nationalist and Monarchist exiles between 1948 and 1954. That these missions were in any case betrayed to Albania via Russia by the British traitor Kim Philby didn't help matters. But relations between Great Britain and Albania had hit the rocks as early as 1946. On 22 October of that year two British destroyers, the *Saumarez* and the *Volage*, sailing apparently without permission in Albanian waters in the Straits of Corfu, ran into a minefield and were severely damaged, with the loss of forty-four lives. Britain complained to the United Nations Security Council, which turned the matter over to an International Court, which found in favour of the UK, though Albania denied all knowledge of the mines, pointed out that she did not have the capacity to produce them, and wondered what British warships were doing in her territorial waters in the first place. Less discussed in Albania today is an earlier incident in 1946, when two British cruisers, the *Orion* and the *Superb*, were fired on in the Corfu Channel from Sarandë.

The facts of the 'Corfu incident' are hard to trace with any accuracy, since there are accounts which favour one side or the other. However, the upshot was that Albania refused to pay the damages awarded by the court, and Britain in retaliation froze a large amount of Albanian gold, allegedly seized by the Allies from the retreating German forces, though some may derive from prewar Albanian foreign investments, and stored in the Bank of England. The gold is now worth about $35 million, and Albania wants it back. 'The bars are even stamped with the eagle and the name of the State Bank of Albania, so there is no question that it is ours,' one Albanian guide told me. As long as the issue remains unresolved, there will be no diplomatic relations between the two countries.

Albania co-operated closely with Yugoslavia during the three years immediately following the war, for Tito saw himself as a kind of big brother to Hoxha. But following the rift between Yugoslavia and Russia in 1948, Hoxha emerged firmly as Stalin's man and remained loyal to Stalinist principles all his life. Stalin seems to have played along with this devotion as soon as he became aware of Albania's strategic importance, though none of the three leaders at the Yalta Conference seems to have thought Albania worth more than a bare mention.

Today Albania protests that the elections which took place in December 1945 and swept Hoxha to power were entirely democratic, and that although there was only one party to vote for not all the candidates were Party members. The fact that in those elections, and in every subsequent one, Hoxha polled well over 90% of the vote, and frequently 100%, vindicates his popular mandate in the Party's eyes. Not surprisingly, westerners are sceptical. This has not endeared them to Albania; but its two staunchest allies fared little better when they began to deviate from Hoxha's reading of Communism.

Russia was Albania's principal ally between 1948 and 1961, when relations were broken off. Principally this was due to Krushchev's denigration of Stalin; but there were other reasons. After the Twentieth Congress of the Communist Party of the Soviet Union at the end of the Fifties, the philosophy of COMECON was that the USSR should enjoy an enhanced economic development in order to catch up with the USA. But this policy failed to take into account the national interests of the smaller member states of COMECON, and Krushchev clearly regarded them as vassal countries. When he visited Albania in 1959, he suggested that the country should be turned into a specialized producer of tropical fruit, tactlessly adding that the country 'had no need to produce wheat, as its total production wouldn't equal the amount the mice ate in the Ukraine'. He condescendingly went on to tell Hoxha that the USSR would supply Albania with grain, and that the little country would be turned into a 'flower garden'. You don't need to be much of an expert on the Albanian character to see that such remarks would be highly inflammatory.

Meanwhile, Albania had begun to exploit her rich natural resources through a series of Five-Year Plans (they still continue, and posters on the streets and on hoardings still glorify them). The Chinese stepped into the gap left by Russia, and Hoxha welcomed them, stating that the Communist Party of China was the only one, apart from his own, not tainted with 'revisionism', that favourite and oddly dated catchword of the communist revolution. The relationship lasted until 1978, though as early as 1972 Hoxha was expressing his unease at President Nixon's visit to Peking. At the same time, however, trade and diplomatic relations had been re-established with France, Italy and Austria. Albania was worth courting: it has oil, bauxite, and bitumen. After South Africa, it is the world's largest producer of chrome. Today it processes all the thirty-odd different ores it mines and exports, and the surplus of electricity is such that it is exported to Greece, Yugoslavia, Austria and beyond. It is strange in such an otherwise poor country to see the towns ablaze with light; Tiranë at night is as bright as London or New York.

Religion was regarded with suspicion by the post-war government because it was associated with the representation of foreign interests. The Catholic priests of the north had always been seen as the agents of Italy, the Orthodox priests of the south as those of Greece. The imams were a reminder of a Turkish dominance and influence which above all Albania wanted to slough off. By the end of the Sixties religious observance, long discouraged, had fallen into such abeyance that a 'spontaneous' Youth Movement to close all religious houses met with no resistance. Shortly afterwards, in response to 'popular pressure', the government declared the practice of religion illegal. The surviving mosques and churches are now monuments, museums, people's cultural centres or gymnasiums. 'Of course people are allowed to observe their religion in private and at home; who is there to see them anyway? But if somebody invited their friends or relations round to worship with them, that would be propaganda and as such illegal and punishable.' One famous case of the early Seventies was that of Father Shtjefen Kurti, a former priest executed allegedly for baptizing a child. The matter was given much publicity in the West, and caused some embarrassment to the Albanians, who did not deny that he had been executed but stated the grounds as espionage, economic sabotage and anti-state propaganda.

As in many other east European countries, the vagueness in which the terms of political offences are defined is frightening; in Albania additionally defence lawyers are required to report anything said to them by their clients which may be deemed 'anti-state'. Sentences are long, though the death penalty by firing-squad is said to be less liberally used now than in Hoxha's day.

In the early Seventies there was a move towards loosening the constraints upon freedom of speech; Hoxha spoke in favour of greater democracy and of the need for greater freedom to criticize both political leadership and managerial policies. Some of this was put into effect, but as far as cultural and literary life was concerned, the opened gates let in too alarming a flood, and after three years there was a clampdown, following 'popular' demands to put an end to 'bourgeois revisionism'. The magazine *Rruga e partisë* even suggested that the country had become 'mired in liberalism and revisionism', echoing sentiments in an article published ten years earlier in *Drita*, entitled 'Revisionism is the Mainspring of all Evil'.

Nevertheless there have been material benefits, especially when coupled with the genuine national pride and patriotism of a new country seeking its own identity, after a hard struggle to achieve independence. Slogans like 'Vigilance and Work! Work and Vigilance!', and 'Think, Work and Live for the Revolution' sound harsh and sinister, but under them effective work-drives have been carried out. Malaria has been eradicated, and the marshlands completely drained and converted to farmland. Olive and citrus-fruit groves swarm over hillsides formerly covered with scrub. Industrial development has been perhaps too ruthlessly pursued.

Standards of medicine and medical treatment have so improved – doctors are among the few Albanians allowed to study abroad – that life expectancy has doubled since the war. Education is compulsory to the age of fourteen and illiteracy has been virtually stamped out. As the small population has much to do, schoolchildren spend one month a year working in farms or factories, and similar proportions of the year are devoted to military training and physical exercise. Especially productive workers and work brigades are singled out for special praise, which is a simple but effective way to maintain a spirit of competition where the rewards are not personal or material; the highest-paid Albanian earns only double the income of the lowest.

30

ROZAFA'S SACRIFICE,
SKËNDERBEG'S TRIUMPH

You arrive at the border after a forty-minute drive from Titograd airport along a road which grows progressively narrower and bumpier. To the right lies Lake Shkodra; a barrier across it marks which waters belong to Yugoslavia and which to Albania. The frontier post is small. A more compelling reason than secrecy for the Albanians only to admit foreign visitors in organized groups is that the country does not have the supplies or the facilities to cope with ad hoc tourism.

The twenty-odd people in our group queued to have their documents inspected by torchlight by the Yugoslavs before carrying or trundling their suitcases across the hundred metres of tarmac which separates the two countries. There was a sky full of stars above, but it was hard to see them beyond the glare of a solitary arc light which imparted a hard, unnatural brightness to the centre of the road. One side of this sloped into and out of a shallow trench, which contained a solution of disinfectant through which lorries entering Albania must drive. Formerly, there was a similar 'dip' for people.

The torchlit inspection was repeated, in deadly earnest, by the Albanians. Here were the first soldiers, in soft kepis and thick greatcoats of an indeterminate colour, keeping their fingers on the triggers of their Chinese machine-guns. The uniforms bore sparing insignia; red stars on the fronts of the kepis glinted.

The customs house was made up of a domestic-looking set of rooms. The walls were washed pale-blue, and hanging on them were beaten-copper pictures showing here a dance and there the profile of a hero. Standard lamps with red shades stood between red-plush armchairs and low satinwood tables, at which we filled in the forms declaring imported currency and valuables, notably cameras. The officers to whom we presented these wore neat suits. Here as elsewhere, chocolate brown was the dominant colour in urban male apparel. Our suitcases were glanced through, our reading matter looked at more thoroughly. Any work on the country not published there is confiscated at the border, along with all other material thought to be politically or morally suspect, or religious. The polite customs officers will give you a receipt, and you can reclaim your copy of *Playboy* or *The Book of Common Prayer* when you leave.

Luckily our group fitted into a small bus, which meant that we could use mountain roads impossible for large coaches. Our two guides and our driver introduced themselves – Agran, Astrid and Bashkim; they would be our companions throughout our trip. This done, we set off for Shkodër, the first town across the frontier, where we arrived at 11.30 p.m., about fourteen hours after leaving London.

The road there was pitch dark, the darkness punctuated once by the headlights of a car, but Shkodër's empty roads were brilliantly lit – the first sign of Albania's opulence in electricity. Once Agran had switched the bus engine off, we were embraced in a lovely quietness. Only a clamour of dogs in the night streets, which didn't scratch the surface of the peace. A cat crossed fussily from pavement to pavement, hurrying but taking its time too, with the foolhardy arrogance cats have.

We stayed at the Hotel Rozafat, one of the fifteen or so in the country which are available to foreigners. Like most of them, it is modern, and although its decor was austere any sense of coldness was dispelled by the friendliness of the people who worked there. It was midnight, we had been delayed over the journey by a couple of hours, but a hot and delicious dinner was awaiting us. Waiters in black ties served pork with garlic and black pepper, with chips (an Albanian staple as well as an English one), preceded by mushroom soup and succeeded by blood oranges ice cold from a refrigerator. Albanian wine, though very cheap, can vary immensely in quality, but the Shkodër region is famous for it. Kallmet was pretty well the most expensive wine anywhere, at about £2.50 a bottle, but it was also the best, like a very dry Burgundy.

The room was comfortable and spotless; the bathroom delivered hot water, and the central heating was, if anything, over-enthusiastic. I mention such details because they were not what travellers' tales had led me to expect.

Awakening next morning, I was once more aware of how soothing silence is – or rather, the absence of traffic noise. It was still early, but it must have been the time of a shift-change, for there was plenty of activity. There were a few buses and one or two jeeps, but otherwise people rode bicycles. The majority walked. Variety of colour in clothing is not something to be found in Albanian towns. Amid a monotony of fawns and greys, a woman's red coat seemed shocking. This is the only east European country in which there does not appear to be one single pair of blue jeans.

Later on, walking in the town by myself, I noticed people's stares. They were not hostile, if anything they were shy; but they were openly curious. If I met someone's eye, however, they averted their gaze, and a smile was rarely returned. There were more bicycles about by this time, and their number seemed to increase as the day wore on. In fact, we weren't to see as many anywhere else. 'Shkodër is a city of bicycles,' Bashkim told us later. 'Each family has two or three at least – even if there are only two people *in* the family!'

We breakfasted on Turkish coffee in large white cups, goat's cheese, and minute, deliciously spicy sausages. The table linen was spotless, and on each table stood a vase with fresh forsythia and quince blossom. Outside the broad windows of the dining room the sun was already washing out the colours in the broad square. It was dominated by a large memorial to a group of resistance fighters of the Second World War (the National Liberation War) and by the severe neo-Classical façade of the town theatre, whose architrave was decorated with a sign extolling the late Enver Hoxha. The personality cult lives on; Hoxha's bust is to be seen in town squares, in parks, and on main streets; his portrait and his sayings are on billboards everywhere; and giant statues have been erected as memorials in Gjirokastër, his birthplace, in Korcë, where he grew up, and in Tiranë, the capital. His name is writ large in arrangements of flowers by roadsides and in whitewashed stones on the sides of mountains. Ramiz Alia seems so far to have kept a low profile by comparison; but already the first modest hoardings and popular portraits are beginning to appear in his praise. He is an amiable-looking, greying man in late middle age, rather like an actor playing a GP in a soap opera. Apart from exhortations to vigilance, labour, emulation, unity, and so on, the one inescapable image is Albania's version of the hammer-and-sickle: the rifle and the mattock, the two tools by which Albania has lived since long before the advent of Communism.

Across one of the broad boulevards which feed into the square a bust of Lenin confronts one of Stalin. Nearby, there is a curious little neo-Gothic castle, about the size of a large villa, which once housed a British consulate. Beyond them, leading northwards, is a street of restored nineteenth-century Italianate houses – the prettiest in Shkodër. Elsewhere, in common with most Albanian towns, the architecture is mainly post-war, and very functional. The street becomes a road and the road leads northwards a short distance out of town to a modern bridge crossing the River Kiri, a broad stream flowing around flat rocks. Next to the modern bridge is a much older one called the Mesi Bridge. This was built by local masons in the Middle Ages to connect Shkodër with the township of Drishti. The narrow, humpbacked stone bridge is built over five arches which leap from rock to rock. On the other side of the river, the Albanian Alps rear up suddenly, grey and dramatic. Our route didn't lie this way; and although there are facilities for skiing and climbing here, at present they are available to Albanians only.

We had attracted a small crowd, almost exclusively male. They wore dusty brown slacks and patterned pullovers whose predominant colours were brown, orange and a startling lime green. Little boys detached themselves from the group and came forward, asking in shy whispers for *gumma* or a *stela*. People here have so little that it is tempting to give in and part with a stick of chewing gum or a biro; but unfortunately to do so only encourages more begging, and Albanians, proud and determined to be self-sufficient, do not like their children to fall into such habits. One little boy was much more interested in discussing football with me. The England–Albania match was due to take place on the following day.

South of Shkodër is the castle of Rozafat, a grey stone ruin which clambers along a hilltop. It is being slowly excavated and restored, though archaeology is not a high priority in Albania. What is visible today was built by the Venetians in the fifteenth century and improved upon by the Turks when they took the town a century later; but the original castle predates both Turkish and Italian rule and was built by a Gheg or even earlier Illyrian chieftain to protect his domain. There was a Roman fortress here, and as the site is on a hill above a river the likelihood is that the place has been settled as long as humans have been in these parts.

There is a harsh legend attached to its foundation. Three brothers worked on building the castle, but no sooner had they completed a wall than overnight it would collapse. They sought the advice of a seer, who told them that the walls demanded the sacrifice of a human life. They decided that whichever of their wives brought them their midday meal the following day should be the victim; but that night the two older brothers secretly explained the situation to their spouses and told them to stay away. Thus Rozafa, the youngest brother's wife, brought the food and was chosen. She did not protest, since her sacrifice would be for the good of everyone, but she asked that when she was walled up holes might be left to enable her to continue to look after her infant son – one hole through which to see him, one through which to suckle him, another for an arm to hold him, and one more for a foot to cradle him. To this day, the walls of Rozafat are said to run with her milk, though it is the limestone which is responsible for the cloudy dew.

Towns here do not trail off into suburbs, they begin and end abruptly. Immediately beyond Rozafat the road thrust south through the countryside. The villagers waved to us from pastures, from little brick cottages, from dusty squares built around standing pumps or wells. Women working with mattocks in the fields were splashes of vivid red and white against the light brown soil, for in the country dress is as bright as it is drab in the towns. Here, in the north, the local surviving tribal costumes are still worn quite ordinarily. Some women had white head-dresses and white trousers under full skirts; others wore black pillbox hats over black wimples. Over forty different clan dresses are still worn in the Shkodër region alone.

Today it is easy to forget what a cosmopolitan place Albania once was. Rich in her own natural resources, she occupied a central position in the ancient world. Her southernmost shore is only separated by a mile or so of sea from Corfu; Durrës is only 150 kilometres across the Adriatic from Brindisi. It is no wonder that Italy has always wanted Albania, for to control both countries is to control the Adriatic. The Romans were able to do so, and the port of Durrës – Dyrrachium – marked the beginning of the land route to Constantinople, the Via Egnatia. Albania was the link between the Eastern and Western Empires.

Even so, it is more recent history that has a greater claim on one's consciousness, Roman Lissus seemed far hazier to me than the medieval town of Lezhë where Skënderbeg lies buried in the church of St Nicholas. The church had been used as a mosque under the Turks for many centuries and is now a ruin, but since 1968, the 500th anniversary of Skënderbeg's death, it has been a national monument. A plain slab marks the hero's resting place, and on it a replica of his helmet, with its goat's-head emblem. The origin of the emblem is explained by one of the many stories surrounding the hero. Outnumbered by the Turks in a forest at night, he was saved by a large herd of wild goats, which made so much noise that the Turks retreated, convinced that enemy reinforcements had arrived.

Across the river, Lezhë is a busy, trafficless modern town built along a dusty main street made up of crumbling new blocks painted in pastel colours. Its main industries, our guides told us, were food-processing and paper. Astrid and Bashkim, who took turns in addressing the group, told us tirelessly and exhaustively about every aspect of modern Albanian life with unaffected pride. Both men had much humour and charm, and were skilled in deflecting questions or comments which were too probing or critical; they were in any case sincerely protective of their country. Early on, Astrid made a short speech in which he told us that we could photograph anything at all, 'except railway stations and trains, and police, soldiers, and military installations'. He also expressed the hope that the photographs we took would reflect the good side of life in Albania, and not 'the many things that are not so good, that we still have to improve upon'. It has to be said, though, that we were shown very little of which he need not have been proud.

We crossed the River Mat. To our left rose the mountains which cover two-thirds of Albania, and to our right lay the flat fertile plain which until the late Forties had been malaria-ridden marshland. Some rice is grown here, but the main crops are wheat and maize. One impressive statistic provided by Bashkim does bear repeating: 'Under Zog, wheat production was eight quintals per hectare. Now, we produce up to 117 quintals.' Not surprisingly, Albanian agricultural technology has become an exportable asset, though the use of chemical fertilizers is lavish. The fields of the reclaimed land in early March were an almost unnaturally vivid green, though already the midday sun was becoming too hot for comfort and farmers were worried at the lack of rain during the winter.

The former king is only ever referred to as 'Zog', and then contemptuously. Under his rule there was no railway, and the total output of electricity was a mere 5000kH. Zog gets barely a mention in the National Museum in Tiranë, and no photograph. But then, five hundred years of Turkish rule are also neatly ignored, and we jump, almost without a nod at the intervening centuries, from Skënderbeg to the freedom fighters of the nineteenth century.

At Fush-Krujë we turned east and followed a road which climbed steadily into the mountains to Krujë. Here stood the castle which was the centre of Skënderbeg's resistance. The town is built on the lower slopes of a vast ridge of grey mountain which rears its cliffs sheer above it. The houses look down on a broad valley scarred by a cement factory, from where we could intermittently hear the sound of blasting for limestone. Krujë has been designated a museum city, and the pleasant buildings are highlighted by a long terrace of medieval craftsmen's shops, now restored. They have low-pitched broad roofs covered with thick red tiles, and stand on a rough, cobbled street. Were it not for the absence of hordes of tourists, one might have been back in Yugoslavia – in Mostar, with its souvenir shops and pretty streets.

The Turks finally captured Skënderbeg's castle ten years after his death, following several unsuccessful attempts which had earned him the admiration of the western world, especially of his ally and near neighbour, Ragusa. Though strengthened by the Turks, it subsequently fell into ruin, and now only one twelfth-century tower remains of the original, a plain-roofed pile reminiscent of the fortified tower-houses built by the feuding clans of northern Albania. The bases of the original walls are still to be seen, and among them, in the original position of the keep, stands a new museum, which has been built along the lines of recently-discovered original plans. The architect concerned was Enver Hoxha's daughter, Pranvera.

The museum houses a collection relating to Skënderbeg's life and campaigns. Little of the period has remained, and there is a number of modern statues and murals of larger-than-life musclebound heroes with particularly huge hands, who look as if they had stepped from the pages of some American super-hero comic. More of these are to be found elsewhere in Albania, especially in the National Museum in Tiranë. They do not make up for the absence of historical artefacts, but for me the building, with its narrow corridors and intricate rooms, is fascinating in itself.

There is a little village within the confines of the castle, the houses behind high walls smothered with vines. Some golden-headed children played with a minute dog in the street, the dusty surface of the ground dazzlingly white in the sun. Just beyond these buildings are the chapels I have mentioned. The larger, Byzantine in plan, was built in the eighteenth century. It, too, is a fine tribute to Albanian architecture.

If national pride is reflected in the care and money spent on key historical buildings, propaganda plays a role too. The infusion of a sense of isolated nationalism was one of the central themes of Hoxha's policy: a kind of *Albania fera da se* which found its way into most aspects of life. At about the time that the Turks resumed power following the death of Skënderbeg, a number of Albanians emigrated across the Strait of Otranto and settled in southern Italy.

'The communities are still there,' Bashkim told me as we took a breather from the museum and looked out across the sunbleached olive groves of the valley. 'They speak the old, pure form of Albanian, which we are trying to reintroduce.'

'How?'

'A number of western and foreign words have crept into our language; gradually, where we can find a counterpart, we are replacing them with their Illyrian forms. Of course, we cannot replace words like, for example, "neutron"!' He spoke English quietly and deliberately, though he was a full-time employee of Albturist of many years' standing. His accent, more pronounced than Astrid's, was indefinable. Encountering it with no clues, one might have shrugged and said, 'Central European'. There is no trace of American in the accent. The generation of English teachers who taught people of Bashkim's age were Chinese. It is a long time since Albania had anything to do with the USA.

The landscape here – as everywhere – is dotted with little domed concrete pillboxes, sometimes with two firing slits, sometimes with only one. The two-slit boxes look like robots, or Daleks, buried up to the eyes. I had assumed them to be left over from the war as many are overgrown with weed, thorn, and other ground-cover. I found this wasn't the case at all; though a few were inherited from the Germans and the Italians nearly all have been built since 1945 as part of the national defence system. The total number throughout the country must be in the thousands, if not the tens of thousands. 'We have no Polaris, no nuclear weapons – we must have some means of defence,' said Bashkim; but this stippling of concrete, in clusters along roads, by railway lines, strung out the length of the coast, sometimes on low hills and – unfathomably – in the middle of fields, seems to border on the paranoid. Three or four times we passed larger concrete emplacements, built into the rockface at the base of hills, where huge, rusty anti-aircraft guns, festooned with webbing, pointed their snouts at the sky.

Everywhere, too, there are soldiers. By day, one can see the colour and texture of their greatcoats. They are a purplish brown, and seem to be made of stiff felt, like carpet underlay. Uniforms seem to be issued with complete disregard for fit, and some soldiers looked desperately uncomfortable as well as hot. I wondered why they couldn't just wear their tunics. As in every east European country, an average of eighteen months' national service is obligatory. It also provides an opportunity for the state to continue to drum its propaganda into the minds of the young, a process which starts at kindergarten. Uniformed police are a far less visible presence. They, too, wear coats, but of lighter weight. These coats are dark blue with brass buttons, and are worn ankle-length.

Krujë, as well as growing olives, is also a centre for other fruit-farming, and we descended from it through dense orchards and vineyards. Later we passed the first graveyard, of which there are many in Albania since, after 500 years of Turkish influence, there is no cremation. Old habits die hard. Since there is no religion the dead are buried according to a brief civil ceremony, or with no ceremony at all. Headstones are usually plain white rectangles, which give the name and dates of the deceased. Later, on the outskirts of Fier, I noticed a cemetery which contained a massive tomb topped by a reclining male nude.

There is nothing to stop you from approaching religious buildings. Many of the churches are splendid Byzantine structures. Most were converted into mosques during the Turkish occupation, but now all, church and mosque alike, are deconsecrated. Occasionally in their grounds one might find a surviving Muslim tomb, its white stone surface still covered with a maze of Arabic, its column still turban-topped.

The drive to Durrës in hot sunshine led through dull countryside – a rocky hill rising every so often from heavily cultivated flatland, punctuated every so often by a pastel-concrete little town, and now and then by a factory, including one vast and bizarre copper refinery. Its huge raggedly lagged pipes stood in the open air like the brainchild of a mad sculptor. By the side of the narrow road ran herds of untidy, shaggy sheep with long fat tails, making forays into the enormous hand-tilled fields of the state farms. The soil looked rich, and every available inch was cultivated. As we drove, our guides fed us information. Thus I can tell you with confidence that Albania is seventy per cent self-sufficient in food, and eighty-five per cent in consumer goods.

Durrës is the more northerly of Albania's two major ports; the other is Vlorë. Rising to fame under the Romans, Durrës was settled before them by the Illyrians, and almost certainly there has been a human presence here since the dawn of mankind. Nowadays it is not only a port but a holiday town. Albanians, lacking hard currency and paid minute wages measured by the western yardstick, do not take their vacations abroad, although no law prevents them from doing so.

The beach is long, greyish yellow and composed of fine sand. At this time of year, still out of season and too cold for swimming, it was deserted except for a huddle of pillboxes, a jogger and a group of young men playing five-a-side football. We discovered that today was National Teachers' Day, and work seemed to be suspended in its honour, for the town was especially crowded. We stayed at the Hotel

Adriatik, one of the best in Albania, built in the Fifties in Stalinist-Aspidistra-Gothic and promising a grandeur which it lacks the means to live up to, though it has a souvenir shop (carved wooden boxes appallingly made, beaten copper artefacts, one or two kelims) and a bookshop, where you can not only get the works of Enver Hoxha (plus one or two with similar titles by Ramiz Alia) translated into French, Italian, German and English, but also maps of the country (no longer available abroad), postcards and stamps. Some of the stamps are beautiful, and the speed of the post from here to the West is faster than from any other east European country.

Along the six kilometres or so of shore separating the hotel from the town there is a string of low buildings, as always built of concrete and painted pastel shades, and as you approach the town some ugly low-level factories and some equally ugly blocks of flats in unfaced brick appear. The bricks are of poor quality and the flats, though quite new, look tumbledown and uncomfortable. Many of the low buildings nearer the hotel are holiday camps for workers. The holiday season is from mid-May to mid-September. Each person averages fifteen days off, and facilities here are similar to those in the other Albanian coastal resorts strung out along the Mediterranean shore.

Durrës itself is a surprisingly large town, and after the relative emptiness of Shkodër the crowds of people came as a shock. There is a small museum which contains a jumble of local Greco-Roman finds, and not far away, though surrounded and partly overbuilt by new houses, is the former amphitheatre. It held 15,000 people, a testimony to the size and importance of the town in Roman times, but so far only a quarter of it has been excavated. What is visible looks neglected and overgrown, though apparently archaeological work continues and a protective roof has been built over the ruins of a sixth-century Christian chapel to Saint Demetrius, built into the wall of the auditorium, together with a small necropolis. Delicate early Christian mosaics of saints peer neglectedly from behind an iron grille. 'In the course of time we will uncover the whole building, and the whole amphitheatre too, although archaeology is a new science in our country, and several houses now occupied will have to be demolished,' Astrid informed us a touch stiffly. It is a pity that Albania's self-imposed isolationism will not allow it to consult and take advantage of the expertise of more experienced foreign archaeologists and scientists, or at least allow its own academics freer access to research material and books published in the West.

In the town the shops' signs are hand-painted on wooden boards above the windows: they are simple, merely describing the goods or the service the shop supplies – BOOKS, BREAD, GREENGROCER, BARBER, and so on. There is strictly no hint of advertising here – beyond, of course, masses of propaganda for Enver and the Party of Labour. Despite their gloomy neon-lit interiors, the shops were not badly stocked. As is usual in eastern Europe, everything is stacked on shelves behind an uncompromising counter.

Dusk had fallen by now, and with the disappearance of the sun the sudden chill reminded me of how early in the year it was still. This did not, however, prevent the *passeggiata*. It was very noticeable that the promenaders were nearly all male, though there were some lovers too, wrapped around each other in a way which would have been frowned on even two or three years ago. It is clear that since Hoxha's death in 1985 there has been a certain amount of welcome social loosening up. Some contact with outsiders will not plunge the country into degeneracy. The clothes people wore were passable but still drab, and the number of colours available was very limited – brown and orange, lime green and mauve. Shoes looked badly made and uncomfortable. I had yet to see either a clothes store or a shoe-shop. Little children were quite often dressed in a patchwork of materials. Sleeves or trouser-legs had been replaced or mended with whatever material was available.

'After dinner,' promised Astrid, 'there will be a programme of folk-music in the bar.' He was a little terse as the several historical errors he had made in his conducted tour of the amphitheatre had been corrected by our group's English courier. The great, echoing, galleried hall of the dining room filled up as a hundred muted English football fans, billeted here because there was no room in Tiranë, filed in for their lamb and chips. My attention was drawn to a florid, grey-haired man, in a pale blue denim jacket and jeans, who seemed to be getting preferential treatment from the staff. He was clearly neither English nor a football fan, and he was certainly not Albanian. He was also very drunk indeed. So drunk, in fact, that I watched in fear lest he should be unable to hold the food which was brought him. He pushed most of it away in favour of a dark red viscous liquid which he drank from a small goblet.

Dinner done, we filed across the main hall with its grand central staircase into the equally cavernous bar, where Beefeater Gin and Johnnie Walker were available at astronomical prices. I stuck to the local raki, which is not aniseed-based but like a plum-brandy, and extremely good. Few people had decided to brave the folk-music, and the band, composed of amateurs who play in the evenings for a little extra cash, did not look too promising for such a soirée, as it was composed of the usual hotel line-up of saxophone, rhythm and bass electric guitars, accordion and drums. We lowered ourselves into deep armchairs and sofas and ordered coffee. The florid man in denims put in an appearance, shook hands with the barman, waved to a couple of girls, then staggered around the open area which was clearly used as a dance floor before homing in on us. Astrid and Bashkim, who had been talking amiably but firmly about the great progress made on all fronts by Albania, stiffened as one.

Florid-Denims sat on the arm of my chair and put an arm round me. 'You Eengleesh?' he grinned. 'Fotbol. Verr' good.' He tickled my ear with his fingers, and leaned closer. 'Don' lissen thiss two,' he said in a very audible whisper, and indicated Astrid and Bashkim with a jerk of his thumb. 'They'll juss' feed you propaganda. Come an' have a drink instead.'

I looked across at my wife, who had accompanied me on my Albanian trip and who was now trying to draw our guides' attention away from my uninvited tête-à-tête with Florid. She was unsuccessful. They regarded him stonily.

'Later, perhaps,' I suggested to Florid. He nodded sagely. 'Thiss your vyfe?' he asked, indicating Nicky.

'Yes.'

'Verr' beyootiful. Come 'n' have a visky. I get you. Jus' you an' your vyfe. Not thiss two.' The thumb jerked again. The fingers of the other hand continued to tickle my ear. Astrid and Bashkim were beginning to look at me sympathetically.

'Later,' I said to Florid. 'Perhaps.'

Unfortunately, Florid took offence, stood up, bowed stiffly to Nicky, gave me a baleful look, and unsteadily withdrew.

'Who is he?' Nicky asked Astrid.

'A Greek captain. His ship is under charter to one of the state export agencies here, so he's frequently at this hotel for the night. He makes plenty of money, so ...' Astrid spread his hands, prepared to be generous, letting the sentence hang. I would have liked to talk to the Greek captain later, but he had left the bar and did not reappear.

The band now struck up, but all they played was a selection of western standards, notably 'Yesterday', which must be the most popular tune in all eastern Europe, and 'Strangers in the Night'. Nicky, disappointed but not surprised, decided to go to bed. I stayed on, nursing my raki, and talked to Astrid and Bashkim, who had suddenly become quite expansive and were obviously pleased that I had not rejected their company in favour of the Greek captain's.

I found out a little more about them. Bashkim, who was born in 1948, had been a Party member since his days as a Pioneer. He'd been with Albturist now for several years, having read modern languages at university. He had two sons, aged ten and fifteen, of whom he was extremely proud. His rheumy eyes softened whenever he spoke of them. Bashkim told me that his own father could neither read nor write, but just as he had improved on that, so he expected his sons to improve on his achievements. To that end, in addition to their schooling, he was teaching them extra English at home, and his wife was teaching them chemical engineering, the subject she had read at university and now taught. Although Bashkim had travelled abroad, nothing he'd seen had made him feel envious or restless about the limitations of Albania. Astrid was less complacent, and although there were not more than eight years between them in age, he represented a younger generation. Not a Party member and only a part-time guide, though he had been doing the job for twelve years, he taught English and Albanian literature in school and was married to a professional musician, a flautist. Astrid had never been out of Albania and was hungry for new impressions and new ideas, although his pride did not let him show this too much. He had given both his young children English first names.

But after a certain amount of personal confidences they withdrew, almost as at a signal, to the safety of general topics. I noticed that they hardly asked me any questions about my life, or about England, though Astrid and I swapped a handful of quotations from Shakespeare, whose plays are popular here. I had the impression that as a foreigner I could only be reached out to so far; I wondered whether they were monitoring each other, though surely only the most loyal and the most trustworthy would be allowed to do such privileged work as theirs. As for contact with other Albanians, it was not discouraged, and in towns where we had time to wander we were allowed to, though not beyond the city limits. In fact there were few opportunities to fraternize because of the limitations set by time, shyness and the language barrier.

Our talk turned to the safe ground of the educational system, which, considering that it barely existed before the war, is now well developed, though it is tightly controlled and used to indoctrinate children from an early age. People need totems. The cults of atheist Albania and anti-religious Romania, to pick the two extreme examples, are strongly based on the idea of the leader as demigod. All of the propaganda programmes on Romanian radio and television take the form, effectively, of prayers or paeans to Ceauşescu; in Albania, it is the image – the statue or picture – of Hoxha which is important.

With Albania's small population and its ambitious work programmes, no one can be spared for long. Maternity leave allows ten months away from work, covering the last month of pregnancy and the first nine of the child's life. The baby is then put into a crêche from 8 a.m. until 3 p.m. every working day until it is three years old. For this the parents are charged a nominal sum. Kindergarten follows for three years, and then compulsory 'eight-year school' until the age of fourteen, after which there is an option to extend schooling to the age of eighteen (twelve-year school). University follows. To get in, a prospective student must choose three possible subjects; for example, Bashkim's older son will apply to do medicine (his first choice), chemistry or history. If his academic track record is up to scratch he will be guaranteed a university place to read one of those subjects, which will be selected for him and which he must accept. He must then go and work in the field and the place where the Party decides he is most needed.

The band now launched into a Thirties medley. I would have talked on, but Bashkim and Astrid stood up and firmly announced that we had an early start tomorrow and a long way to go. I wondered that neither of them had talked himself hoarse after five or six hours of history, anecdote and, above all, detail of agro-industrial achievement. Astrid read the expression on my face correctly, and left me with a parting shot: 'We haven't yet reached the point where freedom of choice ceases to be a self-indulgence and becomes a right.' He didn't say it aggressively. If anything, he said it with regret.

31

THE SILVER CITY

'Today we have a very long drive but we think you will be amused by it,' announced Bashkim solemnly, challenging us to demur. Bashkim shot his cuffs and I noticed that all the buttons on the jacket sleeves of his chocolate brown suit were missing. The same suit and an immaculate white shirt and brown tie were his uniform for the week. Astrid dressed more casually, but it wasn't hard to see that things like replacement buttons and new soles for shoes are not easily come by in Albania

The roads have nearly all been built since the war. They are well-metalled but narrow, and what traffic there is, generally Chinese trucks and tractors, is driven with great ferocity. Cyclists are frequent in towns, and ox- and mule-drawn carts in the country. There are small hoardings every so often along the roadside exhorting people to greater levels of production and heights of loyalty, and small modern concrete memorials to the fallen of the National Liberation War dot the streets in, and on the outskirts of, towns. As we set off south and east towards Lushnjë en route for Fier and Gjirokastër, Astrid reminded us that today was International Women's Day. His tone implied that it would be taken far more seriously in Albania than anywhere else. As we drove through increasingly lovely countryside, we learned that peasants own their cottages, provided by the state free of charge, and also have small plots on which to grow produce which they may sell either privately or to the state, in addition to their work for the state farm to which they are attached. Labour is regimented, as are most aspects of life: teams of twenty farm labourers work under a foreman or forewoman. Women share equal rights and pay with men, but are also expected to fulfil similar quotas. Nevertheless, in a society which owes its traditions to Islam, it was not surprising to see more men idling than women, more women working than men.

Although distances are never great in Albania, the mountainous terrain and small roads often make progress slow, and our journey to the south took most of the day. It ended at the Hotel Butrinti in Sarandë, Albania's southernmost town of any consequence and, except for the archaeological site at Butrint which we would visit the following day, the southernmost point of my entire journey – 1500 kilometres and several worlds away from Gdańsk.

The Hotel Butrinti spoilt us. We were given Room 213. It was a suite which consisted of a large bedroom, bathroom, dressing room and sitting room which came complete with balcony and remote control Europhon colour television. On it, I was able to pick up not only Albania's single channel (which broadcasts faultlessly in

colour and tends to feature folklorique programmes or discussions about agriculture)
but also a Greek channel, an Italian one, and Superchannel, which happened to be
broadcasting an episode of a hoary British thriller series called *The Professionals*.

The first leg of the journey from Durrës lay through more highly cultivated fertile
ploughland, with here and there grassy meadows dotted with sheep and cows.
Scenes already glimpsed repeated themselves contentedly: vividly dressed women in
the fields, old men in black waistcoats and white felt fezzes, sporting handlebar
moustaches, sitting watching children splash themselves at village pumps.

We crossed the River Shkumbin and arrived soon after at Lushnjë, a district
centre which is yet another pastel-shaded concrete industrial town. Women, I had
noticed by now, do not have hairdos. They wear their hair simply, either long,
bobbed, or up. It was only later, in Tiranë, that I saw perms, and even then only a
couple.

We stopped for coffee at Fier, an oil boom-town which is entirely new – it was only
a hamlet before the war. Greater prosperity and improved health services have
brought about a modest population explosion, and with an average age of twenty-
five Albania is the youngest European country.

Despite its modernity and the functional architecture of most of its buildings, Fier
is a lovely town, with broad boulevards and wide green squares. Something
fundamental to familiar culture is missing, though, and after a time you realize that it
is the absence of churches or mosques. Finding your way around Albanian towns
can be a problem as street maps don't exist; but on the other hand no town is big
enough to get lost in.

I found a coffee shop. It was dark, hot and smoky, with a concrete floor, peeling,
ancient paintwork and a mahogany-and-metal bar. The place was crowded, but only
with men. They wore cloth caps, open-necked check shirts and elderly jackets with
wide, Sixties lapels, which were either grey or loudly checked. Most of the younger
ones wore brown or black flared trousers. I might have been in a provincial Turkish
café.

I didn't attract more than cursory glances here. A waiter brought a clean white
tablecloth, a minute cup of treacly coffee and a glass of water. I paid my one lek and
wondered if I'd be able to locate the bust of Stalin which was still somewhere in
town. So far all I had come across was a small one of Hoxha in a minute flower
garden of its own. The Albanians share with the Romanians an apparent passion for
formal public gardens, using humble municipal plants like the marigold and the
begonia but creating ebullient swathes of colour to lift the spirit and gladden the eye.

At the next table a man who looked about thirty-five sat alone. In common with
many white-collar workers he wore a jacket and slacks, with a crisp shirt and
impeccable tie.

'Where are you from?' he asked me in French. He seemed quite happy to talk and
joined me at my table, bringing his own coffee-cognac with him. He turned out to be
a doctor based at the town hospital but attached to one of the co-operatives working
the oilfield. I wondered about the large numbers of people thronging the streets.

'Nearly everyone's on shift-work, so there's always plenty of people around.' The structure of work is, like everything else, highly organized. A worker will get a pay increment every time he goes up a grade, something which is assessed every five years. After fifteen years in the same job he will get a seniority increment in any case. Pay is not high, at an upper level of around 1200 leka a month (about £85.70) paid fortnightly, but rent is cheap at a day's pay per month for a family flat, and services such as electricity and basic foods are heavily subsidized. A suit, however, is expensive at one month's pay. All prices are state-controlled and thus inflation cannot exist, in the sense that wages and prices are adjusted to absorb it. 'So instead of a wage increase, for example, the government might announce that certain prices were to be reduced. Since they're the same everywhere for everyone, and since there's very little difference between one man's income and another's, everyone's happy. At least, that's the theory,' said Ari. 'But the trouble with Utopia is that it can get terribly dull, and it doesn't always work. So take what your Albturist people tell you with a pinch of salt.' He smiled, but wouldn't be drawn any further. I glanced round the room, but still no one was paying any particular attention to us, and Ari seemed quite relaxed.

There was no time left to look for Stalin. I crossed a square and hurried back to the bus. By now I'd acquired a handful of words of Albanian, which is an attractive language that gives occasional flashes of its kinship with ours. Not, however, in the word for hello.

'*Tungjatjeta,*' I said to a group of four elderly men sitting on a bench, twirling worry-beads and staring at me. I was delighted that they all smiled broadly and shook hands. It was a pity that our conversation couldn't get any further. ORGANIZATION − DISCIPLINE − EMULATION: the words are spelled out on the balcony walls of a block of flats nearby. They are nearly the same in Albanian as they are in English. Clearly no Illyrian substitutes have yet been found.

After Fier we turned south-east, leaving the green plain and heading up into the mountains. They are suddenly there − the Mallakaster and Shpirag ranges, and then the higher Shendelli − gigantic cliffs, the highest capped with snow like clouds. There is no doubt that Albanian mountain country, unblemished by tourism, contains some of the most beautiful terrain in Europe.

In the middle of the long, giant valley which cuts through the mountains following the course of the River Vjose, lies the mining town of Memaliaj, and just to the south of it is Tepelenë, a place with great romantic connotations since it was here that Ali Pasha had his palace, and here that he was visited by Byron. But now nothing remains except ruins; earthquakes have done their worst. A small modern agricultural town occupies the spot today. However, there are compensations. The milky-turquoise River Vjose clambers fast over rocks under the dramatic humpback of Mount Dragot, and a village clings to the mountain's lower slopes. The scene is unforgettable and, except for the intensive cultivation of every available space, unchanged since Byron saw it. Certainly the mountain is as untamed, the village as remote.

Below Tepelenë the Vjose turns east, to rise through Përmet and then on south-east again into Greece, where it becomes the Vikos, reaching its source in the barren range of the Timfi Óros. The valley which leads to Gjirokastër is now commanded by the Drina, which joins the Vjose at Tepelenë.

The road by the Drina to Gjirokastër follows one of the most breathtaking routes in Europe, and the silvery grey town, perched on a hill at the end of it, does not disappoint. Easy to defend, high and solidly established on rock, the old town has survived earthquake and siege, commanding a swathe of countryside like the inner curve of a wave. It is dominated by a huge, elliptical fortress and by a vast monument to Hoxha, erected in 1988.

The streets, paved with blocks of the same silvery grey stone which goes to build the houses and, in shards, to tile the roofs, climb steeply away from a square. The fortress, used as a prison of terrifying reputation by Zog, is now partly a gloomy war museum. The dark ground floor with its high tenebrous archways contains dusty Italian and German armoured cars and field guns from the Second World War. 'Trophies of our struggle for freedom,' Astrid explains. From these dark chambers we moved into the open air, onto a battlement, now covered with scruffy grass and commanding a fine view over the town, its grey buildings swarming over hills on both sides of the castle. At the far end of a terrace, in the protecting shadow of a flinty wall, a slowly decaying jet, painted silver and bearing United States markings, is parked. It is a sky-plane which was forced down by the Albanian air force thirty years ago. 'We let the pilot go, but we kept his aircraft. Inside the castle you have seen trophies of the war. Here is a trophy of the peace,' Astrid told us, with rather theatrical bitterness. Beyond this terrace, an amphitheatre opens out around a wide space dominated by an ugly clock tower. Here a national folk festival and competition is held every five years.

Most of the houses were built in the first half of the nineteenth century, though there are examples from the seventeenth and eighteenth as well. Gjirokastër was an administrative and governmental centre during the last century of Turkish rule, and its buildings reflect the prosperity and culture of its inhabitants. It was also the home of the two Topulli brothers, Bajo and Çerçiz, Albanian nationalists of the turn of the century. Their house, built into rock at the top of the town, with its plain, almost Georgian lines and windows placed high in the walls for security, is one of the most attractive, and typical of the earlier design.

To reach it one has to climb steep paths scattered with a shingle of crumbled grey stone, but it is impossible to get lost as all paths interconnect and a circular route brings you back via the edge of a forest to the centre. People here are friendly and relaxed, despite the fact that this was the day when England had beaten Albania two-nil at the Qemal Stafa football stadium in Tiranë. A woman standing in the doorway of her house gave us sprigs of basil as we passed. In front of the principal mosque (built in the seventeenth century, and now a cultural centre) a man greeted us in Greek.

The streets which meet at a crossroad in the town centre are lined with small shops, one of which sold souvenirs and had a notice in English. Almost all had signs hanging outside them from pretty wrought-iron brackets. There was a bookshop, but it had little available beyond the voluminous works of Enver. Albanian books in translation are sold at very low prices: I bought Hoxha's *With Stalin*, a collection of short stories by Nasi Lera, and the contemporary epic poem *Mother Albania* by Dritëro Agolli, which Bashkim told me had the power to move him to tears. I thought it odd that they had no copies of the novels of Ismail Kadare, since he is Albania's most applauded living author. In fact I was never able to track down any book of his, though Bashkim made up for this by giving me his own copy of *The Wedding* as a parting present. All these books had to be posted home from Tiranë, since they would have been confiscated by the Yugoslavian authorities if they had found them. The package took only two days to reach London. Next to the bookshop was a toyshop, which was exclusively stocked with plastic dolls that looked as if they'd escaped from the chorus line of a Busby Berkeley movie. On a corner, where the descending street debouches into the main square, there was a clothes shop. It was closed, but peering through the windows I could see a wooden counter running the length of the store, a scattering of shirts and pullovers behind its glass front, and sparsely stocked shelves from which cotton frocks in textiles of Fifties design drooped from hangers.

Taking the street at the crossroads which leads away from the fortress, one arrives after a while at the splendid house which was the birthplace of Enver Hoxha. It is much grander than it was in 1908, for since that time two houses have been knocked into one, expanded and much restored to provide a home for what is now a combination of museum and shrine.

Lower down the slopes there are clusters of modern blocks of flats, five or six storeys high, cheaply run up in concrete and unfaced brick. There are also some small factories; industry here is devoted to leather, shoemaking, cigarettes and chemicals. None of this detracts aesthetically from the old town. Even the modern hotel which dominates the main square at its foot doesn't intrude. Gjirokastër is probably the most attractive town in Albania. I liked it because it is uncluttered by advertising, by souvenir shops, cafés and noise. However, the town is not without its vulgarity. The fortress is surmounted, as many ancient hilltop citadels are, by large red letters spelling out a Party message, lit up at night.

We continued south through the dusk, then turned westward again, passing on the dark hills the glimmering lights of the mainly ethnic Greek villages here. Following the course of the River Bistrice, we also passed the two major power stations that bear its name and which generate electricity for export to Greece. And so, as night fell, we arrived at the little port of Sarandë.

No lunch or dinner we had in Albania contained fewer than four courses. Now as we sat down to another immense meal, lubricated by a delicious, dry red wine called Shesh-i-Kis, which cost perhaps fifty pence a bottle, I managed to buttonhole Bashkim and ask him a handful of questions which had been nagging me during the day.

'Of course after university you do not have to stay in the same workplace forever,' he said, answering the first one. 'Take my son, for example. When he graduates, he will go where he is sent and stay there for maybe five, maybe seven years, to repay his debt to the state. Thereafter he will be free to come home to Tiranë if he wishes –

or to go and work wherever he chooses – within reason, and provided work's available.' Everybody who is capable of work has to work.

I wanted to know more about how the rites of birth, marriage and death were conducted in the world's first entirely atheist state, as Hoxha described it. No ceremony approximating to baptism exists; the new baby is simply given a name, which is registered. There may be a small party to mark the child's arrival. Marriage is more complicated and retains traditions of the tribal society which existed before the revolution. Although arranged marriages officially no longer exist, they still frequently happen, but the children involved cannot be forced into matrimony as was the case in the past. Bashkim's own marriage was arranged. A period of engagement lasts about two years. During this, the couple see a lot of each other, and get to know each other better, with the right to cry off if they don't like what they find. If all is well the wedding, which is a short civil ceremony, follows. The family celebrations, however, go on for a week and are clearly based on much older rituals, with a formal system of visits made and returned by both the families involved, ending with a visit to the bride's family by the groom's relatives, who then take the bride back with them. She brings all her possessions from her old home to her new one. The culmination of the nuptial celebrations is a dance between the bride and groom. Men dance twirling a handkerchief. In this case it is dipped in raki and set alight. As he dances with his bride, the groom whirls it around her. When it has been consumed by fire the girl is considered to be fully married to the man. They retire to the bedroom, but not before the old women of the family have ritually thrown a male child onto the bed, to ensure that the couple's first-born will be a boy.

Bashkim attracted a good deal of attention with his account, and grew more coy and boyish himself as it progressed. His own marriage had been conducted with every detail of the ritual he'd described. Astrid and his wife, more modern, had simply followed the register-office wedding with a party. They had met at university. Astrid was inclined to be disparaging of the old forms, and I could see that he was embarrassed by them and thought we might consider Albania primitive because of them. He pointed out that divorce was not only allowed and equally accessible to either sex, but socially tolerated and on the increase. He added severely that it was always due to the breakdown of a relationship, and never to adultery, which clearly in his mind was the main cause of marital break-up in the fleshpots of the West. He didn't tell us that a person suing for divorce has to present his or her case to a council of the People's Court and answer any questions they see fit to ask. Many of Albania's laws are designed to limit privacy and encourage snooping.

The extended family unit is still a strong one, and immediate family members live together. Traditionally the oldest male child stays with the parents, even when married and with children of his own. Thus three generations live together, but the family bond is close, and in practical terms the oldest generation, retired from work, contributes by looking after domestic matters such as housework and shopping. The old are, in fact, still very much included in an active social life. Pensions are set at seventy-five to eighty-five per cent of the wage, and retired people may supplement this by returning to work for a few hours a day at full pay to give trainee and apprentice workers the benefit of their experience. Miners retire at forty-five (as elsewhere in eastern Europe), teachers at fifty. The majority retire between sixty and sixty-five, and women stop work five years earlier than men.

The middle generation works, the children concentrate on their education. One month per year in the school timetable is designated for children to work either on building or land-clearance projects. 'In a small country with much to do, everyone cheerfully pitches in,' Astrid said. Certainly the clearance of scrub and marshland for agriculture is a success story to match Israel's.

In a country with cheap rents, guaranteed accommodation, subsidized essential products and no private ownership of cars, I wondered what people spent their savings on. 'We save for holidays, and most people want to have a television.' A television costs the equivalent of six or seven months' income, but the rooftops of every town are a forest of aerials. Bashkim told me that Albanians were free to travel abroad, to visit relatives in Italy or Greece, for example, but that the trip would probably have to be underwritten by those relatives, as the lek has no value outside Albania and ordinary people have no access to hard currency. Travel abroad is, of course, freely available to Albanians working in either the import/export areas of business and in the diplomatic corps.

I was unable to find out accurately about the allocation of space to a family, but from what I could see, though dwellings are very simple, they are not cramped. Country people appear to be better off, with their individual houses and little gardens.

I had already found out a little about the Albanian way of death. 'But no civil ceremony is necessary,' said Bashkim; 'apart from registering the death, nothing formal need be done. My uncle died a few months ago. We dressed him in his best clothes, laid him in his coffin and took him to the civic cemetery. All the family gathered with his friends, and I read a memorial speech – just about what he'd done in his life. Then we went back home and had a wake. And that was all.'

We opened another bottle of Shesh-i-Kis and continued. I probed unsuccessfully for their reaction to the problem of Kosovo, but no one would express a personal opinion. 'What we want seems to us entirely reasonable,' said Astrid. 'Equal rights for the Albanians there, and the right of self-determination. After all, that area used to be part of Albania. We are perfectly contented with our present frontiers,' he added, forestalling any suggestion that Albania might have territorial pretensions, 'but the Serbs have always made trouble for us.' In a sense he is right; and Albania's mistrust of foreigners stems squarely from having for so long been surrounded by inimical ones.

Sarandë looked pretty enough from the hotel suite's balcony the next morning, though it was some distance away. A string of low white buildings lined the shore, while beyond them along the far curve of the bay the familiar low-rise modern blocks rose on the slope of a small hill. Across the sea, eight kilometres away, the grey hulk of Mount Pantokrator on Corfu loomed like a giant's ghost in the haze. Temptingly close, it might as well have been on the other side of the moon for most Albanians, though I wondered if anyone had ever tried to make a break for it from here and succeeded. Penalties for trying to leave the country illegally are tough.

Our own route for that day lay away from Sarandë; there would be time for the disillusion of closer acquaintance later. After a breakfast of delicious but cold omelette, we set off for Butrint. The road leads due south, running between the sea and Lake Butrint. Astrid pointed out the fish farms which had been established in the lake, from where young fish are transported to stock other lakes and reservoirs around the country. Apart from Yugoslavia, no other country I visited offered such plentiful supplies of food or greater availability of fruit. Oranges, apples, grapes and plums were served in generous quantities at every meal. The scrublands on either side of the road have been cleared over the past ten years by young people during their month's 'voluntary' labour (as the Albanians insist on calling it) and planted with citrus groves, mainly lemon trees. Among the groves there was a workers' holiday centre. A fortnight's holiday here costs seventy leka per person, forty per cent of the total cost, the difference being made up by the trade union. The centre was a pleasant building reminiscent of any modest modern seaside hotel.

Corfu is so close, across the strait at Butrint, that you can practically reach out and touch it. The villages and houses along its north-eastern coast are clearly visible. On the Albanian shore an eighteenth-century castle of Ali Pasha stands near a horse ferry. Its walls are disfigured with white daubed graffiti in giant letters extolling Enver Hoxha ('Enver the Inevitable' as someone maliciously dubbed him). Nearby is a mussel farm; the mussels are exported to Italy, where they are in great demand. We turned away and passed through a gate in an old, overgrown brick wall into what appeared to be a lush, Marvellian garden.

The Roman port of Butrint is now on the lake shore. Italian archaeologists, vigorously accused of having taken a good many of the treasures with them when they left, started excavations in the Thirties, but although the Albanians have continued they lack the expertise or the money to make much headway. Progress is therefore slow and the city, built on the massive stone walls and foundations of a former Illyrian settlement, is overgrown with an astonishing fecundity of flora. This place must be as much of a joy to the botanist as to the archaeologist. There had been a heavy rainfall not long before, and the standing water had not drained away. The floor of the Roman theatre was one large brown shallow pool, and elsewhere many floors, almost certainly covered with mosaics, were hidden under stagnant water already soupy with algae. Elsewhere, as in a baptistery converted by early Christians from an original Roman building, the mosaics were invisible beneath a protective polythene sheet over which grey gravel had been strewn, though one or two had been left exposed. It is frustrating to be told that under the gravel there are seven concentric circles of coloured mosaics, depicting flowers, geometric patterns and, in the principal circles, birds and animals. All I could see was one dusty ibis. Near the baptistery is a church of a much later period, though only its shell remains, its floor carpeted with wildflowers. The colours of the stone here are interesting: they range from a soft yellow, like Cotswold stone, through to the dark grey of the early Illyrian building.

The Illyrians built massively, huge block upon huge block, and much of their original fortification remains, incorporated by the Romans into their city. The beauty of Butrint, one soon comes to realize, is that it has been left alone, though it may be sentimental to find beauty in decay and to be pleased that this site has not been cleaned up and signposted but instead lies lost and sprawling among dripping trees. The brick gymnasium stands in the centre of a shallow lake bordered by a chaos of wildflowers. Hornbeams hang their green blossom over a nymphaeum which looks like a forgotten folly in the grounds of an eighteenth-century mansion. Climbing through the city, you pass through an ancient narrow gate decorated by a simple relief group of a lion attacking a bull. The animals are fused together. Everywhere, the city lies under a soft green shroud of ivy and moss, enriched by the discreet colours of thousands of tiny flowers. In the angle of a building, at the corner of an ancient street, an iridescent tree-frog squats. After all this, the brand-new impeccably designed museum in a restored Roman villa at the top of the hill is almost a disappointment. The objects on display are few. 'Nearly half the city is still underground, and the other half is below the waters of the lake,' Bashkim told me with a curious complacency as we descended. He paused to show me a head of Apollo mounted on a column. 'This is a reproduction; but we do have the original. It is in the museum in Tiranë. We made the Italians give it back in 1935.'

Above all the emptiness and the silence allow the atmosphere of Butrint to express itself, in a pleasurably melancholy way. The only fly in the ointment was a custodian dressed in a mauve rollneck and severely belted tan raincoat, who shadowed us throughout our visit. His eyes were quite vacant and his face set in a scowl, his lips clamped around a black plastic holder through which he continuously smoked pungent cigarettes.

On the way back to Sarandë we stopped for lunch at the restaurant attached to the state citrus and olive farm at Ksamil. A kind of light bouillabaisse was followed by a large and very meaty fish. The bottle of milky white Skënderbeg white wine tasted musky and promised afternoon headaches, but they didn't occur. Set on a knoll above a small bay, the restaurant looked out over Corfu. In the bay was a small group of little islands covered with dense vegetation and surrounded by neat, pristine beaches. A similar beach traced the curve of the bay. The water was clear and clean. Two or three pillboxes had been erected, but there was nobody about. I imagined the crowded beaches on Corfu a mile or so across the water and put away the thought of what developers, given a free hand, would do to this magic place. But the pillboxes along this coast, with their freshly whitewashed interiors, are all very definitely in commission.

32

A SAINT IN A BOX

It is impossible not to regret how much of Corfu has been spoilt by tourism. In Sarandë the imprint of concrete has wrought similar damage in a different way. At first sight the town is as attractive as its setting. The narrow beach is lined with a handful of low buildings which formed the fishing village that lies at the core of the town. There is no shop, no bar, no restaurant, though a new public garden is being built and old men sit on park benches playing chess. Others squat round broken flagstones marked in chalk with concentric squares or map out a similar board in the dusty earth, using stones for counters, and play 'nines' or 'threes', a form of draughts which I was never able to fathom. In any capitalist country such a seafront would be at the centre of a busy tourist resort, buzzing with shops and cafés.

There is palpable silence here, but apart from curious sidelong glances the townspeople do not communicate. A smile was met by stoniness. The lack of friendliness was so noticeable by comparison with elsewhere in Albania that one immediately sought reasons for it – suspicion? shyness? Or does proximity to Corfu and perhaps knowledge of the vulgar freedom of the island breed a kind of resentment? The only good-humoured people were a couple of cops outside the large modern police station on the seafront. Not far from it is the cream-painted hospital. Through its barred windows, women in dressing gowns talked to their friends and relatives outside. One man had hoisted himself up by the bars to be closer to his wife. Near him on the broken pavement, emphasizing the forlorn quality of Sarandë, lay a smashed jar of greyish apricot jam.

There was a playground on the front, with brightly-painted swings, a roundabout and a see-saw. But the children used them in silence. There was no one on the broad, newly-paved promenade. Grass made a brave attempt to grow in the new gardens among the spiky palms, still littered with concrete pipes and white edging stones.

One block in from the sea a wide road runs the length of the bay. It is crossed by smart streets rising by flights of steps away from the sea. Here, the broad balconies carry oleanders and orange trees. The paintwork is new and bright. We cheered up a little, telling ourselves that as soon as the gardens were completed the front would look delightful. But then we caught people's sullen eyes, and wondered. Nowhere more than here does the likelihood of Albania's integration with the rest of Europe seem more remote.

Walking up the town we found a *gjelltore*, a bar-restaurant. It was a concrete bunkhouse painted puce, and tired men in grubby clothes sat all along its front façade, facing a dismal square. Inside, along one wall were large cauldrons of boiling stew. We tried a glass of punch – a local liqueur, vivid umber in colour and often drunk as an alternative to raki or the local cognac – which tastes like sweet Cointreau, though the flavour is more tangerine than orange. Heads turned briefly, but any conversation was clearly out of the question. We felt self-conscious and unwelcome, and soon left. Occasionally, in our wanderings around the town, we would encounter other members of our group, looking equally adrift.

'Are they like this because the town's so close to Butrint? Do they see too many tourists down here? Or is this an especially secure area because it's so close to Corfu?' We knew that Albanian propaganda never painted westerners in a flattering light, but hitherto there had been no evidence that people actually paid any attention to it.

Beyond the *gjelltore* and as the town climbs the slope away from the sea, the more attractive houses are replaced by the familiar five-to-seven-storey new blocks of unfaced brick, which stand cheek by jowl or group around squares which are patches of waste ground. On their more humble balconies firewood is stacked, and in the courtyard of one group of buildings we saw a water tanker parked. People with buckets and churns queued; there is no running water in these flats. Not far away there was a small parade of shops, the handmade glass of their windows distorting the few goods on display inside, the pale blue paintwork peeling. Unexpectedly I suddenly received a dazzling smile from an elderly woman in black supervising a children's game of football.

The disparity between the houses down by the sea and the new development in the upper town is very evident. In the same way, the gloomy men sitting in the *gjelltore* contrasted very much with the smart Albanians in elegant suits and dresses who patronized the hotel's *sala familjare* and the restaurant; they looked cheerful, even exchanged smiles; but genuine equality does not exist in human society. However, the five-year plans by which Albania still functions seem to work, although inevitably the shoddiness of building and the poor quality of brick make you suspicious in that area alone that standards may be sacrificed to quota-fulfilment, in the true Stalinist tradition.

Albania sees its progress in terms of a very rigid programme: the five-year plans are part of twenty-year forward prognoses. Into these, everything else must fit. You can't have Utopia at all, of course, but it seems that in the view of the Albanian leadership the closest you can get is through relentless progressive development, the course of which may not be deviated from. That in turn means the sacrifice of democracy. Woe to any dissident voice, therefore. Everyone must fit into the grand scheme, or it will not work. There can be no margins, no room for thinking outside the structure, and in this respect Albania's isolation helps her leaders, for the glimpses ordinary Albanians get of the world outside are few. For those of us used to the principle of freedom, the system here seems harsh indeed, and yet people don't appear to be unhappy. But, human nature being what it is, all the ordinary people I managed to talk to wanted to be free to choose for themselves, wanted access to western goods, and even felt that Albania would have made greater progress if it had adopted a western outlook and gone into partnership with the West.

'The question is very complicated, but what if the Nationalists or even the Royalists had emerged in the war as the leading resistance group? We wouldn't be under the thumb of an outmoded ideology then, but equally our own culture might have been swamped by the West. That's why Hoxha was so against western influences. We've only been really free for forty-five years, and we do owe that to Hoxha's strength and stubbornness. Now he's gone, inevitably there will be change. But how long it will take, I don't know. I certainly don't want to see our coastline turned into the mess that tourism has made of it in Greece or Yugoslavia. So I think that, for as long as we can, we are right to stay aloof from the borrowing and spending that has affected every other country in the world. The question is, can we do that and at the same time open the doors to foreign influences and ideas?' This came at the end of a conversation with a student which had started badly, for I had praised the delicious coarse white Albanian bread we had been eating. I should have known better, for I was quickly reminded that as a tourist I was in a privileged position. I was asked if I had tasted maize bread yet. 'It is a shame that you westerners do not get a chance to look behind the scenes. You come here and you see the country as a spectator sees a stage set: you do not know what is real and what is made of canvas and wood.'

The student who said all this to me over rakis in a bar in Tiranë reflected a common attitude of loyalty and nationalism, coupled with a desire not to be deprived of western goods any longer. The Albanian government still feels that any foreign influence will undermine the grand plan. Private thoughts and desires must continue to be subordinated to what it deems is the national good. And freedom of expression is not something the Balkans have ever been used to.

But western influences there are. After dinner that night in Sarandë we went down to the hotel's nightclub, which was in an unmarked and unsignposted basement. It was almost deserted, except for a group of jolly Englishmen marking the last night of their four-day tour by drinking from an apparently endless supply of canned East German beer: the delicious Radeberg I remembered from the beginning of my journey. The cavern-like basement was painted red, and on a small stage opposite the bar a band was playing. They were very good indeed, and interspersed the inevitable 'Yesterday' with Gershwin and Cole Porter as well as Albanian songs, for which a stick-thin singer emerged from their midst. The leader was a clarinettist/saxophonist, a plump, curly-haired thirty-year-old who played his old silver alto sax and his reedy B flat clarinet with professional polish and infectious enthusiasm. His ten-year-old son sat behind him all evening, a solemn boy in a red zipper jacket who watched his father with admiration.

The two most striking things about their performance were the relaxed seriousness with which they played and the contrast in the sound of the clarinet when it switched from familiar songs like 'Autumn Leaves' to the wild, remote melodies of Albania – a music which beckons you and makes you want to fly and soar with it, though I never heard it played better than here. The band were all amateurs. The leader was the local barber, and the drummer drove one of the little two-stroke three-wheeler delivery vans which busy about in every Albanian town. As their wind-up number, they sang 'My Bonny Lies Over the Ocean', word-perfect. I wonder if they'd learned it at school.

The following morning we set off early, and Bashkim took his place at the microphone. Both he and Astrid had relaxed considerably as they got to know us better, though their guard was never completely dropped. I happened to be sitting near Bashkim, and he leaned over to me confidentially:

'Did you have a good time last night?'

'I enjoyed the music, and I helped the raki co-operative meet its quota.'

He laughed. 'It isn't a co-operative, it's an enterprise.' Then he fell silent and weighed the microphone in his hand, thinking. 'What,' he asked, 'have I not told you about? Have I told you about marriage?'

'Yes.'

'How about education?'

'We've had quite a bit about that too.'

'Agricultural history?'

'No, we haven't had that.'

He beamed, and switched the microphone on. Thus it was that, among many other things, I learned that very recently Albania made the modest discovery that knocking olives off the trees by throwing sticks at them damages the trees and jeopardizes the following year's crop. The switch resulting from this discovery to hand-picking led to a production yield in 1988 which was fifty per cent higher than that of 1987. Every single fruit tree in Albania, be it lemon, orange or olive, has a number attached to it so that the crop in the different groves and different areas can be assessed down to the last detail, along with the quotas achieved by the various brigades responsible for different groups of trees. In this way a basis is provided from which future targets can be set.

'Ultimately, we will replace all the scrubland with groves of fruit trees,' Bashkim told me. 'There is a long-term land-clearance and planting scheme which is under-taken by young volunteers.' Since the scrubland maintains quite a large number of non-productive wild trees, I couldn't help wondering if their wholesale dis-appearance might in some way account for the unexpectedly low rainfall of recent years, which is beginning to cause concern. Bashkim glowed with pride at the rolling acres of cultivated land through which we were now passing, and told me that he himself had planted an orange grove just south of Vlorë when he was a youth volunteer in 1967. I made him promise to show them to me.

Back in the country, we were among friendly people again. A small group of gaily-dressed Gypsies laughed and waved at us. No Gypsy I saw in eastern Europe ever seemed to have any trouble in getting hold of bright floral materials, however drably the other locals dressed. I hadn't seen many in Albania. I wondered how they fitted into the system.

'Nowadays they are fully integrated Albanian citizens,' Astrid told me rather grandly. 'They are settled and have jobs, though they are still allowed to follow their wandering nature.' I guessed that this would be within limits; there are no statutory travel restrictions on Albanian citizens within the country, but here as anywhere exigencies of work and availability of money can be limits in themselves.

'What sort of work do they do?'

'The women tend to be roadsweepers. As that's a night-time job, they have their days free to do what they like.' By the road, a couple of the smaller Gypsy children had started to dance. The older ones formed a loose circle, clapping. Dazzling teeth shone in copper faces and eyes the colour of molasses glowed. There was an uncompromised freedom in them.

Bashkim had moved on from agriculture to the national health service, and was telling us that all medical care is free. Very few people indeed had the poor teeth or the malformed or diseased eyes which I had seen frequently elsewhere in eastern Europe. Other diseases, like rickets and goitre, I didn't notice at all in Albania, nor did I see anyone terribly crippled or half-starved as I had in Romania. One curiosity was that virtually nobody wore spectacles.

The narrative was interrupted as the bus swerved to avoid one of the Romanian-built box-like ARO jeeps which most of the agricultural co-operatives use. From Sarandë we had taken the coast road, stopping briefly at Himare. There is a modern village by the sea shore, but the old village (a rare sight in Albania) which Edward Lear must have visited is on a hill immediately above. It is a pretty place, with a well-kept cemetery, one of the few that was bright with flowers. The headstones carried tiny oval metal photographs of the deceased, as is the European custom east of Germany, in addition to the laconic name and dates.

From Himare the road, already passing through lovely countryside, becomes ravishing. The giant rugged mountains of the Çike range are fringed with snow, and on their foothills wander herds of shaggy silver goats. Inland, the terra-cotta soil is so baked and parched that only goats could live on the sparse scrub that grows. There are low stone farmsteads clamped to the slopes, while on the other side of the road, closer to the coast, the land abruptly turns green again and endless citrus groves tumble down to the sea, separated from it by long pencil lines of startlingly white, deserted beaches. There are workers' holiday centres dotted along the shore, but only one modest building for perhaps every four miles of beach. Inevitably, on the wild face of a nearby mountainside the words PARTI ENVER are laid out in huge letters of white stone. More modestly, an isolated flowerbed was arranged in numbers to commemorate 45 years of Albanian Communism.

Bashkim showed me his orange grove and we drove into Vlorë, Albania's second port and her principal naval base. It is a large and prosperous-looking modern town, with noticeably better built blocks of flats along broad, tree-lined boulevards. A mosque stands in the centre of an intersection. It is now an artist's workshop. Not far beyond it stands one of the curiosities of modern statuary. Long after most of eastern Europe has abandoned it, Albania clings to Socialist Realism. God knows whom it has ever convinced or fooled, for it has about as much to do with realism as the illustrations in a Superman comic, and the beetle-browed Peasant or Worker or Freedom Fighter represented is a static, wooden non-figure. The Martyrs'

Monument in Vlorë, a mighty pile of figures striking heroic poses, is Socialist Realism in its purest, silliest form.

Vlorë is an ancient foundation, but it is the successor to a still older city. Apollonia lies some 20 kilometres to the north. A Greek river-port of major importance in antiquity, its decline began in the third century AD and was hastened when an earthquake diverted the course of the river on which its prosperity depended. Today the small site is deep in the countryside, near an abandoned Byzantine monastery which has been renovated as a museum to house the finds from the slow excavation of the Greek city. The monastery church of St Mary is exquisite, though shored up with great wooden supports after being badly damaged in a recent earthquake: it is thus impossible to enter. Its portico is decorated with slim Romanesque columns set in pairs, and each is topped by a capital carved with delightful medieval beasts and devils. The texture of the complicated brickwork of the monastery walls, the glow of its colour in the dying sunlight against the dark green of the surrounding fields, and the loneliness of the place create a profound sense of peace and beauty.

The Greek city is of pale stone, and beyond traces of its massive walls little remains, or has been uncovered, to give an impression of the greatness of the town, though something of it is apparent in the workmanship of the isolated façade of the town hall, the ambulatory and the Odeon. It is hard to believe now that this was a major Mediterranean trading centre and a seat of Greek culture so renowned that it attracted the mighty of the Roman world – Cicero praises it, and Octavius Caesar stayed here – but there is a ghostly magnificence about it still, and at least there is more to see now than there was when Lear visited the spot: 'I went at sunrise to the single Doric column – the only remaining token of Apollonia above ground. It stands on a dreary little hill, covered with long grass and brambly thorn, and a more lonely and forlorn record of old times cannot well be contemplated.'

Nightfall brought us to Berat, originally settled by the Illyrians on the north bank of the River Osum. The main street, which follows the line of the river as it cuts dramatically through a gorge, is broad, lined on one side by modern buildings and shops and on the other by a large, formal garden which overlooks the river and contains a modest bust of Lenin. At one end of the boulevard is the Hotel Tomori, across a square from the Leaden Mosque, so-called because it has a lead roof. It is now a museum of architecture. At the other end of the boulevard is the Bachelor's Mosque. It is now a modest arts and crafts museum. The works on display are not impressive, but the original woodcarving and decoration inside are beautiful.

'Why is it called the Bachelor's Mosque?'

'Because it was founded by a rich bachelor,' said Bashkim; but doubt was very evident in his voice.

Behind it, a labyrinth of narrow cobbled streets climb the hill on which the citadel stands. The houses here are mainly nineteenth-century, but those within the walls of the fortress are considerably older. Three or four beautiful and virtually intact red-brick Byzantine churches cling to the sides of the hill below the walls. The most impressive exterior is St Michael's, but there are two churches within the citadel which not only are accessible but contain works by the Berati iconographer-priest

Onufri and his son Nikolla. Onufri is one of the greatest icon-painters of his period (the sixteenth century), and he worked well beyond the confines of his home town, not only all over Albania but also in Macedonia and Greece.

The citadel is a medieval town, one of the last fortified cities of Europe still to be inhabited. The fortunate occupants of the houses have simply inherited them; there is no favouritism attached to ownership, because houses, once allocated, remain with the same family until altered circumstances or a break in continuity demand a change.

The dominating features of the view from the silvery grey castle are the two mountains which protect the town – Shpirag and the giant Tomor. Tomor is not Albania's highest mountain, but is certainly her greatest. He is the father of the nation, the symbol, the unifier which in the end will be more enduring than Enver Hoxha. The legend which unites mountains, river and town is this: two brothers loved the same girl, but she could not decide between them, so they fought a duel. In the fight, each mortally wounded the other. The girl wept over their bodies: her tears became the river. In her grief, she turned to stone and became the castle. The brothers' bodies are Shpirag and Tomor.

Much is being done to renovate and restore the castle. At its centre lies a small Byzantine Eastern Orthodox church with a superb iconostasis – not by Onufri, but largely by nineteenth-century painters; Berat was a centre for icon-painting for several hundred years. The church is gradually recovering from a sad state of repair, but the paintings and most of the woodwork is safe. There are curiosities. Like chestnut wood, ostrich-egg shells are believed to repel spiders, and they were incorporated into the decorated chains from which chandeliers were hung in churches such as this. Very few examples survive, but here there are five or six. In the area behind the iconostasis we found an old wooden box within which were some brown paper bags containing human bones.

'An unidentified saint,' said the curator when I asked him about them. 'They've been there for years but I'm afraid we still haven't got round to doing anything about them.'

We were already on friendly terms with the curator, Fatos, having met him the night before in the hotel bar. He was sitting with a group of friends at the table next to ours. Presently a series of accurate cartoons of some of us began to emanate from his group. He had drawn them. He'd just left Enver Hoxha (formerly Tiranë) University, where he'd read Fine Art and Russian.

The collection of icons in the small two-storey museum attached to the church contains many by Onufri. He was an artist ahead of his time, famous for the fluidity of movement in his figures, a degree of realism not found in the work of contemporaries, and the beginnings of psychological insight in facial expressions. He is also famous for his matter-of-fact angels. 'Albanian angels do not float, they walk,' said Fatos, pausing in front of an Annunciation in which a businesslike angel strides towards a politely interested Mary. The angel has wings, but they are unfurled behind him in a decorative way; the artist has not even bothered to relate them to his body. Onufri's son Nikolla follows his father's style with marginally less success; a smaller church nearby, which was under massive restoration, is entirely covered with frescoes by him. The Balkan saints, Demetrius and George, are much in evidence.

'It is a pity,' said Fatos, 'that Onufri never left his son the secret of his wonderful reds.' The Onufri red is unique, and so distinctive that it alone is enough to identify his work. The colours he uses are lurid, and probably symbolic in a way I do not recognize. Composition and style, especially in the landscape backgrounds, reminded me of Mantegna. I liked one of his characteristics: he was proud of his home, and when he travelled he would describe himself as 'a citizen of the lovely city of Berat'.

At the door of the museum Fatos pointed out one more icon to us. 'This is worth looking at. It shows the sick being healed at a fountain of holy water. You can see that the city had both Christians and Muslims in it, because there are minarets in the background. But look – there's a wall which separates the two religions, and keeps the Muslims away from the fountain.'

He accompanied us from the castle and showed us the way through the narrow whitewashed streets back down the hill into town. He told me that he wanted to become an art historian, and seemed optimistic that he would be able to travel later – notably to Italy and France – to continue his studies and gain access to the books he wanted. 'But as I want to specialize in silver icons, I expect most of my research will be in Greece and Russia.' He also wanted to keep up his own painting. To my astonishment he had read Hemingway and Theodore Dreiser extensively, and to my relief he was happy to talk to me about them rather than to ask questions.

On the way down the hill in the hot sun, we passed a primary school. It was playtime and the children were in the yard outside. When they saw us they flocked over, chorusing in the faultless accents of the English middle class: 'How do you do?'

33

MOTHER ALBANIA

On the road the next day Astrid gave us a brief lecture about Albania's penal system. He told us that there were virtually no political prisoners and very few criminals. In any case the Albanian system was more concerned with re-educating the malefactor or dissident than with punishing him. Murder was virtually unknown, but the death penalty still existed for treason and premeditated homicide. Astrid could not remember when it was last applied. The Amnesty International report on the Albanian judiciary is less sanguine about the country's liberality. Awkward questions were deflected with a fairly light touch: 'We are a young country ... We are a small country ...' The implication every time was, 'We cannot afford to indulge ...'

Not far from Tiranë a funeral was in progress. The coffin, covered by a reddish-brown cloth, was being carried towards a black minibus by at least twelve men. Some way behind them, dozens of women followed, all wearing white headscarves. The presence of the parked hearse caused chaos for the traffic on the narrow road – our bus, one oncoming lorry, and a two-stroke tractor pulling a cart – since no one wanted to give ground, but finally, after a good deal of Italianate gesturing, we conceded the road to the lorry and pulled onto the grass verge.

The outskirts of Tiranë, and indeed most of the town itself, consist of ranks of apartment blocks, their paintwork peeling. Five colours predominate: beige, orange, pink, green and grey. This is a new city. In defence of the functional architecture, Bashkim told me that Albania has successfully managed to maintain a building programme to keep pace with a population increase that has trebled the number of Albanians to about three million since the war. 'New housing developments,' he explained in his pedantic way, 'are built by local communities, and everyone helps with the unskilled labour in their spare time. That means that the professional builders can concentrate on the work which really requires their expertise.' Bashkim added that in the country many people build their own houses privately. When I asked him where they got the materials to do so, he replied enigmatically that the trees and stones which occurred naturally provided them.

The seat of government was moved to Tiranë from Vlorë in 1920, and what had been a minor provincial town, chosen for its central position, was converted into a capital with remarkable speed. At its centre is Skënderbeg Square, a massive rectangle on which all the town's principal public buildings stand. From it a wide boulevard leads south, the Avenue of the Martyrs of the Revolution. This lovely tree-lined street starts just behind the self-important equestrian statue of Skënderbeg in its little garden. Beyond it lie the Italian-designed buildings of the ministries, faced in pale yellow with attractive mouldings and topped by the usual exhortations to Loyalty, the Party and so on in large red letters. Beyond them on the left is a modern art gallery whose terrace is dotted with Socialist-Realist bronzes, among which is a famous figure of a worker holding a rifle and brandishing a pickaxe, which sometimes replaces the mattock as the second national symbol. Near him a much larger statue of Lenin stands on a high plinth. He faces across the street what must be the last full-size statue of Stalin anywhere – in a Napoleonic pose, complete with greatcoat and cap and an impossibly benign expression on his face.

Skënderbeg Square is defined by a series of massive buildings: the National Bank, the Palace of Culture, which comprises opera house, theatre and ballet as well as a cinema, and the National Museum. A huge modern mosaic on its façade groups Albanians from Skënderbeg's to modern times defensively around a rifle-brandishing young woman of striking beauty – Mother Albania. The mosaic well reflects the 'us-against-the-world' attitude encouraged here. Between the Palace of Culture and the museum stands the new Hotel Tiranë, built to rival intercontinental hotels anywhere in the world and virtually indistinguishable from them. It is, however, only the second-best hotel in town according to the locals. The best is the much older, Italian-built Dajti some way down the Avenue of the Martyrs on Lenin's side, and if one could see a fair cross-section of the Albanian bourgeoisie at the bar of the Tiranë it was outside the Dajti that most of the large Mercedes and Volvos were parked. 'You get better service at the Tiranë, but somehow the Dajti just has more class,' a young journalist called Ruzhdi told me. Near the Tiranë, and dwarfed by it, is a local hotel for Albanians. It is more down-to-earth in every sense. At the Tiranë an Albanian will pay 40 leka for a room, about four times the rate at an ordinary hotel. Foreigners, doomed in any case to the 'international' standard hotels, pay a lot more. Hard currency is needed just as much in Albania as anywhere else in the Eastern Bloc. The ever-present irony throughout my entire trip was that the US dollar and the American Express card were the most welcome means of payment everywhere.

From our room in the hotel there was a sweeping view across the square, along the front of the Palace of Culture to the clock tower and the Ethem Bey Mosque, both survivors of the original town. Beyond them stretches the Avenue of the Martyrs, terminating in the central block of the University, which was founded in 1957. On the Avenue, about halfway down, we could see the white inverted funnel of the new Enver Hoxha Museum. I wonder how long it will be before Skënderbeg Square is renamed Enver Hoxha Square. At its centre an enormous golden statue of the great man has stood since 1988, a partner to the memorials erected in Gjirokastër and Korçë. It is curiously magnificent. Beyond the town the bare hills rise protectively. Despite its size – it has a population of about 300,000 – Tiranë stops and starts almost as abruptly as other Albanian towns.

We were too late for the bookshops, which had closed at 4 p.m., and the only thing on at the Palace of Culture that night, a selection of arias from operas including

Madame Butterfly and *Il Trovatore*, started at 6 p.m. and was sold out. At the hard-currency shop in the Dajti we bought a new kelim and a copper coffee pot for making mocha. The People's Store behind the Palace of Culture had the appearance of what a Middle American Woolworth's might have looked like in the Thirties, but as it was already closed we could only peer through the windows at the pale wood-and-glass counters and the scant selection of everything from trilbys to colanders.

The ornamental fountains in the square were illuminated alternately red and blue. We made our way to the post office, which was divided into two sections, one for telephoning, the other for postal services. The second section was all but deserted. There was no queue; the girl who served us was efficient and courteous and charged us something like fifty pence to airmail our books back to England. 'We don't send many letters in Albania,' Astrid told me later as I marvelled at the lack of a queue. The section for telephoning was packed. Albanians like to ring each other up, although the number of private telephones is minute.

As the sun sank lower in the sky and work ended for the day, Lowry-like figures poured from the side-streets into the square. Apart from newish red-and-white buses there was still very little traffic, and fewer bicycles than in Shkodër. People were beginning to trickle into the Avenue of the Martyrs for the evening's *passeggiata*, and we joined them. Young men idly twirled sprigs of yellow flowers and eyed the girls. Older men in stained caps rattled worry-beads. The Avenue and the square, apart from a few pretty Italianate streets behind the Palace of Culture, *are* the town. The rest is a uniform sea of brick blocks.

The Enver Hoxha Museum had only just opened at the end of 1988 and was thronged with local people. Demand for tickets had been such that only now for the first time were foreigners being allowed to buy them. The museum was designed by Enver Hoxha's son-in-law, and it is a beautiful piece of modern architecture. Faced in white marble, it is in the shape of a shallow funnel. At its apex is a horizontal red star, but you would only be able to see it from directly above the building. From above, the white marble is seen to represent rays of light emanating from the star. The marble rays are alternated with top-to-bottom glass panels. The building is at its best caught in the rays of the setting sun.

Inside it is dominated by another giant statue of Hoxha seated in an armchair, reminiscent of the statue of Lincoln in Washington. Otherwise the contents are dull, unless one is an avid student of Enver's life. The fact that he has virtually a whole floor of the National Museum dedicated to him as well indicates that the cult has been developed *ad absurdum*.

Opposite the museum in a little garden there are three busts arranged in a semicircle. They are of the Frashëri brothers – a poet, a politician, and a philosopher, who worked towards Albanian independence at the end of the nineteenth century, by which time Turkish control was notional. As I am shortsighted, I went towards them to get a better look. This was a mistake, for a soldier emerged from behind a bush and rattled his machine-gun at me. I think he was merely bored, for the following morning when I passed that way again the man on duty smiled and waved, but it is not pleasant to be at the receiving end of a machine-gun held by a dull-looking teenager. He was protecting a Ministry, hidden behind the trees on the other side of the garden.

By now, night had fallen, for the dusk is short. The streets rapidly emptied, and we returned slowly to the hotel. A folklorique evening had been arranged in the nightclub of the Hotel Tiranë for the convocation of tourists staying there. Apart from mentioning how odd it was suddenly to be together with other west Europeans again – there were French, Swedish and Italian groups – I will draw a veil over the event. We made an early escape and found a bar in town where we managed to get a glass of vermouth. An inebriated old man immediately flung himself at us with violent imprecations. A handful of other customers held him back with good-natured apologies before he could do any damage, and he subsided, muttering. That was the only incident that came even close to unpleasantness.

Edith Durham describes her frustration at not being able to prevent Albanian women at the turn of the century from swaddling their babies so tightly and heavily that they often died. Any innovation she attempted was greeted by a stolid refusal to have anything to do with what ran counter to established custom. It is possible that the heavy swaddling was originally introduced to ensure that only the healthiest babies made it to the age of two, when they were relieved of their rugs and allowed into the daylight. Even today in Albania babies are carried around in heavy rugs which cover them from head to toe. I saw a couple of mothers with such unhappy-looking bundles the following morning. I'd got up early in order to walk the mile-long Avenue of the Martyrs before our day's programme began. The two mothers were the only civilians I saw. I later found out that if I'd been up at about 4.30 a.m. I would have seen plenty of people queueing to do their food shopping before going on shift. As it was, I had the Avenue to myself in the sharp early morning sunshine, except for the soldiers.

To the west of the Avenue lie the embassies, and on its western side, as you approach the university, the parliament buildings and offices. This isn't hard to deduce as a line of soldiers in unusually good quality uniforms and boots are posted along the pavement about every three yards. Every so often, a bulky senior man might emerge from a building, dressed in a plain khaki overcoat. As in Bucharest, you have to cross the road and walk on the other side. Apart from the Hoxha Museum there is little of architectural interest, but the walk itself was pleasant. It would have been pleasanter without the presence of so many armed, uniformed men, but this was something I never got used to and always found oppressive.

I returned early and killed a little time by walking up the street which led north from the hotel. One building was a kind of theatre, though it looked as anonymous as all the others in the block. It housed a permanent circus, a form of entertainment of which the Albanians are fond and which seems to be popular throughout eastern Europe. Further on in a grey building were the newspaper offices of *Zëri i Popullit*, and nearer the square large glass display cases contained colour photographs of workers who had been especially commended for surpassing their quotas. I noticed that the names of older people still reflected the Muslim past, but younger women had names like Katrina, Violeta, Natasha and Zadefka. Bashkim, born just after the revolution, told me that his own name meant 'unity'. Behind the street were little side-alleys, where life was much more relaxed and natural. An old handcart stood propped against a wall, a tortoiseshell cat basked in the early sunshine, and a toddler in a T-shirt squatted to pee in the gutter.

The National Museum, built in 1981, traces Albania's history and culture since the Stone Age. Inevitably, the first object to meet the eye is a large statue of Hoxha, almost identical to the giant in the square outside. In a series of rooms off to his right the prehistory and early Illyrian culture of the country are marvellously exhibited, and so by stages one is conducted through to Skënderbeg's time. A number of original artefacts have been preserved, among them the head of Apollo from Butrint, and they are supported by careful reproductions of, for example, the Romanesque columns from St Mary's Church at Apollonia. Large fibreglass Socialist-Realist statues of medieval heroes are distributed through the rooms as well. Overmuscled, with lantern jaws and huge hands, they would be a gift to any society where satire was allowed, but Albanians are neither humorous nor cynical where nationalism is concerned. Bashkim referred with absolute dedication to 'Our beloved leader, Comrade Enver Hoxha', and it is well to take seriously the respect in which he is held.

After Skënderbeg there is an abrupt jump to the nineteenth century and the rebirth of Albanian nationalism, although Onufri is represented by one icon and there are a couple by his eighteenth-century successor, David Selenica. There are reproductions of the busts of the Frashëri brothers, and there is a dignified statue of Ismail Qemal, who declared his country a sovereign state in 1912. It seems odd that so few contributors to the achievement of Albania's independence before Hoxha are allowed public monuments, but that is what the cult of personality is all about. Only Skënderbeg is permitted house room, and he is presented as a kind of ideological ancestor of Comrade Enver. In fact his main concern in withdrawing from the Turkish forces at Niš was probably to protect his own estates. But then Hoxha wasn't the first politician to bend history to his own ends, and the practice is not restricted to communist leaders.

The early twentieth century is covered by contemporary documents and photographs, and politics take centre stage. As soon as Hoxha enters the arena, the museum becomes a reflection of his life. It ends with a long exhibition on postwar development under his rule. Of course former comrades since disgraced, like Mehmet Shehu, are not included.

From here I went out of town a little way, through pleasant parkland containing Zog's former palace, now a people's cultural amenity, and up a hill to the Martyrs' Cemetery, from where there is a fine view over Tiranë. 'Because they died for their country, we buried them here in its bosom,' Astrid told me with passionate seriousness. The Albanians who perished fighting the Germans and the Italians between 1941 and 1944 lie in serried ranks beneath plain slabs, under the shadow of a monument to Mother Albania. The stone figure, hair and clothes streaming in the wind, holding a red star aloft, was built – the word springs more readily to mind than 'sculpted' – by three Sculptors of the People. At her foot is the red marble rectangle marking the tomb of Enver. The gravestone simply carries his name and dates on it in gold. It is surrounded by fresh flowers of the season; on that day they were pansies. New flowers are brought every day. Those which are replaced are sent to hospitals. Two soldiers stand guard: the only soldiers one is allowed to photograph, though they are not typical. Their uniforms are of the best quality, and they wear peaked caps, not the usual soft kepis.

There is, inevitably, an 'Albania Today' exhibition on permanent display a short drive away, with large-scale models of caustic soda factories, oilfields, electricity plants, and power stations. Tractors and lathes stand gleaming behind red rope barriers. Glass cases around the walls contain every conceivable Albanian product. There are ponderous television sets (brand names: LURA and DAJTI), radios (BUTRINT), calculators, and computers made by URT of Durrës. There are cigarettes, wines, pharmaceuticals, toys, arts and crafts, and even samples of grain and eggs.

Next door, in the same hangar-like building, is the Ethnographic Museum, containing exquisite examples of embroidery and filigree-work – crafts which were practised by men – huge and luxurious kelims, reconstructed domestic interiors mainly in the form of peasant and rural rooms of the early twentieth century, and some examples of the 146 different clan costumes still worn within the frontiers of present-day Albania. The most impressive was of a type apparently unchanged for 3000 years: a woman's skirt of heavy black felt cut into a conical shape and reminiscent of those worn in ancient Cretan statuettes. It was decorated with transverse stripes of black velvet or satin. Before the death of Skënderbeg these stripes were brightly coloured, but thereafter they were black, in mourning.

We set out for home so early in the morning that we arrived at the frontier before dawn, although enough light had broken in the sky for the silhouettes of soldiers to be visible. Finally, a massive metal gate emblazoned with the double-headed eagle was slid back, and the familiar pink frontier building came into view. Astrid gave us a smile and a perfunctory wave; Bashkim was more formal.

The Albanian frontier officials were as polite as ever, and beyond asking us to show that we had not left our cameras behind they only gave our baggage a glance. We walked slowly back to the Yugoslav side, where a sleek Mercedes bus was waiting. I was trailing a little, and must have been among the last to leave Albanian soil. As I did, I accidentally caught the eye of one of the border guards. I thought that at least I would say goodbye.

'*Mirupafshim*,' I said.

The eyes softened and the jaw relaxed. He smiled. '*Mirupafshim*,' he replied.

The journey was over.

EPILOGUE

It seems incredible that when I was in Czechoslovakia I was unable to meet Vaclav Havel because at the time, on the 20th Anniversary of the Prague Spring, he was encircled by security police, a virtual prisoner. His presidency now is the result of twenty-two years and more of dogged persistence, of putting up with humiliation and discomfort, of risking his life and his personal freedom. It is the bravery of individuals like him, and Lech Wałęsa, and of course many others in the countries dealt with in this book, which forms the cornerstone for radical political change, because such people will not be silenced. What has happened in eastern Europe is that a forty-year cycle has ended; those that were in their prime and in control at the beginning grew old, and so rotten had the system they had lived by become that it could not survive them. Yet we should not forget the great achievements of the Iron Curtain countries under their rule, without recourse to the enormous economic aid furnished by America or the investments of Japan, and for the most part handicapped by the economic millstone the Soviet Union deliberately placed around their necks. With that millstone removed, what may their achievements be?

INDEX